JOHN V. WATKINS
THOMAS J. SHEEHAN

Florida Landscape Plants
Native and Exotic

Revised Edition

Drawings by

MARION RUFF SHEEHAN

and other delineators

A   UNIVERSITY   OF   FLORIDA   BOOK

THE UNIVERSITY PRESSES OF FLORIDA
GAINESVILLE / 1975

08 07 06 05 04 03   12 11 10 9   8   7

Library of Congress Cataloging-in-Publication Data

Watkins, John Vertrees. 1901–
   Florida landscape plants.
   "A University of Florida book."
   Includes index.
   1. Plants, Ornamental—Florida.   2. Tropical
plants—Florida.   3. Landscape gardening—Florida.
I. Sheehan, Thomas John, 1924– , joint author.
II. Title.
SB407.W38   1975   635.9'09759   75-22365
ISBN 0-8130-0861-1

http://www.upf.com

Preface

OVER the years *Florida Landscape Plants* has become a standard manual for university students, nurserymen, and homeowners in the Lower South. To assure its continued usefulness we have expanded the text, and we have made necessary editorial changes. There are many fresh, new illustrations in this revised edition.

Although there are more than 400 entries in this book, a few favorite landscape plants may be absent because it would be impossible to describe and illustrate all of Florida's horticultural material in a single volume of popular size. However, due to placement of some illustrations, a family may be misplaced one or more units.

Manual of Cultivated Plants (L. H. Bailey, New York: Macmillan, rev. ed., 1949) is the authority for plant names, their pronunciations, and their derivations. Plant heights in the present volume represent average sizes of aged specimens growing in Florida, and may vary from dimensions printed in Bailey's *Manual*. Systematic arrangement used here for your convenience, and for orderly presentation, follows phylogeny in that great work.

JOHN V. WATKINS
THOMAS J. SHEEHAN
MARION R. SHEEHAN

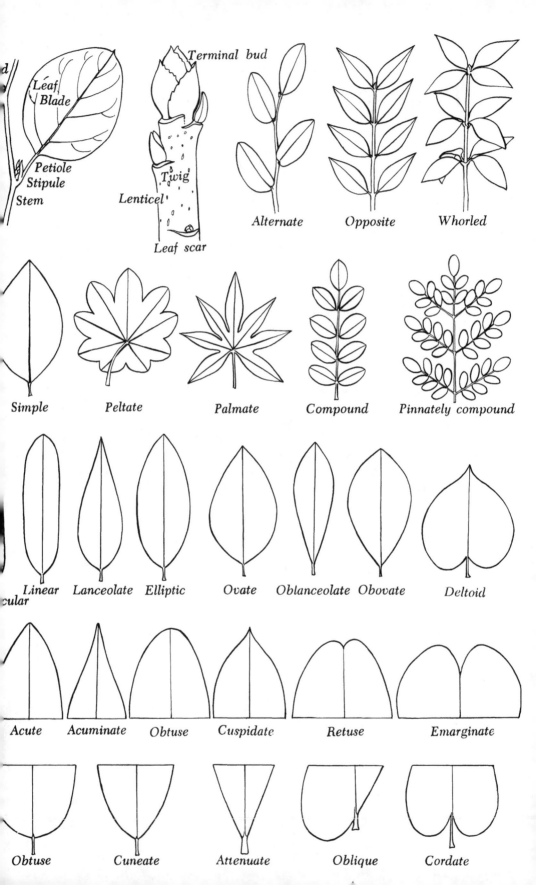

d

Leaf Blade

Petiole
Stipule
Stem

Terminal bud

Twig
Lenticel
Leaf scar

Alternate   Opposite   Whorled

Simple   Peltate   Palmate   Compound   Pinnately compound

Linear   Lanceolate   Elliptic   Ovate   Oblanceolate   Obovate   Deltoid
cular

Acute   Acuminate   Obtuse   Cuspidate   Retuse   Emarginate

Obtuse   Cuneate   Attenuate   Oblique   Cordate

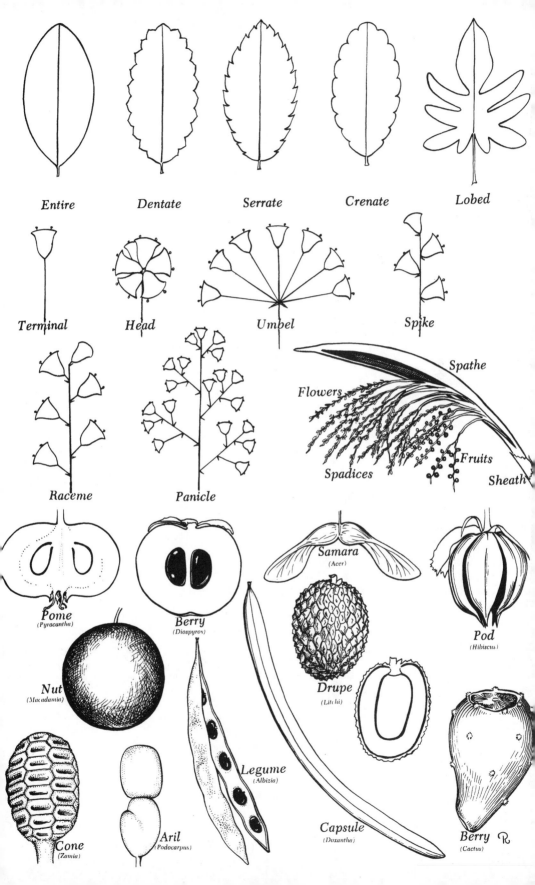

Entire   Dentate   Serrate   Crenate   Lobed

Terminal   Head   Umbel   Spike

Raceme   Panicle

Spathe
Flowers
Spadices   Fruits   Sheath

Pome
(Pyracantha)

Berry
(Diospyros)

Samara
(Acer)

Pod
(Hibiscus)

Nut
(Macadamia)

Drupe
(Litchi)

Cone
(Zamia)

Aril
(Podocarpus)

Legume
(Albizia)

Capsule
(Doxantha)

Berry
(Cactus)

Contents

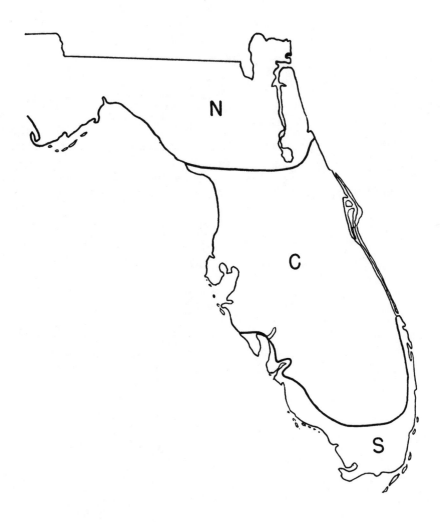

Zone map for Florida gardeners

N = NORTHERN FLORIDA
C = CENTRAL FLORIDA
S = SOUTHERN FLORIDA

Introduction

PROFESSOR John Watkins' book *Florida Landscape Plants, Native and Exotic* has been a best seller for the past six years, but progress in scientific research **requires** revision of any gardening book after a certain number of years. **Now** Dr. Thomas J. Sheehan has joined Professor Watkins in revising **this book**, which is one of Florida's best garden manuals.

In the new edition **some** fifty new plants have been added, along with four pages of color. The text has been updated and the information on pest control removed. Methods of pest control change constantly and information on this is best obtained locally from county agricultural agents. An index of family names has been added as have a large number of new illustrations.

Dr. Sheehan, who is professor of ornamental horticulture at the University of Florida, adds his vast experience to that of Professor Watkins to give the reader a most authoritative book. All residents of Florida who like to garden will find much useful information to help them with their garden problems in this revised book.

JOHN POPENOE, *Director*
Fairchild Tropical Garden
Miami, Florida

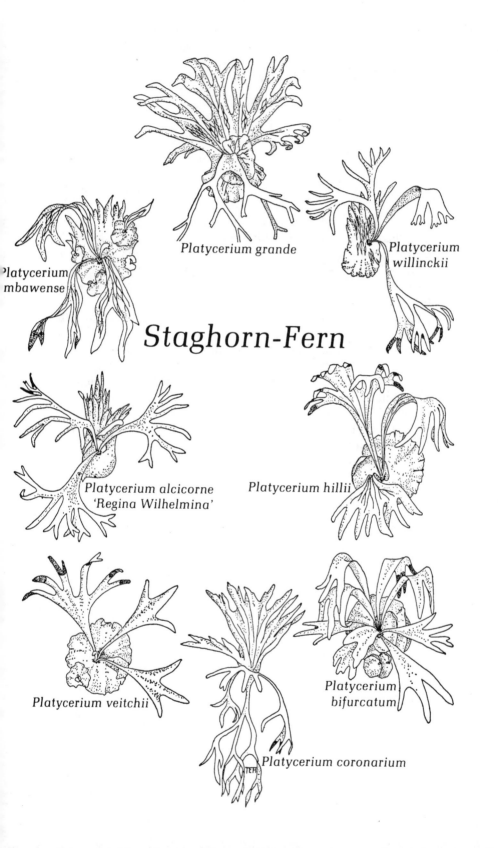

Platycerium grande

Platycerium
willinckii

Platycerium
mbawense

Staghorn-Fern

Platycerium alcicorne
'Regina Wilhelmina'

Platycerium hillii

Platycerium veitchii

Platycerium coronarium

Platycerium
bifurcatum

3
Staghorn-Fern

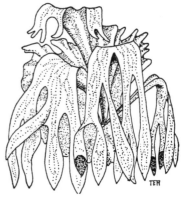

Platycerium (platty-SEAR-ee-um): Greek for broad horn.
SPP.: several species grow in Florida.

FAMILY: Polypodiaceae.   RELATIVES: Holly-fern and leather-leaf fern.
TYPE OF PLANT: Epiphytic perennial.   HEIGHT: 3'. ZONE: S
HOW TO IDENTIFY: These spectacular tree-dwelling ferns have leaves of
    2 types—the flat, rounded, brown sterile fronds that contrast with
    the outward-thrusting, antler-forked, green fertile fronds.
HABIT OF GROWTH: Brown sterile fronds grow tight on the substratum
    and send out attractive, lobed, green fertile fronds.
FOLIAGE: Of two sorts—parchment-like, round, flat, barren fronds lie
    flat to the substratum, while freestanding, forked, green reproduc-
    tive leaves thrust outward.
FLOWERS: Absent.
FRUITS: Sori, in dense pads, are produced near the tips of fertile
    fronds.
SEASON OF MAXIMUM COLOR: Little seasonal variation.
LANDSCAPE USES: To cast the spell of the tropics and to add interest
    to a patio wall, nothing surpasses staghorn-fern. In frostless areas,
    specimens thrive on palm trunks or on branches of woody trees.
    These great epiphytes are quite fashionable.
HABITAT: Eastern tropics.
LIGHT REQUIREMENT: Reduced light is optimum; staghorns will not en-
    dure the Florida sun.
SOIL REQUIREMENT: Osmundine, sphagnum moss, tree fern, or combi-
    nations of these.
SALT TOLERANCE: Not tolerant.
AVAILABILITY: Nurseries on the peninsula have staghorn-ferns in con-
    tainers upon occasion.
CULTURE: Fasten to a slab of pecky cypress, redwood, or tree fern with
    a blanket of one or more of the media mentioned above; keep con-
    stantly moist and shaded; supply liquid fertilizer once a month
    during warm weather.
PROPAGATION: Division; or sowing spores on moist, sterile peat.
PESTS: Mites and chewing insects.

4
House Holly-Fern

Cyrtomium (sir-TOE-me-um): Greek word for bow.
falcatum (fal-KAY-tum): sickle-shaped, alluding to the form of the pinnae.

FAMILY: Polypodiaceae. RELATIVES: Leather-leaf fern and staghorn-fern.

TYPE OF PLANT: Herbaceous perennial.   HEIGHT: 24″. ZONE: N,C,S

HOW TO IDENTIFY: Upright, very shaggy stems bear dark, heavy pinnae that resemble holly leaves.

HABIT OF GROWTH: Compact, forming tight, knee-high evergreen clumps.

FOLIAGE: Dark, heavy, remotely resembling holly foliage.

FLOWERS: Absent.

FRUITS: Large sori scattered over the undersides of fertile fronds.

SEASON OF MAXIMUM COLOR: No seasonal variation.

LANDSCAPE USES: As a ground cover for very shady locations, and for planters under eaves, house holly-fern has long been a favorite in Florida. As a porch plant, it has served generations of Floridians.

HABITAT: Warm parts of eastern Asia.

LIGHT REQUIREMENT: Shady locations are necessary.

SOIL REQUIREMENT: Tolerant of varying soils throughout Florida.

SALT TOLERANCE: Tolerant of salt air back from the strand.

AVAILABILITY: House holly-ferns are available in retail nurseries.

CULTURE: Plant in a shaded location; protect from frost; water moderately during periods of drought.

PROPAGATION: Division of matted clumps.

PESTS: Mites, caterpillars, grasshoppers, and a leaf-spotting disease.

5
Leather-Leaf Fern

Polystichum (pol-ɪs-tee-cum): Greek for many rows, alluding to sori.
adiantiforme (aye-dee-ant-ee-ꜰᴏʀᴍ-ee): resembling adiantum.

FAMILY: Polypodiaceae.   RELATIVES: Boston-fern and holly-fern.
TYPE OF PLANT: Herbaceous perennial.   HEIGHT: 3′. ZONE: N,C,S
HOW TO IDENTIFY: Triangular fronds, which may grow as much as a
   yard high, are made up of stiff, leathery, coarse-toothed, heavy-
   textured pinnules.
HABIT OF GROWTH: Compact, clump-forming.
FOLIAGE: Bold, heavy, leathery, sometimes 3′ high, of excellent keep-
   ing quality when cut.
FLOWERS: Absent.
FRUITS: Spores are borne in prominent sori midway between the edges
   and the midribs of the pinnules.
SEASON OF MAXIMUM COLOR: No seasonal variation.
LANDSCAPE USES: For many years leather-leaf fern has been popular
   as a pot plant for porches, and it is often planted, too, in earth of
   shaded garden spots and patios. Grown commercially for florists,
   cut leather-leaf fern is often used instead of the old stand-by *Aspar-
   agus plumosus.*
HABITAT: World tropics.
LIGHT REQUIREMENT: Broken shade of hammocks, or constant shade of
   porches.
SOIL REQUIREMENT: Tolerant of varying soils.
SALT TOLERANCE: Grows back from the strand with some protection.
AVAILABILITY: Frequently seen in containers on retail sales lots.
CULTURE: Plant divisions slightly deeper than the plant grew originally;
   water periodically when there is little rain; fertilize with balanced
   fertilizer in water solution during warm months.
PROPAGATION: Division or sowing spores on sterilized, moist peat.
PESTS: Mealy-bugs, leaf-hoppers, and leaf-miners.

6
Tree
Fern

Alsophila (al-soph-ill-a): Greek for grove-loving.
Cibotium (si-boat-ee-um): Greek for little seed-vessel.
Cyathea (si-ath-ee-a): Greek for cup referring to the fruiting bodies.
Dicksonia (dick-son-ee-a): for J. Dickson, English botanist.
spp.: species from each of these genera grow in Florida.

FAMILY: Cyatheaceae.   RELATIVES: The tree ferns.
TYPE OF PLANT: Tree fern.   HEIGHT: 20′. ZONE: C,S
HOW TO IDENTIFY: Striking tree fern with distinct trunk.
HABIT OF GROWTH: Single, brown trunks bear beautiful heads of lacy
  fern foliage.
FOLIAGE: Evergreen, huge, feather-leaved, of fine texture and yellow-
  green color.
FLOWERS: None.
FRUITS: Fruiting bodies on the backs of some mature leaf segments.
SEASON OF MAXIMUM COLOR: No variation.
LANDSCAPE USES: For creating true tropical effects nothing can sur-
  pass tree ferns.
HABITAT: Tropics of both hemispheres.
LIGHT REQUIREMENT: Partial shade or dense shade of live oaks is suit-
  able.
SOIL REQUIREMENT: Almost any reasonably fertile, well-drained soil is
  suitable.
SALT TOLERANCE: Not tolerant.
AVAILABILITY: Certain specialty nurseries have tree ferns in containers.
CULTURE: Plant with care in well-made site; water faithfully; keep at-
  mosphere moist by frequent misting; fertilize every month during
  growing weather.
PROPAGATION: By sowing spores.
PESTS: Mites and mealy-bugs.
NOTE: Under any name, a tree fern is a topflight landscape plant where
  winter temperatures do not cause its death.

7
Ceratozamia

Ceratozamia (ce-rat-o-ZAY-me-a): Greek for horn and Latin for pine nut.
mexicana (mex-i-CAY-na): Mexican.

FAMILY: Cycadaceae.

RELATIVES: Queen sago and coontie.

TYPE OF PLANT: Cycad.

HEIGHT: 4′–8′. ZONE: C,S

HOW TO IDENTIFY: Palm-like with rosettes of stiff, pinnate leaves. The 3′-long leaves will have 15–20 pairs of leaflets. Leaf petioles are armed, the spines scattered and encircling petioles.

HABIT OF GROWTH: Medium-sized, palm-like plant.

FOLIAGE: Mature fronds with stiff, leathery pinnae to 12″ long and 1½″ wide. Leaves medium to dark green.

FLOWERS: Borne in cones; scales with horns.

FRUITS: Small, drupe-like fruits.

SEASON OF MAXIMUM COLOR: When seeds ripen on mature plants.

LANDSCAPE USES: A fine plant to use as a freestanding specimen. Often used in palm groupings and for tropical effects.

HABITAT: Mexico; in Florida, central and southern areas.

LIGHT REQUIREMENT: Partial shade to full sun.

SOIL REQUIREMENT: Thrives on well-drained, sandy soils.

SALT TOLERANCE: Not tolerant on front line.

AVAILABILITY: Limited quantities are for sale in containers.

CULTURE: Like most cycadaceous plants, *Ceratozamia* requires little care once it becomes established.

PROPAGATION: Seedage.

PESTS: Occasionally defoliated by caterpillars.

NOTE: *Ceratozamia mexicana* is deserving of wider landscape use, since it has few pests and is of easy culture.

8
Coontie

Zamia (ZAY-me-a): Latin for pine nut.
floridana (flor-ee-DAY-na): Floridian.

FAMILY: Cycadaceae.   RELATIVE: Queen sago.

TYPE OF PLANT: Dwarf herbaceous perennial.   HEIGHT: 3′. ZONE: N,C,S

HOW TO IDENTIFY: Feather-like, evergreen leaves emerge from a very large storage root; there are very often reddish-brown reproductive cones at the ground line.

HABIT OF GROWTH: Dwarf herbaceous perennial of fern-like appearance.

FOLIAGE: Evergreen, fern-like, fine in texture, in tones of green.

FLOWERS: Borne in cones.

FRUITS: Large, reddish-brown reproductive cones at ground level; staminate and pistillate cones on separate plants.

SEASON OF MAXIMUM COLOR: No seasonal variation.

LANDSCAPE USES: No native plant is better for foundation plantings for low, rambling houses of contemporary design. Set 1½′ o.c. As a transition plant for larger species and in planters and urns, coontie excels, as it does as an atmosphere-creator when planted by pine trunks in woodland developments.

HABITAT: Sandy soils throughout the state.

LIGHT REQUIREMENT: Full sun or dense shade, latter preferred.

SOIL REQUIREMENT: Tolerant of various types of well-drained soil.

SALT TOLERANCE: Tolerant of salt drift.

AVAILABILITY: Coonties are often sold in retail sales lots.

CULTURE: Coontie is most difficult to transplant because of the far-reaching tap root. Plant in well-drained locations; water with moderation; protect against red scale.

PROPAGATION: Seedage. This is difficult and high mortality is the rule.

PESTS: Florida red scale, a major pest, must be controlled by regular spraying, lest it cause the death of plants.

9
Dion

Dion (di-on): Greek for two and egg (each scale covers 2 ovules).
edule (ED-you-lee): edible.

FAMILY: Cycadaceae.

RELATIVES: Zamia and other cycads.

TYPE OF PLANT: Cycad.

HEIGHT: 6′–8′. **ZONE:** C,S

HOW TO IDENTIFY: Cycad-like with hard, green, stiff, pinnate leaves. Leaflets entire in adults but often toothed at apex in younger plants. Differs from cycas in flowers and fruit.

HABIT OF GROWTH: Stout, unbranched stem with rosette of leaves at apex.

FOLIAGE: Evergreen; dark-green, leathery pinnae; side nerves 12 or less.

FLOWERS: Borne in large, gray, felty cones.

FRUITS: Drupe-like seeds.

SEASON OF MAXIMUM COLOR: When seeds ripen on mature plants.

LANDSCAPE USES: For tropical effects. Excellent as a freestanding specimen.

HABITAT: Mexico; in Florida, southern and central area.

LIGHT REQUIREMENT: Grows in full sun as well as in partial shade.

SOIL REQUIREMENT: Tolerant of a variety of soil types.

SALT TOLERANCE: Not tolerant of front line.

AVAILABILITY: *Dion* is available from many nurseries in containers.

CULTURE: Requires little care once established.

PROPAGATION: Seedage.

PESTS: None serious; caterpillars occasionally may attack leaves.

NOTE: Plants are hard to separate from some other cycads when young. Once mature and flowering, *Dion* can be identified without difficulty.

10
Queen Sago

Cycas (sy-kus): Greek name for a palm tree.
circinalis (sir-sin-al-is): coiled.

FAMILY: Cycadaceae.   RELATIVES: The cycads, including coontie.
TYPE OF PLANT: Cycad.   HEIGHT: 20′. ZONE: S
HOW TO IDENTIFY: Palm-like with dark green feather-leaves; the foot-long pinnae, with flat margins, droop gracefully.
HABIT OF GROWTH: Stout, unbranching trunk with beautiful drooping foliage atop.
FOLIAGE: Evergreen, pinnate, of fine texture and darkest green color.
FLOWERS: Felty inflorescence in the center of the leaf mass.
FRUITS: Orange-colored, smooth, the size and form of bantam eggs.
SEASON OF MAXIMUM COLOR: When seeds ripen on mature plants.
LANDSCAPE USES: Because of its tropical aspect, and very graceful habit, queen sago is highly regarded as a freestanding specimen for large properties in areas that are nearly frostless.
HABITAT: Tropical Africa; in Florida, warmest spots only.
LIGHT REQUIREMENT: Shade is quite suitable, but not necessary.
SOIL REQUIREMENT: Tolerant of varying soil types.
SALT TOLERANCE: Not tolerant.
AVAILABILITY: Queen sago is popular and rather widely available in containers.
CULTURE: When well established in a frost-protected location, queen sago grows well with usual care.
PROPAGATION: Seedage or division of offsets.
PESTS: Scales and leaf-spotting disease.
NOTE: *Cycas revoluta,* the hardy relative that is seen in northern Florida, is not recommended because of its susceptibility to leaf-spotting disease. A colorless fungicide, applied frequently, may afford protection against leaf-spotting.

11
Florida Torreya

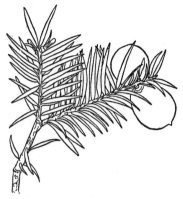

Torreya (TOR-ee-a): for John Torrey, American botanist of the nineteenth century.
taxifolia (tacks-ee-FOL-ee-a): yew-leaved.

FAMILY: Taxaceae.　　　　　　　　RELATIVES: English yew and Florida yew.
TYPE OF PLANT: Tree.　　　　　　　　　　　　HEIGHT: 40′. ZONE: N
HOW TO IDENTIFY: Evergreen, linear leaves, 1″ long × ⅛″ wide, lustrous above, with 2 narrow, white stomatal bands beneath. Crushed leaves and twigs have a fetid odor which has given this plant the vernacular name "stinking-cedar." Purple, egg-shaped fruits, deeper than broad, mature in late summer. The foliage tips are sharp-prickly.
HABIT OF GROWTH: Conical, open crown, formed by slender, drooping branches.
FOLIAGE: Evergreen, 2 white bands beneath, aromatic, of fine texture, deep green color.
FLOWERS: Cones in March; those of different sexes are produced on separate trees.
FRUITS: Egg-shaped, 1½″ long, deeper than broad, purple at maturity.
SEASON OF MAXIMUM COLOR: Late summer when purple fruits mature.
LANDSCAPE USES: Advanced horticulturists in western Florida might like to culture one torreya tree as a freestanding specimen because of its extreme rarity. Like Florida yew, this is one of Florida's truly rare plants, and culture should be undertaken with forethought to assure success.
HABITAT: Very restricted area on the shore of the Apalachicola River.
LIGHT REQUIREMENT: Broken shade.
SOIL REQUIREMENT: Superior alluvial soil.
SALT TOLERANCE: Not tolerant.
AVAILABILITY: Usually not to be found in Florida nurseries.
CULTURE: Very narrow limits in soil and moisture tolerances exist. A slightly acid, well-drained, fertile, porous soil must be supplied. Water faithfully and fertilize once in late winter.
PROPAGATION: Cuttage.
PESTS: Scales and possibly mushroom root-rot.

12
Florida Yew

Taxus (TACKS-us): ancient Latin name.
floridana (flor-e-DAY-na): Floridian.

FAMILY: Taxaceae.   RELATIVES: English yew and stinking-cedar.
TYPE OF PLANT: Tree; shrub-like for years.   HEIGHT: 20'. ZONE: N
HOW TO IDENTIFY: Small tree that has evergreen leaves in 1 plane, and light red, pulpy fruits. The leaves are simple, thick, dark green above, paler beneath, with edges rolled under and thick-ended. The foliage is very soft to the touch.
HABIT OF GROWTH: Short trunks support many stout, spreading branches.
FOLIAGE: Evergreen, of fine texture and dark green color.
FLOWERS: Inconspicuous catkins; those of different sexes are borne on separate trees.
FRUITS: Light red, pulpy fruits, ½" across, broader than deep, mature in autumn.
SEASON OF MAXIMUM COLOR: Autumn when fruits mature.
LANDSCAPE USES: For the curiosity of Florida's only yew, this plant might find limited use as a freestanding specimen in gardens of advanced amateurs on the Panhandle. Arboretums, city parks, and college campuses should have specimens, properly labeled.
    This is one of our truly rare native plants, being found in only one little area in the entire world.
HABITAT: Very restricted area on the eastern shore of the Apalachicola River.
LIGHT REQUIREMENT: Broken shade.
SOIL REQUIREMENT: Superior alluvial soil.
SALT TOLERANCE: Not tolerant.
AVAILABILITY: Usually not to be found in Florida nurseries.
CULTURE: Very narrow limits in soil and moisture tolerances exist. A slightly acid, well-drained, fertile, porous soil must be supplied. Water faithfully and fertilize once in late winter.
PROPAGATION: Cuttage.
PESTS: Scales and possibly mushroom root-rot.
NOTE: English yew, so popular in northern gardens, is likely to be disappointing in Florida.

13
Fern
Podocarpus

Podocarpus (po-do-CAR-pus): Greek for foot and fruit.
gracilior (gra-SILL-ee-or): more graceful.

FAMILY: Podocarpaceae. RELATIVES: The genus stands alone.

TYPE OF PLANT: Tree, often a shrub in Florida. HEIGHT: 20′. ZONE: S

HOW TO IDENTIFY: Evergreen, narrow foliage is held by gracefully drooping branches.

HABIT OF GROWTH: Tree with drooping leader and pendulous branches.

FOLIAGE: Evergreen, very fine in texture, medium green in color, except new growth which is silvery.

FLOWERS: Inconspicuous catkins or scale-enclosed ovules.

FRUITS: Drupe-like, each standing above its edible red aril.

SEASON OF MAXIMUM COLOR: New growth in springtime is silvery.

LANDSCAPE USES: Fern podocarpus is an outstanding accent plant and atmosphere-creator for tropical plantings on the warmer part of the peninsula. As an espalier on a north wall, as a specimen near a terrace, or as a screening plant, it is most highly recommended.

HABITAT: South Africa; in Florida, sparingly planted in warm locations.

LIGHT REQUIREMENT: Tolerant of shade, but grows equally well in full sun.

SOIL REQUIREMENT: Tolerant of varying soils.

SALT TOLERANCE: Grows back from the strand with some protection.

AVAILABILITY: Infrequently seen in containers on retail sales lots.

CULTURE: Plant carefully in fertile, well-drained soil; water moderately; keep lawn grasses from encroaching; fertilize twice annually.

PROPAGATION: Cuttage and marcottage.

PESTS: Usually none of major importance.

14
Nagi

Podocarpus (po-do-CAR-pus): Greek for foot and fruit.
nagi (NAG-eye): native Japanese name.

FAMILY: Podocarpaceae. RELATIVES: The genus stands alone.

TYPE OF PLANT: Tree; used as a shrub in Florida. HEIGHT: 40′.
ZONE: N,C,S

HOW TO IDENTIFY: Strong central leader, hatrack-type branching, evergreen leaves, the broadest in the genus (1″ × 3″).

HABIT OF GROWTH: Strongly upright central leader with symmetrical branching in geometric pattern.

FOLIAGE: Evergreen, medium in texture, dark green in color.

FLOWERS: Inconspicuous male catkins or ovules in scales on separate plants.

FRUITS: Drupe-like, ½″ in diameter, purple, with bloom.

SEASON OF MAXIMUM COLOR: No seasonal variation.

LANDSCAPE USES: As a strong accent, no plant excels *Podocarpus nagi*. Thus, it is rather widely used throughout the state. For cut foliage this plant excels, as the cut branches stand up very well in flower arrangements. Pistillate plants that bear heavy crops of fruit are likely to exhibit yellow-tipped foliage.

HABITAT: Japan; in Florida, popular in foundation plantings.

LIGHT REQUIREMENT: Tolerant of shade, grows equally well in full sun.

SOIL REQUIREMENT: Tolerant of varying soils.

SALT TOLERANCE: Endures salt drift back from the strand.

AVAILABILITY: Many nurseries offer plants in containers and B & B.

CULTURE: Plant carefully in fertile, made-up sites; water moderately; keep lawn grasses from encroaching; fertilize twice annually while young.

PROPAGATION: Seedage and cuttage.

PESTS: Usually none of major importance.

15
Yew
Podocarpus

Podocarpus (po-do-CAR-pus): Greek for foot and fruit.
macrophylla (mac-roe-PHIL-a): large leaf.

FAMILY: Podocarpaceae.　　　　　　RELATIVES: The genus stands alone.

TYPE OF PLANT: Tree; usually a shrub in Florida.　　　　HEIGHT: 50'.
　　　　　　　　　　　　　　　　　　　　　　　　ZONE: N,C,S

HOW TO IDENTIFY: Evergreen, flat linear leaves about 2"–3" long, with prominent midrib, lighter green beneath. Green seeds stand above purple arils on pistillate plants.

HABIT OF GROWTH: Compact, dense, heavily foliated well to the ground.

FOLIAGE: Evergreen, very fine in texture, dark green in color.

FLOWERS: Inconspicuous, male catkins or ovules in scales on separate plants.

FRUITS: Drupe-like, green, ovoid, ½" in diameter, each standing above its purple, edible aril.

SEASON OF MAXIMUM COLOR: No seasonal variation.

LANDSCAPE USES: Podocarpus is one of Florida's leading landscape plants. As an accent in foundation plantings, for interest in skyline above an enclosing shrubbery barrier, as a clipped hedge, it serves with distinction.

　　　There are several excellent named varieties that have been chosen for one or another outstanding characteristic.

HABITAT: Japan; in Florida, planted everywhere as a garden shrub.

LIGHT REQUIREMENT: Tolerant of shade, grows equally well in full sun.

SOIL REQUIREMENT: Tolerant of varying soils.

SALT TOLERANCE: Endures salt drift back from the strand.

AVAILABILITY: All nurseries sell podocarpus plants in containers or B & B.

CULTURE: Plant carefully in fertile, made-up sites; water moderately; keep lawn grasses from encroaching; fertilize twice annually while young.

PROPAGATION: Seedage and cuttage.

PESTS: Usually none of major importance.

16
Japanese Plum-Yew

Cephalotaxus (sef-al-oh-TACKS-us): Greek for head and taxus.
harringtonia (hair-ing-TONE-ee-a): no doubt honors a Mr. Harrington.
'Drupacea' (drew-PAY-see-a): drupe-like.

FAMILY: Cephalotaxaceae. RELATIVES: This genus is alone in its family.
TYPE OF PLANT: Dwarf shrub.   HEIGHT: 6'. ZONE: N
HOW TO IDENTIFY: Stiffly upright habit of growth; evergreen leaves in 2
   rows, with 2 glaucous bands beneath; with staminate heads on
   stalks ¼" long.
HABIT OF GROWTH: Stiffly upright.
FOLIAGE: Evergreen, 2" long, abruptly pointed, very fine in texture.
FLOWERS: Inconspicuous catkins.
FRUITS: Usually none in Florida.
SEASON OF MAXIMUM COLOR: No variation.
LANDSCAPE USES: In seeking for dwarf, fine-scale shrubs, we must not
   overlook this slow-growing, shade-tolerant plum-yew. As an edging,
   plant it 14" o.c.; as a facer shrub in front of larger, leggy kinds,
   plant 18" o.c.
      With contemporary architecture demanding minimum plant ma-
   terial and with the wide use of planter bins under broad eaves, this
   diminutive shrub is very useful.
HABITAT: Japan; in Florida, landscape plantings in northern counties.
LIGHT REQUIREMENT: Shade-tolerant, a very good north-side plant.
SOIL REQUIREMENT: Fertility and moisture-holding capacity above av-
   erage are needed for good appearance.
SALT TOLERANCE: Not tolerant of front-line conditions.
AVAILABILITY: Some nurseries in northern Florida display specimens.
CULTURE: On good soil, with northern exposure, plant carefully; water
   with moderation; fertilize once each spring.
PROPAGATION: Cuttage.
PESTS: Nematodes.

17
Bunya-Bunya

Araucaria (ah-rah-CARE-ee-a): from Arauco, a province in southern Chile.
bidwillii (BID-will-ee-eye): for J. Bidwill, a nineteenth-century botanist.

FAMILY: Araucariaceae.   RELATIVES: Araucaria trees of both hemispheres.

TYPE OF PLANT: Tree.   HEIGHT: 70'. ZONE: N,C,S

HOW TO IDENTIFY: Juvenile leaves lanceolate. 2″ long; adult leaves spirally imbricated, ovate, ½″ long; woody cones 9″ long × 8″ in diameter.

HABIT OF GROWTH: Upright, symmetrical from single central leader.

FOLIAGE: Evergreen, fine in texture, dark green in color.

FLOWERS: Inconspicuous in tight catkins.

FRUITS: Very conspicuous cones 9″ long × 8″ in diameter.

SEASON OF MAXIMUM COLOR: No seasonal change.

LANDSCAPE USES: Bunya-bunya is recommended as a strong, single accent for large developments. Small trees are popular urn subjects for patios, terraces, and Florida rooms. In this plant, northern Floridians can have hardy monkey-puzzle-like specimens.

HABITAT: Australia; in Florida, infrequently planted as a lawn tree.

LIGHT REQUIREMENT: Full sun for best compact, symmetrical growth.

SOIL REQUIREMENT: Sandy soil of varying acidity is acceptable.

SALT TOLERANCE: Probably tolerant of salt drift back from the strand.

AVAILABILITY: Upon rare occasion, small trees may be found in containers.

CULTURE: Plant carefully in prepared site; water well, and repeat when there is no rain; fertilize twice or thrice annually while young.

PROPAGATION: Seedage or cuttage.

PESTS: None of major concern.

NOTE: *Araucaria* is represented by 12 species in both hemispheres. This is the most hardy and the one most often seen, therefore, in sections where frosts occur annually. Bunya-bunya is usually quite dependable under home-garden conditions in Florida.

18
Norfolk-
Island-Pine

Araucaria (ah-rah-CARE-ee-a): from Arauco, a province in southern Chile.
excelsa (ex-SELL-sa): tall.

FAMILY: Araucariaceae. RELATIVES: Damar-pine and bunya-bunya.
TYPE OF PLANT: Large tree. HEIGHT: 50'. ZONE: C,S
HOW TO IDENTIFY: Strong, straight, central leader with horizontal branches in symmetrical whorls; tiny, sharp-pointed, evergreen leaves.
HABIT OF GROWTH: Geometrically symmetrical with branches in even whorls.
FOLIAGE: Evergreen, very fine in texture, dark green in color.
FLOWERS: Inconspicuous.
FRUITS: Cones 3"–6" in diameter almost globular with spiny scales.
SEASON OF MAXIMUM COLOR: Little seasonal change.
LANDSCAPE USES: As a strong, single accent to enhance a feeling of the tropics, this striking tree is popular, and well-grown lawn specimens are highly prized. Small trees are admired as urn subjects for patios, terraces, and Florida rooms.

While there are a dozen species in this genus, Norfolk-Island-pine is by all odds the most popular in Florida. In some resort cities, specimens of this subtropical plant are well known for the mood that they create.
HABITAT: Norfolk Island; in Florida, warmer coastal positions.
LIGHT REQUIREMENT: Full sun for best, compact, symmetrical growth.
SOIL REQUIREMENT: Sandy soil of varying acidity is acceptable.
SALT TOLERANCE: Quite tolerant of salt air back of the first dune.
AVAILABILITY: Retail sales lots offer beautiful little trees in containers.
CULTURE: A well-made planting hole containing an acid, fertile mixture is recommended to give a young tree a good start. Careful watering, a mulch, and annual fertilization should be supplied.
PROPAGATION: Cuttage of terminal shoots for symmetrical trees.
PESTS: Scales and mushroom root-rot.

19
Callitris

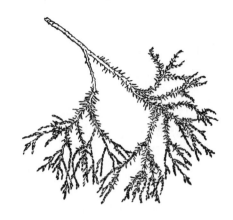

Callitris (cal-IT-ris): Greek for beautiful.
robusta (roe-BUS-ta): robust.

FAMILY: Pinaceae.

RELATIVES: Pine and cedar.

TYPE OF PLANT: Tree.

HEIGHT: 45'. ZONE: N,C,S

HOW TO IDENTIFY: Scale-like, evergreen leaves; jointed, angled branch-lets; subglobose cones 1" through. The graceful habit is character-istic.

HABIT OF GROWTH: Very compact, dense, symmetrical evergreen.

FOLIAGE: Evergreen, minute, of finest texture and dark green color.

FLOWERS: Staminate flowers in small catkins, pistillate cones of 6 un-equal scales.

FRUITS: Subglobose cones about an inch across.

SEASON OF MAXIMUM COLOR: No variation.

LANDSCAPE USES: As an unusually dense, graceful, freestanding speci-men, callitris is notable. It is almost universal in its appeal while young because of its neat, compact growth.

There are 3 or 4 species in Florida, all likely to be mislabeled in nurseries. Very popular in the nineteen-twenties, callitris has lost ground as a specimen plant partly because of its susceptibility to mushroom root-rot and partly because the same effect can be had more easily, more quickly, and more cheaply with Australian-pines.

HABITAT: Australia; in Florida, sparingly planted on the peninsula.

LIGHT REQUIREMENT: Full sun for symmetrical, compact growth.

SOIL REQUIREMENT: Tolerant of sandy soils.

SALT TOLERANCE: Tolerant of light salt drift at some distance from the sea.

AVAILABILITY: Nurseries in central Florida may stock this and other species.

CULTURE: Plant with reasonable care in enriched sites; water faithfully during the first year; thereafter little or no care is needed.

PROPAGATION: Seedage.

PESTS: Mushroom root-rot, which can be very serious.

20
Pines

Pinus (PI-nus): ancient Latin name for pines.
SPP.: several species grow in Florida.

FAMILY: Pinaceae.
RELATIVES: Cedar and Douglas-fir.
TYPE OF PLANT: Evergreen tree.
HEIGHT: To 100'. ZONE: N,C,S
HOW TO IDENTIFY: Resinous, usually upright trees with two types of leaves. Small, scale-like leaves fall early and long, needle-like leaves persist for several years. Needle-like leaves in clusters of 2s, 3s, or 5s, from a few inches to 10"–12" long. Most trees have strong central leaders and are often shaped like inverted cones. Some common species in Florida are sand pine (*Pinus clausa*), slash pine (*P. elliotti*), spruce pine (*P. glabra*), and longleaf pine (*P. palustris*).
HABIT OF GROWTH: Mostly narrow-upright.
FOLIAGE: Medium green and fine-textured, often sharp-pointed.
FLOWERS: Male flowers in catkins, female in cones.
FRUITS: Cones, up to 15" long in some species.
SEASON OF MAXIMUM COLOR: None.
LANDSCAPE USES: Excellent trees for giving an illusion of depth to plantings and for framing. Widely used for bonsai.
HABITAT: North America, China, Japan, Korea, and other areas.
LIGHT REQUIREMENT: Full sun.
SOIL REQUIREMENT: Most Florida soils.
SALT TOLERANCE: Not tolerant of front-line dunes; however, pines thrive back of the strand.
AVAILABILITY: Most nurseries have pines in cans. Year-old, bare-root seedlings can be obtained from State Forest Service.
CULTURE: Plants can be set out from cans at any season of the year and are easy to establish. Seedlings, watered well when set out, will establish rapidly.
PROPAGATION: Seedage.
PESTS: Usually no serious problems.
NOTE: Pines are of great economic importance in the South for lumber and paper pulp.

21
China-Fir

Cunninghamia (cunning-HAM-ee-a): for J. Cunningham, its discoverer.
lanceolata (lance-ee-oh-LAY-ta): lance-shaped.

FAMILY: Taxodiaceae.　　RELATIVES: Cypress, redwood, and sequoia.
TYPE OF PLANT: Tree.　　　　　　　　HEIGHT: 60'. ZONE: N

HOW TO IDENTIFY: Narrow, evergreen leaves, 2½" long, with 2 white bands running lengthwise beneath, and the bases running down the twigs. Tree *always* suckering around the base.

HABIT OF GROWTH: Narrowly upright, always with suckers around the base.

FOLIAGE: Evergreen with 2 white bands below. The leaf bases run down the twigs.

FLOWERS: Inconspicuous.

FRUITS: Roundish cones with leathery, toothed, pointed scales.

SEASON OF MAXIMUM COLOR: No seasonal change.

LANDSCAPE USES: In northern Florida where freezes occur, China-fir can be used as a freestanding specimen to approach the effect that the more tender monkey-puzzle-trees give in warmer sections. Cold-tolerant and disease-resistant, China-fir is planted rather widely in northern Florida and it is deeply appreciated for its many good qualities in states just north of the Florida line. Where China-fir can serve, if it is in the spirit of the scene, it is most highly recommended as a maintenance-free evergreen.

HABITAT: China; in Florida, northernmost counties only.

LIGHT REQUIREMENT: Full sun or north-side location in the shade.

SOIL REQUIREMENT: Tolerant of many soils found in northern Florida.

SALT TOLERANCE: Not tolerant.

AVAILABILITY: Some few nurseries may display small China-fir trees in gallon containers, but these are not widely offered in Florida.

CULTURE: After establishment in superior soil, no care is needed.

PROPAGATION: Cuttage or seedage.

PESTS: None of major importance.

22
Italian
Cypress

Cupressus (coo-press-us): a classical name.
sempervirens (sem-per-vie-rens): evergreen.

FAMILY: Cupressaceae.   RELATIVES: Arbor-vitae and juniper.

TYPE OF PLANT: Tree.   HEIGHT: 50'. ZONE: N

HOW TO IDENTIFY: Strict, upright habit of growth, much taller than broad; needle-like foliage that does not turn plum-colored during cold weather.

HABIT OF GROWTH: Narrow, upright, much taller than broad.

FOLIAGE: Evergreen, needle-like, of fine texture, dark green color.

FLOWERS: Inconspicuous.

FRUITS: Cones 1" in diameter with 8–14 scales, usually not seen in Florida.

SEASON OF MAXIMUM COLOR: No seasonal change.

LANDSCAPE USES: As a strong accent, Italian cypress, in the variety 'Stricta,' which is the one most often seen, is unequaled. This columnar tree is unsuitable for home landscaping; rather, its use will be restricted to college campuses and arboretums where plantings on a large scale could be complemented by strong accents 50' in height.

HABITAT: Southern Europe; in Florida, northern tier of counties.

LIGHT REQUIREMENT: Full sun.

SOIL REQUIREMENT: Fertile soil.

SALT TOLERANCE: Not tolerant.

AVAILABILITY: Italian cypress is rarely seen in Florida nurseries.

CULTURE: Plant in well-prepared site; water periodically until well established; thereafter, no attention will be needed.

PROPAGATION: Cuttage or marcottage.

PESTS: None of major concern.

23
Portuguese Cypress

Cupressus (coo-press-us): a classical name.
lusitanica (loo-si-tan-ee-ca): Portuguese, but native in Central America.

FAMILY: Cupressaceae. RELATIVES: Arbor-vitae and juniper.
TYPE OF PLANT: Tree. HEIGHT: 50′. ZONE: N
HOW TO IDENTIFY: Reddish bark, pendulous branches, usually blue-green foliage.
HABIT OF GROWTH: Dense, compact, beautifully symmetrical.
FOLIAGE: Evergreen, needle-like, of fine texture, blue-green color.
FLOWERS: Inconspicuous.
FRUITS: Cones ½″ in diameter composed of 6–8 scales, with glaucous bloom.
SEASON OF MAXIMUM COLOR: No seasonal change.
LANDSCAPE USES: Clonal propagations from special trees that have good habit, pendulous branches, and glaucous foliage are very popular as freestanding specimens in northern Florida. These are rare and hard to come by. Seedlings, grown from imported seeds, are easy to bring along, but they are quite variable in form, habit, and color, and most of them lack the strong appeal of the selected blue clones. The latter will be hard to find and expensive to buy.
HABITAT: Mountains of Central America; in Florida, northern section.
LIGHT REQUIREMENT: Full sun.
SOIL REQUIREMENT: Fertile, well-drained soil in the northern counties.
SALT TOLERANCE: Not tolerant of dune conditions.
AVAILABILITY: Portuguese cypress is rare in nurseries.
CULTURE: Plant in well-prepared site; water moderately until well established; thereafter, no attention, other than light fertilization, will be needed.
PROPAGATION: Cuttage is used for best blue clones, but cuttings root slowly. Seedlings grow easily, but they are quite variable and very subject to damping-off disease.
PESTS: None of major consequence.

24
Japanese Juniper

Juniperus (june-ɪᴘ-er-us): old classical name.
chinensis (chi-ɴᴇɴ-sis): Chinese.
'Columnaris' (col-um-ɴᴀʀᴇ-is): columnar.

FAMILY: Cupressaceae.   RELATIVES: True cypress and false-cypress.
TYPE OF PLANT: Tree.   HEIGHT: 30'. ZONE: N,C
HOW TO IDENTIFY: Tree-like, owing to strong, single, central leader with
   2 kinds of leaves (needle-like and scale-like) on every branch.
HABIT OF GROWTH: Columnar, with a strong, erect trunk.
FOLIAGE: Evergreen, of 2 types, needle-form and scale-form, on every
   branch. Texture is fine and color is dark green, even during the
   winter.
FLOWERS: Inconspicuous.
FRUITS: Usually not formed in Florida.
SEASON OF MAXIMUM COLOR: No seasonal changes.
LANDSCAPE USES: For accent, both freestanding, and in shrubbery
   groups, Japanese juniper is the best exotic, columnar, needle-
   leaved evergreen for Florida. It rightly enjoys considerable popu-
   larity.
HABITAT: China; in Florida, cultured in northern counties.
LIGHT REQUIREMENT: Full sun for compact growth.
SOIL REQUIREMENT: Fertile, well-drained soils are recommended for
   good growth.
SALT TOLERANCE: Not tolerant.
AVAILABILITY: Northern Florida nurseries display plants B & B or in
   containers.
CULTURE: On well-drained, reasonably fertile soil, no special measures
   are needed except to control juniper blight and mites upon occa-
   sion.
PROPAGATION: Cuttage.
PESTS: Juniper blight and mites.

25
Pfitzer Juniper

Juniperus (june-ip-er-us): old classical name.
chinensis (chi-nen-sis): Chinese.
'Pfitzeriana' (fits-er-ee-ane-a): of Herr Pfitzer.

FAMILY: Cupressaceae.   RELATIVES: True cypress and false-cypress.

TYPE OF PLANT: Dwarf shrub.   HEIGHT: 5'. ZONE: N,C

HOW TO IDENTIFY: Low shrub of horizontal-spreading growth, with branch tips always outward-pointing, or slightly nodding, never upright.

HABIT OF GROWTH: Horizontal-spreading.

FOLIAGE: Evergreen, very fine in texture, light gray-green in color.

FLOWERS: None in Florida.

FRUITS: None in Florida.

SEASON OF MAXIMUM COLOR: No seasonal changes.

LANDSCAPE USES: As a transition plant and planter subject, this dwarf, needle-leaved evergreen is very useful in western Florida. Southward, down the peninsula, Pfitzer juniper becomes increasingly less good as a garden shrub. Unfortunately, there is confusion in naming in nurseries.

HABITAT: China; in Florida, the northern counties.

LIGHT REQUIREMENT: Full sun only.

SOIL REQUIREMENT: Looks best on fertile, well-drained land.

SALT TOLERANCE: Tolerant of salt air well back of the dunes.

AVAILABILITY: Nurseries in northern Florida feature Pfitzer junipers B & B during the winter season. There is often incorrect labeling.

CULTURE: In northern Florida, fertile, well-drained earth that has adequate moisture is a requirement for success.

PROPAGATION: Cuttage, using tips in December–January.

PESTS: Mites and juniper blight.

Shore Juniper

Juniperus (june-IP-er-us): old classical name.
conferta (CON-FERT-a): crowded.

FAMILY: Cupressaceae.   RELATIVES: True cypress and false-cypress.

TYPE OF PLANT: Dwarf shrub.   HEIGHT: 2'. ZONE: N

HOW TO IDENTIFY: Evergreen leaves all needle-like in whorls of 3, each with 2 longitudinal lines on the upper surface. Most branch-tips upward-pointing.

HABIT OF GROWTH: Low, mat-forming.

FOLIAGE: Evergreen, needle-form with 2 white lines, very fine in texture and light gray-green in color.

FLOWERS: Inconspicuous.

FRUITS: None, usually, in Florida.

SEASON OF MAXIMUM COLOR: No seasonal variation.

LANDSCAPE USES: Shore juniper excels as a low transition plant or ground cover for positions in full sun. In sunny planters it looks particularly fine. This, the best of the ground-clinging conifers for our state, enjoys considerable popularity in northern counties.

HABITAT: Japan; in Florida, northern counties.

LIGHT REQUIREMENT: Full sun for compact growth.

SOIL REQUIREMENT: Sandy soils are acceptable.

SALT TOLERANCE: Tolerant of moderate salt spray.

AVAILABILITY: Shore juniper, in containers or B & B, is widely stocked.

CULTURE: On reasonably fertile sandy soil in upper Florida, no special care is needed. The usual watering and fertilization will suffice.

PROPAGATION: Cuttage.

PESTS: Mites and juniper blight.

27
Southern Red-Cedar

Juniperus (june-ip-er-us): old classical name.
silicicola (sill-ee-sick-oh-la): having silicles (capsules broader than long).

FAMILY: Cupressaceae. RELATIVES: True cypress and false-cypress.
TYPE OF PLANT: Tree. HEIGHT: 25'. ZONE: N,C,S
HOW TO IDENTIFY: Coniferous, evergreen tree with reddish-brown, very thin bark; green, flexible twigs that contain two kinds of leaves, the juvenile form being sharp-pointed and spreading, the adult form scale-like, closely appressed, and 4-ranked.
HABIT OF GROWTH: Very symmetrical while young, becoming picturesque, flat-topped, often windswept with age.
FOLIAGE: Evergreen, minute, finest texture, and dark green color.
FLOWERS: Inconspicuous strobili (sexes on different trees) in very early spring.
FRUITS: Succulent, dark blue, drupe-like cones, less than ¼" long, in winter.
SEASON OF MAXIMUM COLOR: Little variation except for brown cones.
LANDSCAPE USES: As a freestanding specimen, southern red-cedar has long been popular. For beach cottages and woodland plantings, it excels. Windbreaks made by planting these trees in double, staggered rows have been used for centuries.
HABITAT: Limestone areas of Florida as far south as Sarasota County.
LIGHT REQUIREMENT: Full sun or partial shade of hammocks.
SOIL REQUIREMENT: Calcareous soils are acceptable, as are beach-front locations.
SALT TOLERANCE: Tolerant of salt; recommended for dune planting.
AVAILABILITY: Some commercial nurseries sell 1-year seedlings in containers and B & B, and some state agencies distribute seedlings for reforestation.
CULTURE: Set in moderately fertile soil if possible; water until well established, and during dry times thereafter; fertilize once or twice annually.
PROPAGATION: Seedage.
PESTS: Juniper blight is a very serious disease that browns the interiors of infected plants. Mites attack junipers, too.

28
Oriental
Arbor-Vitae

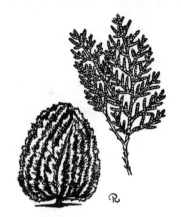

Thuja (THOO-ya): classical name.
orientalis (oh-ree-en-TAL-is): Oriental.

FAMILY: Cupressaceae.   RELATIVES: Cypress, cedar, and juniper.
TYPE OF PLANT: Tree or shrub.   HEIGHT: 40'. ZONE: N,C,S
HOW TO IDENTIFY: Narrow-leaved, coniferous evergreen that produces
   its branchlets in vertical plane; shape of the plant often runs to the
   globular or columnar.
HABIT OF GROWTH: Columnar or globular, with dense foliage.
FOLIAGE: Evergreen, very fine in texture, in various tones of green
   and/or yellow according to the variety. Fall color often purple to-
   ward tips of foliage.
FLOWERS: Inconspicuous.
FRUITS: Cones ½"–1" long, usually 6 woody scales.
SEASON OF MAXIMUM COLOR: Winter, when foliage is purple.
LANDSCAPE USES: Florida landscape developments are best completed
   without this strongly geometrical shrub; nonetheless, oriental arbor-
   vitae is very popular with homeowners and is much planted.
HABITAT: Orient; in Florida, widely cultivated.
LIGHT REQUIREMENT: Full sun for best compact habit.
SOIL REQUIREMENT: Tolerant of varying soils.
SALT TOLERANCE: Not tolerant.
AVAILABILITY: Widely offered in many cultivars in containers and
   B & B.
CULTURE: Plant with reasonable care; water faithfully until well estab-
   lished; fertilize very lightly because of rapid growth. Juniper blight,
   a very serious disease, can be controlled by very frequent appli-
   cations of fungicides.
PROPAGATION: Cuttage.
PESTS: Juniper blight and mites.

White-Cedar

Chamaecyparis (cam-ee-sɪp-ar-is): Greek for dwarf cypress.
thyoides (thigh-oy-dez): like thuja.

FAMILY: Cupressaceae.   RELATIVES: China-fir, cypress, and arbor-vitae.
TYPE OF PLANT: Tree.   HEIGHT: 80'. ZONE: N
HOW TO IDENTIFY: Attractive ascending growth; tiny, evergreen leaves,
    closely overlapping or spreading at apex, on leading shoots, with
    conspicuous glands on the back.
HABIT OF GROWTH: Attractive, symmetrical, dense crown.
FOLIAGE: Evergreen, of fine texture, medium green color.
FLOWERS: Inconspicuous.
FRUITS: Cones about ¼" across that have a glaucous bloom while im-
    mature, turn brown at maturity.
SEASON OF MAXIMUM COLOR: No variation.
LANDSCAPE USES: As a strong, permanent accent, this native tree may
    serve well. For woodland or public plantings, white-cedar is highly
    recommended.
        This is another example of a native tree that is not nearly as
    widely planted as it should be. Completely adapted to our state, of
    course, notably resistant to insects and diseases, beautifully sym-
    metrical in growth, white-cedar should appear in more plantings.
    Seeds germinate satisfactorily and growth is moderately rapid.
    There is seedling variation in form, but this is not objectionable.
HABITAT: Moist soils in certain locations in northern Florida.
LIGHT REQUIREMENT: Native in wooded areas, but grows well in sun.
SOIL REQUIREMENT: Native stands grow on fertile, moist soils.
SALT TOLERANCE: Not tolerant.
AVAILABILITY: Although this is one of our very best needle evergreens,
    it is not often found in nurseries.
CULTURE: Plant small seedlings in moist, organic soil, and no addi-
    tional care will be required.
PROPAGATION: Seedage.
PESTS: None of major consequence.

30
Common
Screw-Pine

Pandanus (pan-DAY-nus): Latinized Malayan name.
utilis (YOU-till-us): useful.

FAMILY: Pandanaceae.　　　RELATIVES: This genus stands alone.
TYPE OF PLANT: Tree.　　　HEIGHT: 25'. ZONE: S
HOW TO IDENTIFY: Stout, branching tree with many brace roots; outward-pointing leaves 3' long by 3" broad, with many sharp, ascending, red spines on margins and midrib. During parts of the year there are conspicuous rough fruits hanging on stout cords.
HABIT OF GROWTH: Coarse tree with scaffold-like branches that support groups of spirally arranged, ribbon-like leaves at their tips.
FOLIAGE: Evergreen, ribbon-like, yard-long, spine-edged, reddish-toned.
FLOWERS: Ball-like, 8" in diameter, hanging from cord-like peduncles.
FRUITS: Round, rough, compound fruits, with prism-like sections, on pistillate trees.
SEASON OF MAXIMUM COLOR: No seasonal variation.
LANDSCAPE USES: To create the atmosphere of the tropics, use pandanus as a freestanding specimen. For terrace, patio, or Florida room, potted individuals are in favor.
HABITAT: South Sea islands; in warmest parts of Florida.
LIGHT REQUIREMENT: Full sun for fruiting specimens; small plants endure shade.
SOIL REQUIREMENT: Grows well in soils of many different types.
SALT TOLERANCE: Not tolerant of dune conditions but thrives near tidal lagoons.
AVAILABILITY: Most nurseries and garden centers market screw-pines.
CULTURE: Set in a site that has been improved by the addition of organic matter; water periodically until established; thereafter keep lawn grasses away from the root zone; fertilize twice each year.
PROPAGATION: Division or seedage.
PESTS: Scales.
NOTE: Veitch pandanus (*P. veitchii*), much used as a pot plant, has spiny leaves with white bands at the margins.

Sander pandanus (*P. sanderi*) with denser, more tufted foliage, has golden yellow bands from midrib to margin. Botanical status is uncertain and labeling may not always be correct.

31
Alexandra Palm

Archontophoenix (ar-kon-toe-FEE-nicks): Greek for majestic palm.
alexandrae (alex-AN-dree): for Alexandra, Queen Dowager of Great Britain.

FAMILY: Palmaceae.　　　　　　　　RELATIVES: The palm trees.
TYPE OF PLANT: Palm tree.　　　　　　HEIGHT: 45'. ZONE: S

HOW TO IDENTIFY: A slender palm that grows from a single, thin, ringed trunk with a swollen base that holds pinnate leaves with heavy side ribs and red fruits ½" across. The fruits are held by green spadix-branches which are quite long.

HABIT OF GROWTH: Neat, upright, symmetrical from single, ringed trunk.

FOLIAGE: Evergreen, pinnate, medium-fine in texture, medium green in color. The rachis curves gracefully to give a very pleasant aspect.

FLOWERS: Inconspicuous, in many-branched spadices below the crown-shaft. The spadix-branches are green, the tiny flowers white.

FRUITS: Red, ½" in diameter on green, many-branched clusters below the crownshaft.

SEASON OF MAXIMUM COLOR: When fruits mature.

LANDSCAPE USES: As a single specimen, as a framing tree, and as an avenue tree, Alexandra palm is well liked. It will serve as a container subject, too, for years. This species is very tender to cold.

HABITAT: Queensland; in Florida, most nearly frost-free locations.

LIGHT REQUIREMENT: Full sun or broken, shifting shade.

SOIL REQUIREMENT: Reasonably fertile, well-drained soil seems best.

SALT TOLERANCE: Not recommended for direct exposure to the surf.

AVAILABILITY: Nurseries in the warmest part of the state.

CULTURE: Plant carefully in well-prepared, frost-protected sites; water faithfully in dry times; protect the foliage against scale insects, the roots against grass.

PROPAGATION: Seedage.

PESTS: Scales and caterpillars.

NOTE: The identity of this palm, and closely related *Archontophoenix cunninghamiana*, is not always clearly defined in nurseries and parks in Florida. The last-named species is much the hardier of the two and has lilac flowers and broader pinnae.

32
Cabbage Palm

Sabal (SAY-bal): unexplained.
palmetto (pal-MET-oh): little palm.

FAMILY: Palmaceae.   RELATIVES: The palm trees.
TYPE OF PLANT: Palm tree.   HEIGHT: 90'. ZONE: N,C,S

HOW TO IDENTIFY: Smooth-edged petioles continue through the palmate blades of the leaves. The trees are quite variable in aspect and foliage color.

HABIT OF GROWTH: Variable as to trunk diameter, curvature, and presence of boots, yet with a small, dense crown of deeply cut, palmate leaves. Rarely specimens with branched trunks and 2, 3, or 4 crowns of foliage are seen in Florida.

FOLIAGE: Evergreen, with petiole continuing through the blade, variable in color.

FLOWERS: Inconspicuous, hermaphroditic, in branched inflorescences.

FRUITS: Black, globular berries with short, tapering bases.

SEASON OF MAXIMUM COLOR: No variation.

LANDSCAPE USES: As peerless avenue tree, 20'–40' o.c. As a framing tree for buildings, as a member of a palm group, as a freestanding specimen, and as a patio or terrace tree, the native cabbage palm cannot be excelled.

This is Florida's state tree, and here it is appreciated for its many sterling qualities.

HABITAT: Much of Florida is inhabited by this picturesque palm.

LIGHT REQUIREMENT: Sun or shade.

SOIL REQUIREMENT: Extremely tolerant of varying soil conditions.

SALT TOLERANCE: Very tolerant of salt; recommended for seaside plantings.

AVAILABILITY: Landscape-size trees are dug from the wild upon order.

CULTURE: Plant deeply in well-prepared sites during summer months; water copiously for a time; after new growth is well under way, no more attention will be needed.

PROPAGATION: Seedage.

PESTS: Palm leaf skeletonizer and palmetto weevil.

NOTE: *Sabal peregrina*, 25' high, planted in Key West, has very fruitful spadices that are shorter than the leaves.

33
Sabal Palms`

Sabal (SAY-bal): unexplained.
SPP.: several species are grown in Florida.

FAMILY: Palmaceae.
TYPE OF PLANT: Palm tree.
RELATIVES: The palm trees.
HEIGHT: Variable. ZONE: N,C,S
HOW TO IDENTIFY: Mainly trees, but some trunkless, with fan-shaped leaves and presence of boots. Flowers small in long-branched inflorescences. *S. causiarum*: Puerto Rican hat palm, very stout tree to 60′. The boots fall, leaving a clear trunk. The massive, fan-shaped leaves are divided about 2/3 of their length, with many filaments. Inflorescence exceeds crown (illustrated above) (Puerto Rico). *S. minor*: Dwarf palmetto or blue palm, this fan-leaved palm is stemless with glaucous or pale green foliage. Leaves are segmented with middle segments split to half their length, and the remainder split to almost 2/3. The inflorescence exceeds the leaves (Georgia to Florida to Texas).
HABIT OF GROWTH: Palm trees.
FOLIAGE: Coarse-textured foliage forms massive fans of medium to pale green color.
FLOWERS: Small, cream-colored, insignificant.
FRUITS: Small, dark drupes with very thin flesh and 1 seed.
SEASON OF MAXIMUM COLOR: No variation.
LANDSCAPE USES: As street trees, for palm groupings, sabal palms are outstanding.
HABITAT: Puerto Rico; Georgia to Florida to Texas.
LIGHT REQUIREMENT: Full sun to partial shade.
SOIL REQUIREMENT: Will tolerate a wide variety of soil types.
SALT TOLERANCE: Tolerant of salt spray.
AVAILABILITY: Sabal palms are found in nurseries specializing in palms.
CULTURE: Plant deeply in summer in a well-prepared site; water frequently until new growth develops. Will require little attention afterwards.
PROPAGATION: Seedage.
PESTS: Scales, mites, and leaf skeletonizers.

34
Coconut Palm

Cocos (COKE-os): Portuguese for monkey.
nucifera (noo-SIF-er-a): nut-bearing.

FAMILY: Palmaceae. RELATIVES: The palm trees.
TYPE OF PLANT: Palm tree. HEIGHT: 60'. ZONE: S
HOW TO IDENTIFY: Palm with leaning, slender, bulbous trunk, heavy crown of graceful, pinnate foliage, and nuts, much of the year.
HABIT OF GROWTH: Graceful, bending trunks hold heavy, graceful crowns.
FOLIAGE: Evergreen, pinnate, of medium texture, medium green.
FLOWERS: Unisexual, in panicles among the leaves.
FRUITS: The well-known coconuts.
SEASON OF MAXIMUM COLOR: Little seasonal variation.
LANDSCAPE USES: The ubiquitous coconut is greatly beloved and deeply appreciated by those persons who dwell in hot countries. As an avenue tree, coconut palm can stand at intervals of 25'–35'. As a background tree, as a framing tree, and as a freestanding specimen, it is without peer for frost-free locations.

There are strains that have been selected for different characters. One of the most popular now is the so-called dwarf yellow, or dwarf golden, with its bright, little fruits. Another is the dwarf green, whose fruits are vivid green at maturity.
HABITAT: Tropics around the world; in Florida, southern counties.
LIGHT REQUIREMENT: Intense light of tropical seashores.
SOIL REQUIREMENT: Tolerant of many diverse soils.
SALT TOLERANCE: Unexcelled for salt tolerance.
AVAILABILITY: Small coconut palms are available in containers in nurseries in southern Florida.
CULTURE: After establishment, no care is required save for semiannual fertilization.
PROPAGATION: Seedage; set coconuts into the earth about one-half their depth.
PESTS: Nematodes, virus diseases, lethal yellow, and fungi.
NOTE: In areas where lethal yellow is a problem, the Malayan dwarf coconut should be planted.

35
Canary Island Date Palm

Phoenix (FEE-nicks): ancient Greek name for the date palm.
canariensis (can-ar-ee-EN-sis): of the Canary Islands.

FAMILY: Palmaceae.

RELATIVES: The palm trees.

TYPE OF PLANT: Palm tree.

HEIGHT: 60'. ZONE: N,C,S

HOW TO IDENTIFY: Stocky, single trunk marked with diamond pattern from the sloughed boots, pinnate leaves with murderous thorns on the petioles and small, orange, decorative dates borne by pistillate individuals.

HABIT OF GROWTH: Straight, single trunk with heavy head of pinnate leaves.

FOLIAGE: Evergreen, feather-leaved with stiffish pinnae, murderous thorns at the bases of the leaf stalks. The foliage is of fine texture and yellow-green color.

FLOWERS: Unisexual, inconspicuous, in short spadices amidst the leaves.

FRUITS: Ovoid, about 1" in length, of a bright orange-yellow color.

SEASON OF MAXIMUM COLOR: Early summer when fruits are fully colored.

LANDSCAPE USES: As an avenue tree, spaced 50' apart, when there is a sufficiently broad planting strip, Canary Island date palm is unsurpassed. For single specimens on lawns of public buildings it is majestic. Its huge bulk makes this palm unsuitable for residences.

HABITAT: Canary Islands; in Florida it is planted in every community.

LIGHT REQUIREMENT: Full sun for best development.

SOIL REQUIREMENT: Any well-drained soil will suffice.

SALT TOLERANCE: Tolerant of salt back from the front-line dunes.

AVAILABILITY: Most nurseries offer these date palms in containers.

CULTURE: Plant in reasonably fertile sites; water moderately; mulch the root zone; keep lawn grasses back; protect the leaves from leaf-spotting diseases while young, and from palm leaf skeletonizer when mature.

PROPAGATION: Seedage.

PESTS: Leaf-spot, palm leaf skeletonizer, and palm weevil in old age.

NOTE: Hybridization within the genus *Phoenix* has been recognized in Florida for many years. Many garden palms may be crossbred.

36
Date and
Wild Date Palms

Phoenix (FEE-nicks): ancient Greek name for the date palm.
SPP.: several species grow in Florida.

FAMILY: Palmaceae.
TYPE OF PLANT: Palm tree.

RELATIVES: The palm trees.
HEIGHT: 100'. ZONE: N,C,S

HOW TO IDENTIFY: Two very stately feather palms with grey-green foliage. Leaflets usually 2-ranked, becoming 4-ranked before becoming spine-like at the base. *P. dactylifera*, date palm: grey-green foliage covered with bloom. Shoots develop at base; it will be clump-forming if shoots are not removed. *P. sylvestris*, wild date palm: foliage not covered with bloom; single trunk. On mature specimens roots may appear on the sides of the trunk as high as 6' above ground.

HABIT OF GROWTH: Clump-forming or single-stemmed.

FOLIAGE: Pinnate leaves to 10' long, grey-green, of coarse texture.

FLOWERS: Small to 10,000 per cluster. Sexes on different trees (e.g., *P. dactylifera*).

FRUITS: Dates, yellow-orange when mature.

SEASON OF MAXIMUM COLOR: In summer when fruit matures.

LANDSCAPE USES: As an avenue tree, space 40'–50' apart. Excellent freestanding specimens for parks and areas around large buildings.

HABITAT: North Africa or India.

LIGHT REQUIREMENT: Full sun.

SOIL REQUIREMENT: Thrives on well-drained, dry, sandy soils; even grows in brackish soils.

SALT TOLERANCE: Tolerant if kept back from the front-line dunes.

AVAILABILITY: Carried by most nurseries specializing in palms.

CULTURE: Plant in well-drained soil; water moderately until established; fertilize once or twice a year. Keep lawn grasses back for a few years.

PROPAGATION: Seedage. Commercially, date palms are increased by division of offsets.

PESTS: Leaf-spot and palm leaf skeletonizer.

NOTE: To have dates you need both a male and a female tree. Dates do not always mature in Florida. Fruit of the wild date is of no value. Trees can be tapped and will yield up to 8 pounds of sugar annually.

Pygmy Date Palm

Phoenix (FEE-nicks): ancient Greek name for the date palm.
roebelenii (roe-bell-EEN-ee-eye): for Mr. Robeleni.

FAMILY: Palmaceae.

RELATIVES: The palm trees.

TYPE OF PLANT: Dwarf palm tree.

HEIGHT: 8'. ZONE: C,S

HOW TO IDENTIFY: A dwarf palm of fine proportions with delicate pinnate leaves and murderous thorns at the bases of the leaf-stalks.

HABIT OF GROWTH: A graceful, fine-scale crown above a single, straight or curving trunk.

FOLIAGE: Evergreen, pinnate, of fine texture, with spines on the petiole.

FLOWERS: Unisexual, inconspicuous, in short spadices among the leaves.

FRUITS: Cylindrical, little, jet-black dates about 1" long.

SEASON OF MAXIMUM COLOR: No variation unless fruits mature.

LANDSCAPE USES: Unquestionably one of Florida's leading dwarf palms, pygmy date is used as a freestanding specimen, planter subject, or urn plant for patio, terrace, or Florida room.

Thousands are propagated here and sold for landscape use and for shipping to northern markets.

HABITAT: Burma; in Florida, protected spots on the peninsula.

LIGHT REQUIREMENT: Partial shade or full sun.

SOIL REQUIREMENT: Well-drained, fertile soil with moderate moisture.

SALT TOLERANCE: Not tolerant.

AVAILABILITY: Most retail nurseries on the peninsula, many chain stores everywhere, offer this excellent little palm for sale.

CULTURE: Plant in fertile soil; water moderately; fertilize three times each year; protect from frost.

PROPAGATION: Seedage.

PESTS: A leaf-spotting disease, scales, and caterpillars.

NOTE: Pygmy date palms hybridize with other members of their genus.

38
Senegal
Date Palm

Phoenix (FEE-nicks): ancient Greek name for the date palm.
reclinata (reck-lin-AH-ta): leaning.

FAMILY: Palmaceae.

RELATIVES: The palm trees.

TYPE OF PLANT: Palm tree.

HEIGHT: 35'. ZONE: N,C,S

HOW TO IDENTIFY: A clump-forming palm with many leaning, bowed trunks and feather-leaves whose pinnae are stiffish and sharp-tipped. The petioles are heavily armed with very sharp spines.

HABIT OF GROWTH: Clump-forming by gracefully curving stems.

FOLIAGE: Evergreen, pinnate, with thorns at the bases of the leaf-stalks. The texture is fine, the color medium green.

FLOWERS: Unisexual, inconspicuous, in short spadices amidst the foliage.

FRUITS: Ovoid little dates about 1" in length of bright orange color.

SEASON OF MAXIMUM COLOR: In early summer when fruits turn orange.

LANDSCAPE USES: As a freestanding specimen to create atmosphere or mood, Senegal date, or cluster date as it is frequently called, is highly regarded and much used in landscape compositions.

HABITAT: Africa; in Florida, all areas.

LIGHT REQUIREMENT: Full sun or partial shade.

SOIL REQUIREMENT: Any well-drained soil seems to be adequate.

SALT TOLERANCE: Tolerant of salt air back from the strand.

AVAILABILITY: Senegal date palms are fairly abundant in small sizes in containers. Landscape-size B & B specimens are rare and expensive.

CULTURE: Plant in fertile soil; water moderately; fertilize once or twice a year; keep lawn grasses from encroaching upon the root zone for a few years.

PROPAGATION: Seedage and/or division of suckers from the base of old trees.

PESTS: Palm leaf skeletonizer and leaf-spot.

NOTE: Cliff date (*Phoenix rupicola*) grows with a single bowed trunk which supports leaves with soft, drooping pinnae emerging from a single plane. Hybridization within the genus *Phoenix* is widespread in Florida, and many garden specimens are crossbred palms.

39
Chinese Fan Palm

Livistona (liv-is-TONE-a): for Livistone, Scotland.
chinensis (chi-NEN-sis): Chinese.

FAMILY: Palmaceae.

RELATIVES: The palm trees.

TYPE OF PLANT: Palm tree.

HEIGHT: 25'. ZONE: C,S

HOW TO IDENTIFY: The ringed trunk is usually straight; the palmate leaves have long, bifid segments that hang downward with age. The bases of the green petioles of young plants are edged with downward-pointing, single spines.

HABIT OF GROWTH: Gracefully fountain-like, causing this species to be called Chinese fountain palm in some localities.

FOLIAGE: Evergreen, palmate, with bifid segments that bend sharply downward.

FLOWERS: Inconspicuous, bisexual, in thin spadices amidst the foliage.

FRUITS: Black, olive-like, ellipsoid-oblong, 1" in length.

SEASON OF MAXIMUM COLOR: No seasonal variation.

LANDSCAPE USES: As a freestanding specimen the little Chinese fountain palm is noted for its outstanding beauty, and as an urn subject a young seedling is much admired as well. Although Chinese fan palm has long been known to horticulture, it has not been much planted by homeowners within its climatic range. It is hoped that this may be remedied as gardeners learn of this fine little palm.

HABITAT: China; in Florida, sparingly planted over the peninsula.

LIGHT REQUIREMENT: Shade while young, sun is tolerated in maturity.

SOIL REQUIREMENT: Soil of moderate fertility is recommended.

SALT TOLERANCE: Not tolerant.

AVAILABILITY: Nurseries offer small Chinese fan palms in containers.

CULTURE: Plant in reasonably fertile soil; shade while young; mulch with organic litter; water during dry spells; fertilize thrice annually.

PROPAGATION: Seedage.

PESTS: Scales.

40
Fountain Palms

Livistona (liv-is-TONE-a): for Livistone, Scotland.
SPP.: several species grow in Florida.

FAMILY: Palmaceae. RELATIVES: The palm trees.
TYPE OF PLANTS: Palm tree. HEIGHT: Variable. ZONE: C,S

HOW TO IDENTIFY: Stately palms with single trunks; ringed and palmate leaves with a distinct ligule. Leaf-stems with varying degrees of armament. *L. australis*, Australian cabbage-palm; leaves round to 4' in diameter, cut below the middle into many segments, tips forked or entire; leaf-stems with spines on entire length. *L. decipens*: loose, open head, with palmate leaves to 5' in diameter, narrow segments cut almost to base. Leaf petiole with small spines continuing out onto margins of the blade. *L. mariae*: loose head of palmate leaves, up to 6' long; almost orbicular. Leaves split to middle with a thread in each sinus. Leaf-stem with many stout, short spines; spines also on leaf-blade. Leaves often with a red tinge.

HABIT OF GROWTH: Single-stemmed palms.

FOLIAGE: Coarse, palmate leaves, medium to dark green.

FLOWERS: Small, cream-colored, insignificant.

FRUITS: Small, purplish-black drupes.

SEASON OF MAXIMUM COLOR: No seasonal variation.

LANDSCAPE USES: Livistonas are outstanding as freestanding specimens. Young palms also make ideal patio plants when grown in tubs or urns. This genus deserves wider use in the landscape.

HABITAT: Australia.

LIGHT REQUIREMENT: Young plants thrive in shade, but mature plants thrive in full sun.

SOIL REQUIREMENT: Grows best in well-drained, fertile soils.

SALT TOLERANCE: Not tolerant.

AVAILABILITY: Found in nurseries specializing in palms.

CULTURE: Plant in fertile soil; water frequently until plants are established. Livistonas require little care after establishment. Fertilize 3 or 4 times per year.

PROPAGATION: Seedage.

PESTS: Scales.

Camellia japonica

Camellia
p. 261

Wisteria sinensis

Wisteria
p. 203

Illicium floridanum
Florida Anise-Tree
p. 160

Jasminum nitidum

Shining Jasmine
p. 324

Tradescantia

Wandering-Jew
p. 89

Gardenia jasminoides

Gardenia
p. 392

Euphorbia milii

Crown-of-Thorns
p. 224

Hibiscus tiliaceus

Sea Hibiscus
p. 252

Crossandra infundibuliformis

Crossandra
p. 381

Bougainvillea glabra

Bougainvillea
p. 148

Spathodea campanulata

African Tulip-Tree
p. 363

Cryptanthus sp.

Cryptanthus
p. 83

41
European Fan Palm

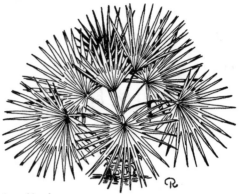

Chamaerops (cam-EE-rops): Greek for dwarf bush.
humilis (HUME-ill-is): dwarf.

FAMILY: Palmaceae.

TYPE OF PLANT: Palm tree.

RELATIVES: The palm trees.

HEIGHT: 15′. ZONE: N,C,S

HOW TO IDENTIFY: Clump-growing; palmate foliage is held by armed petioles. The leaf segments do not droop.

HABIT OF GROWTH: Clump-forming by suckers around the base.

FOLIAGE: Evergreen, palmate, of attractive form, and gray-green color.

FLOWERS: Inconspicuous, in dense spadices among the leaves.

FRUITS: Small, globular berries, reddish or yellowish in color.

SEASON OF MAXIMUM COLOR: No variation in color.

LANDSCAPE USES: As a tiny lawn specimen; many seedlings never grow over 5′ in height. As a part of a palm group, set these dwarfs 5′ o.c. As an urn subject for terrace, patio, or Florida room, European fan palm excels.

HABITAT: Southern Europe; in Florida, all sections.

LIGHT REQUIREMENT: Sun or shade.

SOIL REQUIREMENT: Tolerant of many kinds of soil.

SALT TOLERANCE: Tolerant of light salt drift, back from the dunes.

AVAILABILITY: Only rarely is this little palm found in nurseries, yet it warrants much wider use.

CULTURE: Set in well-prepared planting sites; water faithfully; keep lawn grasses back from the root zone. Fertilize lightly once or twice during the rainy season.

PROPAGATION: Seedage or division.

PESTS: Scales.

NOTE: There are some named clones, there is extreme seedling variation, and many individuals may never reach the maximum height of 30′ but remain for many years true dwarfs.

42
Fiji
Fan Palm

Pritchardia (prit-CHAR-dee-a): for W. Pritchard, an Englishman.
pacifica (pa-SIFF-ee-ca): of the Pacific Ocean.

FAMILY: Palmaceae.

RELATIVES: The palm trees.

TYPE OF PLANT: Palm tree.

HEIGHT: 30'. ZONE: S

HOW TO IDENTIFY: Straight, slender bole; 5-foot leaves, deeply and neatly pleated, held by 3-foot, spineless petioles; globe-like fruit clusters hung on 3-foot cords.

HABIT OF GROWTH: Neat, distinctive, fan-leaved crown atop a slender, straight trunk.

FOLIAGE: Evergreen, palmate, neatly pleated to form a beautiful design in dark green.

FLOWERS: Inconspicuous, bisexual, in globes at the ends of cords.

FRUITS: Globular ½" black berries with tapered bases borne in large balls on yard-long cords.

SEASON OF MAXIMUM COLOR: No color variation.

LANDSCAPE USES: As a framing tree or as a freestanding specimen in a protected garden in extreme southern Florida, Fiji fan palm is without superior. It is easily injured by wind and frost.

HABITAT: Fiji Islands; in Florida, protected locations only.

LIGHT REQUIREMENT: Partial shade is desirable.

SOIL REQUIREMENT: Fertile, well-drained organic soil is recommended.

SALT TOLERANCE: Very intolerant of salt air.

AVAILABILITY: Fiji fan palm will be found in containers in some specialty nurseries in the warmest parts of the lower peninsula.

CULTURE: Plant this delicate palm carefully in a well-prepared site in a very protected location; water faithfully; mulch and fertilize three times a year.

PROPAGATION: Seedage.

PESTS: Scales, mites.

NOTE: Thurston fan palm (*Pritchardia thurstonii*) thrusts its fruits well beyond the leaves on 6-foot cords. This one grows to about 15' in height and has beautifully pleated leaves. There are numerous other species in *Pritchardia*, but these are rare in Florida gardens.

43
Fishtail Palm

Caryota (carry-oh-ta): Greek name first applied to the cultivated date.
mitis (MY-tis): mild.

FAMILY: Palmaceae.

RELATIVES: The palm trees.

TYPE OF PLANT: Palm tree.

HEIGHT: 25′. ZONE: S

HOW TO IDENTIFY: Clump-growing palm whose leaf-blades are divided into many segments, each of which resembles the tail of a fancy goldfish.

HABIT OF GROWTH: Clump-growing by many suckers around the base.

FOLIAGE: Evergreen, of fishtail form and medium texture.

FLOWERS: Inconspicuous, in scurfy, much-branched spadices amidst the foliage.

FRUITS: Globose drupes, ½″ in diameter, bluish-black in color.

SEASON OF MAXIMUM COLOR: No seasonal variation.

LANDSCAPE USES: As a part of shrubbery borders and foundation plantings for large buildings, fishtail palms are popular, but perhaps their best use is for urns for household decoration.

HABITAT: Tropical Asia; in Florida, warmest locations only.

LIGHT REQUIREMENT: Resistant to deep shade.

SOIL REQUIREMENT: Tolerant of varying soils, but fertile soil is best.

SALT TOLERANCE: Not tolerant.

AVAILABILITY: Fishtails are in high demand, and they are widely offered in containers by nurseries in warmest sections of the state.

CULTURE: Plant in carefully made sites; water faithfully; keep lawn grasses from encroaching upon the root zone.

PROPAGATION: Seedage or division.

PESTS: Red spider mites and scales.

NOTE: Wine palm (*C. urens*), seen in southern Florida, may grow to a height of 80′ or more to become too large to use with small homes. This species does *not* sucker at the base.

44
Gru-Gru Palm

Acrocomia (ack-roe-com-ee-a): from a tuft of leaves at the top.
spp.: several species are grown in Florida.

FAMILY: Palmaceae.

RELATIVES: The palm trees.

TYPE OF PLANT: Palm tree.

HEIGHT: 50′. ZONE: C,S

HOW TO IDENTIFY: Vicious thorns arm the trunk and leaf-stalks.

HABIT OF GROWTH: Straight-trunked palm that develops a bulge in middle age.

FOLIAGE: Evergreen, pinnate, fine in texture, light green in color.

FLOWERS: Inconspicuous, in branched, drooping spadices, among the leaves.

FRUITS: Large, round, oil-bearing, sometimes edible.

SEASON OF MAXIMUM COLOR: Possibly when fruits mature.

LANDSCAPE USES: For palm groups, because of the curiosity of the heavily armed trunks, gru-grus must be included.

Palms of this genus have real atmosphere-creating character, much appreciated by tourists to lands of the Caribbean.

HABITAT: Tropical America; in Florida, warm locations.

LIGHT REQUIREMENT: Full sun.

SOIL REQUIREMENT: Tolerant of sandy soils of many types.

SALT TOLERANCE: Tolerant of salt drift, back of front-line dunes.

AVAILABILITY: Gru-gru palms in containers will be found in specialty nurseries.

CULTURE: Plant in enriched site during warm months; water faithfully; keep lawn grasses back; fertilize during each rainy season.

PROPAGATION: Seedage.

PESTS: Scales and palm weevils in old age.

45
Household Palms

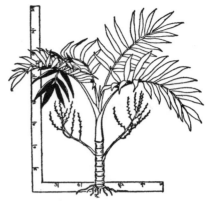

Chamaedorea (cam-ee-DORE-ee-a): Greek for dwarf and gift.
SPP.: several species are grown in Florida.

FAMILY: Palmaceae.

RELATIVES: The palm trees.

TYPE OF PLANT: Dwarf palm trees.

HEIGHT: 10'. ZONE: S

HOW TO IDENTIFY: Dwarf, pinnate palms, with single or multiple trunks and branched spadices among the leaves. The Chamaedoropsis complex, to which they belong, is incompletely understood.

HABIT OF GROWTH: Upright, with tiny, symmetrical crowns.

FOLIAGE: Evergreen, pinnate, of fine texture and pale green color.

FLOWERS: Inconspicuous, unisexual flowers, borne on separate plants.

FRUITS: Globular little drupes.

SEASON OF MAXIMUM COLOR: None.

LANDSCAPE USES: As urn subjects for shady locations, for planter bins, and for accents in north-side foundation plantings, these tiny palms are in high favor in frostless locations. *Chamaedorea elegans* (illustrated) is usually single-trunked. Widely planted because it is so readily available and because of its small size. *Chamaedorea erumpens* is a clump-grower that requires full shade and freedom from frost. The horticultural variety 'Fairchild' is characterized by foliage in which terminal pinnae are united into two broad blades. *Chamaedorea seifrizii* is a scrambling palm that may endure more light than the others in this group. Other species in *Chamaedorea* are offered by nurserymen in southern Florida.

HABITAT: Central America; in Florida, shady sites in nearly frostless locations.

LIGHT REQUIREMENT: Shade is necessary for health and a deep green color.

SOIL REQUIREMENT: Fibrous leaf mold with fertility above average.

SALT TOLERANCE: Not tolerant.

AVAILABILITY: Chain stores, filling stations, and garden centers offer household palms in containers. Specialty nurseries stock rarer species and varieties.

CULTURE: Shade is a requirement; limey soil is tolerated if it is open and fibrous; protection from frost is necessary for success with these diminutive tropical palms.

PROPAGATION: Seedage.

PESTS: Mites, nematodes, and scales.

46
Lady Palm

Rhapis (ʀᴀʏ-pis): Greek for needle.
excelsa (ecks-ꜱᴇʟʟ-sa): tall.

FAMILY: Palmaceae.
TYPE OF PLANT: Dwarf palm.
RELATIVES: The palm trees.
HEIGHT: 10′. ZONE: N,C,S

HOW TO IDENTIFY: Growing in matted clumps, lady palm makes a dense mass of foliage. The blades of the leaves are 5- to 10-parted nearly to the base, 1⅛″ wide at the middle; the apexes are short-toothed.

HABIT OF GROWTH: Clump-forming by underground, running stems.

FOLIAGE: Evergreen, digitate, attractively divided, of medium green color.

FLOWERS: Inconspicuous, unisexual, in branched spadices among the leaves.

FRUITS: Small, 1- to 3-seeded berries.

SEASON OF MAXIMUM COLOR: No color variation.

LANDSCAPE USES: For foundation plantings on north sides of buildings, lady palms are in great favor. As urn subjects for terrace, patio, or Florida room, they are unexcelled. Lady palms are among the most wanted dwarf palms in Florida, and, as a consequence, they are rare and expensive. One rare clone has variegated foliage.

HABITAT: Eastern Asia; in Florida, shady locations in all areas.

LIGHT REQUIREMENT: Shade is requisite for success with lady palms.

SOIL REQUIREMENT: The best-looking plants grow on moist, fertile soil.

SALT TOLERANCE: Not tolerant.

AVAILABILITY: Nurseries offer small seedlings or little divisions in containers, but large specimens are rare and expensive.

CULTURE: Plant only in shady locations, in well-prepared, fast-draining soil that is high in organic matter. Water faithfully but moderately.

PROPAGATION: Division; seedage when seeds are to be had.

PESTS: Scales and caterpillars.

NOTE: Dwarf lady palm (*Rhapis humilis*) has more slender stems and narrower (¾″) leaf segments. There is confusion in naming in the genus *Rhapis*.

47
Licuala Palm

Licuala (lick-you-ALE-a): aboriginal Moluccan name.
grandis (GRAN-dis): large.

FAMILY: Palmaceae.

RELATIVES: The palm trees.

TYPE OF PLANT: Dwarf palm tree.

HEIGHT: 8'. ZONE: S

HOW TO IDENTIFY: Dainty, shade-demanding, dwarf, single-trunked palm with orbicular, yard-broad, undivided, much-pleated leaves.

HABIT OF GROWTH: Single-stemmed, with the dainty, pleated leaves held by slender, spiny petioles.

FOLIAGE: Evergreen, palmate, bold in design, dark green in color.

FLOWERS: Inconspicuous, mostly perfect.

FRUITS: Showy clusters of scarlet, pea-like, pointed drupes.

SEASON OF MAXIMUM COLOR: When fruits mature.

LANDSCAPE USES: As a diminutive subject for an urn in a patio or Florida room, licuala palm is ideal. While this species is perhaps the best known, it is not the only one in *Licuala*. These scale-model palms require shade and warmth.

HABITAT: New Britain Island; in Florida, greenhouses, nurseries, and patios.

LIGHT REQUIREMENT: Dense shade is a requirement for success.

SOIL REQUIREMENT: Moderately fertile, well-drained medium.

SALT TOLERANCE: Not tolerant.

AVAILABILITY: Specialty nurseries may have small licuala palms in gallon containers.

CULTURE: Plant in good soil in a shaded spot; water faithfully; fertilize twice annually; keep grass back. Protection must be supplied on cold nights.

PROPAGATION: Seedage.

PESTS: Nematodes, scales, and mites.

48
Madagascar Palm

Chrysalidocarpus (kris-al-id-oh-CAR-pus): Greek for golden fruit.
lutescens (loo-TESS-enz): becoming yellow.

FAMILY: Palmaceae.

TYPE OF PLANT: Palm tree.

RELATIVES: The palm trees.

HEIGHT: 30'. ZONE: S

HOW TO IDENTIFY: Clump-growing palm with ringed, bamboo-like stems and yellow leaf-ribs.

HABIT OF GROWTH: Clump-forming by means of gracefully bending stems.

FOLIAGE: Evergreen, pinnate, of fine texture and yellow-green color.

FLOWERS: Inconspicuous in short clusters below the crownshaft.

FRUITS: Oblong, ¾" in diameter, nearly black when mature.

SEASON OF MAXIMUM COLOR: No seasonal variation.

LANDSCAPE USES: This beautiful soft palm is one of Florida's favorites for use in foundation plantings, as a featured patio plant, or as an urn subject for terrace or Florida room. Madagascar palm is injured by cold.

Gardeners know this attractive plant under various names, and so nursery labels may designate it as areca palm, bamboo palm, yellow palm, or cane palm. Under any appellation this is one of the most useful palms of the tropics the world around.

HABITAT: Madagascar; in Florida, widely planted in nearly frostless sections.

LIGHT REQUIREMENT: Tolerant of rather dense shade in patios or Florida rooms.

SOIL REQUIREMENT: Grows best in fairly rich soil, slightly acid in reaction.

SALT TOLERANCE: Quite intolerant of salt.

AVAILABILITY: Most nurseries in southern Florida offer Madagascar palms in varying sizes in containers.

CULTURE: Plant in fertile, acid soil; water moderately during dry periods; protect against scale insects and frost.

PROPAGATION: Seedage or division.

PESTS: Scales followed by sooty-mold.

49
Manila Palm

Veitchia (VEECH-ee-a): for the English horticultural family.
merrillii (MER-ril-ee-eye): for E. Merrill, American horticulturist.

FAMILY: Palmaceae.

RELATIVES: The palm trees.

TYPE OF PLANT: Palm tree.

HEIGHT: 25'. ZONE: S

HOW TO IDENTIFY: Resembles small royal palm, with broad, flat pinnae. Prominent clusters of bright red fruits are borne below the crownshaft in winter and spring. The stocky trunk is ringed.

HABIT OF GROWTH: Straight-trunked palm tree of stocky appearance.

FOLIAGE: Evergreen, pinnate, with flat, broad pinnae, of fine texture and light green color. The rachis bends gently to give a graceful effect.

FLOWERS: Inconspicuous, unisexual, in branched spadices below crownshaft.

FRUITS: Drupe-like, bright red, 1" in diameter, very showy; gracefully placed on bone-white spadix in winter and spring.

SEASON OF MAXIMUM COLOR: Late winter and early spring when fruits mature.

LANDSCAPE USES: Avenue tree, plant 25'–35' apart; framing tree; member of a palm group.

Manila palm is usually called adonidia palm in the Miami area. Under any name this lime-enduring, sturdy little tree, that resembles a scale-model royal, is worthy of the high esteem with which it is regarded in frostless areas. Important dividend is the highly decorative red fruits that are produced during the height of the tourist season.

HABITAT: Philippine Islands; in Florida, warmest locations.

LIGHT REQUIREMENT: Full sun when mature, partial shade while young.

SOIL REQUIREMENT: Tolerant of the limestone soils of southern Florida.

SALT TOLERANCE: Tolerant of salt air back from the beach.

AVAILABILITY: Manila palm is very popular in extreme southern Florida where it is widely available in nurseries in all sizes.

CULTURE: Set slightly deeper than former level in well-made sites; water faithfully; keep lawn grasses away from root zone; fertilize thrice annually.

PROPAGATION: Seedage.

PESTS: Scales.

50
Paurotis Palm

Paurotis (paw-ROE-tis): Greek for small ear, application unclear.
wrightii (RIGHT-ee-eye): for C. Wright, American botanist.

FAMILY: Palmaceae.

RELATIVES: The palm trees.

TYPE OF PLANT: Palm tree.

HEIGHT: 30'. ZONE: C,S

HOW TO IDENTIFY: Clump-growing, small-scale fan palm with armed petioles. Slender trunks grow with tufts of fan leaves atop, always with many suckers around their bases.

HABIT OF GROWTH: Clump-forming by many slender trunks.

FOLIAGE: Evergreen, palmate, tropical in appearance, medium green.

FLOWERS: Inconspicuous, on long, branching spadices among the leaves, but protruding beyond the leaf mass in untidy array.

FRUITS: Shining, black, globular drupes ⅜" in diameter.

SEASON OF MAXIMUM COLOR: When flowers open in early summer.

LANDSCAPE USES: In highest favor for landscaping houses of contemporary design, for palm groups, and for parts of enclosing borders, is this native of the Florida Everglades. Beloved of landscape architects and palm fanciers, most available native clumps have been transplanted to landscape compositions. Paurotis palms, also known as Cape Sable palms, are attractive while small and trunkless, yet they are particularly picturesque and handsome in maturity, when several leaning trunks reach roof-tree height. Old fruiting stalks should be pruned out regularly for neat appearance, as should old leaves that turn brown.

HABITAT: Moist locations in the Everglades and Caribbean islands.

LIGHT REQUIREMENT: Full sun or partial shade.

SOIL REQUIREMENT: Tolerant of many soils, native in wet places but grows well on elevated, sandy soil; tolerates alkalinity.

SALT TOLERANCE: Tolerant of salt air, slightly brackish water.

AVAILABILITY: Some nurseries will offer small seedlings in containers.

CULTURE: Set slightly deeper than the palm grew formerly, into fertile, acid soil; water periodically until the palm is well established. Keep lawn grasses back from the roots.

PROPAGATION: Seedage and/or division.

PESTS: None of major concern.

NOTE: *Acoelorrhaphe wrightii* is the proper name of this palm.

51
Pindo
Palm

Butia (BEW-tee-a): corruption of a native name.
capitata (cap-ee-TAY-ta): in compact head.

FAMILY: Palmaceae.

RELATIVES: The palm trees.

TYPE OF PLANT: Palm tree.

HEIGHT: 20'. ZONE: N,C,S

HOW TO IDENTIFY: Blue-green, pinnate leaves have strongly recurving leaf-stems that emerge from heavy, stocky trunks. Decorative orange dates may mature in summertime.

HABIT OF GROWTH: Stout trunks hold recurving, graceful leaves.

FOLIAGE: Evergreen, pinnate, fine in texture, blue-green in color.

FLOWERS: Small, in dense spadices about 3' long, amidst the foliage.

FRUITS: Decorative, orange, date-like, in showy clusters.

SEASON OF MAXIMUM COLOR: Summer when dates color.

LANDSCAPE USES: As a freestanding specimen on large properties, or as a member of a palm group, this hardiest of pinnate palms is highly recommended. Much space is required for the short, broad top to develop. There is great variation among pindo palms in Florida landscape plantings; botanical status is unclear. In years past this palm was known as *Cocos australis*.

HABITAT: Brazil; in Florida, every community in the state.

LIGHT REQUIREMENT: Full sun for best fruiting and compact habit of growth.

SOIL REQUIREMENT: Tolerant of varying soils throughout Florida.

SALT TOLERANCE: Tolerant of salt air back from the strand.

AVAILABILITY: Pindo palms are available in retail nurseries.

CULTURE: After careful planting in fertilized earth, periodic watering and the removal of encroaching lawn grasses will assure good growth.

PROPAGATION: Seedage.

PESTS: Palm leaf skeletonizer.

NOTE: A striking palm is a natural cross between pindo palm and queen palm. This bigeneric hybrid is a beautiful, hardy plant that has many of the good qualities of each parent.

52
Queen
Palm

Arecastrum (ary-CAST-rum): *Areca*-like.
romanzoffianum (roman-zof-ee-AY-num): for N. Romanzoff of Russia.

FAMILY: Palmaceae.

RELATIVES: The palm trees.

TYPE OF PLANT: Palm tree.

HEIGHT: 40'. ZONE: C,S

HOW TO IDENTIFY: Single, usually straight, ringed trunk with untidy boots just below foliage; pinnate, unarmed leaves; decorative, orange fruits during cool months.

HABIT OF GROWTH: Straight, single trunk, and graceful crown of soft leaves.

FOLIAGE: Evergreen, pinnate, fine in texture, dark green in color.

FLOWERS: Inconspicuous, on very large, interfoliar spadices.

FRUITS: Decorative, orange, drupe-like, 1-seeded dates.

SEASON OF MAXIMUM COLOR: Cool months when dates mature.

LANDSCAPE USES: Central Florida's most popular palm is used for avenue plantings (25'–35' o.c.), as a framing tree, as a background tree, and as a member of palm groups.

There is considerable seedling variation in populations of queen palms.

HABITAT: Brazil; in Florida, widely planted on the middle peninsula.

LIGHT REQUIREMENT: Full sun for best habit and fruiting.

SOIL REQUIREMENT: Tolerant of various types of sandy soil.

SALT TOLERANCE: Not very tolerant.

AVAILABILITY: Queen palms in containers and B & B are for sale in almost all nurseries in central Florida. They are often labeled *Cocos plumosa*.

CULTURE: If planted in holes made up with fertile compost, watered during dry times, and fertilized at the beginning of the rainy season, queen palms should grow well.

PROPAGATION: Seedage; volunteers often appear under fruiting trees.

PESTS: Scales; mineral defiency on calcareous soils.

NOTE: A notable palm is a natural cross between queen palm and pindo palm. This bigeneric hybrid is a beautiful, hardy plant that has many of the good qualities of each parent.

53
Royal Palm

Roystonea (roy-STONE-ee-a): for R. Stone, an American engineer.
SPP.: two species grow in Florida.

FAMILY: Palmaceae.

RELATIVES: The palm trees.

TYPE OF PLANT: Palm tree.

HEIGHT: 75'. ZONE: S

HOW TO IDENTIFY: Majestic palm trees with cement-gray trunks that are thickened at about the middle or above; bright green crown-shafts and beautiful heads of soft, pinnate leaves.

HABIT OF GROWTH: Majestic, clean, upright.

FOLIAGE: Shedding at maturity, unarmed, of medium texture and bright green color.

FLOWERS: Inconspicuous, unisexual, in huge spadices below the crown-shaft.

FRUITS: Black or bluish drupes about ½" long.

SEASON OF MAXIMUM COLOR: Perhaps when fruits mature.

LANDSCAPE USES: Southern Florida's most popular palm tree is widely used for avenue plantings (30'–50' o.c.), for framing large buildings, and for palm groups. The species most used in landscaping is Cuban royal palm (*Roystonea regia*). Less frequently planted by nurseries is our own native Floridian royal palm (*R. elata*). This one, so effectively employed at the famed Hialeah racecourse, has the thickening toward the upper part of the bole, with a shoulder at the top; the pinnae lack longitudinal nerves, and the black fruits are nearly round.

HABITAT: Tropical America; in Florida, nearly frostless locations.

LIGHT REQUIREMENT: Full sun or broken, shifting shade.

SOIL REQUIREMENT: Rich soil is best.

SALT TOLERANCE: Tolerant of salt drift.

AVAILABILITY: Small trees in containers and B & B are offered by most nurseries in southern Florida.

CULTURE: Start off well by setting in fertile holes and supplying adequate moisture; during dry times water as needed; fertilize young trees twice each year.

PROPAGATION: Seedage.

PESTS: Scales while young.

NOTE: *Roystonea* species vary from island to island in the West Indies, but the palm was never found on the Florida keys.

54
Seaforthia Palm

Ptychosperma (tie-koe-SPERM-a): folded seed.
elegans (ELL-ee-gans): elegant.

FAMILY: Palmaceae.
RELATIVES: The palm trees.
TYPE OF PLANT: Small palm tree.
HEIGHT: 25'. ZONE: S
HOW TO IDENTIFY: Small size, ringed single trunk, 3"–4" in diameter, thickened near the base; open head of small, pinnate leaves above a green crownshaft; red fruits hanging below the crownshaft.
HABIT OF GROWTH: Small-scale, erect little palm from a single, slender trunk.
FOLIAGE: Evergreen, pinnate, medium fine in texture, bright green in color.
FLOWERS: Inconspicuous, below the crownshaft in bushy spadices.
FRUITS: Bright red, oblong, ¾" long.
SEASON OF MAXIMUM COLOR: Warm months when fruits color.
LANDSCAPE USES: For small home grounds, this small-scale palm can serve as a framing tree or as a patio subject. As a tubbed specimen it has been grown for generations, north and south, as "Seaforthia elegans." It has a long history of popularity in American horticulture, despite confusion in nomenclature.
HABITAT: Tropical islands of the Old World; in Florida, warmest areas.
LIGHT REQUIREMENT: Tolerant of shade.
SOIL REQUIREMENT: Tolerant of many different soils.
SALT TOLERANCE: Not tolerant of front-line dune conditions.
AVAILABILITY: Small seaforthia palms in containers are offered by nurseries in southern counties.
CULTURE: Set slightly deeper than formerly in made-up planting site; water faithfully until well established; apply mulch; keep grasses from the root zone.
PROPAGATION: Seedage.
PESTS: Scales and mites.
NOTE: MacArthur palm (*Ptychosperma macarthurii*), with its clustered slender stems and red fruits, is very popular in the Miami area for planters and urns. There are other species and there are some hybrids, all of which are rare in Florida gardens.

55
Sentry Palms

Howeia (HOW-ee-a): for Lord Howe Islands in the southern Pacific Ocean.
SPP.: two species are grown in Florida.

FAMILY: Palmaceae.

RELATIVES: The palm trees.

TYPE OF PLANT: Palm trees.

HEIGHT: 35'. ZONE: S

HOW TO IDENTIFY: Erect, smooth, single trunk; pinnate leaves 8' long with rachises gently curving downward.

HABIT OF GROWTH: Appealing, neat, and clean.

FOLIAGE: Evergreen, pinnate, of fine texture and dark green color.

FLOWERS: Inconspicuous, unisexual, in spadices amidst the foliage.

FRUITS: Yellow-green, ovoid drupes the size of pecans.

SEASON OF MAXIMUM COLOR: No difference in color.

LANDSCAPE USES: As urn subjects, sentry palms (or kentia palms) have been prime favorites for generations. In southern Florida they serve as small framing trees and as lawn specimens with distinction.

  Howeia belmoreana "makes like a bell," and is notably the more graceful of the two. This one has short petioles.

  Howeia forsteriana, Forster's sentry palm, has leaves with long petioles and fewer pinnae and these stand away from the rachis horizontally for half their length, then become pendant. The fruits of Forster's are long-attenuate to the apex, not beaked. Forster's sentry palm is the more rapid grower.

  Sentry palms are very sensitive to cold.

HABITAT: Lord Howe Islands; in Florida, frost-free locations.

LIGHT REQUIREMENT: Tolerant of shade in patios, terraces, and Florida rooms.

SOIL REQUIREMENT: Fertile, well-drained, organic soils for best growth.

SALT TOLERANCE: Not tolerant.

AVAILABILITY: Specialty nurseries have small sentry palms (they call them kentias) in containers.

CULTURE: Plant carefully in acid compost; water faithfully; protect from cold, from lawn grasses, and from scale insects.

PROPAGATION: Seedage.

PESTS: Scales of many types.

Spindle Palm

Mascarena (mass-car-EE-na): for the Mascarene Islands, home of the palm.
verschaffeltii (ver-sha-FELT-ee-eye): for A. Verschaffelt, Belgian horticulturist.

FAMILY: Palmaceae.

RELATIVES: The palm trees.

TYPE OF PLANT: Palm tree.

HEIGHT: 25'. ZONE: S

HOW TO IDENTIFY: The straight, smooth, gray trunk is swollen prominently just below the green crownshaft. The leaves are short-petioled,
and a prominent yellow band extends the full length of the midrib. Fruit clusters are sent out just below the crownshaft.

HABIT OF GROWTH: Dwarfish palm with straight, heavy, bulging trunk,
holding a very close, compact head of short, pinnate leaves.

FOLIAGE: Evergreen, pinnate, with very short petiole; unarmed.

FLOWERS: Inconspicuous, yellowish, very numerous in spadices below
the crownshaft.

FRUITS: Plum-like, less than 1″ long, produced abundantly.

SEASON OF MAXIMUM COLOR: Little seasonal variation.

LANDSCAPE USES: For the curiosity of the markedly bulging trunk and
the yellow-banded midribs, spindle palm may be set as a freestanding specimen.

HABITAT: Mauritius; in Florida, warmest locations.

LIGHT REQUIREMENT: Full sun or broken shade.

SOIL REQUIREMENT: Many soils appear to be suitable.

SALT TOLERANCE: Tolerant of salt drift back from the strand.

AVAILABILITY: Specialty nurseries in southern Florida may carry a few
Mascarena palm seedlings in containers.

CULTURE: Plant with care in a place that has been enriched with peat;
water carefully; place a mulch over the root zone, and keep lawn
grasses clear of the mulched area.

PROPAGATION: Seedage.

PESTS: Mites, scales, and nematodes.

NOTE: Bottle palm (*Mascarena lagenicaulis*), also from Mauritius, has
the bulge nearer the base of the trunk to lend a bottle-shape to the
stout, little, cement-gray stem.

57
Washington Palm

Washingtonia (wash-ing-TONE-ee-a): for G. Washington.
robusta (roe-BUS-ta): robust, referring to the height of the tree.

FAMILY: Palmaceae.
RELATIVES: The palm trees.
TYPE OF PLANT: Palm tree.
HEIGHT: 60'. ZONE: N,C,S
HOW TO IDENTIFY: Leaves palmate, with many gray threads, petioles heavily armed; growth rapid.
HABIT OF GROWTH: Straight trunk and close, compact head with shag.
FOLIAGE: Evergreen, palmate, bold in aspect, medium green in color.
FLOWERS: Bisexual, inconspicuous, in long, panicled spadices among the leaves, but longer than the foliage mass.
FRUITS: Black, shining drupes that are ellipsoid in shape.
SEASON OF MAXIMUM COLOR: No variation.
LANDSCAPE USES: As an avenue tree, plant 25'–35' apart. Washington palm serves admirably as a central feature in a palm group in large public landscape plantings, but it is too tall for small home ground plantings.
HABITAT: Mexico, in Sonora and Baja California; in Florida, ubiquitous.
LIGHT REQUIREMENT: Full sun for best growth, yet it endures some shade while young.
SOIL REQUIREMENT: Tolerant of light, open sands of low fertility.
SALT TOLERANCE: Tolerant of salt drift back of the front dunes.
AVAILABILITY: Small Washington palms are offered by nearly all nurseries.
CULTURE: After proper planting, no special attention is needed.
PROPAGATION: Seedage.
PESTS: Scales while young, palm weevil in old age.
NOTE: California Washington palm (*Washingtonia filifera*), indigenous to California and so widely used as an avenue tree there, is not often seen in Florida. The Californian has a thicker, heavier trunk and is less tall than its Mexican relative. The shag of hanging dead leaves adds to the picturesque quality, but it presents a fire hazard and a breeding place for rats, so it is unlawful to leave the shag in some California communities.

58
Windmill Palm

Trachycarpus (tray-key-CAR-pus): Greek for rough fruit.
fortunei (FOR-tune-eye): for R. Fortune, Scottish botanist.

FAMILY: Palmaceae.

TYPE OF PLANT: Palm tree.

RELATIVES: The palm trees.

HEIGHT: 20'. ZONE: N,C

HOW TO IDENTIFY: Slender palm with single trunk clothed in brown fiber and yard-broad palmate leaves attached to rough-edged petioles.

HABIT OF GROWTH: Upright, from a single, erect trunk with neat crown.

FOLIAGE: Evergreen, palmate, coarse in texture, gray-green in color.

FLOWERS: Small, yellow, in small, branching spadices among the leaves.

FRUITS: 3-parted, angled fruits, the size of peas, if present.

SEASON OF MAXIMUM COLOR: No seasonal variation.

LANDSCAPE USES: This diminutive, slow-growing palm is of greatest usefulness with structures of contemporary design. In foundation plantings or in shrubbery borders it may serve as an excellent accent.

Popular in Mediterranean gardens and in tropical arboretums, too, windmill palm is enjoying public favor in Florida. *Trachycarpus* will not be injured by cold, and will remain in scale for many, many years. It has, in truth, many admirable qualities.

HABITAT: Eastern Asia; in Florida, infrequently seen in gardens of the upper peninsula and the Panhandle.

LIGHT REQUIREMENT: Tolerant of shade, yet grows in full sun, too.

SOIL REQUIREMENT: Fertility above average is recommended.

SALT TOLERANCE: Tolerant of salt air back of the front-line dunes.

AVAILABILITY: Windmill palm is found in specialty nurseries.

CULTURE: Make sites carefully with an acid, organic mixture; plant a little below original growing depth; water faithfully; keep lawn grasses back from the root zone. Fertilize twice or thrice annually.

PROPAGATION: Seedage.

PESTS: Scales.

59
Galingale

Cyperus (si-PEAR-us): ancient Greek name for these plants.
SPP.: several species are grown in Florida.

FAMILY: Cyperaceae.   RELATIVES: Bulrushes and sedges.
TYPE OF PLANT: Herbaceous perennial.   HEIGHT: Variable. ZONE: N,C,S
HOW TO IDENTIFY: Triangular stems bear tufts of leaves atop. Strong
    clumps of many stems are formed under good conditions.
HABIT OF GROWTH: Upright, symmetrical form.
FOLIAGE: Leaves round or flat, clustered at the tips of the triangular
    stems somewhat like the ribs of umbrellas.
FLOWERS: Inconspicuous, in spikelets covered by subtending bracts.
FRUITS: Tiny achenes of sedges.
SEASON OF MAXIMUM COLOR: Little seasonal variation.
LANDSCAPE USES: In conjunction with water gardens, lily pools, or
    basins in Florida rooms, the galingales are very useful in helping
    to create the feeling of tropical living. Actually, these plants grow
    in garden soil as well.
HABITAT: World-wide tropics.
LIGHT REQUIREMENT: Tolerant of shade; grows equally well in full sun.
SOIL REQUIREMENT: Tolerant of varying soils; grows well in water.
SALT TOLERANCE: Endures salt drift back from the strand.
AVAILABILITY: Many nurseries offer plants in containers.
CULTURE: Plant in a boggy place and forget.
PROPAGATION: Division of matted clumps. Small plants arise from leaf
    axils if foliage heads are placed in moist sand. These are potted
    separately.
PESTS: Mites.
NOTE: Umbrella-plant (Cyperus alternifolius), with many long, flat
    spreading leaves, the most common species, is pictured above. There
    is a clone with mottled foliage. Papyrus (C. papyrus), with many
    long, wire-like clustered leaves, is preferred for water gardens.
    Papyrus grows two or three times the height of umbrella-plant. For
    tiny water-garden arrangements, there is C. haspan 'Viviparus', the
    smaller, right-hand sketch. Dwarf, broad-leaved Cyperus diffusus
    makes an attractive pot plant for pool or Florida room.

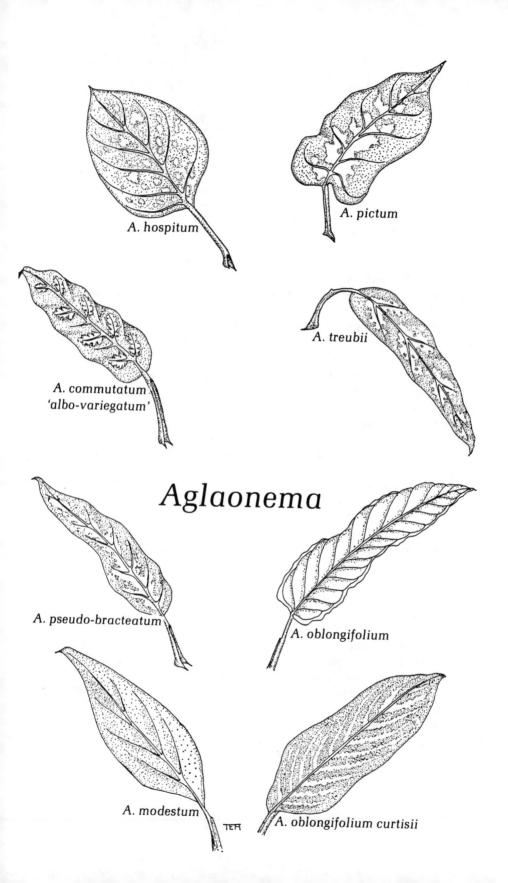

A. hospitum

A. pictum

A. commutatum 'albo-variegatum'

A. treubii

Aglaonema

A. pseudo-bracteatum

A. oblongifolium

A. modestum

A. oblongifolium curtisii

61
Aglaonema

Aglaonema (ag-low-NEE-ma): Greek for bright thread, referring to the stamens.
SPP.: several species grow in Florida.

FAMILY: Araceae.   RELATIVES: Monstera and philodendron.
TYPE OF PLANT: Herbaceous perennial.   HEIGHT: Variable. ZONE: S
HOW TO IDENTIFY: Round, thumb-sized stems bear attractive leaves by
    ensheathing petioles that are equal to, or shorter than, the blades.
    Tiny spadices are protected by little green or yellow spathes which
    soon wither to reveal attractive red or yellow fruits.
HABIT OF GROWTH: Neat, upright-spreading, with leaves attractively
    arranged at stem-ends.
FOLIAGE: Bold and attractive, held horizontally by ensheathing petioles
    shorter than blades. Patterns of white markings vary with the spe-
    cies or variety.
FLOWERS: Little spadices with tiny spathes resemble diminutive callas.
FRUITS: Conspicuous, bright red or yellow, in little clusters, held on
    slender stalks.
SEASON OF MAXIMUM COLOR: Late summer when fruits ripen.
LANDSCAPE USES: For locations with reduced light, aglaonemas are
    outstanding. Use them in planter bins, urns, pots, or, in frostless
    areas, in north-side arrangements in the foundation scheme.
HABITAT: Malaysia.
LIGHT REQUIREMENT: Tolerant of reduced light that would be unsuit-
    able for many tropical exotics.
SOIL REQUIREMENT: Fertile, nematode-free compost is highly suitable,
    yet aglaonemas will survive in peat and perlite, in sand, or in water
    if fertilizer salts (in small amounts) are added regularly.
SALT TOLERANCE: Not tolerant of dune conditions.
AVAILABILITY: Nurseries and garden centers offer aglaonemas.
CULTURE: These plants should not be subjected to low temperatures,
    nor should they be planted in media that might contain nematodes.
    Regular applications of dilute fertilizers should be made during
    growing weather.
PROPAGATION: Cuttage and marcottage.
PESTS: Nematodes, pythium root-rot under some conditions, and mites.
NOTE: Chinese evergreen (*Aglaonema modestum*), illustrated above,
    is the most popular of the several species grown in Florida.

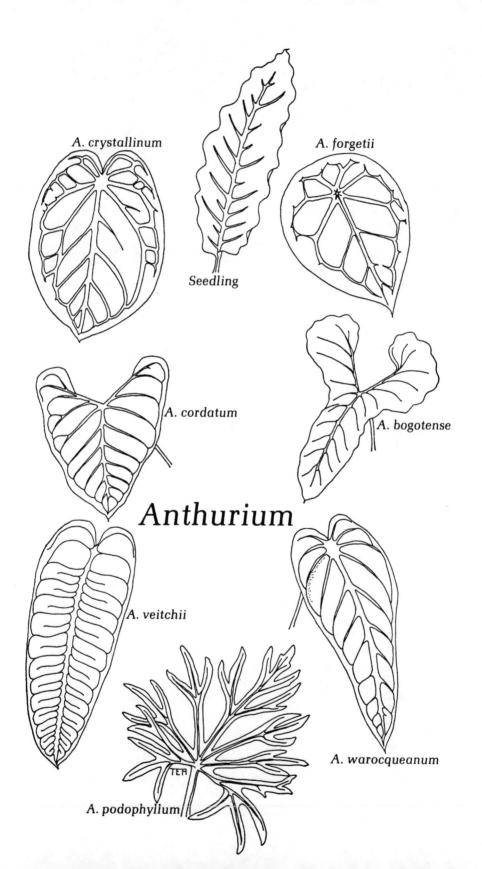

A. crystallinum

Seedling

A. forgetii

A. cordatum

A. bogotense

Anthurium

A. veitchii

A. warocqueanum

A. podophyllum

63
Anthurium

Anthurium (an-THOO-ree-um): Greek for flower and tail.
SPP.: several species and many hybrids are found in Florida.

FAMILY: Araceae.   RELATIVES: Alocasia and colocasia.
TYPE OF PLANT: Herbaceous perennial.   HEIGHT: Variable. ZONE: S
HOW TO IDENTIFY: Many anthuriums are grown for their very showy, highly decorative spathes, the most colorful in the aroid family. These are called "flamingo-flowers." Others are cultured for their decorative leaves (the rat-tail anthuriums).
HABIT OF GROWTH: Compact herbaceous perennial.
FOLIAGE: Extremely variable, usually decorative, bold, and persistent.
FLOWERS: Extremely variable; flamingo-flowers are most beautiful; rat-tail types are considerably less attractive.
FRUITS: Fleshy berries.
SEASON OF MAXIMUM COLOR: Warm months when blossoms appear.
LANDSCAPE USES: As specimens in frostless, shady spots outdoors, or in pots, anthuriums are greatly admired. Flamingo-flowers, noted for their beautiful clear colors and amazing keeping quality, are popular corsage subjects.
HABITAT: American tropics.
LIGHT REQUIREMENT: Reduced light is optimum.
SOIL REQUIREMENT: Organic potting compost, sawdust, peat, osmundine, and tree fern fragments, or combinations of these, are used as growing media for anthuriums.
SALT TOLERANCE: Not tolerant.
AVAILABILITY: Small plants in containers are for sale in some nurseries and garden centers on the peninsula.
CULTURE: Plant slightly deeper than the plant grew formerly; water carefully daily; fertilize once each month during the summer.
PROPAGATION: Cuttage and seedage.
PESTS: Mites, nematodes, scales, mealy-bugs, and grasshoppers.
NOTE: Possibly a dozen of the 500 species in *Anthurium* have been used to make hybrids. Both wild types and hybrids of complex lineage are popular in Florida, and some of each are illustrated on the facing page. Above right is a sketch of a flamingo-flower, a hybrid of *Anthurium andreanum*.

Fancy-Leaved Caladium

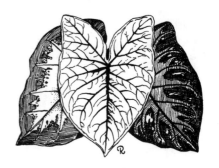

Caladium (cal-AYE-dee-um): name of East Indian origin.
SPP.: at least 2 species have been used to make the many hybrids.

FAMILY: Araceae.   RELATIVES: Monstera and aglaonema.
TYPE OF PLANT: Tuberous perennial.   HEIGHT: 2'. ZONE: N,C,S
HOW TO IDENTIFY: The strikingly beautiful, fancy-leaved caladiums are
    so well known that description should be unnecessary. There is re-
    markable variety in form and color of leaf.
HABIT OF GROWTH: Bright leaves on tall stems arise from tubers to form
    clumps.
FOLIAGE: Deciduous, variously heart-shaped or of lance-form, in a
    multitude of color combinations.
FLOWERS: Boat-shaped, persistent spathes enclose somewhat shorter
    spadices.
FRUITS: Fleshy berries may mature after pollination.
SEASON OF MAXIMUM COLOR: Warm months.
LANDSCAPE USES: For bright spots of summertime color in front of
    green shrubbery, or in planters, fancy-leaved caladiums have long
    been great favorites. Best landscape effects are attained when many
    plants of a single clone are bedded together, but some homeowners
    prefer to mass mixed foliage for a great riot of color.
HABITAT: Tropical America.
LIGHT REQUIREMENT: Full sun or high, shifting shade.
SOIL REQUIREMENT: Rich, organic earth is best.
SALT TOLERANCE: Not tolerant.
AVAILABILITY: Garden centers offer, at appropriate seasons, both dor-
    mant tubers and potted plants in full leaf.
CULTURE: Plant tubers when days lengthen in springtime; water during
    dry times; and fertilize once each month. As days shorten (October–
    November), the leaves may be cut away. In northern Florida, where
    freezes are the rule, tubers should be dug at this time and stored
    in dry peat until the following spring.
PROPAGATION: Division of offsets from old tubers, or by division of the
    tuber (chips) as long as each chip has one eye (bud).
PESTS: Soil-borne fungus diseases, mites, and grasshoppers.

65
Dieffenbachia

Dieffenbachia (deef-en-BOCK-ee-a): for J. Dieffenbach, German physician.
SPP.: several species, and many varieties are grown in Florida.

FAMILY: Araceae.   RELATIVES: Philodendron, monstera, and caladium.
TYPE OF PLANT: Herbaceous perennial.   HEIGHT: 8'. ZONE: C,S
HOW TO IDENTIFY: Ringed, hose-like stems, with many prominent root
   initials and bold, variegated leaves with long petioles which clasp
   or ensheath the stems.
HABIT OF GROWTH: Stems bent or almost upright, usually unbranched,
   with the huge, alternate, evergreen leaves growing out in all direc-
   tions.
FOLIAGE: Evergreen, large, bold, usually variegated in striking patterns.
FLOWERS: Spadices within thick, persistent, boat-like spathes.
FRUITS: Fleshy, densely packed, ripened ovaries.
SEASON OF MAXIMUM COLOR: No seasonal variation.
LANDSCAPE USES: Dieffenbachias are in great demand as accent plants
   in outdoor plantings and as urn subjects for Florida rooms, patios,
   and terraces.
HABITAT: Tropical America; in Florida, widely cultured indoors, and
   out.
LIGHT REQUIREMENT: Very tolerant of shade, yet grows in sun.
SOIL REQUIREMENT: Tolerant of many soil types and reactions, but
   grows best with moderate moisture and freedom from nematodes.
SALT TOLERANCE: Not tolerant of dune conditions.
AVAILABILITY: All nurseries and garden center stores offer dieffenbach-
   ias.
CULTURE: Plant in moderately fertile soil of acid reaction; water with
   moderation; fertilize lightly once each month during growing
   weather; control mealy-bugs.
PROPAGATION: Cuttage of stem pieces, and marcottage.
PESTS: Mealy-bugs, mites, scales, nematodes, and root-rot.
NOTE: The genus *Dieffenbachia* contains a score of species that have
   been used to make many varieties. Naming may not be consistent.
   Above is *Dieffenbachia amoena*, popular, fast-growing, king-size
   dumbcane.

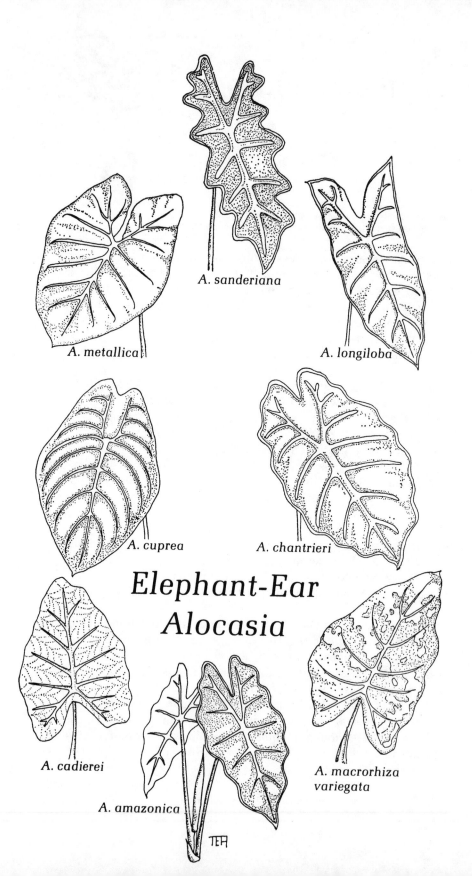

A. sanderiana

A. metallica

A. longiloba

A. cuprea

A. chantrieri

Elephant-Ear
Alocasia

A. cadierei

A. amazonica

A. macrorhiza
variegata

TEH

67
Elephant-Ear

Alocasia (al-o-CAZ-ee-a): name made from *Colocasia*.
Colocasia (col-o-CAZ-ee-a): old Greek name.
Xanthosoma (zan-tho-so-ma): Greek for yellow body, referring to the stigma.
SPP.: many species and innumerable varieties belong in this great complex.

FAMILY: Araceae.   RELATIVES: Aglaonema and dieffenbachia.
TYPE OF PLANT: Tuberous or rhizomatous perennial.   HEIGHT: Variable.
ZONE: N,C,S

HOW TO IDENTIFY: Bold, shield-like leaves (peltate or sagitate) are held
   by fleshy petioles. Leaf colors, sizes, shapes, and ornamentation
   beggar description.

HABIT OF GROWTH: Huge, coarse, sprawling, clump-forming.

FOLIAGE: Bold, decorative, variable in size, color and form.

FLOWERS: Spadices are protected by boat-like spathes.

FRUITS: Fleshy berries, if present.

SEASON OF MAXIMUM COLOR: Warm months when fresh leaves appear.

LANDSCAPE USES: To enhance the feeling of the tropics, elephant-ears
   may be grouped at the far end, or a low corner, of the out-of-door
   living area. The outsize foliage does not combine well with that of
   most woody shrubs. As pot plants, the diminutive, fancy-leaved
   types (see opposite page) are very popular. For planters, medium-
   sized clones can be selected.

HABITAT: The tropics the world around.

LIGHT REQUIREMENT: Full sun or broken, shifting shade, depending
   upon the kind.

SOIL REQUIREMENT: Rich, organic, moisture-retentive earth is best.

SALT TOLERANCE: Not tolerant.

AVAILABILITY: Garden centers sell canned plants.

CULTURE: Once they are established, the large elephant-ears growing
   in the earth receive little attention. The miniature, pot-plant types,
   on the other hand, require reasonable care in the matter of watering and fertilization.

PROPAGATION: Division of underground storage organs.

PESTS: Soil-borne fungus diseases.

NOTE: Uncounted numbers of aroids in this huge complex are grown
   in Florida for garden ornament; yet, in tropical lands, the world
   around, these are important sources of dietary starch.

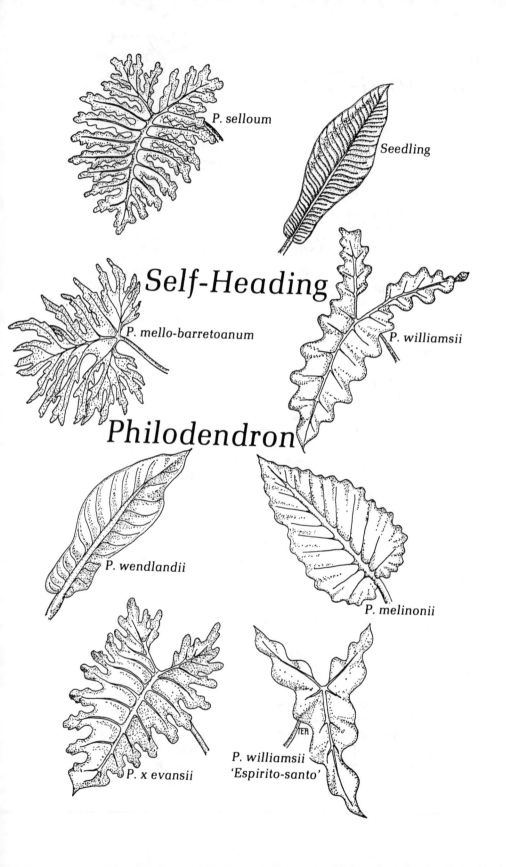

P. selloum

Seedling

Self-Heading

P. mello-barretoanum

P. williamsii

Philodendron

P. wendlandii

P. melinonii

P. x evansii

P. williamsii 'Espirito-santo'

69
Self-Heading Philodendron

Philodendron (fil-oh-DEN-dron): Greek for tree-loving.
SPP.: many species and countless varieties grow in Florida.

FAMILY: Araceae.   RELATIVES: Caladium and ivy-arum.
TYPE OF PLANT: Herbaceous perennial.   HEIGHT: Variable. ZONE: S
HOW TO IDENTIFY: Arborescent herbaceous perennials with leaves in an infinite variety of shapes, sizes, and colors.
HABIT OF GROWTH: Very compact.
FOLIAGE: Highly variable in size, shape, and color; usually bold and showy.
FLOWERS: Spadices within thick, persistent, boat-like spathes.
FRUITS: Fleshy, densely packed, ripened ovaries.
SEASON OF MAXIMUM COLOR: Summer when new growth appears.
LANDSCAPE USES: Landscape planners and homeowners use philodendrons in every conceivable landscape application. They excel as subjects for planters in Florida rooms and for urns on terraces.
HABITAT: Tropical America.
LIGHT REQUIREMENT: Variable: some thrive in sunlight, others in shade.
SOIL REQUIREMENT: Fertility and moisture-holding capacity above average are needed for good appearance.
SALT TOLERANCE: Not tolerant of front-line conditions.
AVAILABILITY: Most nurseries display specimens.
CULTURE: After establishment in nearly frostless locations, philodendrons require reasonable attention in the matter of watering and fertilization.
PROPAGATION: Self-heading philodendrons are propagated by seedage.
PESTS: Mites and scales.
NOTE: The genus *Philodendron* contains 200 species; with these, countless hybrids have been produced. On the opposite page are leaf drawings of self-headers. Naming is not always consistent. Above is the popular *Philodendron cannaefolium*.

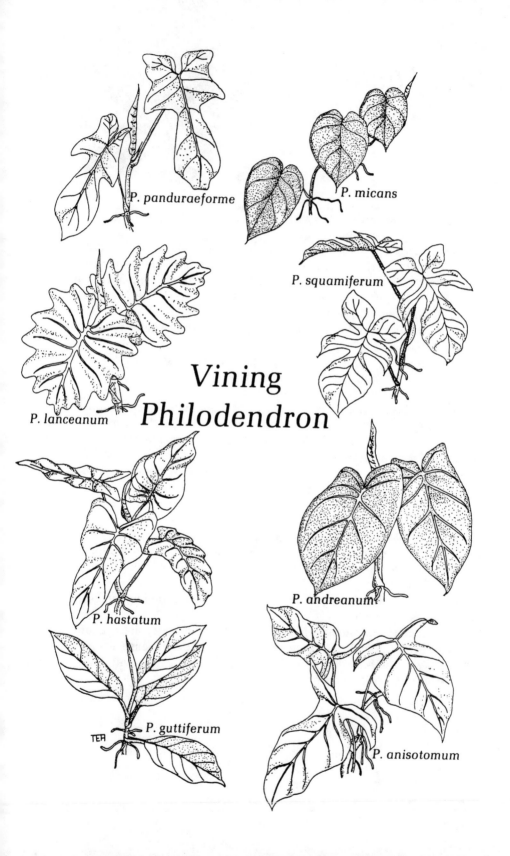

P. panduraeforme

P. micans

P. squamiferum

P. lanceanum

Vining
Philodendron

P. hastatum

P. andreanum

P. guttiferum

P. anisotomum

Vining
Philodendron

Philodendron (fil-oh-DEN-dron): Greek for tree-loving.
SPP.: many species and countless varieties grow in Florida.

FAMILY: Araceae.   RELATIVES: Caladium and ivy-arum.
TYPE OF PLANT: Vine.   HEIGHT: Variable. ZONE: S

HOW TO IDENTIFY: Vigorous tropical lianas, with leaves in infinite variety of shapes, sizes, and colors. Strong, brown, twine-like roots hold tenaciously to supporting trees or walls.

HABIT OF GROWTH: Vining herbaceous perennial.

FOLIAGE: Variable, always evergreen, usually of bold form, variable in color, frequently dark green, sometimes variegated.

FLOWERS: Spadices within thick, persistent, boat-like spathes.

FRUITS: Fleshy, densely packed, ripened ovaries.

SEASON OF MAXIMUM COLOR: No seasonal variation.

LANDSCAPE USES: Landscape planners and homeowners use philodendrons in every conceivable landscape application. For planters in Florida rooms or for urns on terraces philodendrons are highly approved. The vining types are ever popular for training on trees and patio walls.

HABITAT: Tropical America; in Florida, widely cultured indoors and out.

LIGHT REQUIREMENT: Variable: some thrive in sunlight, others in shade.

SOIL REQUIREMENT: A fertile, well-drained, organic soil, slightly acid in reaction, is always best.

SALT TOLERANCE: Not tolerant of dune conditions.

AVAILABILITY: All nurseries and garden centers offer philodendrons.

CULTURE: After establishment in nearly frostless locations, philodendrons require reasonable attention in the matter of watering and fertilization. They are not temperamental plants, and they respond well to moderately good care and mulching.

PROPAGATION: Vining types by cuttage; self-headers by seedage.

PESTS: Scales.

NOTE: The genus *Philodendron* contains 200 species; with these countless hybrids have been produced.

Ivy-Arum

Scindapsis (sin-DAP-sis): Greek name for some kind of vine.
SPP.: 2 species and a number of varieties grow in Florida.

FAMILY: Araceae. RELATIVES: Calla and spathiphyllum.
TYPE OF PLANT: Vine. HEIGHT: Variable. ZONE: S
HOW TO IDENTIFY: Huge, variegated, ovoid leaves with 1 or more deep clefts are produced by wrist-thick, vigorous, climbing vines.
HABIT OF GROWTH: Rampant tropical vine that climbs into tallest trees.
FOLIAGE: Gigantic, bizarre, mottled leaves, often with clefts, are characteristic of vines growing vigorously on vertical supports in the open. Indoors and on earth-bound individuals, leaves may be heart-shaped, about 6" long.
FLOWERS: Densely packed spadices within white, deciduous spathes, when present.
FRUITS: Typical, cone-like, aroid fruits, if present.
SEASON OF MAXIMUM COLOR: Springtime when colors of new growth are fresh.
LANDSCAPE USES: To highlight palm trunks, ivy-arums are in great favor in most nearly frost-free sections. As ground cover, earth-bound vines are excellent for shady spots. For indoor decoration, these plants are popular as pot items, planter-bin subjects, and for growing in bowls of water.
HABITAT: Tropical islands of the Pacific.
LIGHT REQUIREMENT: Tolerant of shade, but color is better in full light.
SOIL REQUIREMENT: Tolerant of many soil types.
SALT TOLERANCE: Endures mild salt air back from the strand.
AVAILABILITY: Chain stores, garden centers, and retail nurseries offer ivy-arums in pots.
CULTURE: Plant slightly deeper than formerly; water faithfully during dry times; fertilize during warm months.
PROPAGATION: Cuttage of stem joints.
PESTS: Scales, mites, and mealy-bugs.
NOTE: Many choice varieties of *Scindapsis aureus* are available from nurseries.

73
Monstera

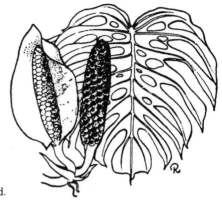

Monstera (mon-STER-a): name unexplained.
deliciosa (de-lis-ee-OH-sa): delicious.

FAMILY: Araceae.   RELATIVES: Dieffenbachia and philodendron.

TYPE OF PLANT: Vine.   HEIGHT: Variable. ZONE: S

HOW TO IDENTIFY: Yard-long, thick, evergreen leaves that are pinnately cut with elliptic spaces, from a rampant, fast-growing tropical vine, also known as ceriman in some localities.

HABIT OF GROWTH: Rampant vine that climbs by strong aerial rootlets.

FOLIAGE: Evergreen, huge, of tropical appearance and dark green color.

FLOWERS: Thick, densely flowered spadix about a foot long.

FRUITS: Thick, densely packed fruits cohering into a cone-like body.

SEASON OF MAXIMUM COLOR: No variation.

LANDSCAPE USES: For creating a tropical atmosphere, outdoors or in the house, nothing can surpass ceriman, and it is widely employed, in consequence, in every conceivable landscape and interior decorating use in Florida.

HABITAT: Tropical American mainland; in Florida, widely cultured.

LIGHT REQUIREMENT: Shade of forests is natural habitat.

SOIL REQUIREMENT: Rich forest soils are best.

SALT TOLERANCE: Not tolerant.

AVAILABILITY: Monsteras are for sale in almost every nursery and garden center.

CULTURE: In a nearly frostless location, plant pieces of stem; water faithfully during dry times; fertilize thrice annually; protect from scale insects and from frost.

PROPAGATION: Cuttage of pieces of the stem, and marcottage.

PESTS: Scales, mites, mealy-bugs.

Swiss-Cheese Plant

Monstera (mon-STER-a): name unexplained.
friedrichstahlii (freed-rick-STALL-ee-eye): for a man named Friedrich Stahl.

FAMILY: Araceae.   RELATIVES: Dieffenbachia and philodendron.

TYPE OF PLANT: Vine.   HEIGHT: Variable. ZONE: S

HOW TO IDENTIFY: Foot-long leaves bear many elliptical holes, all or most of which are enclosed and do not penetrate the margins to make deep lobes, as in *M. deliciosa*.

HABIT OF GROWTH: Vine.

FOLIAGE: Elliptical, 10″–12″ long, perforated with many holes, few or none of which break the margins to form lobes.

FLOWERS: Typical spadices of the Araceae.

FRUITS: Typical cone-like bodies of this family.

LANDSCAPE USES: As an urn subject, if vertical support such as redwood or tree fern is supplied, this tropical liana is well liked. For adding interest to palm or oak trunks, it is useful as well.

HABITAT: Tropical America.

LIGHT REQUIREMENT: Reduced light of forests is optimum; full sunshine is not recommended.

SOIL REQUIREMENT: Rich, organic soils are best.

CULTURE: In nearly frostless locations, plant pieces of stem, or a plant from a container; water faithfully during dry times; fertilize thrice annually.

PROPAGATION: Cuttage of pieces of the stem.

PESTS: Mites, scales, and mealy-bugs.

NOTE: Usually the plants seen in Florida landscaping belong to the one species; there are no horticultural variants reported as yet, but, as so many tropical exotics appear in variegated forms, it is quite likely that a Swiss-cheese plant with white-marked leaves will be discovered, described, and named as a clone.

75
Schismatoglottis

Schismatoglottis (skis-mat-o-GLOT-is): Greek for falling tongue, referring to the shedding spathe.
picta (PICK-ta): painted.

FAMILY: Araceae.　　　　　　　　RELATIVES: Aglaonema and dumb-cane.

TYPE OF PLANT: Herbaceous perennial.　　　HEIGHT: Variable. ZONE: S

HOW TO IDENTIFY: Very closely allied to dumb-cane, schismatoglottis is most difficult to differentiate. The leaves are held in much the same fashion, variegation is similar to that in some dumb-canes, and growth habits are much alike.

HABIT OF GROWTH: Stems usually upright, unbranched, with large, alternate, evergreen leaves growing out in all directions.

FOLIAGE: Bold and attractively marked with white, some cultivars show translucent spots. The sheathing petiole is longer than the blade.

FLOWERS: Unisexual flowers in spadices, typical for the family; the stamens are free, the ovaries 1-celled, the spathe falls free.

FRUITS: Oblong, green or yellowish.

SEASON OF MAXIMUM COLOR: Possibly when the little fruits develop color.

LANDSCAPE USES: Schismatoglottis enjoys the same popularity for indoor uses as do its close relatives dieffenbachia, aglaonema, and monstera. This aroid serves well in planters that receive reduced light.

HABITAT: Malaya.

LIGHT REQUIREMENT: Reduced light found in Florida rooms and patios is satisfactory.

SOIL REQUIREMENT: A fertile, well-drained, organic soil, slightly acid in reaction, is always best, yet mixtures of peat and perlite are frequently used for schismatoglottis.

SALT TOLERANCE: Not tolerant of dune conditions.

AVAILABILITY: Chain stores, garden centers, and nurseries offer potted plants of this species under a variety of names.

CULTURE: Regular attention to watering, fertilization, and pest control will keep plants growing satisfactorily.

PROPAGATION: Cuttage and marcottage.

PESTS: Mites, nematodes, and scales.

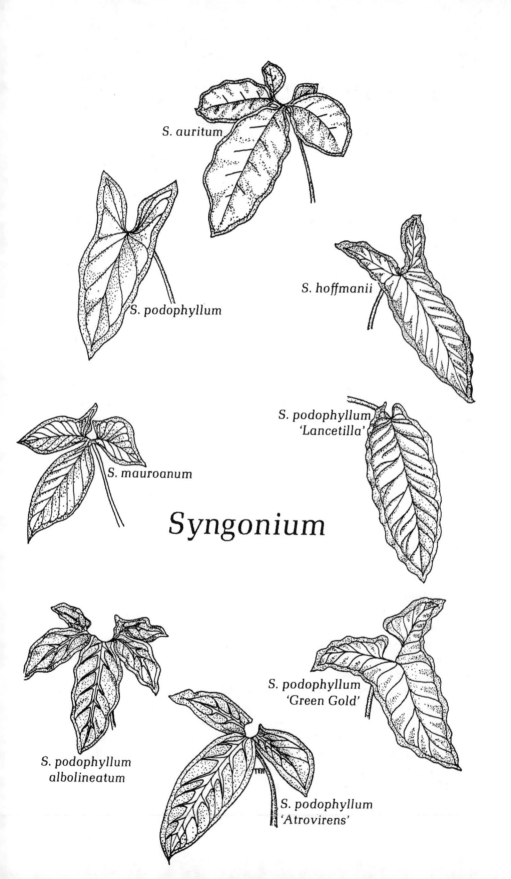

S. auritum

S. podophyllum

S. hoffmanii

S. mauroanum

S. podophyllum
'Lancetilla'

Syngonium

S. podophyllum
albolineatum

S. podophyllum
'Green Gold'

S. podophyllum
'Atrovirens'

77
Syngonium

Syngonium (sin-GO-nee-um): Greek, referring to cohesion of the ovaries.
SPP.: several species and many cultigens are in Florida.

FAMILY: Araceae.   RELATIVES: Elephant-ear and caladium.
TYPE OF PLANT: Herbaceous perennial.   HEIGHT: Variable. ZONE: S
HOW TO IDENTIFY: These creeping plants bear small, delicate, more or
    less lance-shaped leaves while young, then huge, peltate, deeply
    lobed foliage on long petioles at maturity. The rooting stems yield
    milky sap when wounded. Juvenile leaves remotely resemble those
    of fancy-leaved caladiums.
HABIT OF GROWTH: Fast-growing tropical vine.
FOLIAGE: More or less lance-shaped or 3-pointed; marbled with white
    while young; giant, lobed, nearly green leaves borne by old vines.
FLOWERS: Yellowish or greenish spathes surround shorter spadices.
FRUITS: Black seeds may mature after pollination.
SEASON OF MAXIMUM COLOR: Spring, when new growth emerges.
LANDSCAPE USES: For Florida room urns, juvenile syngoniums are very
    popular, as they grow well and are most attractive, delicate, little
    aroids. Yard syngoniums assume mammoth sizes as they adorn
    palm trunks to enhance the tropical effect.
HABITAT: Tropical America.
LIGHT REQUIREMENT: Reduced light of dwellings is acceptable, as is the
    high, shifting shade from palms.
SOIL REQUIREMENT: Moderately fertile, fibrous, slightly acid compost.
SALT TOLERANCE: Not tolerant.
AVAILABILITY: Chain stores and nurseries carry potted syngoniums.
CULTURE: Be cautious in watering and fertilization in order that com-
    pact, nonclimbing, juvenile form with bright variegation may be
    maintained.
PROPAGATION: Cuttage and seeds.
PESTS: Nematodes, mites, and soil-borne diseases.
NOTE: Named varieties in Florida are many, some of the choicest
    being illustrated on the opposite page. Juveniles are delicate, little,
    variegated-leaved pot plants; old vines on palm trunks become
    jungle giants with wrist-thick stems that hold huge, fingered, out-
    size leaves. Above right is shown *Syngonium wendlandii*.

78
Spathiphyllum

Spathiphyllum (spath-i-FIL-um): Greek for leaf-spathe.
SPP.: 2 species and several hybrids grow in Florida gardens.

FAMILY: Araceae.   RELATIVES: Elephant-ear and ivy-arum.
TYPE OF PLANT: Herbaceous perennial.   HEIGHT: 2′. ZONE: C,S
HOW TO IDENTIFY: Thin, lanceolate, sharp-acuminate, plantain-like
    leaves are held gracefully by long petioles; flowers with persistent
    white (or greenish-white) spathes are produced freely during warm
    months. Usually spathiphyllums in Florida grow as clusters of
    leaves, without an above-ground stem.
HABIT OF GROWTH: Clump-growing herbaceous perennial.
FOLIAGE: Foot-long, lanceolate, sharp-acuminate, dark-green leaves are
    held by petioles of about their same length.
FLOWERS: Bisexual, fertile flowers are packed on little spadices which
    are backed by attractive white or greenish spathes.
FRUITS: Fleshy, berry-like.
SEASON OF MAXIMUM COLOR: Spring and summer when blossoms are
    out.
LANDSCAPE USES: As ground cover for shady spots, as pot plants, or as
    components of planter arrangements, spathiphyllums are good for
    those who would like to have easy-to-grow white anthuriums.
HABITAT: American tropics.
LIGHT REQUIREMENT: Tolerant of considerable shade.
SOIL REQUIREMENT: Reasonably fertile soil that is free of nematodes is
    best.
SALT TOLERANCE: Not tolerant.
AVAILABILITY: Many nurseries, garden centers, and chain stores offer
    plants in containers.
CULTURE: Turn a specimen out of its container; plant at the same level
    at which it grew formerly; water during periods of drought; and
    fertilize each month during the summer.
PROPAGATION: Division of matted clumps and seedage.
PESTS: Mites, scales, and mealy-bugs.

79
Aechmea

Aechmea (eke-ME-a): Greek, referring to the pointed sepals.
SPP.: several species and numerous hybrids grow in Florida.

FAMILY: Bromeliaceae.   RELATIVES: Pineapple and billbergia.
TYPE OF PLANT: Herbaceous perennial.   HEIGHT: 3′. ZONE: S
HOW TO IDENTIFY: Stiff rosettes of scurfy or smooth, usually spine-edged, variously colored leaves make up the plants that hold aloft spikes of usually bright-colored bracts in winter and springtime. Some are epiphytic, others terrestrial.
HABIT OF GROWTH: Clump-growing by offsets of stiff leaves.
FOLIAGE: Stiff rosettes of leaves of varying widths and colors.
FLOWERS: Usually spectacular spikes of varying bright bract color.
FRUITS: Many-seeded berries.
SEASON OF MAXIMUM COLOR: March–April when blossoms are out.
LANDSCAPE USES: For adding interest to trees, for planters, urns, and for earth-culture in warm locations, aechmeas, like so many bromeliads, are very popular. These are indicated for general landscapes and are much admired by hobbyists.
HABITAT: Tropical America.
LIGHT REQUIREMENT: Shifting light-and-shade is acceptable; some highly colored varieties may pale in reduced inside light.
SOIL REQUIREMENT: Osmundine; a mixture of peat, leaf-mold, and sand; or rotted leaves worked into the earth beneath oak trees.
SALT TOLERANCE: Not tolerant of dune conditions.
AVAILABILITY: Most nurseries in Florida have aechmeas in containers.
CULTURE: Fasten to branches of rough-barked trees with copper or aluminum wire; pot in your chosen medium in containers or plant in the rotted leaf-mold beneath live oak trees. Keep the cups full of water and apply dilute liquid fertilizer to the growing medium once each summer month.
PROPAGATION: Division of offsets or seedage.
PESTS: Scales; mosquitoes may breed in the water standing in the cups of outdoor aechmeas.
NOTE: Hybridization has been extensive within this very large genus (140 species) and with other genera, with the result that many hybrid forms are seen in Florida landscape arrangements.

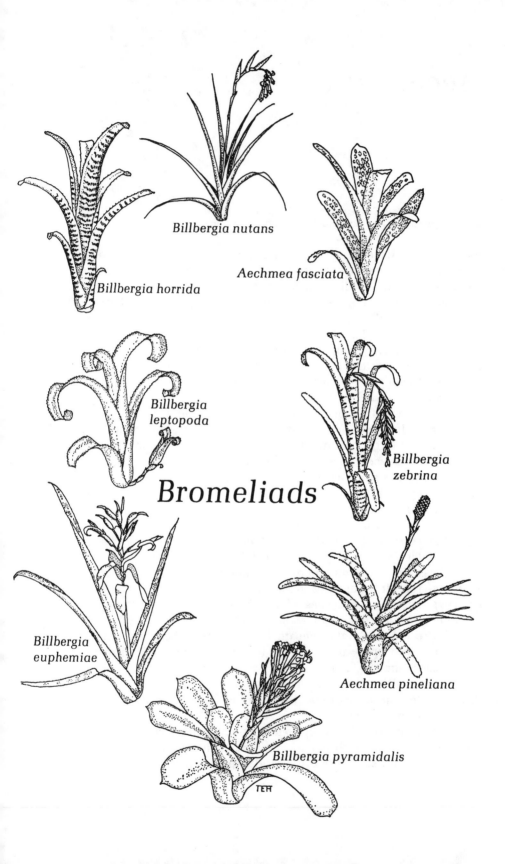

Billbergia nutans

Billbergia horrida

Aechmea fasciata

Billbergia leptopoda

Billbergia zebrina

Bromeliads

Billbergia euphemiae

Aechmea pineliana

Billbergia pyramidalis

81
Billbergia

Billbergia (bill-BURR-jee-a): for J. Billberg, Swedish botanist.
SPP.: several species and numerous hybrids grow in Florida.

FAMILY: Bromeliaceae.   RELATIVES: Aechmea and Spanish-moss.
TYPE OF PLANT: Herbaceous perennial.   HEIGHT: 3'. ZONE: S
HOW TO IDENTIFY: Plants composed of stout rosettes of scurfy or smooth, usually spine-edged leaves, that may be spotted or blotched. Some are epiphytic, others terrestrial.
HABIT OF GROWTH: Clump-growing by offsets of stiff leaves.
FOLIAGE: Stiff rosettes of mostly spine-edged leaves in varying color patterns.
FLOWERS: Usually spectacular spikes contain bright, showy bracts beneath the true flowers.
FRUITS: Many-seeded berries.
SEASON OF MAXIMUM COLOR: Late summer and early fall when spikes appear.
LANDSCAPE USES: For adding interest to trees, for planters, urns, and for earth-culture in warm locations, billbergias, like so many bromeliads, are very popular, especially in hobby collections.
HABITAT: Tropical America.
LIGHT REQUIREMENT: Ordinarily billbergias thrive in fairly bright light. Intensity of coloration may be lost inside some homes.
SOIL REQUIREMENT: Osmundine; a mixture of peat, leaf-mold, and sand; or rotted leaves worked into the earth beneath oak trees.
SALT TOLERANCE: Not tolerant of dune conditions.
AVAILABILITY: Nurseries and garden centers carry billbergias in pots.
CULTURE: Fasten to limbs of rough-barked trees with copper or aluminum wire, or pot in chosen medium. Keep cups at leaf bases full of water and apply dilute liquid fertilizer to the growing medium once each summer month.
PROPAGATION: Division of offsets and seedage.
PESTS: Scales; mosquitoes may breed in water held in cups of outdoor billbergias.
NOTE: This genus, among the most popular of the bromels, has been used extensively in plant breeding. Shown opposite are some of Florida's favorites; above right is 'Fantasia'.

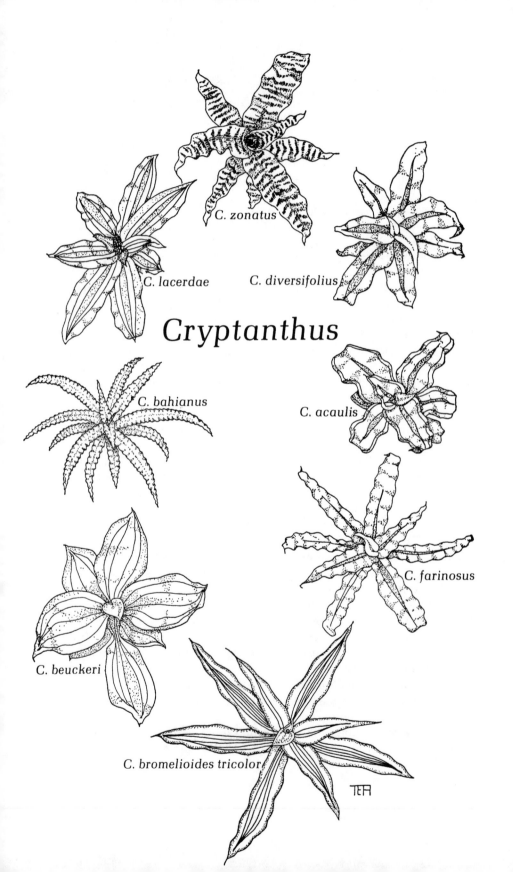

C. zonatus

C. lacerdae

C. diversifolius

Cryptanthus

C. bahianus

C. acaulis

C. farinosus

C. beuckeri

C. bromelioides tricolor

TEA

83
Cryptanthus

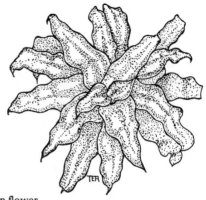

Cryptanthus (crip-TAN-thus): Greek for hidden flower.
SPP.: several species and a number of hybrids grow in Florida.

FAMILY: Bromeliaceae.   RELATIVES: Aechmea and billbergia.
TYPE OF PLANT: Epiphytic perennial.   HEIGHT: 2"–10". ZONE: S
HOW TO IDENTIFY: These are the pygmies of the Bromeliaceae. Tiny,
   flat rosettes of smooth or scurfy, spine-edged leaves are typical.
   Flowers are hidden in the hearts of the rosettes, and mature speci-
   mens usually produce offsets in abundance.
HABIT OF GROWTH: Tight, little rosettes of stiff leaves.
FOLIAGE: Diminutive rosettes are formed by little, undulate, prickly
   leaves. These may be all green, all red, or variously striped, banded,
   or spotted.
FLOWERS: Inconspicuous white flowers hide in the hearts of the ro-
   settes.
FRUITS: Tiny, dry berries.
SEASON OF MAXIMUM COLOR: Springtime when new growth emerges.
LANDSCAPE USES: For little indoor planters and dish gardens, these
   miniature bromels are much admired. They are used also outdoors
   as ground cover or for decorating limbs of rough-barked trees.
HABITAT: Tropical America.
LIGHT REQUIREMENT: Shifting sun-and-shade or reduced light of dwellings.
SOIL REQUIREMENT: Osmundine, or a mixture of peat, leaf-mold, and
   sand.
SALT TOLERANCE: Not tolerant of dune conditions.
AVAILABILITY: Small plants in pots are offered by nurseries, garden
   centers, and chain stores.
CULTURE: Fasten to limbs of rough-barked trees with aluminum wire,
   or pot in your chosen medium. Keep water in leaf bases, and the
   medium moist, and set potted plants out in the rain during warm
   weather. Apply dilute liquid fertilizer to the growing medium once
   each summer month.
PROPAGATION: Division of offsets (these will be unrooted).
PESTS: Scales; mosquitoes might breed in water-holding leaf bases of
   outdoor plants.

84
Variegated Pineapple

Ananas (an-NAN-as): from the aboriginal name.
comosus (com-MOE-sus): with long hair.
'Variegatus': variegated.

FAMILY: Bromeliaceae. RELATIVES: Ball-moss and Spanish-moss.
TYPE OF PLANT: Herbaceous perennial. HEIGHT: 4'. ZONE: S
HOW TO IDENTIFY: Rosettes of long, spine-edged, striped leaves; fruits growing out of the centers of maturing rosettes; underground ratoons growing out to form large clumps.
HABIT OF GROWTH: Low perennial.
FOLIAGE: Rosettes of spine-edged, variegated leaves.
FLOWERS: Central spikes of inconspicuous, complete flowers.
FRUITS: The world-famous, delicious tropical fruits.
LANDSCAPE USES: Variegated pineapples are planted for the tropical effect that they create, and for horticultural curiosity. Use in rock-'n'-sand gardens, in planters, alone in redwood tubs, or along garden paths in protected locations. The foliage is the thing, yet home-grown pineapples are worthwhile dividends for southern Floridians.
HABITAT: Tropical America.
LIGHT REQUIREMENT: Full sun for fruiting, yet container-grown plants kept for foliage effect will survive in reduced light.
SOIL REQUIREMENT: Moderately fertile, open, gritty, fast-draining soil is suitable.
CULTURE: After establishment, moderate watering and thrice annual fertilization should assure adequate growth. Mealy-bugs are certain to infest pineapples, so spray often.
PROPAGATION: Divide suckers from the bases of mature fruits, and divide ratoons from around established plants.
PESTS: Mealy-bugs, nematodes, and mites.
NOTE: 'Variegatus' is but one of the striped-leaved pineapples grown in Florida for ornament. A dozen or so clones with all-green leaves are cultivated for their delectable fruits and for their curiosity in backyard landscapes.

85
Pinguin

Bromelia (bro-MELL-ee-a): for M. Bromel, a Swedish botanist.
pinguin (PIN-gwin): native vernacular name.

FAMILY: Bromeliaceae.   RELATIVES: Pineapple and Spanish-moss.

TYPE OF PLANT: Herbaceous perennial.   HEIGHT: 3'. ZONE: N,C,S

HOW TO IDENTIFY: Rosettes of stiff, spine-edged foliage; underground ratoons spread the cultures over large areas.

HABIT OF GROWTH: Rosettes of stiff leaves.

FOLIAGE: Evergreen, spine-edged, ribbon-like, gray-green in color.

FLOWERS: Central spikes with bright red bracts hold inconspicuous little flowers.

FRUITS: Small, globular, fuzzy fruits along the upper parts of the spikes.

SEASON OF MAXIMUM COLOR: Springtime when the bracts turn red.

LANDSCAPE USES: To help create a tropical atmosphere, clumps of pinguin are useful. The plants, in vegetative condition, are not in the least dramatic, but in springtime, when reproductive spikes appear, they are most spectacular because of the glowing red bracts. Visitors are invariably pleased with the effect. In tropical lands, hedges of pinguin are used to check livestock.

HABITAT: Tropical America.

LIGHT REQUIREMENT: Full sun or broken shade.

SOIL REQUIREMENT: Tolerant of a wide range of soils.

SALT TOLERANCE: Tolerant of salt.

AVAILABILITY: Pinguin is usually not a nursery item; homeowners may exchange plants.

CULTURE: Pinguin requires no care whatsoever.

PROPAGATION: Division of matted clumps.

PESTS: None of major concern.

Oyster-Plant

Rhoeo (RE-O): name obscure.
discolor (DIS-col-or): of two colors.

FAMILY: Commelinaceae.   RELATIVES: Spiderwort and wandering-Jew.
TYPE OF PLANT: Herbaceous perennial.   HEIGHT: 2′. ZONE: C,S
HOW TO IDENTIFY: Broad, tender, succulent leaves that are green above
    and purple beneath grow in little clumps; conspicuous, boat-shaped
    bracts enclose little, white flowers.
HABIT OF GROWTH: Dense, lanceolate leaves make this a formal, neat,
    little herbaceous perennial.
FOLIAGE: Evergreen, long-lanceolate, green above, purple beneath.
FLOWERS: Inconspicuous, white blossoms are held within boat-shaped
    bracts.
FRUITS: Little capsules mature within the bracts.
SEASON OF MAXIMUM COLOR: No seasonal variation.
LANDSCAPE USES: Oyster-plant enjoys great popularity as a ground-
    cover, as an edging, and for planting bins. Usual planting interval
    is 1′ o.c.
        There is a variety 'Vittata' or 'Striata' that has longitudinal lines
    of yellow down the centers of leaves.
        Tender to cold, oyster-plant must be taken indoors for the winter
    in northern counties.
HABITAT: American tropics; in Florida, ubiquitous where winters are
    not severe.
LIGHT REQUIREMENT: Full sun or deep shade is acceptable.
SOIL REQUIREMENT: Almost any growing medium will support oyster-
    plant.
SALT TOLERANCE: Tolerant of salt air back of the first dune.
AVAILABILITY: Available in almost every plant-merchandising estab-
    lishment.
CULTURE: Oyster-plant has few cultural requirements, and these are
    very easily supplied.
PROPAGATION: Seedage, cuttage, and division.
PESTS: Caterpillars and mites.
NOTE: Taxonomists list this plant as *R. spathacea,* but it is still sold in
    the trade as *R. discolor.*

87
Setcreasea

Setcreasea (set-CREASE-ee-a): derivation unclear.
SPP.: several types are cultured in Florida.

FAMILY: Commelinaceae.   RELATIVES: Spiderwort and wandering-Jew.
TYPE OF PLANT: Herbaceous perennial.   HEIGHT: 14″. ZONE: N,C,S
HOW TO IDENTIFY: Fleshy, hairy leaves grow oppositely from erect or
    trailing stems. Three-petaled, ephemeral blossoms nestle in leaf-
    like bracts in terminal positions. Ubiquitous 'Purple Queen' has
    rich, purple foliage; other types have green leaves or ones striped
    with white.
HABIT OF GROWTH: Sprawling, mat-forming.
FOLIAGE: Succulent, fleshy, with many long, fine hairs; leaf-bases en-
    sheath their stems.
FLOWERS: 3 flaring pink petals, highlighted by golden anthers, charac-
    terize the flowers that nestle within their large, protective, leaf-like
    bracts during warm months.
FRUITS: Tiny, inconspicuous.
SEASON OF MAXIMUM COLOR: Spring when new leaves emerge.
LANDSCAPE USES: As ground cover for frostless locations, setcreaseas
    are in high favor. For sunny, exposed rock-'n'-gravel gardens, in
    shady planters, beneath pines and palms, these creeping perennials
    serve with distinction. Most popular is 'Purple Queen' (large draw-
    ing in center). Cultivated here are all-green 'Pallida' (right-hand
    sketch) and striped 'Striata' (left-hand sketch). Botanical status in
    Setcreasea is unclear.
HABITAT: Tropical America; in Florida, nearly frostless locations.
LIGHT REQUIREMENT: Full sun or broken, shifting shade.
SOIL REQUIREMENT: Rich soil is best, but setcreasea grows in poor sand
    as well.
SALT TOLERANCE: Tolerant of salt drift.
AVAILABILITY: Plants in containers are offered by most nurseries in
    Florida.
CULTURE: Simply stick pieces of stem where plants are wanted; water
    carefully until established, thereafter moderately when rains are
    infrequent; fertilize lightly once each summer month.
PROPAGATION: Cuttage.
PESTS: Mites, but these plants are notably pest-free.

88
Spironema

Spironema (spy-roe-NEE-ma): Greek for spiral thread for winding filaments.
fragrans (FRAY-grans): fragrant.

FAMILY: Commelinaceae.   RELATIVES: Dichorisandra and setcreasea.
TYPE OF PLANT: Herbaceous perennial.   HEIGHT: 4'. ZONE: C,S
HOW TO IDENTIFY: Broad, foot-long leaves encircle their stems in rosette
   form; stolons are readily sent out, many twine-like roots grow from
   these, and maturing individuals send up yard-long spikes of tiny,
   very fragrant flowers.
HABIT OF GROWTH: Mat-forming by stoloniferous growth.
FOLIAGE: Lush, bold, succulent, 4" × 12", green with purple shadings,
   held in rosette form to make a symmetrical plant.
FLOWERS: Yard-long spikes bear little, white, fragrant blossoms in
   summer.
FRUITS: Small pods.
SEASON OF MAXIMUM COLOR: No variation.
LANDSCAPE USES: Spironema usually serves as a pot plant or hanging-
   basket subject, yet it can be used in planters, and as a ground cover
   under large-leaved trees where coarse texture is not objectionable.
   The summertime flower spikes make for an untidy effect. In years
   past, botanists used *Spironema* to study transport of fluids.
HABITAT: Mexico.
LIGHT REQUIREMENT: Full sun or partial shade of porches.
SOIL REQUIREMENT: Tolerant of a wide range of soil types.
SALT TOLERANCE: Not tolerant.
AVAILABILITY: Occasionally spironemas appear in nurseries.
CULTURE: Minimum care keeps spironema in growing condition. Like
   so many members of the Commelinaceae, this plant demands little
   from its owner.
PROPAGATION: Cuttage and division.
PESTS: Mites, but this plant is notably pest-free.

89
Wandering-Jew

Tradescantia (trad-es-CANT-ee-a): for J. Tradescant, English gardener; and
Zebrina (zee-BRINE-a): referring to the striped leaves.
SPP.: several species of both genera grow in Florida.

FAMILY: Commelinaceae.   RELATIVES: Oyster-plant and spiderwort.
TYPE OF PLANT: Herbaceous perennial.   Height: 10″. ZONE: N,C,S
HOW TO IDENTIFY: Wandering-Jew is grown by homeowners so widely
   that description here seems unnecessary.
HABIT OF GROWTH: Sprawling, mat-forming, by horizontal, rooting
   stems.
FOLIAGE: Succulent, soft, furnished with long, sparse hairs; leaf-bases
   ensheath their stems.
FLOWERS: Tiny, nestling within protective leaf-like bracts. Tones may
   vary with the variety.
FRUITS: Tiny, inconspicuous.
SEASON OF MAXIMUM COLOR: Little variation, even when blossoms are
   out.
LANDSCAPE USES: As ground cover for shady, frostless locations,
   wandering-Jew has long been a favorite with Floridians. These
   perennials serve to cover the soil in planters and to soften their
   top lines. Very often single pots of fancy-leaved types are featured
   porch plants.
HABITAT: Tropical America.
LIGHT REQUIREMENT: Reduced light is optimum.
SOIL REQUIREMENT: Tolerant of widely varying well-drained soils.
SALT TOLERANCE: Not tolerant.
AVAILABILITY: Offered in containers by most nurseries in central and
   southern Florida. Frequently received from neighbors.
CULTURE: Simply stick pieces of stems where plants are wanted; water
   carefully until established, thereafter moderately during times when
   rains are infrequent; fertilize lightly at the onset of warm weather.
PROPAGATION: Cuttage.
PESTS: Mites, but these plants are notably pest-free.

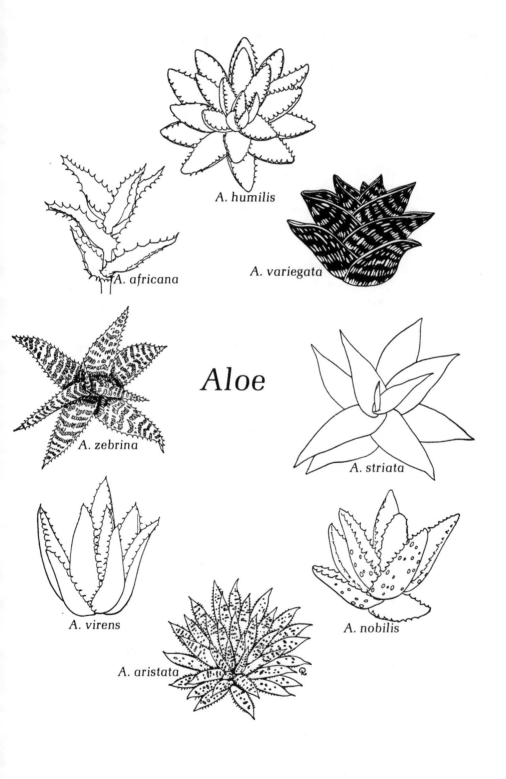

A. humilis

A. africana

A. variegata

A. zebrina

Aloe

A. striata

A. virens

A. aristata

A. nobilis

91
Aloe

Aloe (AL-oh): ancient Arabic name.
SPP.: several species are grown in Florida.

FAMILY: Liliaceae.   RELATIVES: Lily, daylily, and asparagus.
TYPE OF PLANT: Succulent perennial.   HEIGHT: Variable. ZONE: C,S

HOW TO IDENTIFY: Stiff rosettes of thick, succulent, spike-edged, or smooth leaves, usually mottled; erect scapes with red, orange, or yellow tubular flowers.

HABIT OF GROWTH: Compact because of many closely held succulent leaves.

FOLIAGE: Succulent, usually mottled with purple or white.

FLOWERS: Showy spikes of tubular blossoms in tones of red, orange, or yellow produced during warm months.

FRUITS: 3-angled capsules.

SEASON OF MAXIMUM COLOR: Spring, when blossoms unfurl.

LANDSCAPE USES: For a tropical look, for rock-'n'-sand gardens, urns, and sunny planters, and for seaside plantings, aloes excel.

HABITAT: Old World tropics and warm temperate regions.

LIGHT REQUIREMENT: Full sun or shady situations.

SOIL REQUIREMENT: Most soils seem to be entirely adequate. Basic reaction and dry conditions are tolerated.

SALT TOLERANCE: Most tolerant of salt; grows on front-line dunes.

AVAILABILITY: Canned plants in most nurseries in southern Florida.

CULTURE: After establishment, water moderately during periods of extreme drought. Fertilize once at the beginning of the rainy season.

PROPAGATION: Division of offsets from around old plants; seedage.

PESTS: Caterpillars may chew holes in young, tender leaves.

NOTE: Most widely grown is Barbados aloe (*Aloe barbadensis*) illustrated above. Leaves are spiny-toothed; 1″ yellow flowers are produced on 4′ scapes in summer.

Coral aloe (*Aloe striata*) (right opposite) may form a 2′ trunk that bears leaves 4″ × 20″, striate, with entire white margins and spikes of coral-red flowers.

Tree aloe (*Aloe arborescens*) develops a trunk that bears spreading leaves 2″ × 24″ with prickly, wavy margins, and red flowers that are 1½″ long. This is widely grown in the type and is the parent of some hybrids.

Asparagus-Fern

Asparagus (as-PAR-a-gus): from Greek meaning sprout.
SPP.: several species widely grown in Florida.

FAMILY: Liliaceae.   RELATIVES: Daylily and Easter lily.
TYPE OF PLANT: Herbaceous perennial or semi-woody vine.
    HEIGHT: Variable. ZONE: N,C,S
HOW TO IDENTIFY: Evergreen perennial with long, thin, green, wiry
    branches which turn gray at maturity. Leaves fine, often needle-like
    or scale-like, to large sickle-shaped.
HABIT OF GROWTH: Clump-forming or vine-like.
FOLIAGE: Evergreen; mostly fine-textured, soft leaves.
FLOWERS: Small, white, to ½" across.
FRUITS: Small red berries.
SEASON OF MAXIMUM COLOR: When in flower and fruit.
LANDSCAPE USES: Ground cover, hanging baskets, tub specimens for
    patios, as cut foliage, and excellent for use in Japanese gardens.
    A. plumosus: finest foliage (⅛" long), wiry stems, sprays of leaves
    flat or fan-shaped. Widely used as cut foliage. *A. sprengeri*: long,
    arching, green stems, leaves yellow-green to ¾" long. Excellent pot
    or hanging-basket subject. *A. myriocladus*: stiff, upright branching.
    Borne in clusters at nodes, the leaves linear to ¾" long. Fine for
    tub specimens or in Japanese gardens. *A. meyeri*: stems upright,
    plume-like, resembling foxtails, leaves similar to *A. sprengeri*. Good
    pot specimen, used also as cut foliage. *A. falcatus*: woody vine with
    somewhat rampant stems that are heavily armed. Leaves sickle-
    shaped, leathery, to 4" long. Good screening plant, also sold as
    small pot plant.
HABITAT: Mediterranean region to South Africa.
LIGHT REQUIREMENT: Partial shade to full sun.
SOIL REQUIREMENT: Tolerant of most well-drained soils.
SALT TOLERANCE: Not tolerant.
AVAILABILITY: Offered by most nurseries and foliage plant growers.
CULTURE: Plant in hammock-type soils or soils containing ⅓ to ½ or-
    ganic matter for best growth. Watering can be critical until plants
    are established. Then they require minimal care.
PROPAGATION: Seedage or division of parent clumps.
PESTS: Usually not a problem.

93
Cast-Iron Plant

Aspidistra (as-pi-DIS-tra): Greek for small, round shield, describing the stigma.
elatior (ee-LAY-tee-or): taller.

FAMILY: Liliaceae.   RELATIVES: Daylily and Easter lily.
TYPE OF PLANT: Herbaceous perennial.   HEIGHT: 3'. ZONE: N,C,S
HOW TO IDENTIFY: Clusters of tall, broad, evergreen leaves are sent up
    from strong, persistent rhizomes. These tough leaves, either all
    green or striped with white, endure low light intensities and low at-
    mospheric humidity which would be unsuitable to many foliage
    plants.
HABIT OF GROWTH: Clump-forming.
FOLIAGE: Yard-long by 6" broad, atop erect petioles, produced in
    dense clusters from tough rootstocks.
FLOWERS: Inconspicuous, borne close to the earth.
FRUITS: Inconspicuous, little 1-seeded berries.
SEASON OF MAXIMUM COLOR: No seasonal variation.
LANDSCAPE USES: Since earliest times, this has been a dependable
    porch plant, always noted for its ability to endure adverse growing
    conditions. Now contemporary designers approve its use.
HABITAT: China; in Florida, frequently seen in shady gardens.
LIGHT REQUIREMENT: Reduced light is optimum; full sunlight cannot be
    tolerated.
SOIL REQUIREMENT: Moderately fertile, fibrous soil is best, yet cast-iron
    plant shows tolerance for widely varying growing media.
SALT TOLERANCE: Tolerant of moderate salt air back of first-line dunes.
AVAILABILITY: Nurseries offer aspidistras in containers.
CULTURE: Plant slightly deeper than former growing depth in shady lo-
    cations; water during periods of drought; fertilize once each sum-
    mer month.
PROPAGATION: Division of old matted clumps.
PESTS: Leaf-spotting disease.

94
Lily-Turf

Liriope (leer-EYE-o-pee): for the nymph Liriope.
muscari (mus-CARE-ee): referring to musky odor.

FAMILY: Liliaceae.   RELATIVES: Lily and dwarf lily-turf.
TYPE OF PLANT: Herbaceous perennial.   HEIGHT: 1'. ZONE: N,C,S
HOW TO IDENTIFY: This dwarf, rhizomatous herb forms close, green
   mats. The dark-green, grass-like foliage is interspersed with spikes
   of pretty blue flowers in springtime, and conspicuous, shiny, black
   fruits during the winter.
HABIT OF GROWTH: Grass-like, mat-forming.
FOLIAGE: Evergreen, long-linear, grass-like, growing in tufts.
FLOWERS: Lax spikes of pretty blue flowers, ¼" across, in spring and
   summer.
FRUITS: Globose capsules, ⅓" in diameter, persist during fall and win-
   ter.
SEASON OF MAXIMUM COLOR: Spring and summer when blossoms are
   out, fall and winter when fruits mature.
LANDSCAPE USES: As a ground cover for densely shaded spots, lily-turf
   is widely accepted. Plant 6" or 12" o.c. As an edging for shady
   walks, it excels.
HABITAT: Eastern Asia; in Florida ubiquitous in shady gardens.
LIGHT REQUIREMENT: Shady situations are recommended.
SOIL REQUIREMENT: Tolerant of many soil types; however, growth is
   more attractive in fertile earth.
SALT TOLERANCE: Tolerant of salt air back from the strand.
AVAILABILITY: Most nurseries stock lily-turf.
CULTURE: Plant divisions of old matted clumps in well-prepared soil;
   water moderately until well established, then during periods of se-
   vere drought only. Fertilize once each springtime.
PROPAGATION: Division and seedage.
PESTS: Scales and a very serious tip-burn.
NOTE: Confusion exists in this genus, and labeling may be inaccurate.
   Giant, broad-leaved types and others with striped leaves are pop-
   ular in western Florida.

95
Dwarf Lily-Turf

Ophiopogon (o-fee-o-POE-gon): Greek for snake's beard.
japonicus (jap-ON-i-cus): Japanese.

FAMILY: Liliaceae.   RELATIVES: Aloe and cast-iron plant.
TYPE OF PLANT: Herbaceous perennial.   HEIGHT: 10". ZONE: N,C,S
HOW TO IDENTIFY: This is the finest textured of the liliaceous, non-grass
   ground covers. The leaves are ⅛" broad; the flowers are usually
   hidden below the foliage; the fruits, if present, are inconspicuous.
HABIT OF GROWTH: Grass-like, mat-forming by stolons.
FOLIAGE: Evergreen, long-linear, very fine in texture, very dark green
   when growing in the shade.
FLOWERS: Inconspicuous, bluish, 3/16" long, few on short scapes that
   are lower than the leaves.
FRUITS: Small, fleshy capsules when present.
SEASON OF MAXIMUM COLOR: Little change throughout the year.
LANDSCAPE USES: For covering the earth under trees, for shaded
   planters, and to edge woodland walks, dwarf lily-turf excels. Set
   divisions 6" o.c.
HABITAT: Eastern Asia; in Florida, ubiquitous in shady gardens.
LIGHT REQUIREMENT: Full shade is quite acceptable.
SOIL REQUIREMENT: Adapted to many soils.
SALT TOLERANCE: Tolerant of salt air back from the strand.
AVAILABILITY: Most nurseries stock dwarf lily-turf.
CULTURE: Plant divisions of old matted clumps in well-prepared soil;
   water moderately until well established, then during periods of se-
   vere drought only. Fertilize once each springtime.
PROPAGATION: Division.
PESTS: Scales.
NOTE: Dwarf lily-turf is offered for sale under many strange vernacu-
   lar names. Giant types and others with striped foliage are much
   used in western Florida to edge garden walks.

Pony-Tail

Beaucarnea (bo-CAR-nee-a): derivation obscure.
recurvata (ree-curv-ATE-a): recurved, referring to the downward-bending foliage.

FAMILY: Liliaceae.

RELATIVES: Lily, gloriosa, and aloe.

TYPE OF PLANT: Tree.

HEIGHT: 15′. ZONE: C,S

HOW TO IDENTIFY: The greatly swollen trunk base and the recurving, narrow leaves are certain identification.

HABIT OF GROWTH: Upright, with long, flowing, ribbon-like leaves.

FOLIAGE: Evergreen, fine in texture, light green in color.

FLOWERS: Inconspicuous, but borne on large inflorescences.

FRUITS: Usually none are produced in Florida.

SEASON OF MAXIMUM COLOR: None.

LANDSCAPE USES: As an urn subject for terrace, patio, or Florida room, pony-tail excels. As a freestanding specimen out-of-doors it is sometimes seen in frostless locations.

    Pony-tail is one of Florida's most dramatic plants because of its much-expanded trunk at the soil line. This is a tried-and-true conversation piece.

HABITAT: Mexican highlands; in Florida, sandy soils in warm locations.

LIGHT REQUIREMENT: Full sun.

SOIL REQUIREMENT: Sandy, well-drained, neutral soils.

SALT TOLERANCE: Tolerant of salt drift well back from the sea.

AVAILABILITY: Many nurseries sell small pony-tails in containers.

CULTURE: Plant in a well-drained site that is not subjected to low temperatures; fertilize once at the beginning of warm weather; keep lawn grasses back from the trunk.

PROPAGATION: Seedage.

PESTS: Chewing insects; root-rot diseases may cause death on wet soils.

Spider-Plant

Chlorophytum (clor-OFF-it-um): Greek for green plant.
capense (cape-EN-see): of the Cape of Good Hope.

FAMILY: Liliaceae.   RELATIVES: Dwarf lily-turf and lily-turf.

TYPE OF PLANT: Herbaceous perennial.   HEIGHT: 1'. ZONE: S

HOW TO IDENTIFY: Neat rosettes of gaily variegated, smooth leaves form the main plants and bunches of little rooting plantlets are produced at the ends of stolons. These hang for many months.

HABIT OF GROWTH: Low perennial.

FOLIAGE: Linear, bright, smooth, usually lined with white bands.

FLOWERS: Whitish, in racemes ¾" across.

FRUITS: Little pods.

SEASON OF MAXIMUM COLOR: Flowers insignificant.

LANDSCAPE USES: For pots and hanging baskets spider-plant has been popular since earliest times. Usually passed along from one home-maker to another, this dependable lily relative is as much a part of porch-gardening as are begonias and ferns. A modern adaptation is the use of spider-plant for covering the soil in planters, where the hanging stolons, with their clusters of offsets, soften top lines.

HABITAT: South Africa.

LIGHT REQUIREMENT: Partial shade is excellent.

SOIL REQUIREMENT: Moderately fertile, somewhat fibrous soil is acceptable.

CULTURE: Plant offsets from stolon-ends in pots containing fibrous soil; water moderately; shift to larger containers as necessary.

PROPAGATION: Division of offsets from stolon-ends.

PESTS: Mites.

NOTE: Usually striped-leaved varieties are seen in Florida, often under the designation "Anthericum." There is confusion in the nomenclature of these plants.

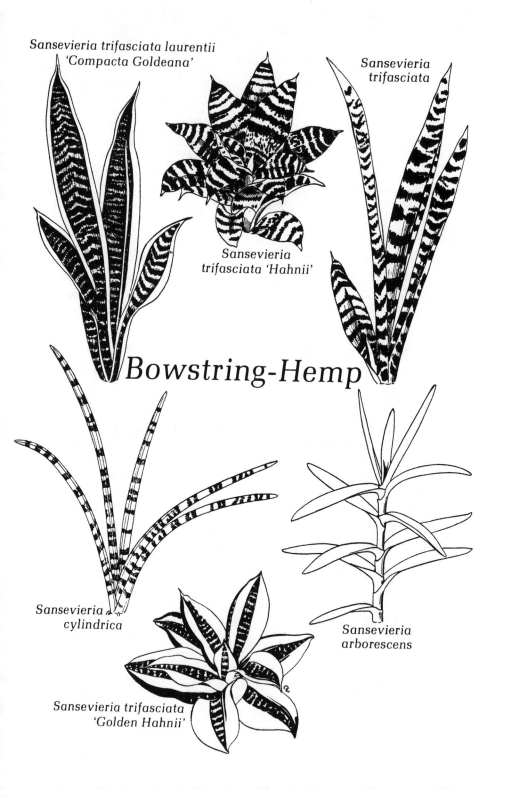

Sansevieria trifasciata laurentii
'Compacta Goldeana'

Sansevieria trifasciata

Sansevieria trifasciata 'Hahnii'

Bowstring-Hemp

Sansevieria cylindrica

Sansevieria trifasciata 'Golden Hahnii'

Sansevieria arborescens

99
Bowstring-Hemp

Sansevieria (san-see-vere-ee-a): for an Italian prince.
spp.: many kinds grow in Florida.

FAMILY: Agavaceae.
RELATIVES: Dracena and ti.
TYPE OF PLANT: Herbaceous perennial.
HEIGHT: Variable. ZONE: S

HOW TO IDENTIFY: Stiff, mottled, blotched or striped leaves, succulent, and fiber-bearing, characterize this great group of tropical exotics. Scapes support white, tubular, very fragrant flowers.

HABIT OF GROWTH: Very compact, rosette-like.

FOLIAGE: Stiff, succulent, mottled, blotched or lined, of many shapes and sizes.

FLOWERS: White, tubular, fragrant, held by scapes that are usually taller than the leaf mass.

FRUITS: Green pods may follow pollination.

SEASON OF MAXIMUM COLOR: Little variation over the seasons.

LANDSCAPE USES: Sansevierias are planted in every conceivable landscape application in Florida. As accent plants in foundation arrangements, in planters, for Florida room urns, as porch plants, even for tiny dish gardens, these African tropicals are in high favor.

HABITAT: Tropical Africa.

LIGHT REQUIREMENT: Full sun or reduced light of dwellings is acceptable.

SOIL REQUIREMENT: Tolerance of widely varying soils is notable.

SALT TOLERANCE: Tolerant of salt air and saline soils.

AVAILABILITY: Usually found in chain stores and nurseries.

CULTURE: Simply plant, water, and forget.

PROPAGATION: Division or leaf cuttage.

PESTS: Caterpillars may chew tender foliage.

Note: Many clones are widely grown in our state. Pictured opposite are popular kinds with their Florida names. As the botany is imperfectly understood, naming is subject to question. New kinds arise in horticultural establishments, and acceptance by the public has been quite marked. Above is the popular birds-nest sansevieria.

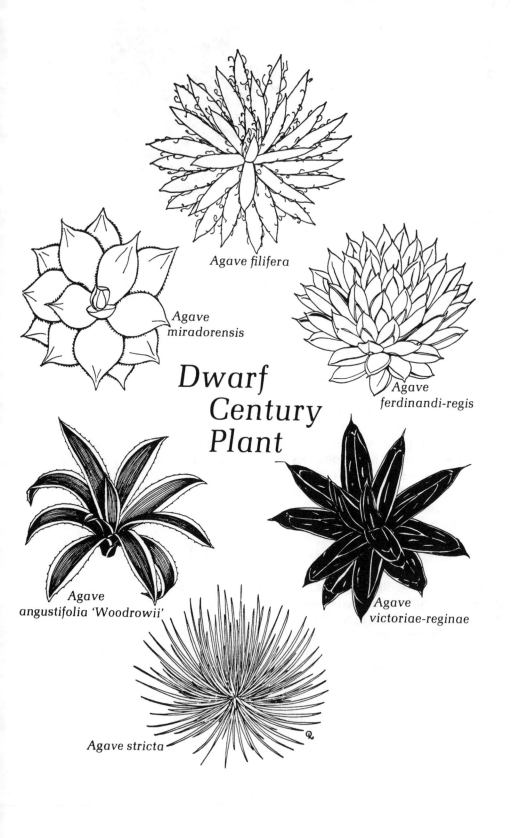

Agave filifera

Agave miradorensis

Agave ferdinandi-regis

Dwarf Century Plant

Agave angustifolia 'Woodrowii'

Agave victoriae-reginae

Agave stricta

101
Century Plant

Agave (a-GAY-vee): Greek for admirable.
americana (a-mer-ee-CANE-a): American.

FAMILY: Agavaceae.   RELATIVES: Spanish bayonet, dracena, and ti.
TYPE OF PLANT: Succulent herbaceous perennial.
                    HEIGHT OF LEAF MASS: 6'. ZONE: N,C,S
HOW TO IDENTIFY: Great, stiff, heavy, persistent leaves in rosettes.
HABIT OF GROWTH: Tight rosettes.
FOLIAGE: Very coarse in texture, gray-green or banded with yellow.
FLOWERS: Yellowish-green on horizontal branches, high in the air.
FRUITS: Capsules the size of large eggs that split to release black seeds
    or germinating seedlings.
SEASON OF MAXIMUM COLOR: No seasonal variation.
LANDSCAPE USES: As a strong accent, where a bold tropical effect is
    wanted, century plant excels. As a tubbed specimen, it may serve,
    if terminal spines are carefully clipped away.
        Here in Florida, landscape architects and homeowners employ
    agaves often in landscape compositions to enhance the feeling of
    the tropics. In spite of their wide use, many, many more could be
    planted. In rock-'n'-sand gardens, agaves make harmonious com-
    positions with tropical succulents.
HABITAT: Dry, sandy regions; in Florida, very widely planted.
LIGHT REQUIREMENT: Full sun for best growth, but endures heavy shade.
SOIL REQUIREMENT: Any well-drained soil is suitable.
SALT TOLERANCE: No plant is better adapted to seaside conditions.
AVAILABILITY: Nurseries, garden centers, and chain stores offer century
    plants of many kinds.
CULTURE: The sharp spines that terminate the leaves must be removed
    so that they do not injure children and pets.
PROPAGATION: Division of clumps, or aerial plants from the inflores-
    cence.
PESTS: Scales, but these are not of great consequence.
NOTE: There are more than 300 species and many varieties of *Agave*.

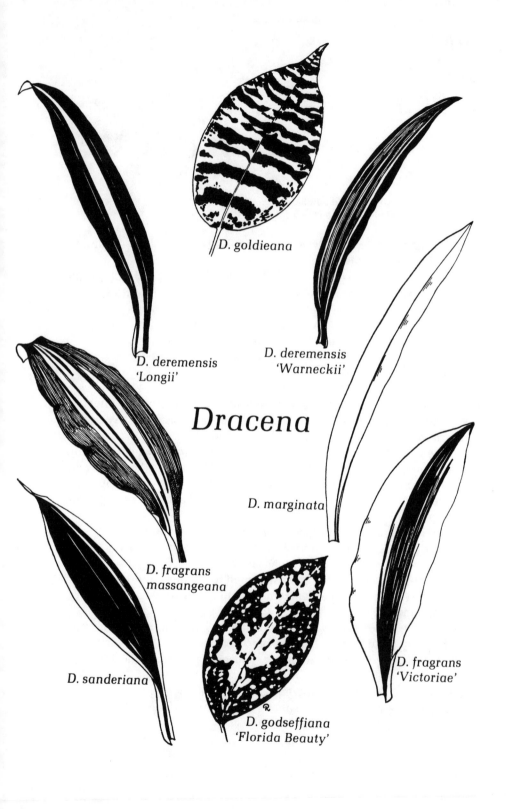

D. goldieana

D. deremensis 'Longii'

D. deremensis 'Warneckii'

Dracena

D. marginata

D. fragrans massangeana

D. fragrans 'Victoriae'

D. sanderiana

D. godseffiana 'Florida Beauty'

103
Dracena

Dracaena (dray-SEEN-a): Greek for female dragon.
SPP.: several species are grown in Florida.

FAMILY: Agavaceae.

RELATIVES: Century plant and ti.

TYPE OF PLANT: Shrub.

HEIGHT: 15'. ZONE: S

HOW TO IDENTIFY: Woody-stemmed shrubs with prominent, corn-like leaves more or less clustered near the tips. The leaves, which may or may not have petioles, are variable in size and color, depending upon the species and variety. Flowers, which are held in branched, upright panicles, have an unpleasant odor.

HABIT OF GROWTH: Strongly ascending, single-trunked in some species, branched in others.

FOLIAGE: Evergreen, without petioles, of bold, tropical aspect, of variable color.

FLOWERS: Inconspicuous, in upright panicles, dark red outside, white inside, with unpleasant odor.

FRUITS: Globose berries with 1 to 3 seeds when present.

SEASON OF MAXIMUM COLOR: No seasonal variation.

LANDSCAPE USES: For the attractive tropical aspect, landscape dracenas are popular in garden compositions in southern Florida. Tender to cold, these tropical exotics must be kept in Florida rooms or in greenhouses in more northerly locations.

HABITAT: Tropical Africa; in Florida, landscape plantings in the southern part; Florida rooms of all sections.

LIGHT REQUIREMENT: Tolerant of considerable shade.

SOIL REQUIREMENT: Fertile, moisture-retentive soils are requisite for good-looking foliage.

SALT TOLERANCE: Not tolerant.

AVAILABILITY: Widely offered in containers in southern Florida.

CULTURE: Plant in reasonably fertile soil that has been made free of nematodes; water moderately and fertilize about three times each year.

PROPAGATION: Cuttage and marcottage.

PESTS: Anthracnose leaf-spot is sometimes serious.

NOTE: Landscape dracenas in Florida are many, botanical status is unclear, and labeling may be inconsistent. Portrayed across are Florida favorites. On this page is delicate, little 'Marginata'.

New Zealand Flax

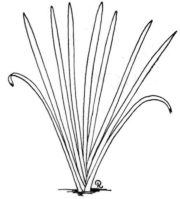

Phormium (FOR-me-um): Greek for basket, referring to uses of the fiber.
tenax (TEE-nax): strong.

FAMILY: Agavaceae.   RELATIVES: Century plant and bowstring-hemp.
TYPE OF PLANT: Herbaceous perennial.   HEIGHT: 6'. ZONE: C,S
HOW TO IDENTIFY: Tall, sword-shaped, equitant, keeled leaves rise to
   man-height from fleshy rhizomes. Tubular, red or yellow flowers
   may be produced on 15' scapes under good conditions.
HABIT OF GROWTH: Stiffly upright by long, lance-form leaves.
FOLIAGE: Man-high, 5" broad, sword-shaped, equitant, highlighted
   with orange-red lines at the keeled midrib and at the margins. Old
   leaves will split at their apexes.
FLOWERS: Tubular, red or yellow, borne in 15' scapes under favorable
   conditions.
FRUITS: Capsules 2"–4" long if present.
SEASON OF MAXIMUM COLOR: Warm months when flowers appear.
LANDSCAPE USES: For the strong tropical character of the tall, dusky
   leaves, New Zealand flax is in high favor with garden designers. An
   established clump may be used near a doorway, gate, or passage,
   particularly with structures of contemporary design. A clump is ef-
   fective near a water feature as well.
HABITAT: New Zealand.
LIGHT REQUIREMENT: Full sun or broken, shifting shade.
SOIL REQUIREMENT: Moist, rich soil high in organic matter is recom-
   mended.
SALT TOLERANCE: Not tolerant of dune conditions but thrives near tidal
   lagoons.
AVAILABILITY: Nurseries offer New Zealand flax in cans.
CULTURE: Once established in good, moist soil, this tough, fiber-bearing
   relative of the century plant requires little care.
PROPAGATION: Division or seedage.
PESTS: Usually none of major importance.
NOTE: Ordinarily the type depicted above is displayed in Florida
   landscape plantings, but the clone 'Variegatum' has striped leaves,
   and a selection with leaves that display a rich, reddish cast is attractive.

105
Adam's Needle

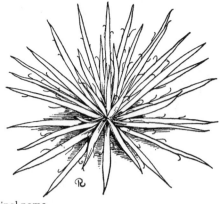

Yucca (YUCK-a): modification of an aboriginal name.
smalliana (small-ee-AY-na): for J. Small, American botanist.

FAMILY: Agavaceae.   RELATIVES: Dracena and century plant.
TYPE OF PLANT: Herbaceous perennial.   HEIGHT: 2½′. ZONE: N,C
HOW TO IDENTIFY: Rosettes of gray-green, lance-shaped, sharp-tipped, thread-edged leaves have led to the use of bear-grass as one local name.
HABIT OF GROWTH: A strong, basal rosette, with no erect trunk.
FOLIAGE: Evergreen, ribbon-like with gray threads, gray-green in color.
FLOWERS: White, nodding, on tall, erect panicles which arise from the center of the foliage rosette. The white petals are edible.
FRUITS: Conspicuous, fleshy capsules, which turn black and dry at maturity.
SEASON OF MAXIMUM COLOR: Early summer when flower spikes are sent up.
LANDSCAPE USES: As a transition plant for a group of Spanish bayonets and/or century plants, bear-grass serves admirably. Set these 2′ apart. To edge driveways or walkways in woodland plantings, use the same interval. This native plant can be used, too, for urns and planters.
HABITAT: Sandy ridges and hammocks in Florida.
LIGHT REQUIREMENT: Full sun or broken shade below tall pines or oaks.
SOIL REQUIREMENT: Any well-drained soil seems to suffice.
SALT TOLERANCE: Very tolerant of salt.
AVAILABILITY: Occasionally nurseries will offer bear-grass plants in containers.
CULTURE: Bear-grass transplants with difficulty; often plants will die after they have been in garden locations for many months. Plant in well-drained sites; water with moderation.
PROPAGATION: Seedage and division of matted, native clumps.
PESTS: Possibly soil-borne diseases cause death in gardens.

Spanish Bayonet

Yucca (YUCK-a): modification of an aboriginal name.
aloifolia (al-low-i-FOL-ee-a): aloe-leaved.

FAMILY: Agavaceae.　　　　　　RELATIVES: Dracena and tuberose.
TYPE OF PLANT: Herbaceous perennial.　　　HEIGHT: 25'. ZONE: N,C,S
HOW TO IDENTIFY: Evergreen, dagger-like leaves, 2½' long × 2½" wide,
　　tipped with sharp spines, grow outward from many inclining thick
　　trunks. Spikes of white nodding blossoms appear in springtime.
HABIT OF GROWTH: Clump-forming, by means of many inclining trunks.
FOLIAGE: Evergreen, dagger-like, coarse in texture, in tones of green.
FLOWERS: White, hanging, cup-like, 3" in diameter are held by erect,
　　terminal panicles in springtime. The petals are edible.
FRUITS: Fleshy capsules 5" long dry and turn black at maturity.
SEASON OF MAXIMUM COLOR: Spring, with spikes of white flowers.
LANDSCAPE USES: For seaside planting, nothing equals Spanish bayo-
　　net. For barriers, enclosures, foundation plantings, set plants or
　　unrooted cuttings 1½'–3' apart. Inland, this native plant serves
　　equally well. The vicious thorns must be removed with sharp pruning
　　shears from the leaf-tips as new foliage unfurls. *Yucca elephantipes*
　　does not have harmful spines.
HABITAT: Well-drained sands in Florida, notably, the coastal dunes.
LIGHT REQUIREMENT: Sun or shade.
SOIL REQUIREMENT: Any well-drained soil.
SALT TOLERANCE: Very tolerant of salt, therefore, highly recommended
　　for dune plantings.
AVAILABILITY: Occasionally Spanish bayonets are offered by nursery-
　　men, but more often they are simply cut from native cultures.
CULTURE: Plant rooted plants or unrooted cuttings in well-drained sites.
　　These need not be fertile or rich in organic matter. Water sparingly
　　at all times.
PROPAGATION: Cuttage, using pieces of any size at any season.
PESTS: Yucca moth larvae may destroy buds of low plants.
NOTE: There are clones with foliage variously striped with gold or
　　gold and pink. A very similar plant with thin, soft leaves and an
　　inflorescence with ascending branches is *Yucca gloriosa*, native to
　　the Deep South. The flowers often have reddish shading. This plant
　　is good for coastal plantings.

Spineless Yucca

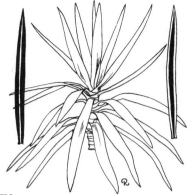

Yucca (YUCK-a): modification of an aboriginal name.
elephantipes (el-e-FAN-ti-pez): elephant foot.

FAMILY: Agavaceae.

RELATIVES: Spanish bayonet and ti.

TYPE OF PLANT: Succulent shrub.

HEIGHT: 25'. ZONE: C,S

HOW TO IDENTIFY: Spanish bayonet-like, but with pliable leaves terminated by harmless tips.

HABIT OF GROWTH: Clump-forming by means of inclining trunks.

FOLIAGE: Evergreen, dagger-like, coarse in texture, colored in tones of green.

FLOWERS: White, cup-like, hanging from erect panicles. The petals are edible.

FRUITS: Purple-black capsules in summertime.

SEASON OF MAXIMUM COLOR: Springtime, when the spikes of white flowers elongate.

LANDSCAPE USES: To enhance the tropical effect wherever Spanish bayonets have been used, this related species may be preferred because of the harmless leaf-tips. As accents in foundation arrangements and for large planters, spineless yucca is highly regarded. In succulent groups by antique brick walls and in rock-'n'-gravel gardens it is almost an essential component.

HABITAT: Central America; in Florida, now widely planted.

LIGHT REQUIREMENT: Sun or shade.

SOIL REQUIREMENT: Any well-drained soil appears to be suitable.

SALT TOLERANCE: Tolerant of salt.

AVAILABILITY: Many nurseries stock this desirable plant.

CULTURE: Plant in well-drained site; water and fertilize with moderation.

PROPAGATION: Cuttage, using pieces of any size.

PESTS: Yucca moth may kill low plants.

NOTE: Spineless yuccas with striped foliage are to be found in some nurseries.

Ti

Cordyline (core-dee-LINE-ee): Greek for club, referring to the thickened roots.
terminalis (ter-min-ALE-is): at the end of the stem.

FAMILY: Agavaceae.   RELATIVES: Dracena and Spanish bayonet.
TYPE OF PLANT: Shrub.   HEIGHT: 8′. ZONE: S
HOW TO IDENTIFY: Showy, persistent leaves of many colors and sizes are always held by distinct, clasping petioles. Flowers are produced on foot-long panicles among the leaves.
HABIT OF GROWTH: Stiffly upright; some forms are branched, others are not.
FOLIAGE: Evergreen, in many colors, with channeled, clasping petioles.
FLOWERS: Inconspicuous, in various tones, held on branched panicles.
FRUITS: Globose berries, rather freely produced by some varieties in Florida.
SEASON OF MAXIMUM COLOR: The year around, if not injured by cold.
LANDSCAPE USES: To enhance the tropical effect, colorful ti is popular in extreme southern Florida. It is set in foundation arrangements, and in bins and urns. A group of 3 ti of a single color forms an effective focal point in front of green shrubbery. The clones are many, some of which have English names, some French, some Japanese, and some Hawaiian. Consistency in naming may not be the rule. Ti is very tender to cold.
HABITAT: Eastern Asia; in Florida, landscape plantings in southern part.
LIGHT REQUIREMENT: Tolerant of considerable shade.
SOIL REQUIREMENT: Reasonably fertile soil that is free of nematodes is best.
SALT TOLERANCE: Not tolerant.
AVAILABILITY: Many nurseries, garden centers, and chain stores offer plants in containers and small pieces of stem in plastic bags for home propagation.
CULTURE: Plant in reasonably fertile soil that has been made free of nematodes; water moderately; fertilize about three times each year; protect the foliage against leaf-spot.
PROPAGATION: Cuttage and marcottage.
PESTS: Anthracnose, leaf-spot, nematodes, and mites.

109
Banana

Musa (MEW-sa): for A. Musa, physician to the first Roman emperor.
paradisiaca (para-dis-EYE-a-ca): of gardens.

FAMILY: Musaceae.   RELATIVES: Heliconia and travelers-tree.
TYPE OF PLANT: Tall herbaceous perennial.   HEIGHT: 20′. ZONE: N,C,S
HOW TO IDENTIFY: Tall, stoloniferous, herbaceous perennial with ever-
     green leaves some 7′ long × 1½′ wide, with a bunch of bananas
     emerging from the axils of mature specimens.
HABIT OF GROWTH: Tree-like, from underground rootstocks.
FOLIAGE: Evergreen, of coarse texture and deep green color when well
     fertilized.
FLOWERS: Terminal hanging inflorescences borne under protective pur-
     plish bracts.
FRUITS: Long, berry-like bodies with thick, shining rinds, hang in
     clusters.
SEASON OF MAXIMUM COLOR: Summer when purple bracts are present.
LANDSCAPE USES: For lending an air of the tropics, nothing surpasses
     banana. Plant bananas in bold clumps behind walls or hardy shrubs
     so that they will not be missed when frost cuts them to the earth.
HABITAT: Tropics around the globe; in Florida, ubiquitous.
LIGHT REQUIREMENT: Full sun or broken shade.
SOIL REQUIREMENT: Fertile, moist soil makes for best growth.
SALT TOLERANCE: Not tolerant.
AVAILABILITY: Most sales lots offer bananas in containers during the
     summer months.
CULTURE: Plant, water, and forget.
PROPAGATION: Division of matted clumps.
PESTS: *Cercospora* leaf-spot, Panama disease, scales, and nematodes.
NOTE: There are many kinds of bananas. Some ornamental types,
     grown for foliage or flowers, make outstanding garden subjects. In
     addition to those with colorful foliage, there are some with very
     attractive inflorescences. *Musa coccinea* has brilliant red bracts, M.
     rosea pink bracts; both hold up very well as cut flowers.

110
Bird-of-Paradise Flower

Strelitzia (strel-IT-zee-a): for the wife of King George III.
reginae (ree-JINE-ee): of the queen.

FAMILY: Musaceae.　　　　　　　RELATIVES: Banana and travelers-tree.
TYPE OF PLANT: Herbaceous perennial.　　　　HEIGHT: 4'. ZONE: C,S
HOW TO IDENTIFY: Two-ranked, evergreen foliage with channeled, erect,
　　succulent petioles which support the waxy blades that are 6" × 18";
　　spectacular bird-like blossoms atop long scapes as tall as, or taller
　　than, the foliage mound.
HABIT OF GROWTH: Clump-forming, trunkless, herbaceous perennial.
FOLIAGE: Evergreen, waxy, bold in form and dark green in color.
FLOWERS: Spectacular orange-and-blue floral parts emerge from hori-
　　zontal, boat-shaped bracts atop vertical, leafless scapes.
FRUITS: 3-angled capsules that split to release seeds that are edible.
SEASON OF MAXIMUM COLOR: Whenever flowers are produced.
LANDSCAPE USES: For the curiosity of the flying birds, strelitzia is much
　　admired. In planters or in front of evergreen shrubbery, clumps
　　may stand with 3' between individuals. Improved strains produce
　　birds which fly well above the foliage. In Florida, bird-of-paradise
　　flower does not always bloom as freely as it does in California.
HABITAT: South Africa; in Florida, sparingly cultured in gardens.
LIGHT REQUIREMENT: In Florida, high shade is recommended during
　　part of the day.
SOIL REQUIREMENT: Rich, moisture-retentive, acid soil is recommended.
SALT TOLERANCE: Not tolerant.
AVAILABILITY: Nurseries on the peninsula offer plants in containers.
CULTURE: Plant in well-prepared sites; water faithfully; protect from
　　cold and scale insects.
PROPAGATION: Seedage or division.
PESTS: Scales.
NOTE: *Strelitzia nicolai,* to 20' in height, with palm-like trunk and
　　leaves, resembles an untidy travelers-tree. In this, the larger, more
　　hardy strelitzia, the spathe is reddish, the sepals white, the tongue
　　blue.

111
Heliconia

Heliconia (hell-i-CONE-ee-a): for Mt. Helicon.
SPP.: several species and variants are cultured in Florida.

FAMILY: Musaceae.   RELATIVES: Banana and travelers-tree.
TYPE OF PLANT: Herbaceous perennial.   HEIGHT: Variable. ZONE: S
HOW TO IDENTIFY: Plants resemble slender or dwarf bananas and produce inflorescences with highly decorative bracts. The plants, their foliage, and their bracts are variable with the species or the variety.
HABIT OF GROWTH: Upright, banana-like.
FOLIAGE: Banana-like and highly decorative.
FLOWERS: Inconspicuous, held within various kinds of highly colored, very beautiful bracts, for which these plants are cultivated.
FRUITS: Blue capsules which break into berry-like parts.
SEASON OF MAXIMUM COLOR: Spring and summer when bracts develop color.
LANDSCAPE USES: For the beautiful, colorful bracts, heliconias are in high favor in frostless locations. While these inflorescences are usually cut for indoor decoration, if left in place they become sure conversation starters.
HABITAT: Tropical America; in Florida not very widely cultured.
LIGHT REQUIREMENT: Full sun or partial shade.
SOIL REQUIREMENT: Fertile, moist soil makes for best growth and flowering.
SALT TOLERANCE: Quite tolerant of salt air back of the first dune.
AVAILABILITY: Retail sales lots offer heliconias in containers.
CULTURE: Plant, water, and continuously protect the foliage against *Cercospora* and *Helminthosporum* leaf-spots. Fertilize once during each summer month.
PROPAGATION: Division of matted clumps.
PESTS: *Cercospora* and *Helminthosporum* leaf-spots, scales, and nematodes.
NOTE: Shown above are some Florida favorites. Common names are many—wild plantain, balisier, flowering banana, and lobster-claw are some of those most frequently heard.

112
Travelers-Tree

Ravenala (rav-en-ALE-a): name of the plant in Madagascar.
madagascariensis (mad-a-gas-car-ee-EN-sis): of Madagascar.

FAMILY: Musaceae.   RELATIVES: Banana and bird-of-paradise flower.

TYPE OF PLANT: Tree.   HEIGHT: 25′. ZONE: S

HOW TO IDENTIFY: Huge leaves are held in two ranks to give a fan-like effect atop a stout, palm-like trunk.

HABIT OF GROWTH: Two-ranked foliage forms a huge, symmetrical fan.

FOLIAGE: Evergreen, bold in aspect, medium green in color.

FLOWERS: Small, white flowers are held in erect series of canoe-like bracts.

FRUITS: 3-celled woody capsules with many indigo seeds.

SEASON OF MAXIMUM COLOR: No seasonal change.

LANDSCAPE USES: To help create a tropical atmosphere, travelers-tree is one of Florida's most popular plants; surely none is more striking. Travelers-tree is used as a freestanding specimen, often as a focal point in the outdoor living area. There is no truth in the oft-heard idea that the foliage fan must face a certain point of the compass.

HABITAT: Madagascar; in Florida, planted as a lawn specimen in warm locations.

LIGHT REQUIREMENT: Full sun for best growth, but small plants in pots may be shaded for a time.

SOIL REQUIREMENT: Fertile soil, high in organic matter is best.

SALT TOLERANCE: Not tolerant of dune conditions.

AVAILABILITY: Most nurseries on the lower peninsula offer plants.

CULTURE: In locations protected from frost, plant in fertile earth; water carefully; fertilize several times during growing weather.

PROPAGATION: Seedage or division.

PESTS: *Cercospora* leaf-spot is a very serious disease.

113
Ginger-Lily

Hedychium (he-DICK-ee-um): Greek for sweet snow, referring to the flowers.
SPP.: several species and hybrids grow in Florida.

FAMILY: Zingiberaceae.　　　　RELATIVES: Ginger and shell-flower.
TYPE OF PLANT: Herbaceous perennial.　　HEIGHT: 6'. ZONE: N,C,S
HOW TO IDENTIFY: This genus produces heavy clumps of leafy stems from strong rhizomes, and terminal inflorescences. In *Hedychium* the fragrant, long-tubed flowers have large, flaring lips. White in the most popular species; yellow or pinkish blooms are borne by lesser-known kinds.
HABIT OF GROWTH: Heavily foliated, stout stems form huge clumps.
FOLIAGE: Evergreen, alternate, 24" × 6", held attractively by man-high stems. Ginger-lily foliage is killed in northern Florida, but may persist in warmer sections.
FLOWERS: Fragrant, long-tubed flowers with lobed lips extend from terminal, bracted heads.
FRUITS: Capsules which split to reveal red seeds.
SEASON OF MAXIMUM COLOR: Warm months when blossoms are out.
LANDSCAPE USES: In common with other gingerworts, hedychiums have long been popular with Floridians for the beauty of the lush foliage and for the interesting inflorescences. Clumps can form parts of herbaceous borders, or they may stand near bodies of water.
HABITAT: Eastern Asia.
LIGHT REQUIREMENT: Full sun or broken, shifting shade.
SOIL REQUIREMENT: Fertile, moist soil makes for best growth and flow-ering.
SALT TOLERANCE: Tolerant of salt air back of the first-line dunes.
AVAILABILITY: Nurseries sell ginger-lilies in cans.
CULTURE: In springtime, plant rootstocks just below the surface of the earth; water moderately; and fertilize once at the beginning of each rainy season.
PROPAGATION: Division of matted clumps.
PESTS: Mites, possibly nematodes in light, open, sandy soils.
NOTE: Most widely grown ginger-lily is white-flowered *Hedychium coronarium*, illustrated above. *H. flavum* has yellow blooms, and *H. gardnerianum* has light yellow blossoms. There are hybrids among these species.

114
Pine Cone-Lily

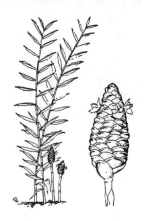

Zingiber (ZIN-gy-burr): classical name.
zerumbet (zur-RUM-bet): aboriginal name.

FAMILY: Zingiberaceae.   RELATIVES: Ginger and shell-flower.
TYPE OF PLANT: Herbaceous perennial.   HEIGHT: 4'. ZONE: N,C,S
HOW TO IDENTIFY: Leafy stems of ginger-like foliage are sent up in
    springtime, to be followed in the autumn by short, bracted in-
    florescences which resemble pine cones. These flower heads, which
    become bright red at maturity, are much admired for indoor deco-
    ration.
HABIT OF GROWTH: Leaning, heavily foliated stems form strong clumps.
FOLIAGE: Alternate, long, narrow leaves like ginger foliage are held
    almost horizontally by the 4' stems. Plants die down during short
    days of autumn.
FLOWERS: Bracted heads form red, pine cone-like bodies on short stems
    after the rainy season.
FRUITS: Capsules.
SEASON OF MAXIMUM COLOR: Fall and winter when bracted heads de-
    velop red coloration.
LANDSCAPE USES: Because they are so popular for indoor arrangements,
    Floridians cultivate pine cone-lilies as separate plantings in the
    out-of-door living area or the service area. During the cold months
    there is nothing above ground.
HABITAT: South Sea islands.
LIGHT REQUIREMENT: Full sun or shifting, broken shade.
SOIL REQUIREMENT: Fertile, moist soil makes for best growth and flow-
    ering.
SALT TOLERANCE: Tolerant of salt air back from the beach.
AVAILABILITY: Retail nurseries throughout the state sell pine cone-lilies.
CULTURE: Plant rootstocks in springtime just below the surface of the
    earth; water moderately; fertilize lightly once during each summer
    month.
PROPAGATION: Division of matted clumps.
PESTS: Mites.
NOTE: Variegated ginger (Zingiber zerumbet 'Darceyi') is admired for
    its glistening white-and-green foliage. It can be grown in herbaceous
    borders and as a pot plant.

115
Shell-Flower

Alpinia (al-PIN-ee-a): for P. Alpinus, early Italian botanist.
SPP.: several species and clones are seen in Florida.

FAMILY: Zingiberaceae.   RELATIVES: Ginger and pine cone-lily.
TYPE OF PLANT: Herbaceous perennial.   HEIGHT: Variable. ZONE: N,C,S
HOW TO IDENTIFY: Bold clumps of heavily foliated stems come up from
    vigorous rootstocks. The persistent leaves may measure a foot in
    length by half this width. In *Alpinia*, flowers are borne at stem-
    ends, not on separate peduncles near the earth.
HABIT OF GROWTH: Dense, graceful, compact clumps are formed by
    leafy stems.
FOLIAGE: Persistent, bright, deep green. Some cultivars are variegated.
FLOWERS: Shell-like, fragrant, in drooping clusters at stem-ends.
FRUITS: Capsules.
SEASON OF MAXIMUM COLOR: Summer and autumn, as flowers open.
LANDSCAPE USES: For the lush effect of the huge clumps and the inter-
    est of the attractive warm-weather blossoms, shell-flowers have
    long been Florida favorites. In warm locations, stems will persist;
    in cold sections, they will be cut to earth each winter, but new
    shoots will appear with the spring.
HABITAT: South Sea islands.
LIGHT REQUIREMENT: Full sun or high, shifting shade.
SOIL REQUIREMENT: Fertile, moist soil makes for best growth.
SALT TOLERANCE: Somewhat salt tolerant, but not for dune plantings.
AVAILABILITY: Nurseries in warmer parts of the state stock shell-flowers.
CULTURE: Plant rootstocks in springtime just below the surface of the
    earth; water periodically until established; and fertilize once at
    the beginning of the summer rainy season.
PROPAGATION: Division of matted clumps.
PESTS: Mites, yet these pests are usually not of major concern.
NOTE: Most popular shell-flower is *Alpinia speciosa*, above right. Its
    clone 'Vittata' has foliage attractively splotched with white. At the
    lower left is depicted *A. mutica* which produces small erect spikes
    of attractive open flowers that are followed by persistent, felty,
    red fruits. The top left sketch illustrates red-ginger, *Alpinia pur-
    purata*, which is distinguished by vivid, terminal clusters of red
    bracts which subtend tiny white flowers.

116
Spiral-Flag

Costus (COST-us): old classical name.
SPP.: perhaps a half dozen species may be found in Florida gardens.

FAMILY: Zingiberaceae.   RELATIVES: Shell-flower and torch-ginger.
TYPE OF PLANT: Herbaceous perennial.   HEIGHT: Variable. ZONE: N,C,S
HOW TO IDENTIFY: Large, lush leaves are spirally arranged around stems
   that arise from underground rootstocks. Terminating these may
   appear bracted, cone-like inflorescences, from which emerge color-
   ful flowers in season.
HABIT OF GROWTH: Sprawling to form huge mounds of spiral-leaved
   stems.
FOLIAGE: Evergreen, abundant, spirally arranged.
FLOWERS: Conspicuous, colorful, in terminal positions, arising from
   cone-like, bracted heads.
FRUITS: Seeds may form between bracts.
SEASON OF MAXIMUM COLOR: Warm months when blossoms appear.
LANDSCAPE USES: Clumps may stand in moist locations near water-
   courses, or they may be featured against masonry walls if the soil
   there is rich and retentive of moisture.
HABITAT: Tropics of both hemispheres.
LIGHT REQUIREMENT: Full sun or high, shifting shade.
SOIL REQUIREMENT: Fertile, moist soil; often planted near water.
SALT TOLERANCE: Tolerant of conditions back of the front-line dunes.
AVAILABILITY: Spiral-flags are staple items in retail nurseries.
CULTURE: Plant rootstocks or offsets in springtime; water moderately
   until established; fertilize once at the beginning of the rainy season;
   keep grasses back from the root zone.
PROPAGATION: Division of matted clumps; separation of offsets that
   form below flower heads; cuttage of stems.
PESTS: Mites, possibly nematodes in light, open, sandy soils.
NOTE: Of the hundred or more species recorded, no more than a half
   dozen are likely to be seen in Florida. *Costus speciosus* (left-hand
   sketch) has foot-long, green leaves that are downy beneath. The
   10-foot stems are topped by bracted cones from which appear
   white, papery flowers. *Costus igneus* (right-hand sketch), orange-
   spiral-flag, grows a foot in height, and bears 6″ leaves that are
   purple beneath.

117
Torch-Ginger

Phaeomeria (fee-o-ME-ree-a): Greek for dark and part.
speciosa (spee-see-OH-sa): showy.

FAMILY: Zingiberaceae.   RELATIVES: Ginger-lily and shell-flower.
TYPE OF PLANT: Herbaceous perennial.   HEIGHT: 12'. ZONE: C,S
HOW TO IDENTIFY: One of the most vigorous plants in its family, torch-
   ginger will form huge clumps of tall, heavily foliated stems under
   good conditions. Spectacular reddish flower heads stand terminally
   on separate, yard-tall, leafless scapes.
HABIT OF GROWTH: Dense, close clumps are formed by leafy stems.
FOLIAGE: Evergreen, lush, and attractive.
FLOWERS: Spectacular reddish or pinkish heads of waxy bracts termi-
   nate separate, 1-flowered, leafless scapes.
FRUITS: Berries massed together somewhat resembling small pine-
   apples.
SEASON OF MAXIMUM COLOR: Autumn, when flowers expand.
LANDSCAPE USES: For the lush, tropical effect of the vigorous foliage
   and the very handsome, waxy inflorescences, torch-ginger enjoys
   popularity in warm sections of the state. Bold clumps standing by
   bodies of water are striking.
HABITAT: South Sea islands.
LIGHT REQUIREMENT: Partial shade is recommended.
SOIL REQUIREMENT: Rich, acid, moist soil is needed for best growth.
SALT TOLERANCE: Tolerant of mild salt air back from the strand.
AVAILABILITY: Most retail nurseries in warm areas sell torch-ginger
   plants in containers.
CULTURE: Plant divisions of old matted clumps in springtime; water
   until established; after that, little care is needed. Fertilize once at
   the beginning of the rainy season.
PROPAGATION: Division of old clumps; seedage.
PESTS: Mites, nematodes on light sandy soils.
NOTE: Formerly in *Amomum*, torch-ginger is now in the genus *Phaeo-
   meria*, also known as *Nicolaia elatior*.

C. lutea

C. zebrina

C. vittata

Calathea

C. medio-picta

C. insignis

C. lietzei

C. ornata 'Sanderiana'

C. princeps

119
Calathea

Calathea (cal-a-THE-a): Greek for basket, referring to the setting of the flowers.
SPP.: many kinds are cultured in our state.

FAMILY: Marantaceae.   RELATIVES: Arrowroot and thalia.
TYPE OF PLANT: Herbaceous perennial.   HEIGHT: Variable. ZONE: S
HOW TO IDENTIFY: Sheathing leaves noted for their appealing markings
    grow during warm, moist months to delight gardeners. To distin-
    guish varieties and species, and to be certain that a plant in ques-
    tion is a calathea and not a maranta, is a most difficult assignment.
HABIT OF GROWTH: Mottled leaves are held gracefully by wiry stems.
FOLIAGE: Very appealing, because of the beautiful patterns of lines,
    blotches, and spots.
FLOWERS: Little spikes, not particularly showy.
FRUITS: Little berries or capsules.
SEASON OF MAXIMUM COLOR: Spring when new foliage comes out.
LANDSCAPE USES: As pot plants, these are very popular because of
    their attractively marked foliage. Protection from cold is essential.
HABITAT: Tropical America.
LIGHT REQUIREMENT: Reduced light is optimum; bright sunlight is not
    recommended.
SOIL REQUIREMENT: Rich, moisture-retentive, but fast-draining soil is
    needed for good growth and bright coloration.
SALT TOLERANCE: Not tolerant of ocean-front conditions.
AVAILABILITY: Nurseries sell calatheas in pots.
CULTURE: Plant at the same level as the plant grew formerly, in a pot
    that has an abundance of coarse material in the bottom to assure
    good drainage and aeration. Supply high humidity and high tem-
    perature continuously, and light fertilization once in each summer
    month.
PROPAGATION: Division.
PESTS: Mites.
NOTE: Above is *C. vandenheckei* 'Wendlinger'; illustrated on the op-
    posite page are some of Florida's most popular calatheas. Clear-cut
    distinctions among these many kinds are hard to define. All of these
    are called marantas in Florida.

120
Arrowroot

Maranta (ma-RAN-ta): for B. Maranta, Italian botanist.
SPP.: many kinds grow in Florida.

FAMILY: Marantaceae.   RELATIVES: Calathea and thalia.
TYPE OF PLANT: Rhizomatous perennial.   HEIGHT: Variable. ZONE: S
HOW TO IDENTIFY: Sheathing leaves, noted for their appealing mark-
   ings, grow during warm, moist months to delight gardeners.
HABIT OF GROWTH: Low perennial.
FOLIAGE: Very appealing because of the beautiful patterns of lines,
   blotches, and spots.
FLOWERS: Little spikes of white flowers, spotted with purple, are pro-
   duced among the leaves.
FRUITS: Little berries or capsules.
SEASON OF MAXIMUM COLOR: All year due to colorful foliage. Flowers
   insignificant.
LANDSCAPE USES: As pot plants, these are very popular because of
   their attractively marked foliage. Protection from cold is essential.
HABITAT: Tropical America.
LIGHT REQUIREMENT: Reduced light is optimum; bright sunlight is not
   recommended.
SOIL REQUIREMENT: Rich, moisture-retentive, but fast-draining soil is
   needed for good growth and bright coloration.
CULTURE: Plant at the same level as the plant grew formerly, in a pot
   that has an abundance of coarse material in the bottom to assure
   good drainage and aeration. Supply high humidity and high temperature continuously, and light fertilization once in each summer
   month.
PROPAGATION: Division.
PESTS: Mites.
NOTE: Clear-cut distinction between arrowroot varieties and calatheas
   is impossible; in fact, they are all called marantas. Great confusion
   in naming exists in Florida, unfortunately.

121
Epiphytic Orchid

1. *Cattleya* (CAT-lee-a): for W. Cattley, English horticulturist.
2. *Dendrobium* (den-DRO-bee-um): Greek for tree and life.
3. *Epidendrum* (ep-ee-DEN-drum): Greek for on trees.
4. *Oncidium* (on-SID-ee-um): Greek for tubercle, for lobed labellum.
5. *Phalaenopsis* (fal-ee-NOP-sis): Greek for moth-like.
SPP.: many kinds are seen in Florida.

FAMILY: Orchidaceae. RELATIVES: The orchids.
TYPE OF PLANT: Epiphytic perennial. HEIGHT: Variable. ZONE: S
HOW TO IDENTIFY: Tree-dwelling perennials that produce white, velamen-coated roots that lodge in bark crevasses. Plants often have pseudobulbs, usually with green leaves.
FOLIAGE: Usually green, persistent, but there are many exceptions.
FLOWERS: Extremely variable, some minute, others large and spectacular, the most wanted blossoms in the plant kingdom.
FRUITS: Angled pods that may contain millions of dust-like seeds.
SEASON OF MAXIMUM COLOR: Usually springtime, but some epiphytic orchids may be found in flower every month in the year.
LANDSCAPE USES: To add interest to lawn trees, epiphytic orchids are wired to branches of trees in nearly frost-free locations. In colder sections, pot culture in greenhouses is standard.
HABITAT: Tropics of both hemispheres.
LIGHT REQUIREMENT: Light, shifting shade is acceptable; dense shade is unsuitable.
SOIL REQUIREMENT: Osmundine, shredded tree fern, or chipped bark from lumber trees can be used to pot epiphytic orchids.
SALT TOLERANCE: Not tolerant.
AVAILABILITY: Orchid nurseries, garden centers, and chain stores sell epiphytic orchids.
CULTURE: Secure landscape epiphytes to branches of rough-barked yard trees with copper wire; pot greenhouse epiphytes after flowering, in one of the media listed above. Soak weekly; syringe lightly each day; tie new growths to wire stake.
PROPAGATION: Division and seedage.
PESTS: Scales, mites, and fungus diseases.

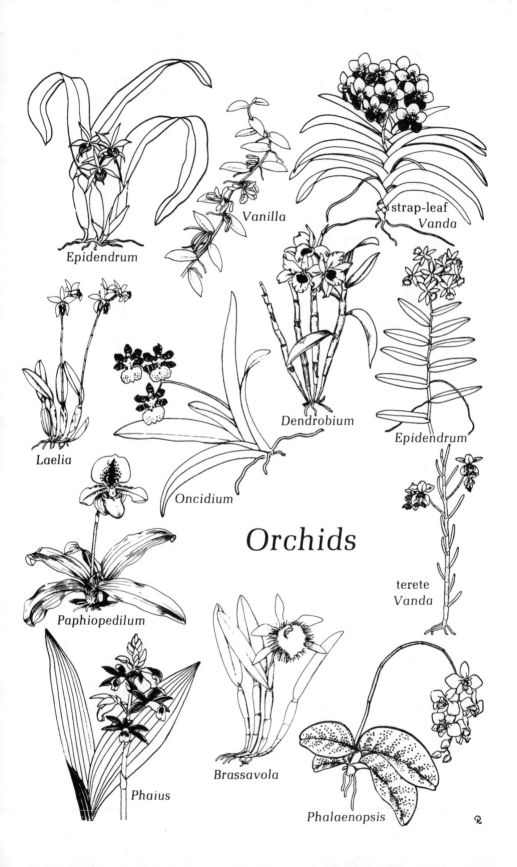

Epidendrum

Vanilla

strap-leaf Vanda

Laelia

Oncidium

Dendrobium

Epidendrum

Paphiopedilum

Orchids

terete Vanda

Phaius

Brassavola

Phalaenopsis

123
Terrestrial Orchid

Phaius (FAY-us): Greek for swarthy, for the color of the flowers.
Vanda (VAN-da): Sanskrit name.
and numerous other genera.
SPP.: many kinds are seen in Florida.

FAMILY: Orchidaceae. RELATIVES: The orchids.
TYPE OF PLANT: Terrestrial perennial. HEIGHT: Variable. ZONE: S
HOW TO IDENTIFY: Positive identification depends upon flowers, as the plants are so variable.
HABIT OF GROWTH: Extremely variable.
FOLIAGE: Extremely variable, evergreen or deciduous.
FLOWERS: True orchids in many sizes and colors.
FRUITS: Angled capsules that may contain myriads of tiny seeds.
SEASON OF MAXIMUM COLOR: Usually springtime, yet terrestrial orchids may flower at other seasons.
LANDSCAPE USES: For the curiosity of orchids as garden flowers, earth-dwellers can form color highlights in frost-free gardens. In cooler sections of Florida these plants are grown in containers in green-houses.
HABITAT: Tropics of both hemispheres.
LIGHT REQUIREMENT: Variable; some demand full sun, others thrive in partial shade, none grow well in deep shade.
SOIL REQUIREMENT: Open, friable, gritty, reasonably fertile, fast-draining soils are needed.
SALT TOLERANCE: Not tolerant.
AVAILABILITY: Terrestrial types are for sale in all orchid nurseries.
CULTURE: Plant carefully, slightly deeper than formerly; water during periods of drought; apply dilute, liquid fertilizer once during each summer month. Furnish wooden trellises for vining types.
PROPAGATION: Cuttage by pieces of stem, or division of clump-growers.
PESTS: Scales.

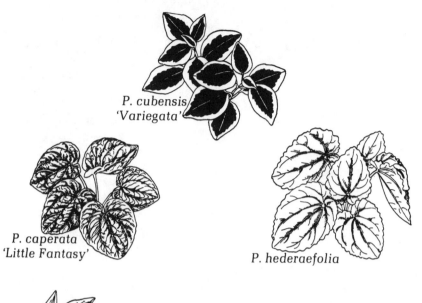

P. cubensis
'Variegata'

P. caperata
'Little Fantasy'

P. hederaefolia

Peperomia

P. metallica

P. bicolor

P. nivalis

P. caperata 'Tricolor'

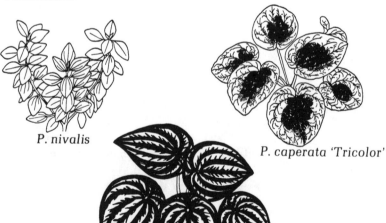

P. argyreia

125
Peperomia

Peperomia (pep-er-OH-me-a): pepper-like.
SPP.: many kinds are seen in Florida.

FAMILY: Piperaceae.   RELATIVE: Pepper of commerce.
TYPE OF PLANT: Herbaceous perennial.   HEIGHT: Variable. ZONE: S
HOW TO IDENTIFY: Small, succulent, clump-growing perennials send up
   decorative leaves of many shapes, sizes, and colors and little spikes
   of inconspicuous flowers.
HABIT OF GROWTH: Diminutive clump-grower.
FOLIAGE: Evergreen, succulent, diverse in size, shape, and color.
FLOWERS: Little spikes of inconspicuous flowers.
FRUITS: Little, thin-coated berries.
SEASON OF MAXIMUM COLOR: Possibly when new growth first emerges.
LANDSCAPE USES: Long favorite pot plants, latterly popular as ground
   cover for shady, frostless spots and for planters, peperomias are to
   be found in many households. They are frequently planted in
   pockets in rockery-water features in home landscapes.
HABITAT: Tropical America.
LIGHT REQUIREMENT: Shaded locations are right for peperomias.
SOIL REQUIREMENT: Rich, fibrous, quick-draining soil is best.
SALT TOLERANCE: Not tolerant.
AVAILABILITY: Peps in containers are offered in chain stores and retail
   sales lots.
CULTURE: After potting in soil described above, keep humidity very
   high by frequently syringing with very light mist.
PROPAGATION: Cuttage and division.
PESTS: Mites, leaf-spots, and rots.
NOTE: To visit Florida nurseries and garden centers and to study the
   7 pages devoted to the genus in *Exotica* is to realize that the culti-
   vars are many, the naming not necessarily consistent. Shown above
   and across are some of Florida's favorite peps.

Australian-Pine

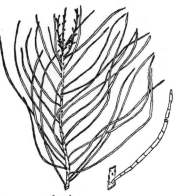

Casuarina (cas-you-are-EYE-na): with branches like cassawary feathers.
equisetifolia (eck-we-seat-ee-FOL-ee-a): with leaves like the horsetail.

FAMILY: Casuarinaceae.   RELATIVES: The genus is alone in its family.
TYPE OF PLANT: Tree.   HEIGHT: 60′. ZONE: S
HOW TO IDENTIFY: Horsetail-like branch-tips, green, leafless; cones very
    short-stalked, globular, ½″ in diameter. This species self-seeds but
    does *not* sucker at the roots.
HABIT OF GROWTH: Spire-like, with open crown; seedlings make huge
    cultures.
FOLIAGE: Absent; branch texture very fine, of dark green color.
FLOWERS: Inconspicuous.
FRUITS: Brown cones, very short-stalked, globular, ½″ in diameter.
SEASON OF MAXIMUM COLOR: No variation.
LANDSCAPE USES: For clipped hedges and topiary near the sea nothing
    surpasses this species. For windbreaks and roadside trees, Austra-
    lian-pines are much used. They serve notably to help hold sand
    and build keys in southern Florida.
HABITAT: Australia; in Florida, warmest locations, often at seaside.
LIGHT REQUIREMENT: Full sun or shady situations.
SOIL REQUIREMENT: Most soils seem to be entirely adequate.
SALT TOLERANCE: Most tolerant of salt, grows on front-line dunes.
AVAILABILITY: Canned trees are stocked by most nurseries in southern
    Florida.
CULTURE: Plant in a prepared site; water until established; thereafter
    prune rigorously to keep within size desired.
PROPAGATION: Seedage. *C. lepidophloia* may be grafted upon *C. equi-
    setifolia*, thus making sucker-free plants.
PESTS: Mushroom root-rot.
NOTE: *C. cunninghamiana*, the hardiest species, has upright, spire-like
    habit, dense green foliage, and brown cones 1″ in diameter.
        C. lepidophloia forms countless suckers to encompass large plots
    of ground. This one does not produce fruits in Florida, and it is *not*
    tolerant of salt.

127
Southern Wax-Myrtle

Myrica (mir-EE-ca): Greek for the tamarisk.
cerifera (sir-IF-era): wax-bearing.

FAMILY: Myricaceae.   RELATIVES: Northern bayberry and sweet gale.
TYPE OF PLANT: Large shrub or small tree.   HEIGHT: 25′. ZONE: N,C,S
HOW TO IDENTIFY: Aromatic leaves are coarsely serrate toward their tips, rusty-glandular on both sides; waxy gray-green fruits are borne by some individuals.
HABIT OF GROWTH: Clump-forming by stolons; picturesque shapes are often seen.
FOLIAGE: Semi-evergreen, alternate, medium in texture, variable in color.
FLOWERS: Inconspicuous, unisexual; there are pistillate and staminate plants.
FRUITS: Grayish-green, waxy drupes are borne by pistillate plants.
SEASON OF MAXIMUM COLOR: Possibly when fruits color in autumn.
LANDSCAPE USES: For enclosure (5′ o.c.) no native shrub is more appreciated. Wax-myrtle becomes too open below for clipped hedges, too large for foundation plantings. As a small specimen tree, it can be a good selection.
HABITAT: Ubiquitous in every county in Florida.
LIGHT REQUIREMENT: Full sun or partial shade.
SOIL REQUIREMENT: Wet swamplands or dry locations on high ground.
SALT TOLERANCE: Tolerant of salt air and saline soils.
AVAILABILITY: Usually not a nursery item, native clumps are dug as needed after permission has been granted by the property owner.
CULTURE: Cut branches back to 10″ stubs and dig clumps with generous mats of roots. Water and forget.
PROPAGATION: Transplant wild clumps with permission of the property owner.
PESTS: Caterpillars tie terminal leaves; cankers may form on old branches.
NOTE: *Myrica pennsylvanica* is the source of wax for bayberry candles.

128
Laurel Oak

Quercus (KWARE-cuss): ancient Latin name.
laurifolia (law-rye-FOL-ee-a): laurel-leaved.

FAMILY: Fagaceae.   RELATIVES: The beeches and the chestnuts.
TYPE OF PLANT: Tree.   HEIGHT: 100'. ZONE: N,C,S

HOW TO IDENTIFY: A fast-growing tree that bears alternate, thin smooth leaves that are shiny on both sides, round acorns that mature the second year and are enclosed for ¼ or less of their height in thin, saucer-like cups.

HABIT OF GROWTH: Upright tree that is taller than broad, with round head.

FOLIAGE: Deciduous or partially evergreen, alternate, medium fine in texture.

FLOWERS: Inconspicuous, in catkins near the branch-tips.

FRUITS: Round acorns, maturing the second year, are enclosed ¼-way in flattish cups.

SEASON OF MAXIMUM COLOR: No variation.

LANDSCAPE USES: Laurel oak grows rapidly, reaches senility, and begins to break up near the half-century mark. For occasional planting on home grounds where fast growth is required and short life is no disadvantage, this native might be indicated. However, ultimate size is great and cost of removal may be considerable. Laurel oak is not recommended for municipal planting because of its comparatively short life.

HABITAT: Moist soil north of the Everglades.

LIGHT REQUIREMENT: Sun or shade; mature specimens require much space in full sun.

SOIL REQUIREMENT: Widely tolerant of the many varying soils found in Florida.

SALT TOLERANCE: Not tolerant.

AVAILABILITY: Most nurseries would dig young laurel oak trees on order.

CULTURE: No special care is needed after properly planted young trees become established.

PROPAGATION: Seedage.

PESTS: Mushroom root-rot.

129
Live Oak

Quercus (KWARE-cuss): ancient Latin name.
virginiana (vir-gin-ee-AY-na): Virginian.

FAMILY: Fagaceae.   RELATIVES: The beeches and the chestnuts.
TYPE OF PLANT: Tree.   HEIGHT: 60'. ZONE: N,C,S
HOW TO IDENTIFY: Noble tree with wide-spreading, horizontal branches covered with deeply corrugated, light gray bark; evergreen, alternate leaves that are thick, shining green above, downy beneath, with revolute edges. The acorns, which mature the first season, are nearly black, elliptical, enclosed for ⅓ their length in top-shaped cups.
HABIT OF GROWTH: Wide-spreading, horizontal branches from short, buttressed trunks which often assume picturesque shapes, allow branch-tips to bend down to the earth.
FOLIAGE: Evergreen, medium fine in texture, dark green above, lighter beneath.
FLOWERS: Inconspicuous, in catkins near the branch-tips.
FRUITS: Elliptical black acorns, enclosed ⅓ their length in deep cups.
SEASON OF MAXIMUM COLOR: No variation.
LANDSCAPE USES: Live oak is Florida's shade tree par excellence. As an avenue tree it has the highest rating; set individuals 90' apart. The life of live oak trees is measured in centuries; stability in high winds is widely recognized; the picturesque forms are admired.
HABITAT: Hammocks and lake margins in every county in Florida.
LIGHT REQUIREMENT: Shade or sun; for maximum development, allow great space in full sun.
SOIL REQUIREMENT: Moist soil of good fertility.
SALT TOLERANCE: Very tolerant of salt and alkaline soil.
AVAILABILITY: Good, small live oak trees are not readily available. Small native seedlings might be dug on order.
CULTURE: Plant carefully in well-prepared planting sites; wrap trunks; water faithfully; fertilize twice a year; remove moss periodically.
PROPAGATION: Seedage.
PESTS: Mushroom root-rot.
NOTE: Twin live oak, *Q. virginiana* 'Geminata', grows on sandy soil, is more upright in habit, has thick revolute leaves and acorns growing as twins.

130
Aluminum-Plant

Pilea (PIE-lee-a): Latin for felt cap, for the fruit cover.
cadierei (cad-YEAR-eye): for M. Cadiere.

FAMILY: Urticaceae.   RELATIVES: Artillery-plant and panamigo.

TYPE OF PLANT: Herbaceous perennial.   HEIGHT: 8″. ZONE: C,S

HOW TO IDENTIFY: The quilted and puckered leaves marked with silver bands are sure identification.

HABIT OF GROWTH: Mat-forming to cover the earth in shady locations.

FOLIAGE: Evergreen, puckered, lined with silver-colored bands.

FLOWERS: Inconspicuous, in little spikes.

FRUITS: Tiny pods.

SEASON OF MAXIMUM COLOR: Early spring when new growth appears.

LANDSCAPE USES: In shaded rock-'n'-sand gardens and indoor planters and pots, aluminum-plant is extremely popular.

HABITAT: Tropical regions.

LIGHT REQUIREMENT: Tolerant of considerable shade; sunlight is unsuitable.

SOIL REQUIREMENT: Rich, fibrous, fast-draining soil is best.

SALT TOLERANCE: Tolerant of salt drift back from the strand.

AVAILABILITY: Almost all nurseries have small plants for sale.

CULTURE: Plant sections of stems in pots, planters, or pockets of the soil mentioned above and maintain high humidity by frequent syringing with light mist.

PROPAGATION: Cuttage and division.

PESTS: Mites.

NOTE: *Pilea involucrata* from Peru is another outstanding herbaceous plant in this genus. The deeply quilted leaves are rich green when grown in the shade and red-brown when grown in bright situations. Red flowers are borne in tight clusters in leaf axils.

131
River Birch

Betula (BET-u-la): ancient Latin name.
nigra (NI-gra): dark.

FAMILY: Betulaceae.   RELATIVES: Alders and hop hornbean.
TYPE OF PLANT: Deciduous tree.   HEIGHT: 50'–60'. ZONE: N,C
HOW TO IDENTIFY: Upright, narrow tree, with short trunk usually dividing into a few large branches; bark smooth, papery, flaking in small pieces. Young branches are very slender, smooth, and reddish-brown. Leaves alternate, ovate to 2½" long with double-toothed margins. Flowers in spring before leaves appear.
HABIT OF GROWTH: Narrow, upright tree.
FOLIAGE: Simple, shiny, smooth, medium green.
FLOWERS: Staminate and pistillate catkins on separate trees.
FRUITS: Small, nut-like.
SEASON OF MAXIMUM COLOR: Spring.
LANDSCAPE USES: Excellent, fast-growing tree for small properties and along stream banks.
HABITAT: Massachusetts to Florida, west to Kansas.
LIGHT REQUIREMENT: Full sun to partial shade.
SOIL REQUIREMENT: Thrives on moist soils, e.g., stream banks and bottom lands.
SALT TOLERANCE: None.
AVAILABILITY: Found infrequently in nurseries.
CULTURE: Once established, plants require little care. River birch can be grown on well-drained sandy soils, with irrigation during periods of drought.
PROPAGATION: Seedage or hardwood cuttings.
PESTS: Twig girdlers are sometimes a problem. Occasionally attacked by caterpillars.
NOTE: This excellent tree should be more widely used in Florida landscapes. The slender twigs move with the wind and the shiny leaves glisten as they move.

132
Dwarf Elm

Ulmus (ULM-us): ancient Latin name for the elm.
pumila (PEW-mill-a): dwarf.

FAMILY: Ulmaceae.
RELATIVES: The elm trees.
TYPE OF PLANT: Tree.
HEIGHT: 25'. ZONE: N,C
HOW TO IDENTIFY: Very rapid, upright growth; deciduous or semi-evergreen foliage with unequal bases, almost simply serrate, pubescent in axils of veins beneath.
HABIT OF GROWTH: Strongly upright, rapid growth.
FOLIAGE: Deciduous or semi-evergreen, of fine texture and medium green color.
FLOWERS: Inconspicuous catkins in early spring, if present.
FRUITS: Small, winged fruit, called samara, if present.
SEASON OF MAXIMUM COLOR: Possibly autumn, when leaves turn yellow.
LANDSCAPE USES: For a very fast growing tree, this little elm is popular. It is not recommended for permanent street use, however, because of rapid growth and possible short life.
HABITAT: Siberia; in Florida, rather widely planted in the northern section.
LIGHT REQUIREMENT: Full sun.
SOIL REQUIREMENT: Any soil seems to be adequate.
SALT TOLERANCE: Not recommended for dune planting.
AVAILABILITY: Nurseries in central and northern Florida offer this elm.
CULTURE: Plant with reasonable care; water until established; fertilize once each winter while young.
PROPAGATION: Seedage by means of imported seeds; cuttage, as well.
PESTS: Mites.
NOTE: There may be confusion with Chinese elm (*Ulmus parvifolia*), which is inclined to have a more weeping habit and smaller leaves. This one may be sold as evergreen elm or weeping evergreen elm in south-central Florida nurseries.

Florida's native winged elm (*Ulmus alata*) has landscape value. Its bark with corky wings adds to the overall attractiveness of this plant. Leaves turn rusty early in autumn due to insect damage.

133
Cecropia

Cecropia (see-CROW-pea-a): Greek, refers to use of wood in wind instruments.
palmata (pal-MAY-ta): divided in a hand-like fashion.

FAMILY: Moraceae.

RELATIVES: Mulberry and ficus trees.

TYPE OF PLANT: Tree.

HEIGHT: 50'. ZONE: S

HOW TO IDENTIFY: Slender trunk with smooth bark, open branching; huge, palmate leaves (right-hand sketch) with white undersurfaces clustered at the ends of branches, cut to middle or below.

HABIT OF GROWTH: Tall, ungainly, open.

FOLIAGE: Evergreen, palmate, of most interesting form, dark green above, white beneath.

FLOWERS: Inconspicuous catkins.

FRUITS: Pencil-like pods to 6" long.

SEASON OF MAXIMUM COLOR: No variation.

LANDSCAPE USES: The curled-inward, dried cecropia foliage is useful in dry arrangements. The tree may stand free as a horticultural curiosity on large grounds in nearly frostless locations.

HABITAT: Tropical America; in Florida, most nearly frost-free areas.

LIGHT REQUIREMENT: Broken shade of wooded areas.

SOIL REQUIREMENT: Fertile soil above average in quality.

SALT TOLERANCE: Not tolerant of seaside conditions.

AVAILABILITY: Specialty nurseries in warmest parts may stock small cecropia trees.

CULTURE: Plant with great care in warmest location; water faithfully; keep lawn grasses from encroaching; fertilize annually.

PROPAGATION: Seedage and/or cuttage.

PESTS: Ants inhabit hollow branches, but apparently do no damage.

NOTE: *Cecropia peltata* (left-hand sketch) has foot-broad leaves divided only ⅓ of the distance to the center, with petiole attached near the center, and with fruits about 3" long. Cecropia trees are killed by frost.

134
Benjamin Fig

Ficus (FYE-cuss): ancient Latin name for the fig.
benjamina (ben-jah-MINE-a): refers, incorrectly, to this as a benzoin source.

FAMILY: Moraceae.   RELATIVES: The fig trees, mulberry, and hops.
TYPE OF PLANT: Tree.   HEIGHT: 50'. ZONE: S
HOW TO IDENTIFY: Weeping habit, no aerial roots in the usual Florida forms; evergreen leaves resistant to thrips; tiny figs become deep red.
HABIT OF GROWTH: Weeping branches drape gracefully from a very symmetrical, dense head; aerial roots are lacking in the usual forms seen in Florida.
FOLIAGE: Evergreen, alternate, thrips-resistant, of fine texture.
FLOWERS: Lacking.
FRUITS: Red figs ⅓" in diameter, in sessile, axillary pairs.
SEASON OF MAXIMUM COLOR: Summer when figs color.
LANDSCAPE USES: As a street tree (set 35'–50' o.c.) benjamin fig is very popular in southern Florida. The beautiful weeping habit, resistance to foliar thrips, and freedom from aerial roots make for its excellence as an avenue tree. There are several selections in this excellent species, one being 'Exotica'.
HABITAT: India; in Florida, very widely planted in frost-free areas.
LIGHT REQUIREMENT: Full sun or broken shade.
SOIL REQUIREMENT: Any soil seems to be suitable.
SALT TOLERANCE: Not tolerant of dune conditions, but grows back of the strand.
AVAILABILITY: Nurseries in southern Florida sell small trees in containers and B & B.
CULTURE: Water during periods of drought; keep lawn grasses back; fertilize annually while young. In maturity, pruning should be all the care that is required.
PROPAGATION: Cuttage and marcottage of very large branches.
PESTS: Scales.
NOTE: Cuban-laurel (*Ficus retusa* 'Nitida') is very widely grown in southern Florida as a clipped hedge or sheared specimen shrub. This upright-growing, robust tree has upright habit, aerial roots emerging from trunk and branches, and foliage that is almost always malformed by the feeding of thrips.

135
Creeping Fig

Ficus (FYE-cuss): ancient Latin name for the fig.
pumila (PEW-mill-a): dwarf.

FAMILY: Moraceae.   RELATIVES: The fig trees, mulberry, and hops.
TYPE OF PLANT: Vine.   HEIGHT: Variable. ZONE: N,C,S

HOW TO IDENTIFY: Vigorous vine that clings by tenacious, aerial root-lets yields milky sap when wounded, and produces large, green figs on stiff, horizontal fruiting branches at maturity.

HABIT OF GROWTH: Vining, with excessively rapid growth on most vertical surfaces.

FOLIAGE: Evergreen, fine texture on vertical shoots, coarse foliage on horizontal branches; the color is usually dark green or medium green.

FLOWERS: Absent.

FRUITS: Green figs the size and shape of hens' eggs, on mature, horizontal branches.

SEASON OF MAXIMUM COLOR: Spring, when new growth is reddish.

LANDSCAPE USES: To soften masonry walls, plant 5'–10' o.c. Do not plant this vine unless time can be devoted to pruning to regulate size, and do not plant near wooden structures.

HABITAT: Eastern Asia; in Florida, ubiquitous in landscape plantings.

LIGHT REQUIREMENT: Not critical; most light intensities are acceptable.

SOIL REQUIREMENT: Not critical; most soils are acceptable.

SALT TOLERANCE: Not critical; endures conditions back of the dunes.

AVAILABILITY: Fig vines in containers are occasionally offered in sales lots.

CULTURE: Creeping fig grows so vigorously that containing the root system in a deep, bottomless container in the earth is recommended. Periodic clipping is essential to keep the vine within bounds.

PROPAGATION: Simple layerage or cuttage.

PESTS: None of major concern.

NOTE: Variety 'Minima' has very small leaves held by slender twigs. *Ficus radicans* has oblong-lanceolate leaves 2″ long. Its variegated form is popular for hanging baskets and planter bins.

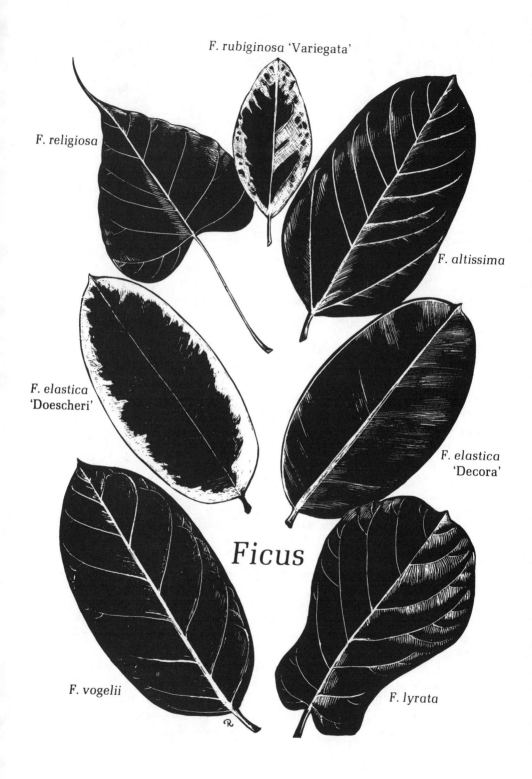

F. rubiginosa 'Variegata'

F. religiosa

F. altissima

F. elastica 'Doescheri'

F. elastica 'Decora'

Ficus

F. vogelii

F. lyrata

137
Large-Leaf Ficus

Ficus (FYE-CUSS): ancient Latin name for the fig.
SPP.: several species and a number of cultivars grow in Florida.

FAMILY: Moraceae.
RELATIVES: Mulberry and cecropia.
TYPE OF PLANT: Tree.
HEIGHT: 50′–120′. ZONE: S

HOW TO IDENTIFY: Milky sap exudes when bark is broken; most species send down aerial roots which become multiple trunks to form huge, spreading trees.

HABIT OF GROWTH: Widely sprawling with aerial roots, multiple trunks.

FOLIAGE: Evergreen, as much as a foot long, bold in aspect.

FLOWERS: Absent.

FRUITS: Figs of various sizes, shapes, and colors.

SEASON OF MAXIMUM COLOR: When figs ripen.

LANDSCAPE USES: Because of their huge sizes, they are useful in public plantings. In homes they are grown in urns.

HABITAT: World tropics; in Florida, warmest locations.

LIGHT REQUIREMENT: Full sun or broken shade.

SOIL REQUIREMENT: Tolerant of many soil conditions.

SALT TOLERANCE: Not tolerant of dune conditions.

AVAILABILITY: Most nurseries in southern Florida sell tropical fig trees.

CULTURE: Plant with a little organic matter around the root ball, water, and forget. For container culture, select a soil mixture that is not excessively fertile; water moderately to control growth.

PROPAGATION: Cuttage or marcottage.

PESTS: Scales.

NOTE: *Ficus lyrata*, fiddle-leaf fig (lower right), has evergreen leaves 15″ long shaped like violins.

F. *vogelii* (lower left) holds pubescent foliage almost horizontally.

F. *elastica* 'Doescheri' has leaves marbled with yellow.

F. *religiosa*, bo tree (upper left), has long-pointed, heart-shaped leaves that hang downward from long flexible petioles.

F. *rubiginosa* 'Variegata' (top) has downy leaves 4″ long, with short, obtuse apices.

F. *altissima*, lofty fig (upper right), has glossy foliage with white veins. The two lowest veins form a distinct V.

F. *elastica* 'Decora' (right center) produces broad, reddish leaves that are quite brilliant while young.

138
Lofty
Fig

Ficus (FYE-cuss): ancient Latin name for the fig.
altissima (al-TISS-ee-ma): highest.

FAMILY: Moraceae.   RELATIVES: The fig trees, mulberry, and hops.
TYPE OF PLANT: Tree.   HEIGHT: 50′. ZONE: S
HOW TO IDENTIFY: Trunks, many; young parts pubescent; evergreen leaves 8″ long, glabrous both sides, light-colored veins form a V at the base of the leaves; orange figs in sessile, axillary pairs.
HABIT OF GROWTH: Broader than tall, with multiple trunks, covering huge areas.
FOLIAGE: Evergreen, very coarse in texture, of medium green color.
FLOWERS: Lacking.
FRUITS: Figs ¾″ in diameter, orange, in sessile axillary pairs.
SEASON OF MAXIMUM COLOR: Summer when figs color.
LANDSCAPE USES: Giant tropical trees of this sort must be limited to use in municipal, park, campus, or arboretum plantings, as they grow too large for home-ground plantings.
HABITAT: Asian mainland and the islands; in Florida, warm areas.
LIGHT REQUIREMENT: Full sun or broken shade.
SOIL REQUIREMENT: Any soil appears to be suitable.
SALT TOLERANCE: Not tolerant of dune conditions.
AVAILABILITY: Most nurseries in southern Florida offer an assortment of tropical fig trees in containers of various sizes and B & B.
CULTURE: Plant in a hole with a little organic matter, water, and forget.
PROPAGATION: Cuttage or marcottage, using huge branches.
PESTS: Scales.
NOTE: This is but one of the 2,000 species of figs planted in hot countries around the globe. True banyan (Ficus benghalensis) has leaves that are rounded at their apexes, and have dull upper surfaces and velvety lower sides. The midvein is very heavy and bears a gland just above the petiole.

Bo-tree (Ficus religiosa) is easily distinguished by the trembling of the long-pointed leaves hanging from their long, flexible petioles.

139
Strangler Fig

Ficus (FYE-cuss): ancient Latin name for the fig.
aurea (ORE-ee-a): golden.

FAMILY: Moraceae.   RELATIVES: The fig trees, mulberry, and hops.
TYPE OF PLANT: Tree; vine-like parasite while young.   HEIGHT: 50'.
ZONE: S
HOW TO IDENTIFY: Strangling habit; oblong, evergreen leaves, about 4"
    long, frequently covered with sooty-mold; stalkless red figs in pairs
    by the leaves.
HABIT OF GROWTH: Vine-like while young; scraggly, unkempt tree in
    maturity.
FOLIAGE: Evergreen, coarse in texture, medium green in color.
FLOWERS: Absent.
FRUITS: Red, globose figs, ¾" across, in pairs in leaf axils.
SEASON OF MAXIMUM COLOR: When figs ripen.
LANDSCAPE USES: For the curiosity of its strangling habit, Florida's
    most abundant fig may be left growing on building sites in southern
    Florida, but it is not recommended for planting in home landscape
    schemes.
HABITAT: Hammocks in southern Florida, rather conspicuous in the
    wild.
LIGHT REQUIREMENT: Shifting shade of hammocks.
SOIL REQUIREMENT: Any soil is suitable.
SALT TOLERANCE: Not tolerant of front-line dune conditions.
AVAILABILITY: Seldom is strangler fig an item of commerce.
CULTURE: Plant in a hole with a little organic matter, water, and forget.
PROPAGATION: Seedage in the wild, but cuttage could be used by man.
PESTS: Aphids and scales followed by sooty mold.
NOTE: Other figs, indeed other plants, including schefflera (no. 308), may
    begin life high in other trees where seeds lodge, and become
    stranglers as aerial roots grow to the earth.

140
Banks
Grevillea

Grevillea (gray-VILL-ee-a): for C. Greville, English patron of botany.
banksii (BANKS-ee-eye): for J. Banks, English patron of horticulture.

FAMILY: Proteaceae.   RELATIVES: Queensland nut and silk-oak.
TYPE OF PLANT: Tree or large shrub.   HEIGHT: 20'. ZONE: S
HOW TO IDENTIFY: Small tree with evergreen, pinnate leaves that have revolute margins and are silky beneath; terminal red blossoms in 4" spikes.
HABIT OF GROWTH: Shrubby little tree.
FOLIAGE: Evergreen, fern-like, of fine texture and gray-green color.
FLOWERS: Red, in dense, erect, terminal spikes in springtime.
FRUITS: Shaggy little capsules less than 1" long.
SEASON OF MAXIMUM COLOR: Spring, when red flowers are out.
LANDSCAPE USES: Banks grevillea serves as a source of red in a shrubbery border, or as a little yard tree. It may grow as an urn subject as well. It is much preferred to its huge relative, the silk-oak, because it does not grow so large. This plant may not be completely successful everywhere in Florida, but gardeners in moderately warm locations should try Banks grevillea.
HABITAT: Queensland; in Florida, sparingly cultured in warmest parts.
LIGHT REQUIREMENT: Partial shade of high tree tops.
SOIL REQUIREMENT: Fertile, well-drained soil that is free of nematodes.
SALT TOLERANCE: Not tolerant.
AVAILABILITY: Specialty nurseries may have small trees in containers.
CULTURE: Plant carefully in soil that has been made free of nematodes; water carefully; fertilize three times each year; mulch the root zone; keep lawn grasses hoed back.
PROPAGATION: Seedage or cuttage.
PESTS: Borers, scales, mites, and nematodes.

141
Silk-Oak

Grevillea (gray-VILL-ee-a): for C. Greville, a patron of botany in England.
robusta (roe-BUS-ta): strong.

FAMILY: Proteaceae.   RELATIVES: Queensland nut and silver-tree.
TYPE OF PLANT: Tree.   HEIGHT: 75'. ZONE: C,S
HOW TO IDENTIFY: Evergreen, dissected leaves, gray-green in color; young branches covered with gray hairs; showy orange blossoms in springtime.
HABIT OF GROWTH: Robustly upright with compact head, and thick trunk.
FOLIAGE: Evergreen, fern-like, of fine texture and gray-green color.
FLOWERS: Showy, orange, in short (4") racemes on old wood.
FRUITS: Broad, assymetrical follicles, about ¾" long.
SEASON OF MAXIMUM COLOR: Springtime.
LANDSCAPE USES: Silk-oak is such a huge tree that there are few places in modern residential arrangements that it will serve. For large municipal developments, within its climatic range, silk-oak may be indicated where rapid growth and great size are acceptable. The trees may stand 50'–60' o.c.
HABITAT: Australia; in Florida, sandy soils of the warmer counties.
LIGHT REQUIREMENT: Full sun for best flowering.
SOIL REQUIREMENT: Open sands of central and southern Florida.
SALT TOLERANCE: Not tolerant.
AVAILABILITY: Most nurseries sell small silk-oak trees in containers.
CULTURE: Within its climatic range, silk-oak grows rapidly without special care.
PROPAGATION: Seedage.
PESTS: Caterpillars and mushroom root-rot.
NOTE: Clones with special characteristics have been selected, but these are not widely grown in Florida.

142
Coral-Vine

Antigonon (an-TIG-o-non): Greek, referring to the jointed flower stems.
leptopus (LEP-to-pus): slender-stalked.

FAMILY: Polygonaceae. RELATIVES: Sea-grape and pigeon-plum.
TYPE OF PLANT: Herbaceous vine. HEIGHT: Variable. ZONE: N,C,S
HOW TO IDENTIFY: This is a tendril-climbing, tender, herbaceous vine with heart-shaped leaves. Showy pink or white flowers are produced during late summer and autumn. Frost cuts coral-vine to the earth.
HABIT OF GROWTH: Climbing by tendrils.
FOLIAGE: Evergreen, heart-shaped, coarse in texture, and light green in color.
FLOWERS: Slender racemes of bright pink, or white; flowers in late summer and autumn.
FRUITS: Three-angled, pointed pods.
SEASON OF MAXIMUM COLOR: Late summer and fall.
LANDSCAPE USES: To veil a fence, pergola, or arbor, coral-vine has long been the choice of many southern homeowners. Where frosts occur, it cannot produce a permanent effect, yet the seasonal flowers are most attractive.
HABITAT: Tropical America; in Florida, ubiquitous.
LIGHT REQUIREMENT: Full sun for best flowering.
SOIL REQUIREMENT: Most soils are suitable.
SALT TOLERANCE: Not tolerant.
AVAILABILITY: Coral-vine is a popular home-gardening plant that is usually given away by people who have old vines; seldom does it appear in nurseries.
CULTURE: Plant with reasonable care; water for a month or so if there is no rain. During the winter, cut the canes back to the ground.
PROPAGATION: Seedage; volunteer seedlings abound under old vines.
PESTS: Caterpillars chew holes in the leaves.

143
Ribbon-Bush

Homalocladium (hoe-mal-oh-CLAY-dee-um): Greek for leaf-like branches.
platycladum (platty-CLAY-dum): wide-branched.

FAMILY: Polygonaceae.   RELATIVES: Coral-vine and sea-grape.
TYPE OF PLANT: Shrub.   HEIGHT: 4′. ZONE: C,S
HOW TO IDENTIFY: One of the distinctive plants of tropical horticulture, this woody shrub bears branches that are flat, jointed, ribbon-like. Leaves may be absent entirely, or restricted to young, sterile shoots.
HABIT OF GROWTH: Scraggly, loose assemblage of many slender, drooping branches.
FOLIAGE: Absent, or if temporarily present on young shoots, lanceolate, lobed at bases, about 2″ long.
FLOWERS: In small clusters at joints in the flattened branches.
FRUITS: Purplish, berry-like, ridged, if present.
SEASON OF MAXIMUM COLOR: Best color is summer green.
LANDSCAPE USES: For the unique, ribbon-form branches, this plant is sometimes included in home-ground arrangements. It may appear as a member of a shrubbery border, or as a conversation piece in an urn on a terrace.
HABITAT: Solomon Islands.
LIGHT REQUIREMENT: High, shifting shade is excellent.
SOIL REQUIREMENT: Moderately fertile, moist, well-drained soil is acceptable.
SALT TOLERANCE: Not tolerant of dune conditions.
AVAILABILITY: Ribbon-bush is occasionally seen in Florida nurseries.
CULTURE: Ordinary care as a pot plant or as a shrub in frost-free gardens should make for success with ribbon-bush.
PROPAGATION: Cuttage.
PESTS: Scales and nematodes.

144
Sea-Grape

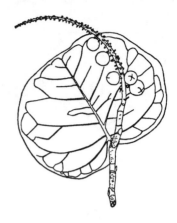

Coccoloba (coco-LOBE-a): Greek for lobed berry.
uvifera (oo-VIFF-er-a): grape-bearing.

FAMILY: Polygonaceae.   RELATIVES: Coral-vine and pigeon-plum.
TYPE OF PLANT: Tree or shrub, depending upon training.

HEIGHT: 25'. ZONE: S

HOW TO IDENTIFY: Evergreen leaves, almost circular in outline, 8" in diameter, red-veined; purple grapes hang in long bunches during warm months.

HABIT OF GROWTH: Low-spreading to form dense shrub clumps, or small trees.

FOLIAGE: Evergreen, almost circular, coarse in texture. Mature leaves have red veins and turn completely red before they fall; young foliage is a beautiful bronze.

FLOWERS: Inconspicuous ivory blossoms in foot-long racemes.

FRUITS: Purple grapes, ¾" in diameter, which are excellent for jelly.

SEASON OF MAXIMUM COLOR: Warm months when grapes ripen.

LANDSCAPE USES: No tropical plant is more dramatic than sea-grape, none better for seashore landscape. Use as a terrace tree or as a part of an enclosing border (set 7'–10' o.c.). Because of its coarse texture and large size, sea-grape is not good for foundation plantings for small homes, but it is in high favor for use with large buildings in tropical settings. There is a clone with strikingly variegated leaves.

HABITAT: Sea beaches in tropical America, including southern Florida.

LIGHT REQUIREMENT: Intense light of ocean front is optimum.

SOIL REQUIREMENT: Beach sand.

SALT TOLERANCE: Most tolerant of salt; widely used on the ocean front.

AVAILABILITY: Nurseries in southern Florida feature sea-grapes.

CULTURE: Plant in moderately rich sites; water faithfully until well established; thereafter, prune to control shape.

PROPAGATION: Seedage.

PESTS: Pith-borer.

NOTE: Pigeon-plum (*C. laurifolia*), also native in southern Florida, becomes a tree 40' in height. The evergreen leaves are oval, 4" long; the purple fruits are smaller than those of sea-grape. This is a most beautiful and desirable landscape tree for seaside locations.

145
Big-Leaf
Sea-Grape

Coccoloba (co-co-lobe-a): Greek for lobed berry.
grandifolia (grand-i-fol-ee-a): large-leaved.

FAMILY: Polygonaceae.   RELATIVES: Coral-vine and native sea-grape.
TYPE OF PLANT: Tree.   HEIGHT: Variable. ZONE: S
HOW TO IDENTIFY: The largest (yard-broad) disc-form leaves of any
   woody plant in Florida horticulture make it easy to identify this
   tropical exotic.
HABIT OF GROWTH: Stout, upward-thrusting trunks, sometimes with
   little branching, hold the huge, circular leaves.
FOLIAGE: Yard-broad, disc-shaped, puckered, with prominent veins,
   rolled-down edges, and rusty pubescence below.
FLOWERS: Small, greenish, in erect, terminal spikes when present on
   mature trees.
FRUITS: Berry-like, if present.
SEASON OF MAXIMUM COLOR: Little seasonal variation.
LANDSCAPE USES: For the striking king-size leaves, this tropical rela-
   tive of buckwheat is cultivated as a freestanding specimen. Certain
   to evoke comment, it can be grown as a tubbed individual, or as a
   point of emphasis in a border of tropical shrubbery.
HABITAT: Tropical America.
LIGHT REQUIREMENT: High, light, shifting shade is quite suitable.
SOIL REQUIREMENT: Gritty, open, moderately fertile, well-drained soil
   is best.
SALT TOLERANCE: Locations just back of front-line dunes are acceptable.
AVAILABILITY: Landscape nurseries in extreme southern Florida might
   stock big-leaf sea-grapes.
CULTURE: Do not overwater or overfeed, lest big-leaf sea-grape grow
   too rapidly.
PROPAGATION: Marcottage or cuttage of large-leaved, juvenile individ-
   uals.
PESTS: Mealy-bugs, mites, scales, and pith-borers.

146
Blood-Leaf

Iresine (eye-ree-SIGN-ee): Greek, alluding to woolly flowers and seeds.
lindenii (lin-DEN-ee-eye): for J. Linden, Belgian horticulturist.

FAMILY: Amaranthaceae.   RELATIVES: Amaranth and cocks-comb.
TYPE OF PLANT: Herbaceous perennial.   HEIGHT: 3′. ZONE: C,S
HOW TO IDENTIFY: Blood-red, opposite leaves about 2½″ long are pro-
   duced in great profusion, to give a very compact habit. Little, round,
   chaffy heads of flowers, greenish to straw-colored, are produced
   during much of the year.
HABIT OF GROWTH: Slender, upright, yet forming dense mounds of red.
FOLIAGE: Opposite, blood-red, 2½″ long, acuminate.
FLOWERS: Prominent, chaffy, or woolly little bracted heads on long
   peduncles.
FRUITS: Little, woolly 1-seeded fruits.
SEASON OF MAXIMUM COLOR: Summer.
LANDSCAPE USES: For a mound of glowing red in full sun, blood-leaf is
   popular. It serves as well as a pot plant in very light shade.
HABITAT: Tropical America.
LIGHT REQUIREMENT: Full sun for best color and compact habit.
SOIL REQUIREMENT: Sandy soil of open character is suitable.
SALT TOLERANCE: Tolerant of salt drift back from the shore.
AVAILABILITY: Nurseries in southern Florida offer blood-leaf in con-
   tainers.
CULTURE: In a sunny spot, plant as a garden perennial after danger of
   frost has passed. Pinch out terminal buds for best compact habit.
   Blood-leaf thrives in light, sandy soil despite presence of nema-
   todes.
PROPAGATION: Cuttage.
PESTS: Mites.
NOTE: The botany of this section of the amaranth family is in need of
   definitive study. A close relative, not to be overlooked, is *Iresine
   herbstii*. The very showy leaves are almost round and have a pronounced notch at the apex. Leaves may be deep red with light red
   veins, or green with very pronounced yellow veins. The stems are
   always red.

147
Parrot-Leaf

Alternanthera (all-ter-NAN-the-ra): refers to the two types of anthers which alternate. *amoena* (am-o-EE-na): pleasant.

FAMILY: Amaranthaceaé. RELATIVES: Amaranthus and celosia.

TYPE OF PLANT: Herbaceous perennial. HEIGHT: 10″–15″. ZONE: N,C,S

HOW TO IDENTIFY: Very dwarf, much-branched plants, seldom more than 6″–8″ tall; opposite, elliptical to lanceolate leaves, 1″–2″ long; often 2 leaf forms will be found on a branch; stems sometimes woody.

HABIT OF GROWTH: Dwarf herbaceous perennial.

FOLIAGE: Medium-fine textured leaves, green, variegated, reddish.

FLOWERS: Very small, borne in dense axillary clusters.

FRUITS: Small capsules, seldom seen.

SEASON OF MAXIMUM COLOR: Grown mainly for its year-round color.

LANDSCAPE USES: Bedding plant; outstanding border or edging plant; widely used in complex garden designs as clocks and emblems.

HABITAT: Brazil.

LIGHT REQUIREMENT: Full sun.

SOIL REQUIREMENT: Most well-drained soils.

SALT TOLERANCE: Not tolerant.

AVAILABILITY: Readily available from bedding plant growers.

CULTURE: Easy to grow; shears well; treated as annual in northern Florida.

PROPAGATION: Division, cuttage, or seedage.

PESTS: Caterpillars eat holes in leaves.

148
Bougainvillea

Bougainvillea (boo-gain-VIL-ee-a): for M. de Bougainville, the French navigator.
SPP.: two species are widely grown in Florida.

FAMILY: Nyctaginaceae.   RELATIVES: Four-o'clock and sand-verbena.
TYPE OF PLANT: Vine.   HEIGHT: Variable. ZONE: C,S
HOW TO IDENTIFY: Long, thorny canes with alternate, heart-shaped leaves and flowers enclosed by conspicuous, highly colored bracts during the cool months.
HABIT OF GROWTH: Sprawling by far-reaching canes. Support is usually provided.
FOLIAGE: Evergreen, of medium texture and medium green color.
FLOWERS: Small, tubular, enclosed by large, showy, highly colored bracts.
FRUITS: Inconspicuous, little ribbed pods.
SEASON OF MAXIMUM COLOR: Winter and spring when this becomes Florida's favorite vine.
LANDSCAPE USES: Bougainvillea sprawling over a masonry wall is a sight long to be remembered. Plant every 10'. Trained beside and across doorways, the vine is very popular, and it is sometimes used to veil wire fences.

Most clear-colored, wanted varieties come from *B. spectabilis,* great bougainvillea. Hardier, cosmopolitan, purple bougainvillea is in *B. glabra.* This one is sometimes trained as a tree.
HABITAT: Brazil; in Florida, central and southern areas.
LIGHT REQUIREMENT: Full sun for best flowering.
SOIL REQUIREMENT: Tolerant of various soils, but may develop chlorosis on calcareous earth.
SALT TOLERANCE: Endures salt air back from the front-line dunes.
AVAILABILITY: Nurseries on the peninsula have bougainvilleas in containers. In the mid-1970s, varieties with multiple bracts, to give a double effect, were introduced.
CULTURE: Plant in carefully made sites of fertile, acid medium in full sun; attend to watering carefully; spray for leaf-chewers and keep lawn grasses off the roots. Fertilize lightly three times each year.
PROPAGATION: Cuttage.
PESTS: Caterpillars and mineral deficiencies on lime-bearing soils.

149
Hottentot-Fig

Carpobrotus (car-poe-BRO-tus): in reference to the edible fruits.
edulis (ed-YOU-lis): edible.

FAMILY: Aizoaceae.　　　　　　　RELATIVES: Ice-plant and stoneface.
TYPE OF PLANT: Perennial.　　　　　　　HEIGHT: 6″. ZONE: C,S
HOW TO IDENTIFY: Stems, which become woody, creep for great distances along the earth and bear 4″ triangular leaves in clusters. Usually in Florida this plant is seen in seaside gardens.
HABIT OF GROWTH: Wide-spreading branches form a mat as they run across the earth.
FOLIAGE: Evergreen, succulent, triangular; keels finely serrate, growing in little bunches along the prostrate stems.
FLOWERS: Yellow to rose-purple, 3″ across, bright, and glistening.
FRUITS: Large and edible, if present.
SEASON OF MAXIMUM COLOR: Summer when flowers are out.
LANDSCAPE USES: For covering sandy expanses, especially at the seashore, Hottentot-fig is extremely popular in Florida, as it is in California. An outstanding demonstration of this use in the Sunshine State is at Marineland. For sunny planters, this African succulent is also very useful.
HABITAT: South Africa.
LIGHT REQUIREMENT: Full sun of tropical and subtropical strands.
SOIL REQUIREMENT: Sandy, fast draining soil of low or moderate fertility is optimum.
SALT TOLERANCE: Very tolerant of salt, recommended for ocean-front planting.
AVAILABILITY: Garden centers and nurseries may supply plants.
CULTURE: Plant sections of stem in open, sandy soil, water moderately until established, then forget.
PROPAGATION: Cuttage and division.
PESTS: A fungous disease attacks Hottentot-fig under some conditions.
NOTE: Taxonomy of the Aizoaceae, which includes many succulent, ground-cover-type plants for sandy locations, is imperfectly understood, and confusion may be the rule.

150
Nandina

Nandina (nan-DEAN-a): Japanese name.
domestica (dough-MES-tee-ca): domesticated.

FAMILY: Berberidaceae.   RELATIVES: Barberry and mahonia.
TYPE OF PLANT: Shrub.   HEIGHT: 8'. ZONE: N

HOW TO IDENTIFY: Many, nonbranching, ringed stems with lacy, compound leaves atop; panicles of white blossoms in springtime followed by bright red berries in winter.

HABIT OF GROWTH: Stiffly upright, unbranching, to give stilt-like effect.

FOLIAGE: Deciduous, alternate, 2- to 3-compound, lacy, to give very fine texture. The summer color is medium green and the fall color is red.

FLOWERS: Small, white, in long terminal panicles.

FRUITS: Berries, ¼" in diameter, bright red by cool weather.

SEASON OF MAXIMUM COLOR: Autumn after fruits color.

LANDSCAPE USES: Singly, or in groups of 3 against pine trunks, nandina looks best. As a facer shrub against larger shrubs, allow 3' between plants. Groups of 3 nandinas at the backs of planters may serve to give interest against masonry walls. Here, the plants can be set 18" o.c. This Japanese shrub does so much better in western Florida than it does on the sandy soil of the peninsula that it is highly recommended for the former area, not endorsed for the latter.

HABITAT: Eastern Asia; in Florida, superior soil of upper counties.

LIGHT REQUIREMENT: Tolerant of shady locations, endures full sun on heavy soils.

SOIL REQUIREMENT: Superior soils of the Panhandle are best for nandina.

SALT TOLERANCE: Not tolerant.

AVAILABILITY: Small plants in gallon cans and larger plants B & B are offered by nurseries in northern Florida.

CULTURE: On good soil, culture is easy, and no special procedures are needed.

PROPAGATION: Seedage and division.

PESTS: Mites, scales, and mushroom root-rot.

151
Oregon Grape-Hollies

Mahonia (ma-HONE-ee-a): for McMahon, American horticulturist.
SPP.: several species grow in Florida.

FAMILY: Berberidaceae.

RELATIVES: Nandina and barberry.

TYPE OF PLANT: Evergreen, woody shrubs.

HEIGHT: 6'–12'.

ZONE: N,C,S

HOW TO IDENTIFY: Woody shrubs, with upright stems with sparse branching. Alternate, compound leaves grow in clusters near branch tips. Flowers borne in racemes near branch tips. *M. fortunei*: leaflets 5–9, lanceolate to 5" long; soft; margins with small sharp spines. *M. lomarifolia*: leaflets 9–15, stiff, almost holly-like, often undulate to 3½" long. Leaflet margins with pointed, spiny lobes. *M. bealei*: leaflets 9–15 usually, large ovate to 5" long, with few large teeth. Leaflets very stiff.

HABIT OF GROWTH: Stiff, upright.

FOLIAGE: Medium to dark green or gray green.

FLOWERS: Small, yellow, fragrant in some species.

FRUITS: Blue berries.

SEASON OF MAXIMUM COLOR: Spring and summer.

LANDSCAPE USES: Excellent foundation plants for the north sides of buildings or for use in shrubbery borders.

HABITAT: China.

LIGHT REQUIREMENT: Partial shade to full sun.

SOIL REQUIREMENT: Most well-drained soils.

SALT TOLERANCE: Tolerant of salt drift back of the strand.

AVAILABILITY: Found in cans in nurseries.

CULTURE: Once established, plants require occasional pruning but little other care.

PROPAGATION: Cuttage or seedage.

PESTS: None serious.

Wintergreen Barberry

Berberis (BUR-bur-is): ancient Arabic name.
julianae (jewel-ee-ANN-ee): for Mrs. Julia Schneider.

FAMILY: Berberidaceae.

RELATIVES: Nandina and grape-holly.

TYPE OF PLANT: Shrub.

HEIGHT: 6'. ZONE: N

HOW TO IDENTIFY: A shrub which bears 3", spiny-toothed leaves and 3-parted spines. Bright yellow inner bark is revealed when outer bark is broken.

HABIT OF GROWTH: Dense, by many stems, under good conditions.

FOLIAGE: Evergreen, alternate, of medium texture, dark green color.

FLOWERS: Yellow, ¼" across, in groups of about 15.

FRUITS: Black berries, about ⅓" across, contain 1 seed each.

SEASON OF MAXIMUM COLOR: When blossoms are out and fruits color.

LANDSCAPE USES: For foundation plantings in extreme northern Florida, set plants 18" o.c. North-side locations are satisfactory. Under high pine shade, wintergreen barberry can be used for low hedges. Set the plants 18" o.c.

HABITAT: China; in Florida, superior soils of the Panhandle.

LIGHT REQUIREMENT: Full sun on superior soils, or part shade from high pines.

SOIL REQUIREMENT: Clay-loam soils support the best plants.

SALT TOLERANCE: Tolerant of light salt drift back from the Gulf shore.

AVAILABILITY: Nurseries in northwestern Florida offer plants in containers.

CULTURE: Plant in heavy soil; water with moderation; fertilize twice annually while young. On the upper peninsula, plant only in heavy soil either on north-side locations or close to pine trunks. Always mulch barberry plants for best growth.

PROPAGATION: Cuttage.

PESTS: Nematodes and mites.

NOTE: Japanese barberry (*Berberis thunbergii*), especially the red-leaved clone, 'Atropurpurea,' behaves well on heavy soil in western Florida, and can be employed where a fine-scale, slow-growing plant is needed in foundation arrangements. Red-leaved barberry looks nice growing by white masonry.

153
Cocculus

Cocculus (COCK-you-lus): Greek for small berry.
laurifolius (laur-ee-FOL-ee-us): laurel-leaved.

FAMILY: Menispermaceae.

RELATIVE: Moonseed.

TYPE OF PLANT: Shrub or small tree.

HEIGHT: 25'. ZONE: N,C,S

HOW TO IDENTIFY: Declinate, round, green branches that hold alternate, evergreen leaves with 3 prominent veins. Little racemes of tiny blossoms appear in April–May.

HABIT OF GROWTH: Weeping, or clambering if supports are available.

FOLIAGE: Evergreen, alternate, coarse in texture, dark green in color.

FLOWERS: Inconspicuous, in axillary racemes, in April–May. Male and female flowers are borne on separate plants.

FRUITS: Subglobose drupes ⅛" in diameter, when present.

SEASON OF MAXIMUM COLOR: Little seasonal variation.

LANDSCAPE USES: As a part of a shrubbery border or as a foundation plant for a very large building, set 5' apart. Cocculus is an excellent shrub that deserves wider use when its large size and coarse texture will not be disadvantageous. Plants will freeze to the ground some winters in unprotected north Florida locations.

HABITAT: Himalayan region; in Florida, warmer parts of the peninsula.

LIGHT REQUIREMENT: Full sun or partial shade.

SOIL REQUIREMENT: Soils of many types are acceptable.

SALT TOLERANCE: Not tolerant of salt wind.

AVAILABILITY: Container-grown plants are in many nurseries in warmer parts.

CULTURE: After cocculus is growing well in moderately fertile soil, little care will be required other than regular pruning.

PROPAGATION: Standard or leaf-bud cuttings under mist in springtime.

PESTS: Scales.

NOTE: Excellent as cut foliage for flower arrangements.

154
Banana-Shrub

Michelia (me-SHELL-ee-a): for P. Michel, a Florentine botanist.
fuscata (fuss-KAY-ta): dark brown.

FAMILY: Magnoliaceae.   RELATIVES: The magnolias and the tulip-tree.
TYPE OF PLANT: Shrub.   HEIGHT: 20'. ZONE: N
HOW TO IDENTIFY: A large, much-branched shrub that bears evergreen, alternate, dark green leaves, buds with fuzzy coverings, and yellow flowers with the odor of banana.
HABIT OF GROWTH: Much-branched, low-headed, compact shrub.
FOLIAGE: Evergreen, alternate, of medium fine texture and dark green color.
FLOWERS: Yellow, magnolia-like, 1½" across, with the odor of banana.
FRUITS: Small, rough burs.
SEASON OF MAXIMUM COLOR: Springtime when little yellow blossoms open.
LANDSCAPE USES: As a freestanding specimen banana-shrub has been a favorite in northern Florida for generations. It can be used as an accent in the foundation planting for a multistoried building and as a member of an enclosing barrier. In this last use, the planting interval may be 5' o.c.
HABITAT: China; in Florida, fairly common in gardens of upper counties.
LIGHT REQUIREMENT: Broken, shifting shade from tall pine trees is ideal.
SOIL REQUIREMENT: Fertile, well-drained soils rich in organic matter are best.
SALT TOLERANCE: Not tolerant.
AVAILABILITY: Small shrubs in containers are offered in many retail sales lots.
CULTURE: Plant in fertile, well-drained soil; water periodically until established; fertilize once each winter; protect from scale insects.
PROPAGATION: Cuttage.
PESTS: Magnolia scale is a very serious pest and must be controlled by periodic spraying; mushroom root-rot.

155
Magnolia

Magnolia (mag-NO-lee-a): for P. Magnol, an early French botanist.
grandiflora (gran-da-FLOR-a): large-flowered.

FAMILY: Magnoliaceae.   RELATIVES: The magnolias and banana-shrub.
TYPE OF PLANT: Tree.   HEIGHT: 75'. ZONE: N,C
HOW TO IDENTIFY: Huge, stiff, evergreen leaves that are shining, dark
    green above and brown-tomentose or light green below; huge, waxy,
    white, fragrant blossoms in springtime.
HABIT OF GROWTH: Upright, often with straight central leader and com-
    pact head.
FOLIAGE: Evergreen, alternate, bold in outline, dark, shining green in
    color.
FLOWERS: Huge, white, waxy fragrant blossoms in springtime.
FRUITS: Cone-like, 4" burs that split to reveal showy scarlet seeds.
SEASON OF MAXIMUM COLOR: Spring, when blossoms unfurl.
LANDSCAPE USES: As a street tree (50'-60' o.c.), magnolia is superb; as
    a freestanding specimen, framing tree, or shade tree in home-ground
    developments it is a long-time favorite. Grouped informally on
    broad highway rights-of-way, this native tree is one of great dis-
    tinction. Some seedlings have leaves that are attractively coated
    with brown tomentum on their lower surfaces.
HABITAT: Hammocks of central and northern Florida.
LIGHT REQUIREMENT: Full sun for best habit and flowering.
SOIL REQUIREMENT: Fertile hammock soil for best growth and flower-
    ing.
SALT TOLERANCE: Quite tolerant of salt drift and dune sand.
AVAILABILITY: Nurseries sell magnolia seedlings in containers or B & B.
CULTURE: In fertile, moist soil, magnolia grows well without special
    attention save for the usual fertilization and watering while young.
PROPAGATION: Seedage, yet fine selections are increased by cuttage or
    graftage.
PESTS: Magnolia scale and algal leaf-spot.

156
Saucer Magnolia

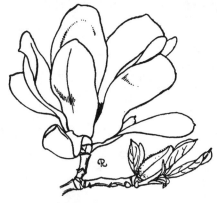

Magnolia (mag-NO-lee-a): for P. Magnol, an early French botanist.
liliflora (lily-FLOR-a): with flowers like a lily.
'Soulangeana' (soo-lon-gee-ANE-a): for the originator, Soulange-Bodin.

FAMILY: Magnoliaceae.   RELATIVES: The magnolias and banana-shrub.
TYPE OF PLANT: Shrub in Florida.   HEIGHT: 25'. ZONE: N
HOW TO IDENTIFY: Shrubby growth, deciduous, alternate leaves that
    emerge from furry buds; showy, tulip-like blossoms in late winter
    from fur-coated buds; the sepals, usually purplish or pinkish out-
    side, are half as long as the petals.
HABIT OF GROWTH: Shrubby, upright-branching.
FOLIAGE: Deciduous, alternate, very coarse in texture, medium green
    in color.
FLOWERS: Showy, upward-pointing, bell-like, purplish or pinkish out-
    side, white inside, with little fragrance.
FRUITS: Cone-like, 4″ burs that are usually few-seeded in Florida.
SEASON OF MAXIMUM COLOR: January, when flowers unfurl.
LANDSCAPE USES: As a freestanding specimen, saucer magnolia is a
    long-time favorite. It may be set into a shrubbery border to lend
    seasonal color interest, as well.
    This group of plants does best in the northwestern section of the
    state, and is not generally recommended for the peninsula. The
    tendency is for the blossoms to appear a few at a time during the
    warm winter weather rather than to make a great burst of color as
    they do farther north where lower winter temperatures keep the
    plants dormant until spring.
HABITAT: Gardens of the temperate zone; in Florida, upper tier of
    counties.
LIGHT REQUIREMENT: Full sun or high, shifting pine shade.
SOIL REQUIREMENT: Superior, well-drained soils of upper counties.
SALT TOLERANCE: Not tolerant.
AVAILABILITY: Saucer magnolias are not widely offered in Florida.
CULTURE: In northwestern Florida, plant with care in fertile, well-
    drained spot; water until established, then during periods of
    drought; fertilize once each winter while young.
PROPAGATION: Cuttage or graftage.
PESTS: Scales, nematodes, and mushroom root-rot.

157
Starry Magnolia

Magnolia (mag-NO-lee-a): for P. Magnol, an early French botanist.
stellata (stel-ATE-a): starry.

FAMILY: Magnoliaceae.   RELATIVES: The magnolias and banana-shrub.
TYPE OF PLANT: Large shrub or small tree.   HEIGHT: 15'. ZONE: N
HOW TO IDENTIFY: Robust shrub or small, many-stemmed tree, with
    showy white blossoms in wintertime that have petals and sepals
    alike. The foliage is deciduous, and all leaves, buds, and new twigs
    are densely pubescent.
HABIT OF GROWTH: Open, upright-branching, large shrub or small tree.
FOLIAGE: Deciduous, alternate, of coarse texture and medium green
    color.
FLOWERS: Showy, white, 3" across, sepals and petals alike, 12 or more
    in number, 2" in length, outward-flaring. There are clones with all-
    pink flowers.
FRUITS: Cone-like burs that are usually few-seeded in Florida.
SEASON OF MAXIMUM COLOR: January–February when blossoms are out.
LANDSCAPE USES: Known for its outstanding beauty in late winter,
    starry magnolia is the best of the Oriental species for Florida.
    Though the white form is the one most often sold here, there are
    other clones that should be used in landscaping. One with pink
    flowers is especially nice. Starry magnolia may be a freestanding
    specimen or a member of a shrubbery border.
HABITAT: Japan; in Florida, better soils of northern counties.
LIGHT REQUIREMENT: Full sun or shifting shade from tall pine trees.
SOIL REQUIREMENT: Fertile, acid, well-drained soils.
SALT TOLERANCE: Not tolerant.
AVAILABILITY: Starry magnolia is not widely offered by retail nurseries.
CULTURE: Plant in fertile, well-drained spot; water periodically until
    well established; mulch the root zone; fertilize once each year
    while young.
PROPAGATION: Cuttage.
PESTS: Scales and nematodes.

158
Sweet Bay

Magnolia (mag-NO-lee-a): for P. Magnol, an early French botanist.
virginiana (vir-gin-ee-ANE-a): Virginian.

FAMILY: Magnoliaceae.   RELATIVES: The magnolias and banana-shrub.
TYPE OF PLANT: Tree.   HEIGHT: 75'. ZONE: N,C,S
HOW TO IDENTIFY: Slender, smooth, gray trunks; alternate evergreen
    leaves, 6" long, silvery beneath, with smooth margins; fragrant,
    white flowers in springtime.
HABIT OF GROWTH: Irregularly rounded crown held aloft by slender
    branches.
FOLIAGE: Evergreen, alternate, silvery beneath to give a light green
    appearance. The texture would be classed as coarse.
FLOWERS: White, fragrant, 3" across, 9- to 12-petaled, in springtime.
FRUITS: Typical magnolia burs that display scarlet seeds in autumn.
SEASON OF MAXIMUM COLOR: All year, silvery foliage; autumn, red
    fruits.
LANDSCAPE USES: For naturalistic developments and for small back
    yards on moist, fertile soil, sweet bay warrants wider use. This,
    like so many native plants, is virtually overlooked by planners but
    this is another indigene that can serve Floridians well, if it were
    indicated more frequently.
HABITAT: Florida bayheads, swamps, and stream banks.
LIGHT REQUIREMENT: Tolerant of shifting shade of wooded environ-
    ments.
SOIL REQUIREMENT: Wet, boggy, fertile soils, but sweet bay will grow
    in garden soils with care in watering during dry spells.
SALT TOLERANCE: Not tolerant.
AVAILABILITY: Sweet bay is not an item of commerce.
CULTURE: Plant in well-prepared, acid, organic site; wrap the trunk as
    protection against borers; water faithfully during all dry periods;
    fertilize once each winter.
PROPAGATION: Seedage or transplanting from woodlots with permission.
PESTS: Sooty-mold, scales, borers, in civilization.

159
Tulip-Tree

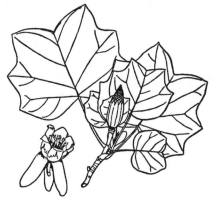

Liriodendron (lear-ee-oh-DEN-dron): Greek for lily-tree.
tulipifera (two-lip-IF-er-a): tulip-bearing.

FAMILY: Magnoliaceae.   RELATIVES: The magnolias and banana-shrub.
TYPE OF PLANT: Tree.   HEIGHT: 100′. ZONE: N,C
HOW TO IDENTIFY: Alternate, deciduous leaves are saddle-shaped at
    their apexes; the greenish flowers are tulip-shaped and the winter
    twigs are spatulate like ducks' bills.
HABIT OF GROWTH: A forest giant that usually grows with a single, cen-
    tral leader and many symmetrically arranged, upward-pointing
    branches.
FOLIAGE: Deciduous, alternate, interesting in pattern, medium green
    in color.
FLOWERS: Handsome, greenish with orange markings, tulip-form, ap-
    pearing in springtime.
FRUITS: Brown cones about 3″ long.
SEASON OF MAXIMUM COLOR: Spring, flowers open; fall, foliage colors.
LANDSCAPE USES: Where a true giant is needed, tulip-tree may be con-
    sidered. For large public plantings, highways, and avenues, this
    native tree will serve, but for the usual home-grounds, it is entirely
    too large.
HABITAT: Moist woods in Florida as far south as Orange County.
LIGHT REQUIREMENT: Full sun or shade of hammocks.
SOIL REQUIREMENT: Moist soils are needed for good growth and long
    life.
SALT TOLERANCE: Not tolerant.
AVAILABILITY: Seldom are tulip-trees offered by Florida nurserymen.
CULTURE: Plant in moist, fertile soil, if possible; lacking this, plant in
    acid, peaty compost; attend to watering during dry periods.
PROPAGATION: Seedage.
PESTS: Aphids followed by sooty-mold.

160
Anise-Tree

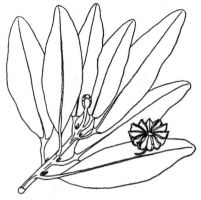

Illicium (ill-ISS-ee-um): Latin for allurement, for the pleasant odor.
anisatum (an-ee-SAY-tum): for the anise-scent of crushed leaves.

FAMILY: Illiciaceae.

RELATIVE: Florida anise-tree.

TYPE OF PLANT: Shrub or tree.

HEIGHT: 20'. ZONE: N,C

HOW TO IDENTIFY: Strong scent of anise is released when leaves are crushed.

HABIT OF GROWTH: Very compact, dense, close to the earth.

FOLIAGE: Evergreen, alternate, bold in pattern, light green in color.

FLOWERS: Very small, nodding, greenish-yellow, not fragrant.

FRUITS: Fluted pods split at pie sections to release dark brown seeds.

SEASON OF MAXIMUM COLOR: No variation.

LANDSCAPE USES: For enclosure, no shrub surpasses anise. Plant 5' o.c. For foundation plantings for massive public buildings, the plants may stand at the same interval. Anise-tree is one of Florida's best large exotic shrubs.

HABITAT: Japan and Korea; in Florida, gardens in upper counties.

LIGHT REQUIREMENT: Very tolerant of shade; grows well in full sun, too.

SOIL REQUIREMENT: Very tolerant of a wide range of soils.

SALT TOLERANCE: Not tolerant of seaside locations.

AVAILABILITY: Rather widely available in nurseries in upper Florida.

CULTURE: Rich soil, moderate moisture, and a mulch over the roots should make for success. Annual pruning is needed if the plant is to be maintained as a shrub.

PROPAGATION: Cuttage, simple layerage, and seedage.

PESTS: Mites, scales upon occasion.

NOTE: Florida anise-tree (*Illicium floridanum*) grows to a height of 20' and bears aromatic leaves; red-purple flowers with 20–30 petals, making each about 1½" across, and much more showy than those on the exotic species. Fruits, the fluted pods, are quite similar.

161
Avocado

Persea (PURR-see-a): ancient name.
americana (a-mer-ee-CANE-ah): American.

FAMILY: Lauraceae.   RELATIVES: Redbay, camphor, and sassafras.
TYPE OF PLANT: Tree.   HEIGHT: 40'. ZONE: C,S
HOW TO IDENTIFY: Evergreen, usually aromatic, huge leaves on green
    twigs and conspicuous pear-shaped or round warty fruits hanging
    from cords.
HABIT OF GROWTH: Symmetrical, dense, usually branching to ground
    while young.
FOLIAGE: Evergreen, variable in size and shape, aromatic, and lustrous
    dark green in color when well fertilized.
FLOWERS: Inconspicuous, greenish, clustered near the ends of twigs.
FRUITS: Conspicuous fleshy drupes, round or pear-shaped, green or
    purple, delicious to eat.
SEASON OF MAXIMUM COLOR: Spring when new leaves emerge.
LANDSCAPE USES: As a fruit-bearing specimen that may double as a
    shade tree or framing tree, for homes in frost-protected areas of
    the peninsula, the avocado tree is highly regarded. There are many
    named varieties that belong to several classes.
HABITAT: American tropics; in Florida, widely cultured in warm areas.
LIGHT REQUIREMENT: Full sun or high, shifting shade.
SOIL REQUIREMENT: Fertile, well-drained soil that can be irrigated dur-
    ing drought.
SALT TOLERANCE: Not tolerant.
AVAILABILITY: Nurseries sell small avocado trees in containers.
CULTURE: Carefully prepare the site in a well-drained location, set the
    tree at the same level that it grew formerly, water moderately until
    well established, and thereafter during drought. Fertilize three times
    each year, use mulch, and keep lawn grasses back from the root
    zone.
PROPAGATION: Graftage.
PESTS: Scales, root-rot, and leaf-spotting diseases.
NOTE: Redbay (*P. borbonia*) is a tree native in hammocks throughout
    the state.

162
Camphor-Tree

Cinnamomum (sin-a-mo-mum): ancient Greek name.
camphora (cam-for-a): of camphor.

FAMILY: Lauraceae.   RELATIVES: Avocado, redbay, and sassafras.
TYPE OF PLANT: Tree.   HEIGHT: 50'. ZONE: N,C,S
HOW TO IDENTIFY: Crushed leaves have the odor of camphor; twigs, petioles, and leaves are all the same color.
HABIT OF GROWTH: Closely branched to make a dense, round, symmetrical head.
FOLIAGE: Evergreen, alternate, aromatic, of medium texture and dark green color.
FLOWERS: Inconspicuous, produced in springtime in axillary panicles.
FRUITS: Shining black berries ⅜" in diameter, produced in abundance to become a nuisance on walks, terraces, and driveways.
SEASON OF MAXIMUM COLOR: Springtime, when new growth emerges.
LANDSCAPE USES: Shade tree for large properties and for avenue plantings, planting distance 50'. Sheared hedges are made from camphor. Set seedlings 2' o.c. and clip very frequently for best appearance. Mature trees have such dense heads that it is difficult to grow grass beneath them.
HABITAT: Eastern Asia; in Florida, ubiquitous.
LIGHT REQUIREMENT: Full sun or light, high shade.
SOIL REQUIREMENT: Tolerant of many soils; may be chlorotic on calcareous earth.
SALT TOLERANCE: Not tolerant.
AVAILABILITY: This is not a lucrative nursery item, as small camphor seedlings grow abundantly under old trees, and many are given away by homeowners.
CULTURE: Camphor-trees transplant with great difficulty in larger sizes, so only plants from gallon containers are recommended. These will grow very rapidly with but little care.
PROPAGATION: Seedage.
PESTS: Scales, mites, and chlorosis on calcareous soils.

163
Hydrangea

Hydrangea (hy-DRAIN-jee-a): Greek for water vessel, from the shape of the capsules.
macrophylla (mak-roe-PHIL-a): large-leaved.

FAMILY: Saxifragaceae. RELATIVES: Saxifrage and philadelphus.
TYPE OF PLANT: Shrub. HEIGHT: 4'. ZONE: N,C
HOW TO IDENTIFY: Huge, opposite, deciduous leaves; prominent axillary
buds; showy blossom-heads in summer.
HABIT OF GROWTH: Compact, much-branched, with up-pointing twigs.
FOLIAGE: Deciduous, opposite, coarse in texture, medium green. Fall
color: spotted yellow.
FLOWERS: Prominent calyces are the showy parts of the inflorescences.
These are usually blue on acid soil, pink on basic, and a dirty white
on earth of neutral reaction. Buds and young leaves are poisonous.
FRUITS: Capsules, seldom formed in Florida.
SEASON OF MAXIMUM COLOR: Early summer.
LANDSCAPE USES: Along north walls or under oak trees, hydrangeas
look best in generous drifts, with about 2' between individuals. The
clones in this species, most popular in Florida, number a score or
more.

Summertime blossoms, deciduous foliage, and very coarse texture limit the usefulness of hydrangeas near houses of contemporary
design, but the blue, pink, or white heads that appear so depend-
ably endear hydrangeas to all garden-lovers. Pruning must be done
immediately after flowering, otherwise new flower buds will be
sacrificed.
HABITAT: Japan; in Florida, north sides of buildings or under trees on
the upper peninsula and on the Panhandle.
LIGHT REQUIREMENT: As indicated above, shade is recommended in
Florida.
SOIL REQUIREMENT: Fertile, well-drained soil is best.
SALT TOLERANCE: Not tolerant.
AVAILABILITY: Many retail sales lots offer hydrangeas in containers.
CULTURE: A shaded site, moderate moisture, fairly high fertility, and
good drainage should be supplied for hydrangeas. Pruning directly
as flowering ends is suggested to keep plants compact.
PROPAGATION: Cuttage.
PESTS: Nematodes, mites, and scales.

164
Oak-Leaf Hydrangea

Hydrangea (hy-DRAIN-jee-a): Greek for water vessel, from the shape of the capsules.
quercifolia (kware-see-FOL-ee-a): oak-leaved.

FAMILY: Saxifragaceae.   RELATIVES: Saxifrage and philadelphus.
TYPE OF PLANT: Shrub.   HEIGHT: 6'. ZONE: N
HOW TO IDENTIFY: Deciduous, opposite, deeply cleft, oak-like leaves, 8″ long, on pubescent twigs, with fuzzy axillary buds; showy white spikes appear in late spring.
HABIT OF GROWTH: Spreading, with up-pointing twigs.
FOLIAGE: Deciduous, opposite, striking in form, light green. Fall color: rusty.
FLOWERS: Showy, elongated panicles, 1' long, calyces white, turning purplish.
FRUITS: Capsules with 2–5 cells, splitting down from the top.
SEASON OF MAXIMUM COLOR: Early summer.
LANDSCAPE USES: For wooded areas, oak-leaf hydrangea can be used effectively against the trunks of large trees. This native shrub is admired by advanced gardeners for its value in landscaping naturalistic areas, but it is seldom seen in home plantings. Here it grows too tall, the foliage is too coarse in texture and, like that of most hydrangeas, it falls to the earth in autumn. This free-flowering outsized shrub is completely maintenance-free when grown on hammock soil in northern counties.
HABITAT: Hammocks of northern Florida.
LIGHT REQUIREMENT: Partial shade of hammocks, north side of tree trunks.
SOIL REQUIREMENT: Fertile, slightly acid, well-drained hammock soil.
SALT TOLERANCE: Not tolerant.
AVAILABILITY: Oak-leaf hydrangea is seldom seen in Florida nurseries.
CULTURE: In hammock soil, when it is planted on the north side of a tree trunk, no attention will be needed after this shrub becomes established.
PROPAGATION: Cuttage and seedage.
PESTS: None of major concern.

165
Pittosporum

Pittosporum (pit-TOSS-poe-rum): Greek for pitch and seeds.
tobira (toe-BYE-ra): native Japanese name.

FAMILY: Pittosporaceae.   RELATIVES: Hymenosporum and sollya.
TYPE OF PLANT: Shrub.   HEIGHT: 15′. ZONE: N,C,S
HOW TO IDENTIFY: Thick, clustered stems bear whorled, revolute, leathery leaves that have a disagreeable odor when crushed. Little, white, fragrant flowers are followed by angled, green capsules containing red-coated seeds.
HABIT OF GROWTH: Compact, much-branched shrub.
FOLIAGE: Evergreen, whorled, medium in texture, dark green in color.
FLOWERS: Fragrant, white, 5-petaled, ½″ long, in terminal umbels.
FRUITS: Angled, globose capsules, ½″ in diameter. In western Florida, these fruits may contain viable, red-coated seeds; on the peninsula, the capsules may be sterile.
SEASON OF MAXIMUM COLOR: Spring when blossoms are out.
LANDSCAPE USES: For hedges (plant 18″ o.c.) pittosporum cannot be excelled; for foundation arrangements, allow 3′ between individuals, and in informal shrubbery borders, set the plants 5′ apart. For seaside plantings and for partially shaded situations, pittosporum is highly recommended.
    For pleasantly variegated foliage that gives an olive-green effect, choose the popular variegated clone. In addition, there are several green-leaved clones that have been selected for one or another outstanding characteristic.
HABITAT: Eastern Asia; in Florida, much used as a garden shrub.
LIGHT REQUIREMENT: Tolerant of shade, recommended for north-side locations.
SOIL REQUIREMENT: A fertile, slightly acid medium is best.
SALT TOLERANCE: Very tolerant; good for seaside plantings.
AVAILABILITY: Green and variegated plants are offered by nurseries.
CULTURE: Plant in enriched, acid site; furnish with mulch; combat cottony cushion scale and *Cercospora* leaf-spot continually.
PROPAGATION: Cuttage and seedage.
PESTS: Cottony cushion scale and *Cercospora* leaf-spot.
NOTE: *Pittosporum undulatum*, rather subject to attack by pests, grows in Florida, but it is not as dependable here as it is in California.

Crassula x
'Tricolor Jade'

Crassula arborescens

Crassula x portulacea

Jade-Plant

Crassula tetragona

Crassula lycopodioides

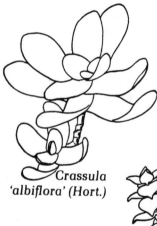

Crassula
'albiflora' (Hort.)

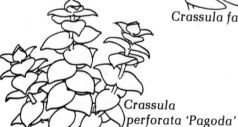

Crassula falcata

Crassula
perforata 'Pagoda'

167
Jade-Plant

Crassula (CRASS-soo-la): Latin for thick.
argentea (are-GENT-ee-a): silvery.

FAMILY: Crassulaceae.   RELATIVES: Kalanchoe and sedum.
TYPE OF PLANT: Shrub.   HEIGHT: 4'. ZONE: S
HOW TO IDENTIFY: A thick, succulent, brown trunk bears thick, succulent branches in comely aspect, which hold very thick, oval leaves clustered near their tips. Growth is very slow, the demand for water small. Resembles a diminutive tree with leaves of jade.
HABIT OF GROWTH: Diminutive, tree-like.
FOLIAGE: Thick, heavy, succulent, oval, not petioled, usually with red edges.
FLOWERS: Jade-plant may grow for many years without blooming. When flowers do appear, they are small, white, or rosy-red in close panicles.
FRUITS: Little pods, when present.
SEASON OF MAXIMUM COLOR: Springtime when foliage matures with full color.
LANDSCAPE USES: For the attractive branching and the tolerance of shade and dry atmosphere, jade-plant has been a household favorite since the beginning of gardening. Alone in a decorative container, or with other little plants in a bin, this South African succulent is sure to please.
HABITAT: South Africa.
LIGHT REQUIREMENT: Tolerant of very dense shade, yet compact habit and attractive red leaf-margins can be had only in bright light.
SOIL REQUIREMENT: Open, free-draining, sandy soil, rather low in nutrients, is recommended.
SALT TOLERANCE: Tolerant of conditions back of the first dunes.
AVAILABILITY: Small plants can be had at most nurseries and chain stores.
CULTURE: Plant in a container, with plenty of drainage, that is filled with a medium as described above; water very lightly, allowing the soil to become quite dry between applications. Keep in a shaded location.
PROPAGATION: Cuttage.
PESTS: Rots if overwatered.

K. marmorata

K. beharensis

K. verticillata

Kalanchoe

K. synsepala

K. blossfeldiana

K. pinnata

K. daigremontiana

K. tomentosa

Marion Ruff Sheehan

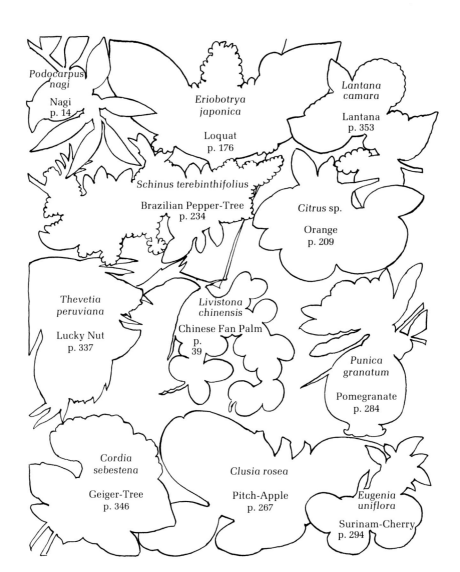

Podocarpus nagi

Nagi
p. 14

Eriobotrya japonica

Loquat
p. 176

Lantana camara

Lantana
p. 353

Schinus terebinthifolius

Brazilian Pepper-Tree
p. 234

Citrus sp.

Orange
p. 209

Thevetia peruviana

Lucky Nut
p. 337

Livistona chinensis

Chinese Fan Palm
p. 39

Punica granatum

Pomegranate
p. 284

Cordia sebestena

Geiger-Tree
p. 346

Clusia rosea

Pitch-Apple
p. 267

Eugenia uniflora

Surinam-Cherry
p. 294

169
Kalanchoe

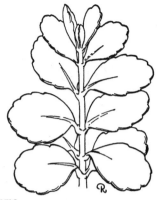

Kalanchoe (cal-ANN-ko-ee): adapted from the Chinese name.
SPP.: several species are grown in Florida.

FAMILY: Crassulaceae.   RELATIVES: Jade-plant and houseleek.
TYPE OF PLANT: Herbaceous perennial.   HEIGHT: Variable. ZONE: S
HOW TO IDENTIFY: Thick, succulent leaves, often with crenatures where small plants arise in profusion. Leaf shape, size, and mottling vary with the species or variety.
HABIT OF GROWTH: Loose habit by several stems that may shed lower leaves.
FOLIAGE: Coarse, bold, often netted with purple or red, usually with crenatures from which plantlets arise for vegetative increase.
FLOWERS: Showy, numerous, in terminal clusters during the warm months. The bell-like corollas hang downward below their calyces.
FRUIT: Little follicles, usually inconspicuous.
SEASON OF MAXIMUM COLOR: Summer and fall when flowers appear.
LANDSCAPE USES: As a ground cover for frostless locations, *Kalanchoe fedtschenkoi*, illustrated above (erroneously called "gray sedum"), is in high favor. All species are wanted for rock-'n'-sand gardens and for planters. Large, fuzzy-leaved species and hybrids are good for urns.
HABITAT: Old World tropics.
LIGHT REQUIREMENT: Full sunlight or partial shade of greenhouses, patios, or Florida rooms.
SOIL REQUIREMENT: Light, gritty, open, well-drained soil of moderate fertility is recommended. Basic reaction, high salt content, and dry conditions are tolerated.
SALT TOLERANCE: Tolerant of salt air and saline sands.
AVAILABILITY: Nurseries and chain stores everywhere sell kalanchoes.
CULTURE: Freedom from frost and invading weeds are necessities for success. One light fertilization at the beginning of the rainy season should supply adequate nutrients for the year.
PROPAGATION: Simply lay a leaf where small plants are wanted, or break plantlets from leaf margins. *K. fedtschenkoi* and *K. blossfeldiana* are grown from conventional tip cuttings commercially.
PESTS: Caterpillars occasionally attack leaves, and leaf-spotting fungi appear on some varieties under humid conditions.

170
Loropetalum

Loropetalum (lor-oh-PET-a-lum): Greek for strap and petal.
chinense (chy-NEN-see): Chinese.

FAMILY: Hamamelidaceae. RELATIVES: Witch-hazel and sweet-gum.
TYPE OF PLANT: Shrub. HEIGHT: 12′. ZONE: N,C
HOW TO IDENTIFY: Compact shrub with outward-pointing branches;
    alternate, simple, rough, evergreen, ovate leaves to 2″ long; white
    or yellowish flowers in clusters in early spring.
HABIT OF GROWTH: Compact, leaves closely packed on outward-pointing
    branches.
FOLIAGE: Evergreen, rough, chlorotic; of medium-fine texture.
FLOWERS: Whitish or yellowish flowers with feathery, strap-shaped
    petals about 1″ long.
FRUITS: Woody capsules that split to release two seeds.
SEASON OF MAXIMUM COLOR: Little variation, even when blossoms are
    out.
LANDSCAPE USES: Foundation plants for small houses, set 3′ o.c. Loro-
    petalum is not very widely planted in Florida, but in some locations
    it performs well. Landscape architects and homeowners have found
    merit in the medium-fine texture of the rough foliage and the hori-
    zontal growth of the branches with the result that loropetalum is
    seen in home plantings.
HABITAT: China; in Florida, sparingly cultured.
LIGHT REQUIREMENT: High, shifting shade or north-side locations.
SOIL REQUIREMENT: Reasonably fertile, acid, moisture-retentive yet
    well-drained soil is a requirement for success.
SALT TOLERANCE: Not tolerant.
AVAILABILITY: Nurseries offer small canned plants.
CULTURE: Plant in sterilized, fertile, slightly acid soil in a shady loca-
    tion, in a planter or on a north side; water faithfully; fertilize thrice
    annually.
PROPAGATION: Cuttage.
PESTS: Mites and mineral deficiency.

171
Sweet-Gum

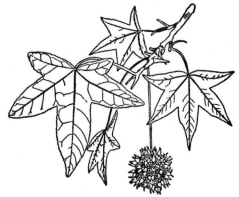

Liquidambar (lick-wid-AM-bar): Latin *liquidus*, fluid, and Arabic *ambar*, for the resin.
styraciflua (sty-ra-SIFF-loo-a): flowing with gum.

FAMILY: Hamamelidaceae.   RELATIVES: Loropetalum and witch-hazel.
TYPE OF PLANT: Tree.   HEIGHT: 100'. ZONE: N,C,S
HOW TO IDENTIFY: Star-shaped, deciduous leaves; pendant, spiny
  fruits; winged twigs that show star-shaped pith in cross-section.
HABIT OF GROWTH: A forest giant that usually grows with a single cen-
  tral leader, which supports a symmetrical, cone-shaped crown
  until old age, when picturesque shapes may be assumed.
FOLIAGE: Deciduous, star-shaped, of medium texture and dark green
  color.
FLOWERS: Inconspicuous clusters in very early spring, before the leaves.
FRUITS: Fruit heads compose a spiny globe 1" in diameter, opening
  with many slits to release seeds.
SEASON OF MAXIMUM COLOR: Fall.
LANDSCAPE USES: For very quick shade, sweet-gum can be planted; it
  can be used, too, for highway and avenue plantings. However, the
  fruits are very objectionable and branches may be carried away by
  strong winds.
    Occasional sweet-gum trees may be left growing where found on
  building sites, but usually they are not items of commerce.
HABITAT: Distributed over the state as far south as Manatee County.
LIGHT REQUIREMENT: Full sun or shade of hammocks.
SOIL REQUIREMENT: Any soil, dry or wet, seems to support sweet-gums.
SALT TOLERANCE: Not tolerant of dune conditions.
AVAILABILITY: Sweet-gum trees are usually not nursery items.
CULTURE: Once planted, sweet-gums grow without care.
PROPAGATION: Seedage; volunteers abound under old trees.
PESTS: Borers and die-back in late years following long dry periods.
NOTE: Formosa sweet-gum (*Liquidambar formosana*) has 3-lobed, de-
  ciduous leaves and twigs without corky wings. Although this Asian
  species grows well in northern Florida, it has never become a good
  nursery item.

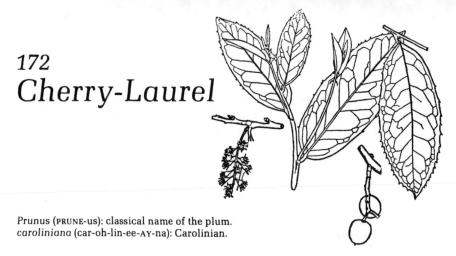

172
Cherry-Laurel

Prunus (PRUNE-us): classical name of the plum.
caroliniana (car-oh-lin-ee-AY-na): Carolinian.

FAMILY: Rosaceae.   RELATIVES: Apple, peach, and pear.
TYPE OF PLANT: Tree, trained as a shrub in gardens.   HEIGHT: 40'.
                                                           ZONE: N,C
HOW TO IDENTIFY: Alternate, evergreen, glossy leaves with taste of
   bitter almond; white flowers in dense clusters that are followed by
   black fruits.
HABIT OF GROWTH: Tree in the wild; clipped shrub in gardens.
FOLIAGE: Evergreen, of medium texture, dark green color. WARNING:
   Cherry-laurel foliage is poisonous.
FLOWERS: White, fragrant flowers, ⅛" across, in axillary racemes.
FRUITS: Black, shining drupes, ½" long.
SEASON OF MAXIMUM COLOR: Springtime when blossoms mature.
LANDSCAPE USES: As a clipped hedge, cherry-laurel has long been a
   southern favorite. Set the plants 18" o.c. As a part of an informal
   enclosing barrier, this native can be kept in shrub form by shear-
   ing. Set plants 5' apart.
      Cherry-laurel is not often planted and grown as a tree, but oc-
   casionally chance seedlings that have grown to maturity may be
   left when housing developments are put in hammock areas.
HABITAT: Hammocks and rich woods of upper Florida.
LIGHT REQUIREMENT: Tolerant of shade.
SOIL REQUIREMENT: Rich soil makes the best-looking specimens.
SALT TOLERANCE: Not tolerant.
AVAILABILITY: Some nurseries in northern Florida will have cherry-
   laurel plants in containers, bare root, or B & B during the winter.
CULTURE: No special cultural requirements need be met.
PROPAGATION: Seedage or by digging suckers around old plants.
PESTS: Mites, stem canker, and caterpillars.

173
Firethorn

Pyracantha (pie-rah-CAN-tha): Greek for fire and thorn.
coccinea (cocks-SIN-ee-a): scarlet.

FAMILY: Rosaceae.   RELATIVES: Hawthorn, loquat, and photinia.
TYPE OF PLANT: Sprawling shrub.   HEIGHT: 20'. ZONE: N,C
HOW TO IDENTIFY: A sprawling shrub that has thorny branches that are gray-tomentose near the tips while young; evergreen, alternate, toothed leaves, 1½" long; conspicuous fruits in fall and winter.
HABIT OF GROWTH: Awkwardly sprawling.
FOLIAGE: Evergreen, alternate, fine in texture, dark green in tone.
FLOWERS: White, showy, ⅓" in diameter, in corymbs on spurs of old wood.
FRUITS: Red or orange pomes ¼" in diameter, very showy in fall and winter.
SEASON OF MAXIMUM COLOR: April for blossoms, November–March for bright fruits.
LANDSCAPE USES: As freestanding specimens, firethorns have long been popular, as they are our best fruiting shrubs. For color interest in shrubbery enclosures, set 5' o.c. A single plant can be trained as an espalier against a masonry wall. Varieties of prostrate habit are used in planters because they will weep over the edges to soften the top line. Set these 3' o.c. There is great confusion in naming.
HABITAT: Southern Europe and western Asia; in Florida, gardens of upper counties.
LIGHT REQUIREMENT: Full sun for best fruiting.
SOIL REQUIREMENT: Tolerant of many different types of soil.
SALT TOLERANCE: Not tolerant of dune conditions.
AVAILABILITY: Small plants in containers are widely offered in nurseries in northern and central Florida. This is the only class of planting stock that is recommended because of the difficulty of transplanting large plants.
CULTURE: Set small plants carefully from containers in well-prepared sites; water faithfully; mulch the roots; protect the foliage against lace bugs and mites. Fertilize twice each year and prune just after flowering, if needed.
PROPAGATION: Cuttage.
PESTS: Lace bugs, mites, scales, thrips, and fire blight.

174
Hawthorns

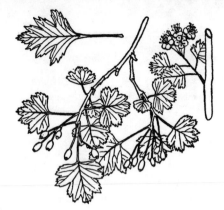

Crataegus (cray-TEE-gus): Greek for strength, for the strong wood.
SPP.: several species grow in Florida.

FAMILY: Rosaceae. RELATIVES: Firethorn, spirea, and loquat.
TYPE OF PLANT: Small trees. HEIGHT: 25'. ZONE: N,C
HOW TO IDENTIFY: Very thorny, small trees with alternate, deciduous leaves, variously lobed; pear-like blossoms of white or pink followed by small pomes of various shades, some noted for jelly-making.
HABIT OF GROWTH: Scraggly, untidy, unkempt.
FOLIAGE: Deciduous, of medium texture and light green color.
FLOWERS: White or pinkish in early spring, conspicuous by their great numbers.
FRUITS: Small pomes containing 1–5 bony, 1-seeded nutlets.
SEASON OF MAXIMUM COLOR: Springtime.
LANDSCAPE USES: In woodland plantings, hawthorn trees are used for seasonal color interest, *C. aestivalis* for the delicious jelly made from its fruits, and *C. marshalli* for the finely toothed, parsley-like leaves. Here is a group of little native trees, always in scale with homes of contemporary architecture, tolerating poor, open sands, yet too seldom used in home landscaping. In the hawthorns some Florida gardeners will find substitutes for northern appleblossoms.
HABITAT: Several species are distributed in northern counties.
LIGHT REQUIREMENT: Full sun or high, shifting shade.
SOIL REQUIREMENT: Various species occur on various soil types.
SALT TOLERANCE: Not tolerant.
AVAILABILITY: Nurseries seldom carry hawthorn trees.
CULTURE: Plant with care in a place that has been enriched with peat; water carefully; mulch and protect the leaves against pests.
PROPAGATION: Seedage or transplanting (with permission) from pasture-lands.
PESTS: Mites, thrips, worms in fruits, bagworms, and lace bugs.

175
India-Hawthorn

Rhaphiolepis (raf-ee-oh-LEP-us): Greek for needle scale.
indica (IN-dee-ca): of the Indies.

FAMILY: Rosaceae. RELATIVES: Loquat, photinia, and quince.
TYPE OF PLANT: Dwarf shrub. HEIGHT: 5'. ZONE: N
HOW TO IDENTIFY: Dwarfish shrub with evergreen, leathery, serrate leaves about 3" long; fragrant, white, ½" flowers that are followed by drupe-like, purplish-black pomes.
HABIT OF GROWTH: Dwarf shrub, open beneath, with leaves clustered at twig tips.
FOLIAGE: Evergreen, sharply serrate, 3" long, of medium texture and dark green color.
FLOWERS: Rose-like, white tinged with pink, ½" in diameter, in loose clusters.
FRUITS: Drupe-like little pomes (⅛" in diameter) that are purplish-black in color.
SEASON OF MAXIMUM COLOR: Fall.
LANDSCAPE USES: As a dwarf seaside shrub, India-hawthorn is excellent. There, in lee-side foundation plantings or planter boxes, set at intervals of 2'. For low hedges, plant 18" o.c. North-side locations are highly suitable.
HABITAT: Southern China; in Florida, sparingly planted in northern counties.
LIGHT REQUIREMENT: Tolerant of shade.
SOIL REQUIREMENT: Soils of good quality grow the best-looking plants.
SALT TOLERANCE: Tolerant of salt drift.
AVAILABILITY: India-hawthorn is sparingly offered in nurseries.
CULTURE: Plant in good soil on lee sides of ocean-front homes; north-side locations are good. In improved, slightly acid soil, set 2' o.c.; water faithfully until well established; fertilize two or three times each year.
PROPAGATION: Cuttage or seedage.
PESTS: Scales, fire blight, and nematodes.
NOTE: Yeddo-hawthorn, *R. umbellata*, has thick leaves that are whitish-tomentose with revolute edges, white blossoms ¾" across that have calyx-lobes which are not red. This latter species is usually taller, more upright, than is *R. indica*.

176
Loquat

Eriobotrya (erry-oh-BOT-ree-a): Greek for woolly cluster, for the felty blossoms.
japonica (jap-ON-ee-ca): Japanese.

FAMILY: Rosaceae.   RELATIVES: Rose, photinia, and firethorn.
TYPE OF PLANT: Tree.   HEIGHT: 20′. ZONE: N,C,S
HOW TO IDENTIFY: Evergreen, alternate leaves, about 10″ long, that are
   coarsely toothed, with sunken veins that go straight to the teeth. Fra-
   grant, whitish, little blossoms appear in the fall to be followed by
   decorative and delicious yellow fruits in wintertime.
HABIT OF GROWTH: A neat little compact tree with upward-pointing
   branches.
FOLIAGE: Evergreen, alternate, very attractive, dark green above, fuzzy
   beneath.
FLOWERS: Fragrant little ½″ white flowers in rusty-pubescent terminal
   panicles in the fall.
FRUITS: Yellow pomes with 1 or several large brown seeds.
SEASON OF MAXIMUM COLOR: Late winter when fruits ripen.
LANDSCAPE USES: Freestanding specimen for fruit and horticultural
   interest, as a part of an informal shrubbery border, as a shade tree
   for patio or terrace, loquat excels. This is unquestionably one of
   Florida's best trees. Its small size, complete hardiness, beautiful
   foliage, appealing fragrance, and delicious fruits endear the loquat
   to all.
HABITAT: China; in Florida, ubiquitous as a yard tree.
LIGHT REQUIREMENT: Full sun for best form, flowering, and fruiting.
SOIL REQUIREMENT: Tolerant of varying soil types.
SALT TOLERANCE: Tolerant of moderate salt air back of first-line dunes.
AVAILABILITY: Seedlings in containers appear in most nurseries.
CULTURE: Plant carefully; water moderately until established; there-
   after just remember to fertilize once or twice a year. A mulch over
   the root zone is recommended.
PROPAGATION: Seedage; superior varieties, increased by graftage, are
   preferred.
PESTS: Scales, caterpillars, and fire blight.

Chinese Photinia

Photinia (foe-TIN-ee-a): Greek for shining, referring to the leaves.
serrulata (ser-you-LATE-a): saw-toothed.

FAMILY: Rosaceae.   RELATIVES: Loquat, India-hawthorn, and pear.
TYPE OF PLANT: Shrub, becoming tree-like with age.   HEIGHT: 15′.
ZONE: N

HOW TO IDENTIFY: Rank, upright growth, heavy twigs that bear sharply
toothed, evergreen leaves to 7″ long, in alternate arrangement.

HABIT OF GROWTH: Stiffly upright, usually bare beneath.

FOLIAGE: Evergreen, strap-shaped, saw-toothed, coarse, dark green.

FLOWERS: White, rose-like, ¼″ across, in flat panicles about 6″ in diameter.

FRUITS: Red, globose pomes, ¼″ across, if present.

SEASON OF MAXIMUM COLOR: Fall, when lower leaves turn red.

LANDSCAPE USES: For screens where large, upright, extremely coarse
shrubs can be used, Chinese photinia could be indicated. Planting
interval is 5′ o.c.

Chinese photinia is a striking outsized shrub on superior soils
in northern sections where winter chilling is experienced, but on
the peninsula's sands where winters are mild, the plant leaves a lot
to be desired. Here, Chinese photinia is not recommended for
home-ground plantings.

HABITAT: China; in Florida, better soils of northern counties.

LIGHT REQUIREMENT: Full sun for compact growth.

SOIL REQUIREMENT: Better soils of northern Florida, only.

SALT TOLERANCE: Not tolerant.

AVAILABILITY: Nurseries in northern Florida offer Chinese photinia.

CULTURE: Plant in well-prepared site; water moderately until established; prune frequently to keep the plant compact and within
bounds.

PROPAGATION: Cuttage.

PESTS: Caterpillars, mites, scales, and fire blight.

NOTE: There is an attractive hybrid between Chinese photinia and
red-leaved *Photinia glabra* that displays desirable characteristics of
both parents.

178
Red-Leaf
Photinia

Photinia (foe-TIN-ee-a): Greek for shining, referring to the foliage.
glabra (GLAY-bra): not hairy.

FAMILY: Rosaceae.   RELATIVES: Loquat, quince, and pear.
TYPE OF PLANT: Shrub.   HEIGHT: 10'. ZONE: N
HOW TO IDENTIFY: Vivid red new leaves turn green at maturity. These
    are evergreen, alternate, 2"–3" long, elliptic in form. The shrub is
    usually bare beneath.
HABIT OF GROWTH: Ungainly, open, bare below.
FOLIAGE: Evergreen, medium in texture, new leaves red, old leaves
    green.
FLOWERS: White, in compact clusters.
FRUITS: Red, berry-like pomes, hollow at the top, ¼" across.
SEASON OF MAXIMUM COLOR: Spring, when new growth emerges.
LANDSCAPE USES: For color accent in a green shrubbery border, plant
    a group of 3 red-leaf photinia, with 3' between plants. During
    seasons when all leaves are a dull green, the plant goes unnoticed.
HABITAT: Japan; in Florida, better soils of northern tier of counties.
LIGHT REQUIREMENT: Full sun for best growth and coloring.
SOIL REQUIREMENT: Better soils of northern Florida.
SALT TOLERANCE: Not tolerant.
AVAILABILITY: Red-leaf photinia and the hybrid are for sale in northern
    Florida.
CULTURE: Prepare rich sites in full sun; plant at the same level; attend
    to watering; prune regularly before flushes of growth to induce
    compact habit.
PROPAGATION: Cuttage.
PESTS: Mites, scales, and caterpillars.
NOTE: There is an attractive hybrid between red-leaf photinia and
    Chinese photinia, that displays desirable characteristics of both
    parents, that may extend the range of photinias down the peninsula
    slightly. Never a subtropical genus, *Photinia* behaves best where
    soil is good, winters are chill.

179
Rose

Rosa (RO-sa): ancient Latin name for roses.
SPP.: several species are grown in Florida; most gardeners grow hybrids.

FAMILY: Rosaceae.

RELATIVES: Photinia and loquat.

TYPE OF PLANT: Evergreen shrub.

HEIGHT: Variable. ZONE: N,C,S

HOW TO IDENTIFY: Upright shrubs, or vine-like due to the long, gracefully arching canes. Stems usually armed with large thorns. Compound, alternate leaves, usually 3–5 leaflets. Leaf petioles often winged near base. Flowers borne either singly or in small clusters at tips of recently matured branches.

HABIT OF GROWTH: Upright or vining.

FOLIAGE: Shiny, light to medium green, sometimes shining red when young.

FLOWERS: Mostly doubles, but singles sometimes are grown; wide range of color.

FRUITS: A green or red hip.

SEASON OF MAXIMUM COLOR: Spring, with scattered flowers all year in C, S zones.

LANDSCAPE USES: For show of color in shrubbery borders and in mass plantings. Excellent for cut flowers.

HABITAT: Civilized areas of the earth.

LIGHT REQUIREMENT: Full sun.

SOIL REQUIREMENT: Most well-drained soils.

SALT TOLERANCE: None.

AVAILABILITY: Most nurseries have plants in cans year round and bare-rooted plants in late fall and early spring.

CULTURE: A well-prepared bed is needed to produce good roses. Some growers prepare a bed 18″ deep, adding organic matter and rotted manure. Once established, roses should receive ½″–1″ of water a week for best growth. Frequent fertilizations during the growing season are recommended. Weekly applications of fungicide and insecticide are needed to keep plants healthy. A well-grown rose plant is the reward of a hard-working gardener.

PROPAGATION: Graftage and budding.

PESTS: Red spider mites and black spot are always serious problems.

NOTE: For best results in Florida, use plants grafted on *R. fortuneana* or Dr. Huey understocks.

180
Southern Crab-Apple

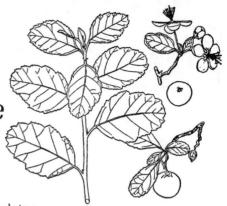

Malus (MALE-us): classical name of the apple tree.
angustifolia (an-gust-ee-FOL-ee-a): narrow-leaved.

FAMILY: Rosaceae. RELATIVES: Apple, peach, and pear.
TYPE OF PLANT: Tree. HEIGHT: 25′. ZONE: N
HOW TO IDENTIFY: Deciduous, alternate, slightly lobed leaves are held by pubescent twigs, and, in springtime, beautiful pink blossoms appear. In the autumn, there are little green apples.
HABIT OF GROWTH: A small tree with broad, open crown.
FOLIAGE: Deciduous, alternate, fine in texture, dull green in color.
FLOWERS: Typical, 5-petaled appleblossoms in tones of blush pink with delightful, characteristic fragrance.
FRUITS: Yellow-green pomes, 1″ in diameter.
SEASON OF MAXIMUM COLOR: March–April when blossoms are out.
LANDSCAPE USES: For delightful appleblossoms, Floridians may plant this, their own native crab-apple, as a freestanding specimen or as a member of an informal shrubbery border. Many troubles beset this beloved tree, and so it probably will never be widely planted in gardens on the peninsula. For the most part, apples are short lived and unproductive in much of the Sunshine State.
HABITAT: Western Florida, along fence rows; in landscape plantings.
LIGHT REQUIREMENT: Full sun for best habit and free-flowering.
SOIL REQUIREMENT: Superior soils of the Panhandle.
SALT TOLERANCE: Not tolerant.
AVAILABILITY: Usually Florida nurseries do not stock southern crab-apples.
CULTURE: Prepare sites carefully; plant at same depth as formerly; wrap trunks; water faithfully; spray to control pests.
PROPAGATION: Seedage.
PESTS: Mites, tent caterpillars, borers, and rust fungus.

181
Reeves Spirea

Spiraea (spy-REE-a): Greek for wreath.
cantoniensis (can-tone-ee-EN-sis): of Canton, China.

FAMILY: Rosaceae.
RELATIVES: Loquat, photinia, and rose.
TYPE OF PLANT: Shrub.
HEIGHT: 6'. ZONE: N

HOW TO IDENTIFY: A shrub of many branches that hold alternate, deciduous leaves which are rhombic-oblong in form and bluish-green in color. In springtime the white blossoms are notable.

HABIT OF GROWTH: Much-branched, ascending.

FOLIAGE: Deciduous, medium-fine in texture, bluish-green in color.

FLOWERS: Conspicuous, white, ½" in diameter, in dense corymbs.

FRUITS: Often not present in Florida.

SEASON OF MAXIMUM COLOR: Springtime, just at the end of azalea season.

LANDSCAPE USES: For glistening white foils with colored azaleas, spirea is superb. Plant 5–7 spireas together, allowing about 3' between plants. In front of all-green shrubbery these snow-white flowers are bright spring accents. Plant as above.

Of the 80 species and many named clones of this group, Reeves spirea is best for Florida. On the Panhandle, other kinds do well as garden shrubs.

HABITAT: China; in Florida, upper tier of counties.

LIGHT REQUIREMENT: Full sun or high, shifting, broken shade.

SOIL REQUIREMENT: Fertile soils of northern counties are best.

SALT TOLERANCE: Not tolerant.

AVAILABILITY: Some nurseries in northern Florida stock spireas.

CULTURE: Plant in moderately fertile land; water faithfully until well established; thereafter, prune after flowering for compact growth; fertilize once in late winter.

PROPAGATION: Cuttage, using long, hard, leafless cuttings in early winter.

PESTS: Aphids and mushroom root-rot.

182
Thunberg
Spirea

Spiraea (spy-REE-a): Greek for wreath.
thunbergii (thun-BERG-ee-eye): for C. Thunberg, Swedish botanist, 1743–1822.

FAMILY: Rosaceae.　　　　　　　RELATIVES: Rose, firethorn, and loquat.
TYPE OF PLANT: Dwarf shrub.　　　　　　HEIGHT: 5'. ZONE: N
HOW TO IDENTIFY: Shrub of weeping habit bears half-evergreen, alternate leaves, 1½" long, with saw-tooth edges on fine, wire-like, arching stems. Tiny white flowers are produced in great quantity in late winter.
HABIT OF GROWTH: Arching, wire-like stems form compact plants.
FOLIAGE: Half-evergreen, alternate, of very fine texture and light green color.
FLOWERS: White, ⅓" across in 3- to 5-flowered groups along the arching stems.
FRUITS: Little pods when present.
SEASON OF MAXIMUM COLOR: January–February.
LANDSCAPE USES: For massing in naturalistic plantings where wintertime white is wanted, this spirea is excellent for northern Florida. To face taller shrubs, and for foundation plantings, it is highly acceptable as well. Planting interval may be about 3' o.c.
　　This fine-scale plant has great usefulness that is not fully appreciated. It is recommended for use on the Panhandle.
HABITAT: Eastern Asia; in Florida, superior soils of northern counties.
LIGHT REQUIREMENT: Shifting shade from high pines is excellent.
SOIL REQUIREMENT: Heavy, well-drained loamy or rocky soil is best.
SALT TOLERANCE: Not tolerant.
AVAILABILITY: Nurseries in northern Florida may offer Thunberg spirea.
CULTURE: Once plants become established on superior soil in northern Florida, culture is simple. Watering during very dry periods, pruning after flowering, and fertilization once each winter are indicated.
PROPAGATION: Cuttage by long, hard, leafless cuttings in December.
PESTS: Aphids and mites.

183
Cassia
Shrubs

Cassia (CASS-ee-a): ancient Greek name.
SPP.: several shrub cassias are widely grown in Florida.

FAMILY: Leguminosae.   RELATIVES: Tamarind and redbud.
TYPE OF PLANT: Shrubs.   HEIGHT: 15′. ZONE: N,C,S
HOW TO IDENTIFY: Upright shrubs that have compound leaves and fall
   and winter blossoms that resemble golden butterflies.
HABIT OF GROWTH: Upright, by means of several stems.
FOLIAGE: Evergreen, compound, of medium texture and light green
   color.
FLOWERS: Terminal spikes of golden yellow in the autumn.
FRUITS: Pods about half a foot long that turn brown at maturity.
SEASON OF MAXIMUM COLOR: Fall and winter.
LANDSCAPE USES: For bright yellow fall and winter color, group three
   cassias in front of green shrubbery. Frost will kill the best of the
   golden-flowered shrub cassias.
      Ringworm cassia (*C. alata*) has erect spikes that resemble fat
   candles before the individual blossoms open. This one should be
   planted only in nearly frostless locations, as the roots may not survive cold winters. In other sections, *Cassia bicapsularis* opens its
   yellow butterflies in October, to be killed to the ground in a month
   or so. The roots usually survive to sprout out again (this species in
   sketch).
HABITAT: Tropical America; in Florida, popular wherever the roots
   will survive.
LIGHT REQUIREMENT: Full sun for best growth and flowering.
SOIL REQUIREMENT: Tolerant of many varying soils.
SALT TOLERANCE: Not tolerant.
AVAILABILITY: Nurseries in southern Florida usually stock both shrub
   cassias; in northern sections, *Cassia bicapsularis* is widely offered
   in bloom in gallon cans in the fall.
CULTURE: After they become established, shrub cassias grow with little
   care. Protect the foliage and blossom buds from caterpillars in the
   fall; cut off at ground level as soon as frost kills back the stems.
PROPAGATION: Cuttage and seedage.
PESTS: Caterpillars consume leaves and flower buds in the autumn.

184
Golden-Shower

Cassia (CASS-ee-a): ancient Greek name.
fistula (FIS-tue-la): Latin for tube for the long, cylindrical pods.

FAMILY: Leguminosae.   RELATIVES: Jerusalem-thorn and redbud.
TYPE OF PLANT: Tree.   HEIGHT: 40'. ZONE: S
HOW TO IDENTIFY: Tree with compound leaves with oval leaflets, 8"
   long, pendant clusters of golden flowers in summertime, followed
   by numerous 2-foot, cylindrical, brown pods.
HABIT OF GROWTH: Upright tree with open crown.
FOLIAGE: Evergreen, compound, lacy in appearance and medium green
   in color.
FLOWERS: Pale yellow, pea-like, in hanging racemes a foot in length.
FRUITS: Huge pods, 1" thick and 2' long, striking, but undecorative.
SEASON OF MAXIMUM COLOR: Summertime.
LANDSCAPE USES: Freestanding specimen for residential properties; on
   avenues set golden-shower trees 25'-35' o.c. This is one of southern
   Florida's favorite summer-flowering trees.
HABITAT: India; in Florida, around the tip of the peninsula.
LIGHT REQUIREMENT: Full sun or partial shade.
SOIL REQUIREMENT: Tolerant of many soil types.
SALT TOLERANCE: Tolerant of mild salt air back from the strand.
AVAILABILITY: Most retail nurseries in warm areas sell golden-shower
   trees in containers.
CULTURE: Once started, golden-shower grows freely in nearly frostless
   locations.
PROPAGATION: Seedage.
PESTS: Caterpillars.
NOTE: *Cassia* is a very large genus that contains some of the tropics'
   most colorful and beloved flowering trees. Among them the various
   pink-showers, pink-and-white-showers, and the spectacular hybrid
   rainbow-shower stand out in hot countries.

185
Cherokee-Bean

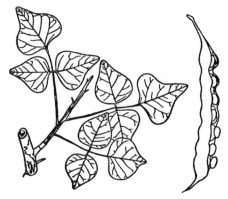

Erythrina (airy-THRINE-a): Greek for red, for the color of the flowers.
herbacea (er-BAY-see-a): herbaceous, not woody.

FAMILY: Leguminosae. **RELATIVES:** Clover and orchid-tree.
TYPE OF PLANT: Herbaceous perennial. **HEIGHT:** 3'. **ZONE:** N,C,S
HOW TO IDENTIFY: Deciduous, compound leaves composed of three spear-shaped leaflets, with prickles on midrib; showy, scarlet, closed blossoms in spring, followed by beans which split to reveal bright scarlet seeds.
HABIT OF GROWTH: Upright, unkempt, often close to trees, sometimes tree-like.
FOLIAGE: Deciduous, compound, of medium texture and medium green color.
FLOWERS: Bright scarlet, 2" long, closed to form tubes, on 15" spikes.
FRUITS: Drooping pods constricted between seeds, split to reveal red seeds.
SEASON OF MAXIMUM COLOR: May–June for flowers, autumn for bright seeds.
LANDSCAPE USES: For woodland plantings, Cherokee-bean is useful for bright highlights of red beside tree trunks. Conspicuous in unspoiled hammocks in springtime, Cherokee-bean is seldom planted in man-made gardens. Here is yet another indigene that warrants much wider planting. For those who want to have more maintenance-free plants in naturalistic arrangements, Cherokee-bean seems to be made to order. True, the effect is transitory, but this is not necessarily a disadvantage.
HABITAT: Hammocks of the state.
LIGHT REQUIREMENT: Broken shade of hammocks.
SOIL REQUIREMENT: Hammock soil.
SALT TOLERANCE: Not tolerant.
AVAILABILITY: Cherokee-bean is not an item of commerce.
CULTURE: Plant in prepared sites by tree trunks; water until established; fertilize in springtime; cut back dead tops in winter.
PROPAGATION: Seedage and cuttage.
PESTS: None of major consequence.
NOTE: The variety *arborea* is a shrub or small tree to 30'.

Cockspur Coral-Tree

Erythrina (airy-THRINE-a): Greek for red, referring to the color of the flowers.
crista-gallii (KRIST-a GAUL-ee-eye): cock's comb, referring to the flowers.

FAMILY: Leguminosae.   RELATIVES: Orchid-tree, redbud, and pea.
TYPE OF PLANT: Tree or shrub.   HEIGHT: 25′. ZONE: C,S
HOW TO IDENTIFY: Stems, petioles, and midribs armed with spines; alternate, compound leaves; showy, red flowers that have standards erect at full flowering; long pods constricted between seeds.
HABIT OF GROWTH: Upright-spreading, with or without distinct trunk.
FOLIAGE: Semi-evergreen, compound, medium in texture and medium green in color.
FLOWERS: Papilionaceous, brilliant crimson, appearing in late summer or fall.
FRUITS: Long pods, constricted between seeds, turn brown at maturity.
SEASON OF MAXIMUM COLOR: Late summer and early fall.
LANDSCAPE USES: As freestanding specimens, this, and other erythrinas, may be cultured for the interest of their reddish, butterfly-like flowers. There are half a hundred species in the genus. Some of the tree species are grown to shade coffee and cocoa in the tropics.
HABITAT: Brazil; in Florida, infrequently cultured as a garden tree in mild sections.
LIGHT REQUIREMENT: Full sun or partial shade.
SOIL REQUIREMENT: Tolerant of many soils, but fertile land is best.
SALT TOLERANCE: Not tolerant of dune conditions.
AVAILABILITY: Nurseries may have limited stocks of erythrina trees in containers.
CULTURE: Once established in nearly frostless districts, erythrina trees grow thriftily with a minimum of attention.
PROPAGATION: Seedage or cuttage.
PESTS: Nematodes, thrips, mites, and twig borers.

187
Colvillea

Colvillea (kol-VIL-ee-a): for Sir Charles Colville, a former governor of Madagascar.
racemosa (ras-e-MO-sa): refers to flower clusters.

FAMILY: Leguminosae. RELATIVES: Royal poinciana and wisteria.

TYPE OF PLANT: Small tree. HEIGHT: 50'. ZONE: C,S

HOW TO IDENTIFY: This small, ascending tree has branches that cross frequently. Trunks are thick and leaves are 2-pinnate with the individual leaf segments ½" long, slightly larger than poinciana. Flowers are borne in dense, pendant, showy clusters, often up to 18" long. Ten or more racemes may be produced at each branch-tip.

HABIT OF GROWTH: Ascending, with many crossing branches.

FOLIAGE: Deciduous, fine-textured, medium-green leaves.

FLOWERS: Buds burnt orange, felt-like; flowers yellow-orange.

FRUITS: Round pods.

SEASON OF MAXIMUM COLOR: Late summer.

LANDSCAPE USES: Excellent street tree; framing tree for small homes.

HABITAT: Africa.

LIGHT REQUIREMENT: Full sun.

SOIL REQUIREMENT: Most well-drained soils.

SALT TOLERANCE: Not tolerant.

AVAILABILITY: Found in some southern Florida nurseries.

CULTURE: Easy to establish and needs no special treatment.

PROPAGATION: Cuttage or seedage.

PESTS: None serious in Florida.

188
Dwarf-Poinciana

Daubentonia (dob-en-TONE-ee-a): for L. Daubenton, an eighteenth-century naturalist.
punicea (pew-NISS-ee-a): reddish-purple.

FAMILY: Leguminosae.   RELATIVES: Wisteria, bean, and lupine.
TYPE OF PLANT: Dwarf tree.   HEIGHT: 8'. ZONE: N,C,S
HOW TO IDENTIFY: A little, flat-topped tree bears deciduous, even-pinnate leaves and scarlet, pea-like, showy blossoms in spring-time, brown pods into the winter.
HABIT OF GROWTH: Flat, umbrella-like head of twiggy growth atop a little, erect trunk.
FOLIAGE: Deciduous, compound, fine in texture, dark green in color.
FLOWERS: Showy racemes of scarlet, pea-like blossoms during spring.
FRUITS: 4-winged, reddish-brown pods, about 4" long, which release brown seeds.
SEASON OF MAXIMUM COLOR: Warm months.
LANDSCAPE USES: For bright color accent in a woodland planting, a few of these red-flowered trees might be indicated. As the seeds are poisonous, pods should be picked as soon as they form.
    This little legume has escaped to become a roadside weed; it could hardly be recommended for landscape plantings.
HABITAT: South America; in Florida, ubiquitous, escaped as a road-side weed.
LIGHT REQUIREMENT: Sun or partial shade.
SOIL REQUIREMENT: Tolerant of many soils, including poorly drained types.
SALT TOLERANCE: Not tolerant of dune conditions.
AVAILABILITY: Small trees might occasionally be found in retail sales lots.
CULTURE: Once established, dwarf-poinciana spreads by seedage, form-ing large colonies; hence, many people do not like this tree.
PROPAGATION: Seedage.
PESTS: None of major concern.

189
Ear-Tree

Enterolobium (enter-o-LOBE-ee-um): intestine-form, for the pods.
cyclocarpum (si-clo-CARP-um): circular fruit, for the pods.

FAMILY: Leguminosae.   RELATIVES: Orchid-tree and royal poinciana.

TYPE OF PLANT: Tree.   HEIGHT: 75′. ZONE: C,S

HOW TO IDENTIFY: A huge, fast-growing tree bears black pods that are shaped like ears of monkeys or humans, and graceful, bipinnate leaves.

HABIT OF GROWTH: Upright, symmetrical form above buttressed trunks.

FOLIAGE: Deciduous, compound, of very fine texture and light green color.

FLOWERS: Globose heads of small, greenish-white flowers in springtime.

FRUITS: Black pods that are twisted so as to resemble anthropoid ears.

SEASON OF MAXIMUM COLOR: Springtime.

LANDSCAPE USES: As a single specimen on a campus, in a city park or botanical garden, ear-tree might be wanted for its interesting pods, but this monstrous legume is too large for home-ground plantings and it is not recommended for city lots, therefore. The brittle wood breaks in strong winds.

HABITAT: American tropics; in Florida, warm locations.

LIGHT REQUIREMENT: Full sun or high, shifting shade.

SOIL REQUIREMENT: Tolerant of various soils, including light sands.

SALT TOLERANCE: Not tolerant.

AVAILABILITY: Ear-trees are seen in nurseries in the warmer parts of the peninsula.

CULTURE: Very rapid growth without care is characteristic of ear-trees.

PROPAGATION: Seedage.

PESTS: None of major concern.

190
Jerusalem-Thorn

Parkinsonia (park-in-SONE-ee-a): for J. Parkinson, English apothecary.
aculeata (a-cule-lee-ATE-a): prickly.

FAMILY: Leguminosae.   RELATIVES: Powderpuff and royal poinciana.
TYPE OF PLANT: Small tree.   HEIGHT: 25'. ZONE: N,C,S
HOW TO IDENTIFY: Thorny, green branches hold deciduous leaves com-
    posed of flattened, twig-like stalks and many small leaflets. Yellow,
    pea-like blossoms come out in springtime, to be followed later in
    the year by brown pods which are flattened between seeds.
HABIT OF GROWTH: Awkward, asymmetrical, open crowns assume pic-
    turesque shapes.
FOLIAGE: Deciduous, compound, very fine in texture, medium green in
    color.
FLOWERS: Yellow, fragrant, pea-like, very showy in spring and sum-
    mer.
FRUITS: Pods 2"–6" long, constricted between the oblong seeds.
SEASON OF MAXIMUM COLOR: Spring and summer.
LANDSCAPE USES: As a freestanding specimen for warm-weather color,
    this splendid little tree is excellent in every section of Florida. To
    shade a part of a terrace, it serves well because of its small size
    and because the leaves fall to let the sun shine through in winter.
    Jerusalem-thorn may stand in a shrubbery border for skyline in-
    terest.
HABITAT: Tropical America; in Florida, it is common as a garden tree.
LIGHT REQUIREMENT: Full sun for best flowering.
SOIL REQUIREMENT: Tolerant of wide variation in soils.
SALT TOLERANCE: Tolerant of salt drift and saline earth.
AVAILABILITY: Many nurseries offer small seedlings in an assortment
    of containers.
CULTURE: After small trees from cans become established, no atten-
    tion will be needed.
PROPAGATION: Seedage.
PESTS: Scales.

191
Manila Tamarind

Pithecellobium (pith-ee-se-LOH-be-um): Greek for monkey's ear.
dulce (DUL-se): sweet.

FAMILY: Leguminosae.   RELATIVES: Royal poinciana and wisteria.
TYPE OF PLANT: Tree.   HEIGHT: 50'. ZONE: S
HOW TO IDENTIFY: Broad, evergreen trees, often spiny when young,
    with 2-pinnate leaves, each pinna having only one pair of leaflets.
    Flowers are borne in dense, pubescent, stemless clusters.
HABIT OF GROWTH: Dense tree.
FOLIAGE: Fine-textured foliage, often with a small bristle at the apex,
    later becoming blunt.
FLOWERS: Usually 5–15 per cluster, forming small, whitish puff-balls.
FRUITS: Reddish-brown, spirally twisted pods.
SEASON OF MAXIMUM COLOR: Summer months.
LANDSCAPE USES: Mainly used as a street tree, but can be used as a
    framing tree for small buildings.
HABITAT: Tropical America.
LIGHT REQUIREMENT: Full sun.
SOIL REQUIREMENT: Thrives best on well-drained soils of southern
    Florida.
SALT TOLERANCE: Endures salt drift just behind front-line dunes.
AVAILABILITY: In cans in nurseries in southern Florida.
CULTURE: *Pithecellobium* is easy to establish and, once established,
    will require only minimal maintenance. Fertilized occasionally
    and watered during periods of excessive dry weather, the plants
    will flourish.
PROPAGATION: Seedage or cuttage.
PESTS: None serious.
NOTE: This plant, in its native environs, supplies man with medici-
    nals (roots, seeds, bark), glue (trunk), oil (seeds), fodder (pods),
    and lumber. In Florida, volunteer seedlings may appear in consid-
    erable numbers under old trees.

Orchid-Trees

Bauhinia (bo-HIN-ee-a): for the brothers Bauhin, sixteenth-century herbalists.
SPP.: several species are grown in Florida.

FAMILY: Leguminosae.   RELATIVES: Redbud, Jerusalem-thorn, bean.
TYPE OF PLANT: Trees.   HEIGHT: 25'. ZONE: C,S
HOW TO IDENTIFY: Tree with 2-cleft, deciduous leaves that resemble the
   print from an ox hoof; orchid-like flowers, followed by many long,
   brown pods.
HABIT OF GROWTH: Small head of many branches from a short, often
   crooked, trunk.
FOLIAGE: Deciduous, 2-cleft, coarse in texture, light green in color; fall
   color, yellow.
FLOWERS: Orchid-like, 3"–4" across, in tones of purple, red, or white.
FRUITS: Flat pods, 1' long, sharp-beaked, long-stalked.
SEASON OF MAXIMUM COLOR: Variable with the species.
LANDSCAPE USES: As freestanding specimens, or as framing for small
   houses, orchid-trees are highly acceptable. They may be fitted into
   shrubbery borders to give interest to the skyline and seasonal color.
      Bauhinia variegata, most popular, produces in winter and spring
   most nearly orchid-like blossoms of purplish casts or pure white in
   variety 'Candida'.
      Bauhinia purpurea, most variable, produces narrow-petaled
   flowers in the fall while leaves are on the trees.
      Bauhinia monandra, single-stamened, flowers in summer.
      Bauhinia blakeana, Hong Kong orchid-tree, most spectacular and
   most wanted bauhinia, bears orchid-like, 6" flowers of rich reddish or
   rose purple during the winter. This one is very tender to cold.
HABITAT: India to China; in Florida, in moderately warm sections.
LIGHT REQUIREMENT: Full sun or high, shifting pine shade.
SOIL REQUIREMENT: Tolerant of widely varying well-drained soils.
SALT TOLERANCE: Not tolerant.
AVAILABILITY: Offered in containers by most nurseries in central and
   southern Florida.
CULTURE: After establishment in made-up planting sites, no special care
   is needed.
PROPAGATION: Seedage; marcottage for rare types.
PESTS: Chewing larvae may despoil foliage.

Pride-of-
the-Cape

Bauhinia (bo-HIN-ee-a): for the brothers Bauhin.
galpinii (gal-PIN-ee-eye): for Mr. Galpin.

FAMILY: Leguminosae.

RELATIVES: Redbud and tamarind.

TYPE OF PLANT: Shrub.

HEIGHT: 10'. ZONE: S

HOW TO IDENTIFY: An evergreen, climbing shrub, with 2-lobed leaves resembling cloven hooves of cattle, having orchid-like flowers in clusters of 6 to 10.

HABIT OF GROWTH: Sprawling shrub or vine.

FOLIAGE: Medium-textured foliage, 2-lobed, medium green, turns yellow before falling.

FLOWERS: Brick-red, with 3 stamens, 1½" across, borne in few-flowered racemes.

FRUITS: Pods to 5" long with dark brown seeds.

SEASON OF MAXIMUM BLOOM: Summer months.

LANDSCAPE USES: As color accent in the shrubbery border or as a free-standing specimen, *Bauhinia galpinii* is outstanding.

HABITAT: Tropical Africa.

LIGHT REQUIREMENT: Full sun for best flowering.

SOIL REQUIREMENT: Tolerates most well-drained soils.

SALT TOLERANCE: Not tolerant.

AVAILABILITY: Offered in containers in many southern Florida nurseries.

CULTURE: Requires little maintenance once established. Occasional pruning of excessively long branches helps keep the plant in shrub form.

PROPAGATION: Seedage or cuttage.

PESTS: Chewing insects despoil foliage on occasion.

Pongam

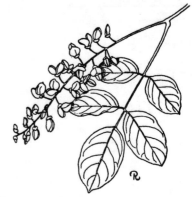

Pongamia (pon-GAM-ee-a): native Malayan name.
pinnata (pin-NAY-ta): feather-formed.

FAMILY: Leguminosae.   RELATIVES: Redbud, wisteria, and orchid-tree.

TYPE OF PLANT: Tree.   HEIGHT: 40'. ZONE: S

HOW TO IDENTIFY: Close, dense head of odd-pinnate, evergreen leaves with 5–7 leaflets that are broadly ovate and about 3" long. The short, thick, brown pods have incurving points and contain only 1 seed.

HABIT OF GROWTH: Heavily foliated; drooping branches from a stout trunk.

FOLIAGE: Evergreen, odd-pinnate, of fine texture and dark green color.

FLOWERS: Pinkish to white, pea-like, in hanging, slender clusters.

FRUITS: Flat, brown pods about 1½" long, with incurving, beak-like points and single brown seeds within each pod. These seeds are poisonous to humans if taken internally.

SEASON OF MAXIMUM COLOR: Springtime when the trees are in flower.

LANDSCAPE USES: Because of its strength, pongam is recommended as a street tree (set 45'-55' o.c.) and windbreak tree (set 25' in double, staggered row) for southern Florida. As a single shade tree for properties back from the dunes, pongam is excellent, as well.

HABITAT: Asian tropics; in Florida, a street tree in the southernmost part.

LIGHT REQUIREMENT: Full sun or partial shade; very resistant to wind.

SOIL REQUIREMENT: Tolerant of many different soils.

SALT TOLERANCE: Tolerant of salt air back of first-line dunes.

AVAILABILITY: Nurseries in warm locations offer pongam trees in cans.

CULTURE: Set pongam trees in fertile soil; water well until well established; fertilize thrice annually while young; keep mulch over the root zone; hoe back grasses; protect the foliage against caterpillars.

PROPAGATION: Seedage.

PESTS: Caterpillars.

195
Powderpuff

Calliandra (cal-ee-AN-dra): Greek for beautiful stamens.
haematocephala (he-mat-oh-SEFF-ah-la): red head.

FAMILY: Leguminosae.   RELATIVES: Mimosa-tree and royal poinciana.
TYPE OF PLANT: Large shrub.   HEIGHT: 15′. ZONE: C,S
HOW TO IDENTIFY: Sprawling growth; compound evergreen leaves; red
   or pink pompons in terminal positions during warm months.
HABIT OF GROWTH: Sprawling to form huge mounds.
FOLIAGE: Evergreen, compound, of medium-fine texture and dark green
   color.
FLOWERS: Globose heads formed by conspicuous red, pink, or white
   stamens.
FRUITS: Straight pods with thickened margins; unattractive.
SEASON OF MAXIMUM COLOR: Warm months.
LANDSCAPE USES: For enclosing barriers, set 5′ o.c.; used as a freestand-
   ing specimen, too. This is one of central Florida's most popular large
   flowering shrubs. Rainbow calliandra is similar, but the new growth is
   mottled with gold.
HABITAT: Brazil; in Florida, central and southern areas, on sandy soil.
LIGHT REQUIREMENT: Full sun for best flowering.
SOIL REQUIREMENT: Tolerant of varying types of sandy soil.
SALT TOLERANCE: Not tolerant.
AVAILABILITY: Small plants can be had at most nurseries in central and
   southern Florida.
CULTURE: After establishment with the aid of adequate water, no par-
   ticular attention is needed other than regular pruning to keep the
   plant within bounds.
PROPAGATION: Marcottage or cuttage, using hardwood cuttings under
   mist.
PESTS: Caterpillars, mites, and thorn bugs.
NOTE: There are other calliandras, but these are usually less striking
   garden shrubs. Possibly selective breeding would bring to Florida
   gardens new powderpuffs of merit.

196
Redbud

Cercis (SIR-sis): ancient Greek name.
canadensis (can-a-DEN-sis): Canadian.

FAMILY: Leguminosae.   RELATIVES: Orchid-tree and Jerusalem-thorn.
TYPE OF PLANT: Tree.   HEIGHT: 40'. ZONE: N,C
HOW TO IDENTIFY: Alternate, heart-shaped, deciduous leaves that are
    palmately veined; buds ovoid; pink, pea-like blossoms in very early
    springtime.
HABIT OF GROWTH: Spreading, broad, irregular head atop a branched or
    bending bole.
FOLIAGE: Deciduous, coarse in texture, medium green in color; fall color,
    brown.
FLOWERS: Rosy-pink, ½" long, pea-like, in very early spring before the
    leaves.
FRUITS: Linear pods, 3½" long, acute at each end, brown and ugly.
SEASON OF MAXIMUM COLOR: January–February.
LANDSCAPE USES: As a street tree (plant 25'–35' apart), as a framing tree
    for small houses, as a shading device for terraces, as a part of an
    informal shrubbery border, redbud excels. A white-flowered form is
    occasionally seen.
HABITAT: Rich hammock areas of northern Florida.
LIGHT REQUIREMENT: Native to shaded hammocks.
SOIL REQUIREMENT: Rich, well-drained, acid soils, high in organic matter.
SALT TOLERANCE: Not tolerant.
AVAILABILITY: Nurseries in northern counties sell redbud trees.
CULTURE: Plant in fertile soil that is well drained; wrap the trunk as
    protection against borers; water faithfully; place a mulch over the root
    zone; fertilize twice a year.
PROPAGATION: Graftage, using redbud seedlings as stocks.
PESTS: Borers, aphids followed by sooty-mold, and root-rot disease.
NOTE: Chinese redbud (*Cercis chinensis*) has flowers that are larger and
    deeper in tone than those of the native species.

197
Barbados Flower-Fence

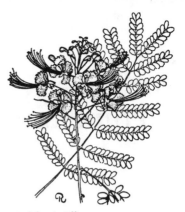

Poinciana (poin-see-AN-a): for M. de Poinci, a governor of the Antilles.
pulcherrima (pull-KARE-ee-ma): very handsome.

FAMILY: Leguminosae.   RELATIVES: Tamarind, cassia, bean, and pea.
TYPE OF PLANT: Shrub.   HEIGHT: 15'. ZONE: S
HOW TO IDENTIFY: Prickly branches bear fine, feathery foliage and
   brilliant scarlet and yellow flowers in erect clusters.
HABIT OF GROWTH: Ungainly, open-branched.
FOLIAGE: Evergreen, compound, very fine in texture, light green in color.
FLOWERS: Scarlet and yellow in erect, showy clusters.
FRUITS: Pods ¾" wide × 4" long; become unsightly when brown.
SEASON OF MAXIMUM COLOR: Much of the warm season.
LANDSCAPE USES: As a bright, informal division hedge, set plants 2' o.c.
   As an accent in front of green shrubbery, this bright legume serves,
   too.
      Barbados flower-fence is very popular in hot countries the world
   around, widely planted in extreme southern Florida.
      Sometimes this poinciana is grown as an annual or as a tender
   herbaceous perennial in sections where frost occurs regularly. The
   roots are quite tender, enduring but a few degrees below freezing for
   a very short period at best.
      Variety 'Flava' has yellow flowers.
HABITAT: Distribution general throughout the tropics.
LIGHT REQUIREMENT: Full sun for best flowering; tolerates some shade.
SOIL REQUIREMENT: Tolerant of varying soils in hot countries.
SALT TOLERANCE: Endures salt drift at some distance from the sea.
AVAILABILITY: Nurseries in southern Florida stock small plants in con-
   tainers.
CULTURE: No special care after new plants become established.
PROPAGATION: Seedage.
PESTS: Scales, nematodes, and mushroom root-rot.

198
Paradise Poinciana

Poinciana (poin-see-AN-a): for M. de Poinci, a governor of the Antilles.
gilliesii (GILL-eze-ee-eye): for G. Gillies, Scottish traveler in South America.

FAMILY: Leguminosae.   RELATIVES: Royal poinciana and cassia.
TYPE OF PLANT: Shrub.
HEIGHT: 10'. ZONE: S
HOW TO IDENTIFY: Scraggly, open shrub with spineless branches that bear feathery foliage with black dots on the undersides of the leaflets. Showy, yellow flowers with brilliant red stamens are in evidence during warm weather.
HABIT OF GROWTH: Scraggly, open.
FOLIAGE: Evergreen, compound, of finest texture and light green color.
FLOWERS: Flamboyant yellow, with contrasting red stamens.
FRUITS: Pods ¾" wide by 4" long, pea-like, brown, and ugly.
SEASON OF MAXIMUM COLOR: Warm months when blossoms appear.
LANDSCAPE USES: As a bright, informal division hedge, set plants 2' o.c. For accent in front of dark green shrubbery use a group of 3 paradise poincianas set on 3' centers.

This poinciana is considered one of the choice shrubs of the tropics, and, like the preceding species it is very tender to cold. The roots will not endure conditions in northern Florida, usually.
HABITAT: Tropical America; in Florida, widely cultured in protected areas.
LIGHT REQUIREMENT: Full sun for best flowering and habit.
SOIL REQUIREMENT: Tolerant of many types.
SALT TOLERANCE: Not tolerant.
AVAILABILITY: Paradise poinciana, under several different names, is widely available in nurseries in southern Florida.
CULTURE: Plant in a reasonably fertile spot; water until well established, then during periods of drought; fertilize three times each year; keep lawn grasses back from the roots.
PROPAGATION: Seedage.
PESTS: Scales, mites, nematodes, and mushroom root-rot.

199
Royal Poinciana

Delonix (de-LON-icks): Greek, referring to the long-clawed petals.
regia (REE-gee-a): royal.

FAMILY: Leguminosae.
RELATIVES: Tamarind and mimosa-tree.
TYPE OF PLANT: Tree.
HEIGHT: 40'. ZONE: S
HOW TO IDENTIFY: Brown pods, 2' long, hang like razor strops; partially or wholly deciduous, compound foliage, and striking scarlet blossoms in early summer facilitate identification of this glory of the tropics.
HABIT OF GROWTH: Wide-spreading branches form a domed top above a stout trunk.
FOLIAGE: Deciduous, compound, fine in texture, medium green in color.
FLOWERS: Striking blossoms in tones of red, 4" across, with 1 striped petal.
FRUITS: Dark brown pods, 2' long x 2" wide, resembling razor strops.
SEASON OF MAXIMUM COLOR: Early summer.
LANDSCAPE USES: As a freestanding specimen, as a shade tree, framing tree, or avenue tree, royal poinciana is world famous because of its riotous summer color. This flamboyant (as it is often called in the tropics), the world's most colorful tree, is greatly admired in hot countries. Color varies slightly in individuals, but all are tender to cold.
HABITAT: Madagascar; in Florida, featured where frosts seldom occur.
LIGHT REQUIREMENT: Full sun for best habit and flowering.
SOIL REQUIREMENT: Tolerant of a wide range of soils.
SALT TOLERANCE: Tolerant of salt air at some distance from the strand.
AVAILABILITY: Nurseries in southern Florida have royal poinciana trees in containers.
CULTURE: Once it becomes established in nearly frostless districts, one annual fertilization and watering during dry times should keep the plant healthy and growing. Protection must be given on cold nights.
PROPAGATION: Seedage.
PESTS: None of major concern.

Sissoo

Dalbergia (dal-BURG-ee-a): for N. Dalberg, a Swedish botanist.
sissoo (SIS-oo): Indian name.

FAMILY: Leguminosae. RELATIVES: Redbud and mimosa-tree.
TYPE OF PLANT: Tree. HEIGHT: 45'. ZONE: C,S
HOW TO IDENTIFY: This shapely tree holds semi-evergreen, or deciduous, pinnate leaves of 3–5 roundish leaflets alternately arranged on a zig-zag rachis. Inconspicuous blossoms are followed by slender brown pods about 4″ long.
HABIT OF GROWTH: Spreading branches form a compact, symmetrical head.
FOLIAGE: Semi-evergreen or deciduous, compound, of medium texture and light green color.
FLOWERS: White, fragrant, inconspicuous, in very short, axillary panicles.
FRUITS: Slender, flat, brown pods, 4″ long, are 1- or 2-seeded in Florida.
SEASON OF MAXIMUM COLOR: Best color is summer green.
LANDSCAPE USES: As a framing tree, as a freestanding specimen, perhaps as an avenue tree, sissoo can be indicated for central and southern Florida. In Lake, Pinellas, and Lee counties, it thrives, and in several restricted areas it has escaped from cultivation. In northern counties sissoo is defoliated by frost, killed by below-freezing temperatures.
HABITAT: India; in Florida, sparingly cultured as a dooryard or campus tree.
LIGHT REQUIREMENT: Full sun, or broken, shifting high shade.
SOIL REQUIREMENT: Tolerant of widely varying soils, enduring both drought and inundation.
SALT TOLERANCE: Not tolerant.
AVAILABILITY: Rarely will sissoo trees be found in nurseries.
CULTURE: Plant in nearly frostless site with reasonable care; water until well established; thereafter, no attention will be needed.
PROPAGATION: Seedage.
PESTS: None of major concern.

201
Sweet Acacia

Acacia (a-KAY-see-a): Greek for point.
farnesiana (far-nes-ee-ANA): for Mr. Farnes.

FAMILY: Leguminosae.   RELATIVES: Poinciana and bauhinia.
TYPE OF PLANT: Shrub or small tree.   HEIGHT: 10'. ZONE: N,C,S
HOW TO IDENTIFY: A thorny, much-branched shrub with bipinnate
  leaves, borne on small, spur-like branches subtended by two spines;
  twigs chocolate-brown and slightly rough. Yellow, very fragrant
  flowers are borne in dense axillary clusters ¼"–½" across. Flowers
  appear after each new flush of growth.
HABIT OF GROWTH: Open shrub.
FOLIAGE: The bipinnate leaves have very small, soft, medium green
  pinnae.
FLOWERS: Small, yellow, puff-ball-like clusters, with delightful
  fragrance.
FRUITS: Brown pods, often borne in clusters of 3 to 5.
SEASON OF MAXIMUM COLOR: All year.
LANDSCAPE USES: Excellent barrier shrub. Can be trained as a small tree
  and used as a freestanding specimen.
HABITAT: Widespread; nativity uncertain; found in North America,
  Asia, and Australia.
LIGHT REQUIREMENT: Full sun.
SOIL REQUIREMENT: Most well-drained soils.
SALT TOLERANCE: Endures salt air back from the strand.
AVAILABILITY: Available in cans in many nurseries.
CULTURE: Easy to grow, but will defoliate if soil is allowed to dry ex-
  cessively.
PROPAGATION: Seedage or cuttage.
PESTS: None serious.
NOTE: This plant is cultivated in the south of France for its flowers
  which are made into a very fine perfume.

Tamarind

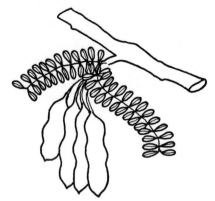

Tamarindus (tam-are-IND-us): from the Arabic.
indica (IN-dee-ca): Indian.

FAMILY: Leguminosae.   RELATIVES: Cassia and Jerusalem-thorn.

TYPE OF PLANT: Tree.   HEIGHT: 65'. ZONE: S

HOW TO IDENTIFY: A large tree that bears evergreen, compound leaves of light green color and plump pods of cinnamon-brown.

HABIT OF GROWTH: Upright tree that develops an enormous domed crown at maturity.

FOLIAGE: Evergreen, compound, very fine in texture, yellowish-green in color.

FLOWERS: Pale yellow, about 1″ in length, held in lax racemes.

FRUITS: Plump, cinnamon-brown pods 3″–8″ long with a thin, brittle shell which encloses a thin, acid pulp.

SEASON OF MAXIMUM COLOR: No seasonal variation.

LANDSCAPE USES: As a single, freestanding specimen for large properties, tamarind might be planted for light shade and for the curiosity of the edible pulp produced around the seeds. While some persons do not relish the pulp out of hand, many esteem it as an ingredient in steak sauces. Tamarind trees will be killed by freezing temperatures.

HABITAT: East Indian islands; in Florida, planted in warmest locations.

LIGHT REQUIREMENT: Full sun for best habit and fruiting.

SOIL REQUIREMENT: Sandy soils are acceptable.

SALT TOLERANCE: Endures salt drift back some distance from the strand.

AVAILABILITY: Specialty nurseries in southern Florida have small trees in containers.

CULTURE: After a tamarind tree becomes established in fertile, sandy soil, no further attention is needed save for the usual applications of fertilizer.

PROPAGATION: Seedage.

PESTS: None of major concern.

203
Wisteria

Wisteria (wis-TEE-ree-a): for C. Wistar, an American professor.
sinensis (sin-EN-sis): Chinese.

FAMILY: Leguminosae.   RELATIVES: Mimosa-tree and royal poinciana.
TYPE OF PLANT: Twining vine.   HEIGHT: Variable. ZONE: N,C
HOW TO IDENTIFY: Rampant vine of twining habit that bears deciduous, compound leaves that have horn-like stipules at the bases of the petioles; showy racemes of blue or white, pea-like blossoms in springtime.
HABIT OF GROWTH: Vigorous twining vine that grows to great heights.
FOLIAGE: Deciduous, compound, lacy in texture, medium green in color.
FLOWERS: Blue or white, pea-like, in drooping racemes before the leaves.
FRUITS: Conspicuous, velvety pods about 6″ long.
SEASON OF MAXIMUM COLOR: Early spring.
LANDSCAPE USES: To cover a pergola or fence, wisteria has always been a favorite in northern Florida. Plants may be trained to tree form by fastening to a vertical pipe until a trunk is developed. With this method, continual pinching is required to head in the rank shoots.
HABITAT: China; in Florida, often seen in the northern part.
LIGHT REQUIREMENT: Broken shade of woodlands is ideal.
SOIL REQUIREMENT: Tolerant of many soils.
SALT TOLERANCE: Not tolerant.
AVAILABILITY: Wisteria is ordinarily not a nursery item, but layers are usually given away by gardeners who have old, established vines.
CULTURE: Simply plant, water, and forget.
PROPAGATION: Simple layerage where stems touch the earth.
PESTS: Thrips and pecan twig girdler.
NOTE: White wisteria (*Wisteria sinensis* 'Alba') is an interesting change from the usual blue-flowered type. It is especially useful when trained to tree form in a naturalistic planting of colored azaleas. Reflected in water, white wisteria trees are very pleasing. The Japanese wisterias and the native American species are not widely cultured in Florida gardens.

204
Yellow-Poinciana

Peltophorum (pel-TOF-o-rum): having a shield.
inerme (in-ER-me): without armature.

FAMILY: Leguminosae.   RELATIVES: Royal poinciana and mimosa-tree.

TYPE OF PLANT: Tree.   HEIGHT: 50′. ZONE: C,S

HOW TO IDENTIFY: Rapidly growing, stately, heavily foliaged tree, very ornamental; bark smooth, grey, pubescent when young, leaves compound; flowers borne on large erect panicles. Entire canopy covered with blooms at flowering.

HABIT OF GROWTH: Upright habit, usually higher than wide.

FOLIAGE: Medium-fine texture, dark green; each leaf may contain up to 200 leaflets, usually 8 to 10 pinnae, with 10 to 20 pairs of leaflets per pinna.

FLOWERS: Small, yellow, to 1″, borne in massive numbers.

FRUITS: Dark, wine-red pods, flat and winged, to 4″ long.

SEASON OF MAXIMUM COLOR: May to September.

LANDSCAPE USES: Excellent street tree; freestanding specimen.

HABITAT: Malaya to Australia.

LIGHT REQUIREMENT: Full sun.

SOIL REQUIREMENT: Most well-drained soils.

SALT TOLERANCE: Usually planted behind front-line dunes.

AVAILABILITY: Often sold by common name in nurseries in southern Florida.

CULTURE: Under normal conditions *Peltophorum* grows with minimal care.

PROPAGATION: Seedage or cuttage.

PESTS: None serious.

205
Womans-Tongue-Tree

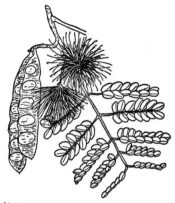

Albizia (al-BIZ-ee-a): for Sr. Albizzi, an Italian naturalist.
lebbeck (LEB-beck): an Arabic name.

FAMILY: Leguminosae.   RELATIVES: Powderpuff and royal poinciana.
TYPE OF PLANT: Tree.   HEIGHT: 50′. ZONE: C,S
HOW TO IDENTIFY: A fast-growing, coarse tree that bears deciduous, pinnately compound foliage, globular, greenish-yellow flowers, and foot-long, brown pods that hang for months.
HABIT OF GROWTH: Horizontal branching from a sturdy trunk.
FOLIAGE: Deciduous, fine in texture, light green in color, fall color yellow.
FLOWERS: Globular heads of greenish-yellow tones.
FRUITS: Foot-long pods, 1½″ wide, that contain many seeds that rattle in the breeze.
SEASON OF MAXIMUM COLOR: Spring.
LANDSCAPE USES: Where a specimen tree is needed in a very short time, womans-tongue-tree can be planted as a single specimen. It attains great size very rapidly, branches break in strong winds, the rattling pods are very annoying, and volunteer seedlings appear in great numbers. This tree is not recommended for home landscaping.
HABITAT: Tropical Asia; naturalized in warm parts of the Western Hemisphere.
LIGHT REQUIREMENT: Full sun.
SOIL REQUIREMENT: Widely tolerant.
SALT TOLERANCE: Somewhat salt tolerant, but not for dune planting.
AVAILABILITY: Nurseries in warmer parts stock womans-tongue-trees in containers.
CULTURE: Simply plant, water, and forget.
PROPAGATION: Seedage.
PESTS: Scales, mites, and mushroom root-rot.

Mimosa-Tree

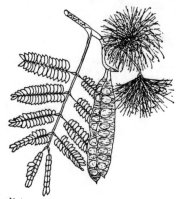

Albizia (al-BIZ-ee-a): for Sr. Albizzi, an Italian naturalist.
julibrissin (jew-lee-BRIS-in): Persian name.

FAMILY: Leguminosae.   RELATIVES: Powderpuff, cassia, and bean.
TYPE OF PLANT: Tree.   HEIGHT: 40′. ZONE: N,C
HOW TO IDENTIFY: This tree has horizontal branching, which makes it
    broader than tall, usually; deciduous, bipinnate foliage; pinkish
    pompons in May; unsightly brown pods thereafter.
HABIT OF GROWTH: Horizontal, bending branches from short, leaning
    trunks.
FOLIAGE: Deciduous, bipinnate, very fine in texture, light green in color.
FLOWERS: Globular heads in shades of pink.
FRUITS: Untidy brown pods that are produced in great numbers.
SEASON OF MAXIMUM COLOR: May, when pompons appear.
LANDSCAPE USES: As a freestanding specimen and as a background tree,
    this well-adapted legume is extremely popular and highly recom-
    mended. As a terrace tree, it is good because the leaves fall to let the
    sun shine through all winter. Most admired are types that produce
    pompons of deep pink tones.
HABITAT: Old World; in Florida, very widely planted in central and
    northern parts.
LIGHT REQUIREMENT: Full sun for best flowering.
SOIL REQUIREMENT: Tolerant of many soils.
SALT TOLERANCE: Tolerant of conditions back of the front-line dunes.
AVAILABILITY: Mimosa-tree seedlings in containers are staple items in
    retail nurseries, but wilt-resistant, cutting-grown individuals are
    preferred.
CULTURE: Under normal, back-yard conditions, mimosa-trees grow
    without attention, though they may be short lived because of the
    prevalence of mimosa wilt.
PROPAGATION: Seedage; wilt-resistant types by cuttage.
PESTS: Mimosa wilt, cottony cushion scale, and mites.
NOTE: Wilt-resistant mimosa-trees, increased by root cuttings, are
    available in a few places.

207
Carambola

Averrhoa (av-er-OH-a): for Averrhoes, an Arabian physician.
carambola (care-am-BOWL-a): vernacular name.

FAMILY: Oxalidaceae.   RELATIVES: Oxalis and nasturtium.

TYPE OF PLANT: Tree.   HEIGHT: 30′. ZONE: S

HOW TO IDENTIFY: Compound, evergreen leaves, with 5–11 leaflets; waxy, 5-ribbed, fleshy fruits, 5″ long, that are very decorative as well as edible out of hand or in preserves.

HABIT OF GROWTH: Upright tree with dense, symmetrical head.

FOLIAGE: Evergreen, compound, of medium texture and dark green color.

FLOWERS: Inconspicuous, white, marked purple, fragrant, in leaf axils.

FRUITS: Fleshy, 5-ribbed, yellow to yellow-brown, 5″ long.

SEASON OF MAXIMUM COLOR: Midsummer when fruits are mature.

LANDSCAPE USES: As a single shade tree for extreme southern Florida, the carambola is popular. The delicious, highly decorative fruits are extra dividends. Related bilimbi (*A. bilimbi*) will grow in southern Florida, is much less frequently seen there.

    Carambola trees usually are very densely foliated when they are well fertilized, so that it is impossible to grow grass beneath them. Possibly a good position in the landscape plan would be near the parking apron. Carambola fruits vary greatly in size, shape, color, and flavor, some being excessively acid, others quite delicious. Usually trees are grown from seeds and named varieties selected for flavor and size are not available.

HABITAT: Malaya; in Florida, most nearly frost-free locations.

LIGHT REQUIREMENT: Full sun or broken shade of hammocks.

SOIL REQUIREMENT: Tolerant of widely varying soils.

SALT TOLERANCE: Not tolerant.

AVAILABILITY: Carambolas are offered by nurseries in southern Florida.

CULTURE: Plant in a carefully prepared site; water periodically; fertilize 2 or 3 times each year for best foliage color and maximum fruit production.

PROPAGATION: Seedage; graftage for superior types.

PESTS: Caterpillars, mites, and scales.

Boxthorn

Severinia (sev-er-IN-ee-a): for M. Severino, an Italian botanist.
buxifolia (bucks-i-FOL-ee-a): box-leaved.

FAMILY: Rutaceae.   RELATIVES: Orange, kumquat, and orange-jasmine.
TYPE OF PLANT: Dwarf shrub.   HEIGHT: 6'. ZONE: C,S
HOW TO IDENTIFY: A dwarf shrub with thorny branches that hold simple,
   oblong, evergreen leaves in alternate arrangement; white, orange-like
   blossoms; shining black fruits.
HABIT OF GROWTH: Very dense and compact, often with pendulous
   branches.
FOLIAGE: Evergreen, alternate, of fine texture and dark green color.
FLOWERS: White, small, orange-like, solitary or in small clusters in axils.
FRUITS: Globular, black berries ⅛" in diameter.
SEASON OF MAXIMUM COLOR: Cool months when fruits are colored.
LANDSCAPE USES: As a sheared hedge, plant 2' o.c.; as a foundation plant,
   use the same interval; as a transition plant for tall, leggy shrubs, set 3'
   apart. Boxthorn is one of the very best dwarf landscape shrubs for
   areas that are not subjected to hard freezes.
HABITAT: Southern China; in Florida, much planted as a garden hedge.
LIGHT REQUIREMENT: Full sun for compact habit, but shade is tolerated.
SOIL REQUIREMENT: Tolerant of most well-drained soils.
SALT TOLERANCE: Not tolerant.
AVAILABILITY: Seedlings in containers are displayed by most nurseries
   on the peninsula.
CULTURE: Plant in enriched holes; water until well established;
   thereafter prune annually; fertilize semi-annually; protect the foliage
   against scale insects.
PROPAGATION: Seedage; selected forms by cuttage.
PESTS: Scales, white-flies, sooty-mold, thrips, mites, and nematodes.
NOTE: Spineless forms have been selected and increased vegetatively,
   but these are not yet widely available.

209
Citrus
Trees

Citrus (sit-russ): ancient classical name.
Fortunella (for-tune-ell-a): for R. Fortune, English traveler.
spp.: several species and many hybrids are widely grown in Florida.

FAMILY: Rutaceae.　　　　RELATIVES: Orange-jasmine and lime-berry.
TYPE OF PLANT: Tree or shrub.　　　HEIGHT: Variable. ZONE: N,C,S
HOW TO IDENTIFY: Evergreen, spiny trees produce yellow, orange, or red
    fruits, many of which are deliciously edible.
HABIT OF GROWTH: Generally dense, much-branched, round-headed
    trees or large shrubs.
FOLIAGE: Evergreen, alternate, variable in size, texture, form, and color;
    aromatic when crushed.
FLOWERS: White, very fragrant, most abundant in springtime.
FRUITS: Yellow, orange, or reddish hesperidiums, among the world's
    most delectable fruits.
SEASON OF MAXIMUM COLOR: Wintertime when fruits color.
LANDSCAPE USES: Plants of the citrus tribe are widely used in landscape
    developments. For shade, framing, backgrounds, hedging, and hor-
    ticultural interest, these beautiful plants excel. No fruits are more
    delicious, no blossoms more fragrant, no trees more beautiful than
    those of the citrus group. This is a very diverse group in which may be
    found kinds for many garden uses.
HABITAT: Eastern Asia; in Florida, much of the peninsula.
LIGHT REQUIREMENT: Full sun for best fruiting.
SOIL REQUIREMENT: Moderately fertile, well-drained soil that can be
    watered during periods of drought is best.
SALT TOLERANCE: Not tolerant.
AVAILABILITY: Trees of many named varieties are offered in containers
    in nurseries, garden centers, and chain stores.
CULTURE: Set carefully in made-up, fertile sites; water faithfully; prevent
    lawn grasses from invading the root zone; protect from pests; fertilize
    thrice annually.
PROPAGATION: Graftage and marcottage.
PESTS: Nematodes, scales, mites, caterpillars, virus, and fungus diseases.

210
Lime-Berry

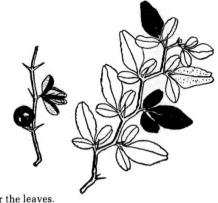

Triphasia (try-FASE-ee-a): Greek, triplex for the leaves.
trifolia (try-FO-lee-a): with three leaf(lets).

FAMILY: Rutaceae.   RELATIVES: Orange-jasmine, orange, and kumquat.
TYPE OF PLANT: Dwarf shrub.   HEIGHT: 6'. ZONE: S
HOW TO IDENTIFY: A shrub, usually low growing, of weeping habit, with
   thorny branches that bear alternate, 3-foliate, evergreen leaves; little,
   white, fragrant flowers which are followed by red berries.
HABIT OF GROWTH: Dense, graceful, compact, weeping.
FOLIAGE: Evergreen, trifoliate, fine in texture, dark green in color.
FLOWERS: White, fragrant, ¾" in diameter, solitary or several in axils.
FRUITS: Red berries, ½" in diameter, decorative; sometimes used in
   jelly-making.
SEASON OF MAXIMUM COLOR: During warm months when flowers or
   fruits are mature.
LANDSCAPE USES: Lime-berry is one of southern Florida's very best
   landscape shrubs. In foundation plantings, set 18" o.c.; for planters or
   for low hedges, use the same interval.
      For use with diminutive structures lime-berry excels because of its
   fine texture, procumbent habit, and pleasing dark green color. The
   white flowers are pleasant accents and the bright red fruits are
   worthwhile highlights. As noted below, nematodes are troublesome
   pests and planting in sterilized soil is recommended most empha-
   tically.
HABITAT: Malaya; in Florida, landscape plantings in most nearly
   frostless areas.
LIGHT REQUIREMENT: Sun or shade.
SOIL REQUIREMENT: Tolerant of varying soils, but very subject to attack
   by nematodes.
SALT TOLERANCE: Not tolerant.
AVAILABILITY: Lime-berry plants are offered in containers of sterilized
   soil by nurseries in southern Florida.
CULTURE: The soil should be enriched and sterilized before planting.
   Water faithfully until well established; place mulch over roots; fer-
   tilize 3 times each year.
PROPAGATION: Seedage or cuttage.
PESTS: Scales, nematodes, white-flies, and sooty-mold.

211
Orange-Jasmine

Murraya (MUR-ay-a): for J. Murray, a botanist of the eighteenth century.
paniculata (pan-ick-you-LATE-a): with flowers in a loose pyramid.

FAMILY: Rutaceae.   RELATIVES: Citrus, boxthorn, and lime-berry.
TYPE OF PLANT: Shrub or small tree.   HEIGHT: 20'. ZONE: C,S
HOW TO IDENTIFY: Attractive, compound, evergreen leaves that are made
   up of pear-shaped or rhombic leaflets; fragrant, white, orange-like
   blossoms which are followed by bright, decorative, red fruits.
HABIT OF GROWTH: Slender, upright, yet with dense head.
FOLIAGE: Compound, evergreen, of fine texture and dark green color.
FLOWERS: White, fragrant, citrus-like, ¾" long, with pointed petals.
FRUITS: Very attractive, pointed, red, ovoid berries, about ½" in length.
SEASON OF MAXIMUM COLOR: Much of the year as flowers or fruits
   mature.
LANDSCAPE USES: One of the tropic's most popular hedge plants comes
   into its own in southern Florida. Set plants 18" o.c. In foundation
   arrangements, allow 2'–3' between individuals, and if orange-jasmine
   is used as informal enclosure, employ a 5' interval. Grown to a single
   trunk, orange-jasmine can make an excellent small terrace or patio
   tree.
      Now, in Florida, there are clonal selections, propagated vegeta-
   tively and sold under name, that are most highly recommended for
   landscaping here.
HABITAT: Tropical Asia; in Florida, landscape plantings in warm locations.
LIGHT REQUIREMENT: Tolerant of moderate shade, but grows well in full
   sun, too.
SOIL REQUIREMENT: Moderately fertile, well-drained earth that is free of
   nematodes.
SALT TOLERANCE: Not tolerant of dune conditions.
AVAILABILITY: Most nurseries in warm locations sell small plants in
   containers. Named clones may be found in some establishments.
CULTURE: Like all members of the citrus family, orange-jasmine must be
   protected against scale insects and nematodes.
PROPAGATION: Seedage or cuttage.
PESTS: Scales, nematodes, and white-flies, followed by sooty-mold.

212
Gumbo-Limbo

Bursera (burr-SER-a): for J. Burser, a European botanist.
simaruba (sim-a-RUBE-a): because of similarity to a tree in the genus *Simarouba*.

FAMILY: Burseraceae.   RELATIVES: This is the only genus in the family.
TYPE OF PLANT: Tree.   HEIGHT: 60′. ZONE: S
HOW TO IDENTIFY: Shining, oily-smooth, brown bark which looks as
   though it had been freshly varnished; the compound leaves are
   deciduous, and mature trees bear angled pods.
HABIT OF GROWTH: Asymmetric, picturesque, with a few huge branches.
FOLIAGE: Deciduous, pinnate, of medium-fine texture and dark green
   color.
FLOWERS: Inconspicuous, greenish, before or with the first leaves in late
   winter.
FRUITS: Three-parted pods, ½″ long, dark red, ripening in summertime.
SEASON OF MAXIMUM COLOR: Possibly when fruits mature.
LANDSCAPE USES: For the curiosity of the distinctive, light-brown,
   peeling bark, gumbo-limbo may be used as a freestanding specimen,
   or as an avenue tree. Nothing quite like this native tree is to be found
   in Florida's plant life; growth is rapid, yet there is marked resistance
   to strong winds, drought, and neglect.
      In tropical lands huge truncheons are driven into the earth close
   together to make living fences; as the gumbo-limbo trees grow, they
   are decapitated with machetes for firewood.
HABITAT: Southern Florida and the offshore islands.
LIGHT REQUIREMENT: Full sun or high, shifting shade.
SOIL REQUIREMENT: Tolerant of many soils, including basic ones.
SALT TOLERANCE: Tolerant of salt drift back from the shore.
AVAILABILITY: Nurseries in southern Florida offer small trees in con-
   tainers.
CULTURE: Once established in a frostless location, little attention need be
   given.
PROPAGATION: Cuttage, using wood of any size.
PESTS: Caterpillars chew the leaves.

213
China-Berry

Melia (ME-lee-a): ancient Greek name.
azedarach (a-ZED-ar-ack): from the Arabic for noble.

FAMILY: Meliaceae.   RELATIVES: Mahogany and Spanish-cedar.
TYPE OF PLANT: Tree.   HEIGHT: 40'. ZONE: N,C,S

HOW TO IDENTIFY: Lacy, bipinnate, deciduous foliage with a characteristic odor; attractive blue blossoms in summertime, followed by sticky, yellow fruits.

HABIT OF GROWTH: Seedlings grow rangy and open; clones have tight, compact heads.

FOLIAGE: Deciduous, bipinnate, fine in texture, and dark green in color.

FLOWERS: Attractive, fragrant, blue flowers are produced in 8" panicles in summer.

FRUITS: Yellow, sticky drupes, ¾" in diameter, smooth and round at first, becoming wrinkled late in the season. These are toxic to humans.

SEASON OF MAXIMUM COLOR: Summer.

LANDSCAPE USES: Since the arrival of the white man, China-berry trees have been used in Florida to furnish shade, and while they helped to make life more comfortable for the pioneers, these fast-growing, weak trees are not in good repute today.

Texas umbrella-tree, known as the variety 'Umbraculiformis', grows with a straight trunk and many, short, straight branches to give the effect of a giant umbrella. This one must be grown vegetatively.

HABITAT: Southwestern Asia; in Florida, ubiquitous.

LIGHT REQUIREMENT: Full sun or shade of hammocks.

SOIL REQUIREMENT: Any soil appears to be suitable.

SALT TOLERANCE: Not tolerant.

AVAILABILITY: Usually seedlings or cuttings are given away.

CULTURE: Once planted, soon forgotten, China-berry takes care of itself.

PROPAGATION: Seedage or cuttage.

PESTS: White-flies followed by sooty-mold.

214
Mahogany

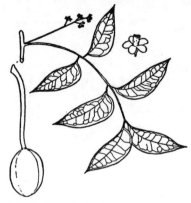

Swietenia (sweet-TEEN-ee-a): for G. von Swieten of the eighteenth century.
mahogani (ma-HOG-an-eye): an aboriginal American name.

FAMILY: Meliaceae. RELATIVES: China-berry and Spanish-cedar.
TYPE OF PLANT: Tree. HEIGHT: 40′. ZONE: S
HOW TO IDENTIFY: Large, high-headed tree bears even-pinnate, deciduous leaves with petioled leaflets; conspicuous brown pods 5″ long hang from cords in wintertime.
HABIT OF GROWTH: Upright tree with broad, rounded, symmetrical crown.
FOLIAGE: Deciduous, compound, of medium texture and medium green color.
FLOWERS: Inconspicuous, greenish, on stalks in axils of current growth.
FRUITS: Ovoid, brown capsules about 5″ long that hang downward from cords.
SEASON OF MAXIMUM COLOR: Possibly when new growth first emerges.
LANDSCAPE USES: As a street tree, 25′–35′ apart, mahogany is in high favor in warm parts. As a framing tree, it serves, too, because it does not cast heavy shade to discourage the growth of grasses beneath, and, furthermore, it is notably storm-fast. Here is another native plant that is good for landscaping in Florida, and many thousands will be needed in future landscape developments.
HABITAT: Native in parts of Dade and Monroe counties; cultured in warm areas of the peninsula.
LIGHT REQUIREMENT: Full sun or partial shade.
SOIL REQUIREMENT: Tolerant of many soils, acid or alkaline.
SALT TOLERANCE: Quite tolerant of salt drift.
AVAILABILITY: Small mahogany trees in containers are in nurseries in southern Florida.
CULTURE: Plant with reasonable care in frost-free locations; water periodically; fertilize twice during each growing season.
PROPAGATION: Seedage.
PESTS: Tent caterpillars must be controlled.

215
Brazilian Golden-Vine

Stigmaphyllon (stig-ma-FILL-on): Greek for stigma and leaf.
littorale (lit-tor-AL-ee): pertaining to the seashore.

FAMILY: Malpighiaceae.   RELATIVES: Thryallis and holly malpighia.

TYPE OF PLANT: Entwining, woody vine.   HEIGHT: Variable. ZONE: C,S

HOW TO IDENTIFY: Robust, tuberous-rooted vine, with brown, entwining stems, leaves opposite, simple, entire; yellow flowers borne in umbel-like heads in leaf axils.

HABIT OF GROWTH: Plants grow upward as branches twine about supports.

FOLIAGE: Simple, entire, dark green leaves, to 5″ long, medium texture; leaves and petioles may be rough to touch.

FLOWERS: Yellow, to ¾″ wide, in small clusters.

FRUITS: Samara, 1 to 3.

SEASON OF MAXIMUM COLOR: Summertime.

LANDSCAPE USES: Golden-vine is widely used as a screening vine on patios and trellises; useful on pergolas.

HABITAT: Brazil.

LIGHT REQUIREMENT: Grows best in full sun to partial shade.

SOIL REQUIREMENT: Most well-drained Florida soils suffice.

SALT TOLERANCE: Normally not planted near front line.

AVAILABILITY: Available from some nurseries in Florida.

CULTURE: Requires little care once established.

PROPAGATION: Seedage or cuttage.

PESTS: None of major concern.

216
Barbados-Cherry

Malpighia (mal-PIG-ee-a): for M. Malphigi, Italian naturalist.
glabra (GLAY-bra): not hairy.

FAMILY: Malpighiaceae.   RELATIVES: Holly malpighia and thryallis.

TYPE OF PLANT: Evergreen shrub.   HEIGHT: 10′. ZONE: C,S

HOW TO IDENTIFY: Opposite-leaved shrub, usually taller than broad. Leaves simple, entire, ovate to lanceolate, up to 3″ long. Flowers borne in clusters of 3 to 8 at branch tips and leaf axils, followed by edible fruit.

HABIT OF GROWTH: Upright habit of growth due to the ascending branches.

FOLIAGE: Opposite, evergreen, fine texture, medium green.

FLOWERS: Insignificant, rose, 3–8 per umbrel, ½″ across.

FRUITS: Red, edible drupes, acid to the taste.

SEASON OF MAXIMUM COLOR: Flowers and fruits throughout the year.

LANDSCAPE USE: For foundation plantings of larger buildings or in the shrubbery border. Often grown for its edible fruit.

HABITAT: Southern Texas to American tropics.

LIGHT REQUIREMENT: Full sun to partial shade.

SOIL REQUIREMENT: A fertile, nematode-free soil is recommended.

SALT TOLERANCE: Not tolerant of dune conditions.

AVAILABILITY: Available in many southern Florida nurseries.

CULTURE: Best if planted in frost-free areas, in nematode-free soil. Requires about two fertilizations per year.

PROPAGATION: Produced readily from seeds or by cuttage.

PESTS: Nematodes, scales, and mites.

NOTE: Vitamin C content of fruit is very high.

217
Holly
Malpighia

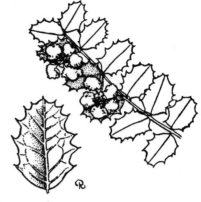

Malpighia (mal-PIG-ee-a): for M. Malpighi, Italian naturalist.
coccigera (cok-SIG-er-a): berry-bearing.

FAMILY: Malpighiaceae.   RELATIVES: Thryallis and stigmaphyllon.
TYPE OF PLANT: Dwarf shrub.   HEIGHT: 3'. ZONE: S
HOW TO IDENTIFY: Dwarf shrub furnished with evergreen, opposite, short-petioled, spiny-toothed leaves; open, pink flowers and red fruits.
HABIT OF GROWTH: Plants of the type grow upright by ascending branches; those of named clones are densely spreading or weeping in habit.
FOLIAGE: Opposite, evergreen, holly-like, of very fine texture and medium green color.
FLOWERS: Pink, flaring, wavy-petaled, ½" across, in axillary cymes.
FRUITS: Decorative, globose, red drupes, ⅓" in diameter.
SEASON OF MAXIMUM COLOR: Much of the year when flowers or fruits mature.
LANDSCAPE USES: For foundation plantings, for planter bins, and as a transition plant, holly malpighia is one of southern Florida's very best dwarf shrubs. Set the plants 2' apart.
    Named clones of weeping habit are most popular, and as a striking accent, a clone with attractively variegated foliage may be chosen.
HABITAT: West Indies; in Florida, landscape plantings in warmest parts.
LIGHT REQUIREMENT: A partially shaded garden spot is highly suitable.
SOIL REQUIREMENT: A good, fertile soil free of nematodes is requisite.
SALT TOLERANCE: Not tolerant of dune conditions.
AVAILABILITY: Nurseries in southern Florida market seedlings of the original type, and cutting-grown plants of the named varieties in containers of sterilized soil.
CULTURE: Plant in frost-free locations, in sterilized soil; water faithfully; fertilize twice during each growing season.
PROPAGATION: Seedage for the type, cuttage for the named clones.
PESTS: Nematodes, scales, and mites.

218
Thryallis

Thryallis (thry-AL-is): old Greek name.
glauca (GLAW-ka): for the dark red fuzz on the new growth.

FAMILY: Malpighiaceae.   RELATIVES: Malpighia and stigmaphyllon.
TYPE OF PLANT: Shrub.   HEIGHT: 9'. ZONE: N,C,S
HOW TO IDENTIFY: Very fine twigs, reddish while young; evergreen, opposite leaves almost, or quite, sessile; yellow flowers in terminal panicles.
HABIT OF GROWTH: Compact because of many fine, close twigs and abundant foliage.
FOLIAGE: Evergreen, opposite, medium in texture, light green in color.
FLOWERS: Showy yellow, in terminal panicles, abundant during much of the year.
FRUITS: Little capsules which split into 3 parts when brown and dry.
SEASON OF MAXIMUM COLOR: Late summer and fall.
LANDSCAPE USES: In foundation plantings, allow 3' between plants; for color in front of green shrubbery, use groups of 3 at 3' intervals between plants. Combine with blue plumbago or blue stokesia for a pleasing effect in complementary colors.

   Where winters are mild, thryallis is one of Florida's very best landscape shrubs. Plants may be injured by a temperature of 28° F.
HABITAT: Tropical America; in Florida, popular landscape shrub on the peninsula.
LIGHT REQUIREMENT: Full sun for best habit and free flowering.
SOIL REQUIREMENT: Dry, well-drained soils of many types are suitable.
SALT TOLERANCE: Tolerant of mild salt drift well away from the sea.
AVAILABILITY: Thryallis is widely available in containers.
CULTURE: No special culture is demanded within the climatic range of the plant.
PROPAGATION: Seedage, sow green fruits; cuttage, take cuttings in July.
PESTS: Caterpillars and mites.

219
African Milk-Bush

Synadenium (sin-a-DEAN-ee-um): Greek, referring to united floral parts.
grantii (GRANT-ee-eye): for a person named Grant.

FAMILY: Euphorbiaceae.   RELATIVES: Castor-bean and poinsettia.
TYPE OF PLANT: Shrub.   HEIGHT: 8'. ZONE: S

HOW TO IDENTIFY: Stiff, thick, sausage-like branches yield milky sap when wounded and hold thick, succulent, obovate, toothed leaves, about 4″ long. These leaves may be more persistent than with some other cactus-like euphorbes. Clusters of red blossoms are produced terminally.

HABIT OF GROWTH: Scraggly, open, by thick, succulent stems.

FOLIAGE: Obovate, thick, succulent, toothed leaves with rounded midribs are perhaps more persistent than are those of other cactus-like euphorbes.

FLOWERS: Clusters of small red flowers are borne terminally.

FRUITS: Capsules, if present.

SEASON OF MAXIMUM COLOR: Warm months when red new growth or red flowers are present.

LANDSCAPE USES: African milk-bush, like other tropical euphorbes, is cultured for its bizarre, exotic effect. It can form striking compositions in frostless locations, and it thrives as an urn subject, too.

HABITAT: Tropical Africa.

LIGHT REQUIREMENT: Full sun or partial shade. 'Rubra' colors best in bright light.

SOIL REQUIREMENT: Any soil, including dune sand and bay-bottom marl.

SALT TOLERANCE: Excellent for ocean-front plantings.

AVAILABILITY: Many nurseries in warmer sections carry plants in containers.

CULTURE: Simply plant a piece of stem in a frostless site; water moderately until established; then forget.

PROPAGATION: Cuttage.

PESTS: None of major consequence.

NOTE: More attractive than the all-green type is its clone 'Rubra'. In this one the stems are reddish and the leaves have a reddish cast above and are a glowing wine-red beneath.

C. variegatum 'Clipper'

Codiaeum spirale

C. variegatum 'Bravo'

C. variegatum Imperialis'

C. variegatum 'Katonii'

Croton

C. variegatum 'Franklin Roosevelt'

C. variegatum 'Hookerianum'

C. variegatum 'Disraeli'

C. variegatum 'Polychrome'

221
Croton

Codiaeum (co-dye-EE-um): Greek for head; croton leaves were used for wreaths.
variegatum (vare-ee-a-GAY-tum): variegated, referring to the mottled foliage.

FAMILY: Euphorbiaceae.   RELATIVES: Copper-leaf and poinsettia.
TYPE OF PLANT: Shrub.   HEIGHT: 10′. ZONE: C,S
HOW TO IDENTIFY: The world's most colorful and variable shrub.
HABIT OF GROWTH: Variable; there are dwarf forms and tree-like varieties.
FOLIAGE: Evergreen, highly variable, usually coarse in texture, brightly variegated in color.
FLOWERS: Inconspicuous, in racemes from leaf axils.
FRUITS: Globose capsules which break into lobes.
SEASON OF MAXIMUM COLOR: The year around!
LANDSCAPE USES: Accents in all-green compositions; use small groups of a single variety in front of neutral, all-green shrubs. Fine-leaved, all green varieties of dwarf habit may be used in planters upon occasion.
   Unquestionably, this is one of the most popular shrubs in hot countries the world around. The varieties are almost without end, but naming is confused.
HABITAT: Malaya; in Florida widely planted in frost-free sections.
LIGHT REQUIREMENT: Variable with variety; some thrive in sun, others in shade.
SOIL REQUIREMENT: Tolerant of many soil types if drainage is adequate.
SALT TOLERANCE: Tolerant of mild salt drift well back of the dunes.
AVAILABILITY: Small crotons in containers are offered by most nurseries on the peninsula.
CULTURE: After plants become established in protected locations, spraying for insect control and pruning for form are needed.
PROPAGATION: Cuttage and marcottage.
PESTS: Scales of many species, thrips, mites, and root-rot diseases.

222
Chenille-Plant

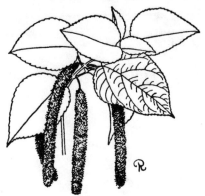

Acalypha (ack-a-LYE-fa): Greek for nettle.
hispida (HISS-pid-a): bristly, referring to the pistillate inflorescence.

FAMILY: Euphorbiaceae.   RELATIVES: Poinsettia and snow-bush.
TYPE OF PLANT: Shrub.   HEIGHT: 8'. ZONE: S

HOW TO IDENTIFY: A vigorous shrub that bears 8", ovate, all-green leaves with pubescence on petioles and veins. Pistillate individuals produce spectacular red spikes of blossoms in cattail form.

HABIT OF GROWTH: Coarse, upright, from many, heavily foliated stems.

FOLIAGE: Evergreen, alternate, very coarse in texture, solid deep green in color.

FLOWERS: Showy, red cattails up to 18" long are borne by female plants.

FRUITS: Usually not seen in Florida.

SEASON OF MAXIMUM COLOR: Warm months when new growth produces red cattails.

LANDSCAPE USES: Chenille-plant attracts a great deal of attention because of its spectacular blossoms. Plant 3 bushes together, with 3' between individuals, in front of all-green shrubbery, as a bright, warm-weather accent. While the red-flowered form is most popular, there is a clone that bears creamy-white cattails. Chenille-plant is tender to cold.

HABITAT: East Indies; in Florida, landscape plantings in warmest locations.

LIGHT REQUIREMENT: Full sun for best flowering.

SOIL REQUIREMENT: Grows well in many types of soil if drainage is adequate.

SALT TOLERANCE: Not tolerant.

AVAILABILITY: Specialty nurseries in southern Florida may have small plants in containers.

CULTURE: After reasonably careful planting in a frostless location, little maintenance is needed. After flowering, prune to keep plant within bounds.

PROPAGATION: Cuttage.

PESTS: Scales, mites, and aphids.

223
Copper-Leaf

Acalypha (ack-a-LYE-fa): Greek for nettle.
wilkesiana (wilkes-ee-ANE-a): for C. Wilkes, a nineteenth-century scientist.

FAMILY: Euphorbiaceae.   RELATIVES: Poinsettia and snow-bush.
TYPE OF PLANT: Shrub.   HEIGHT: 15'. ZONE: S
HOW TO IDENTIFY: A huge, coarse, sprawling shrub with outsize, evergreen, dentate leaves variously mottled in shades of red and purple, green and yellow. These run into many forms.
HABIT OF GROWTH: Huge, coarse, sprawling, many-stemmed shrub of vigorous growth.
FOLIAGE: Evergreen, alternate, dentate, variously mottled and variously shaped, but invariably very large in size.
FLOWERS: Axillary catkins, of no garden value.
FRUITS: Often absent in Florida.
SEASON OF MAXIMUM COLOR: Very colorful the year around.
LANDSCAPE USES: The only approved landscape use of this dazzling, huge shrub is as a bright accent in an all-green shrubbery border. Set one group of 3 plants with 3'–5' intervals between them. There are numbers of clones that display varying leaf forms, but all are very tender to cold.
HABITAT: South Sea islands; in Florida, ubiquitous in landscape plantings in warmest parts.
LIGHT REQUIREMENT: Full sun for best foliage color and compact growth.
SOIL REQUIREMENT: Grows well in many different soils.
SALT TOLERANCE: Not tolerant of dune conditions.
AVAILABILITY: All garden centers and retail nurseries in southern Florida market small copper-leafs (6 or 8 kinds) in containers.
CULTURE: These are among the easiest of all shrubs to grow, yet they are very sensitive to cold.
PROPAGATION: Cuttage, using any kind of wood at any season.
PESTS: Scales and mites.

224
Crown-
of-Thorns

Euphorbia (you-FOR-bee-a): old classical name.
milii (MILL-ee-eye): Baron Milius, once governor of Bourbon.

FAMILY: Euphorbiaceae.   RELATIVES: Poinsettia and Mexican fire-plant.
TYPE OF PLANT: Dwarf shrub.   HEIGHT: 3'. ZONE: C,S
HOW TO IDENTIFY: Milky sap from stems that are densely armed with 1"
    spines; leaves restricted to new growth; bright red bracts, ½" across,
    subtend the true flowers.
HABIT OF GROWTH: Sprawling.
FOLIAGE: Very sparse, restricted to tips of new growth, coarse in texture.
FLOWERS: Inconspicuous, subtended by bright red or pink bracts, ½"
    across.
FRUITS: Not usually formed.
SEASON OF MAXIMUM COLOR: Warm months when red or pink bracts are
    expanded.
LANDSCAPE USES: For planters, and as a ground cover, crown-of-thorns
    is excellent because of its low, weeping habit and its ability to with-
    stand adverse conditions. This is one of the many striking euphorbes
    that help to give Florida a tropical aspect. As noted above, bracts may
    be produced in tones of red or pink, some sorts having larger flowers
    than other varieties.
HABITAT: Madagascar; in Florida, well-drained situations protected
    from frost.
LIGHT REQUIREMENT: Intense light for best habit and flowering.
SOIL REQUIREMENT: Very well drained soil of low fertility is sufficient.
SALT TOLERANCE: Excellent for ocean-front plantings.
AVAILABILITY: Most nurseries in warmer sections carry crown-of-thorns
    in containers.
CULTURE: Overwatering and overfertilization must be avoided.
PROPAGATION: Cuttage.
PESTS: None of great importance.
NOTE: Christ thorn hybrids, shown above left, are in great favor. These
    plants of slow growth and dwarf habit thrive under adverse condi-
    tions.

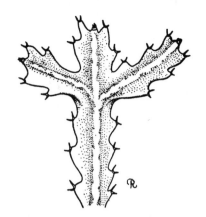

225
Milkstripe
Euphorbia

Euphorbia (you-FOR-bee-a): old classical name.
lactea (LACK-tee-a): milk-white.

FAMILY: Euphorbiaceae.   RELATIVES: Poinsettia and crown-of-thorns.
TYPE OF PLANT: Cactus-like shrub.   HEIGHT: 15'. ZONE: S
HOW TO IDENTIFY: A cactus-like plant with 3- or 4-angled stems that have
    brown spines and exude a milky sap when cut. The stems of this
    species have bands of yellow marbling toward their centers.
HABIT OF GROWTH: Candelabra-like, geometric branching of the angled
    stems.
FOLIAGE: Minute, ephemeral, very fine in texture, light green in color
    when present.
FLOWERS: Inconspicuous, cup-like, in terminal positions when present.
FRUITS: Usually not produced in Florida.
SEASON OF MAXIMUM COLOR: No seasonal color change.
LANDSCAPE USES: To enhance the tropical effect, milkstripe euphorbia is
    much used. It serves as an ocean-front, defensive hedge (set 18" o.c.),
    as a single specimen, and as an urn subject or planter material. This
    plant is very tender to cold.
        Euphorbes can be distinguished from cacti by their milky sap.
HABITAT: East Indies; in Florida, much cultured in most nearly frost-free
    areas.
LIGHT REQUIREMENT: Full sun of dunes or shade of Florida rooms.
SOIL REQUIREMENT: Any soil, including dune sand and bay-bottom marl.
SALT TOLERANCE: Very tolerant of salt, recommended for ocean-front
    planting.
AVAILABILITY: Garden centers and chain stores sell this and other
    euphorbes.
CULTURE: Simply plant a piece of stem in a frostless location, water
    moderately until established, and forget.
PROPAGATION: Cuttage.
PESTS: None of major consequence.
NOTE: Crested milkstripe euphorbia has deformed, gnarled and crested,
    much-shortened branches.

226
Pencil-Tree

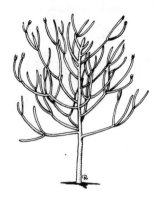

Euphorbia (you-FOR-bee-a): old classical name.
tirucalli (ter-oo-CALL-eye): native Indian name.

FAMILY: Euphorbiaceae.   RELATIVES: Poinsettia and crown-of-thorns.
TYPE OF PLANT: Cactus-like tree.   HEIGHT: 20′. ZONE: S
HOW TO IDENTIFY: A plant that has pencil-size, leafless branches that
   yield milky sap.
HABIT OF GROWTH: Candelabra-like branching of the upward-pointing,
   pencil-form stems.
FOLIAGE: Minute, ephemeral, of very fine texture when present; medium
   green.
FLOWERS: Inconspicuous, cup-like, in sessile clusters at the tops of
   branches.
FRUITS: Capsules, which split at maturity, if present.
SEASON OF MAXIMUM COLOR: Little seasonal change.
LANDSCAPE USES: To enhance the tropical effect, pencil-tree is much
   used in frostless, ocean-front locations. As a defensive hedge (15″
   o.c.), especially on sand dunes, as a planter material, or as an urn
   subject for terrace or Florida room, this succulent is very popular.
HABITAT: Tropical Africa; in Florida, much cultured in most nearly
   frost-free areas.
LIGHT REQUIREMENT: Full sun of ocean dunes, or shade of porches or
   canopies.
SOIL REQUIREMENT: Any soil, including dune sand and bay-bottom marl.
SALT TOLERANCE: Very tolerant of salt, and recommended for dune
   planting.
AVAILABILITY: Widely available wherever plants are sold, pencil-tree is
   a favorite.
CULTURE: Simply plant a piece of stem in frostless location, water
   moderately until established, and forget.
PROPAGATION: Cuttage.
PESTS: None of major consequence.

227
Poinsettia

Euphorbia (you-FOR-bee-a): old classical name.
pulcherrima (pull-KARE-ee-ma): very handsome.

FAMILY: Euphorbiaceae.   RELATIVES: Pencil-tree and crown-of-thorns.
TYPE OF PLANT: Large shrub.   HEIGHT: 12′. ZONE: N,C,S
HOW TO IDENTIFY: Milky latex, huge alternating, simple leaves and red-bracted inflorescences at Christmas time.
HABIT OF GROWTH: Stiffly upright by long, unbranched canes.
FOLIAGE: Evergreen, very coarse in texture, light green in color.
FLOWERS: Inconspicuous, cup-like, subtended by bright red floral leaves called bracts.
FRUITS: Inconspicuous, lobed capsules.
SEASON OF MAXIMUM COLOR: Christmas time.
LANDSCAPE USES: Because of huge size, coarse foliage, and susceptibility to frost injury, poinsettias should be planted in distant parts of shrubbery borders so that their great scale does not show to disadvantage, and so that, when they are killed to the ground, hardy shrubs growing nearby will maintain the form of the garden. Planting interval may be about 5′ o.c.
HABITAT: Central America; in Florida, ubiquitous in plantings about homes.
LIGHT REQUIREMENT: Full sun for best flowering. Nights must be unbroken by light.
SOIL REQUIREMENT: Any well-drained soil is adequate.
SALT TOLERANCE: Not tolerant.
AVAILABILITY: Some nurseries offer poinsettias in containers.
CULTURE: No shrub is of easier culture. Fertilize 2 or 3 times in warm months, cut back in August to induce branching.
PROPAGATION: Cuttage by long, hardwood cuttings stuck directly in the earth.
PESTS: Poinsettia scab in southern Florida, scales, mites, and thrips.
NOTE: There are types with white bracts, others with pink floral leaves, some with many, closely packed red bracts to make heavy heads.

Pedilanthus

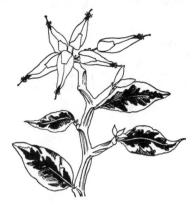

Pedilanthus (peddy-LAN-thus): Greek for slipper-flower.
tithymaloides (tithy-mal-OY-dez): like tithymalus, a euphorbe.

FAMILY: Euphorbiaceae.   RELATIVES: Poinsettia and pencil-tree.

TYPE OF PLANT: Herbaceous perennial.   HEIGHT: 6'. ZONE: C,S

HOW TO IDENTIFY: Zigzag, herbaceous, green stems exude milky sap
   when injured. Alternate, evergreen leaves, about 4" long, are often
   marbled with white, sometimes with pink, in popular varieties.
   Curious little blossoms are slipper-shaped as indicated by the generic
   name.

HABIT OF GROWTH: Stiffly upright by clustered, zigzag stems.

FOLIAGE: Evergreen or deciduous, clustered near tips of branches,
   medium in texture, often marbled with white, sometimes with pink.

FLOWERS: Inconspicuous, cup-like, in dense terminal cymes, the bright
   red bracts, about ½" long, are slipper-shaped.

FRUITS: Lobed capsules about ¼" long.

SEASON OF MAXIMUM COLOR: Warm months when blossoms appear.

LANDSCAPE USES: To enhance the tropical atmosphere, grown in the
   earth or in urns or planter bins, pedilanthus is widely approved. There
   are several popular forms, all of which are known as devils-backbone
   and slipper-flower. Like almost all euphorbes, pedilanthus is tender to
   cold.

HABITAT: Tropical America, warmest parts of Florida included.

LIGHT REQUIREMENT: Full sun or partial shade is satisfactory.

SOIL REQUIREMENT: Many kinds of soils are acceptable.

SALT TOLERANCE: Tolerant of conditions just back of the first dunes.

AVAILABILITY: Garden centers and chain stores offer plants in containers.

CULTURE: Like most euphorbes, pedilanthus is very easy to grow where
   frost is not a factor. Plant, water, and forget; but good growth will be
   the rule if a little fertilizer is thrown near the plant in springtime.

PROPAGATION: Cuttage.

PESTS: Mites and scales.

229
Physic
Nut

Jatropha (JAT-row-fah): Greek, referring to medicinal use.
curcas (CUR-cass): an aboriginal name.

FAMILY: Euphorbiaceae.   RELATIVES: Copper-leaf and poinsettia.
TYPE OF PLANT: Shrubby small tree.   HEIGHT: 15′. ZONE: S
HOW TO IDENTIFY: Milky sap, heart-shaped leaves that have 3–5 lobes,
    oval nuts 1″ in diameter.
HABIT OF GROWTH: Upright, scraggly shrub.
FOLIAGE: Evergreen, of very coarse texture and deep green color.
FLOWERS: Inconspicuous, yellowish-green, in springtime.
FRUITS: Oval nuts, 1½″ long, 3-seeded, POISONOUS.
SEASON OF MAXIMUM COLOR: Not much seasonal variation.
LANDSCAPE USES: As a freestanding specimen, physic nut is sometimes
    seen for the curiosity of its fruits. The plant is very poisonous. The
    nuts are carried by some persons as lucky pocket pieces.
    This euphorbe is not recommended, but it must be known to all
    horticulturists.
HABITAT: Tropical America; in Florida, gardens in warmest parts.
LIGHT REQUIREMENT: Broken shade under tall trees.
SOIL REQUIREMENT: Any soil is suitable.
SALT TOLERANCE: Not tolerant.
AVAILABILITY: Nurseries in southern Florida carry jatrophas of several
    kinds.
CULTURE: Plant, water, and forget.
PROPAGATION: Cuttage or seedage.
PESTS: Mites and mushroom root-rot.
NOTE: Bellyache bush (*Jatropha gossypifolia*), with its purple, lobed, 6″
    leaves is grown for its tropical aspect. The little red flowers are at-
    tractive, yet the plant, like others in the genus, is extremely
    POISONOUS. All jatrophas are tender to frost.

230
Coral-
Plant

Jatropha (JAT-row-fah): Greek, referring to medicinal use.
multifida (mul-TIFF-id-ah): much-cleft.

FAMILY: Euphorbiaceae.   RELATIVES: Copper-leaf and pencil-tree.
TYPE OF PLANT: Shrub.   HEIGHT: 15'. ZONE: S
HOW TO IDENTIFY: Finely cut leaves grow out from the tip of a stout, thorny trunk, whence emerge the clusters of bright, coral-red flowers. Milky sap is released if the bark is scored.
HABIT OF GROWTH: Erect, ungainly, from a single, stout, thorny trunk.
FOLIAGE: Evergreen, deeply cut to become almost fern-like, of fine texture.
FLOWERS: Bright, coral-red in very showy terminal clusters.
FRUITS: Three-cornered pods which turn from green to yellow at maturity.
SEASON OF MAXIMUM COLOR: Warm months when blossoms appear.
LANDSCAPE USES: For a note of bright coral color and the curiosity of its finely cut foliage, coral–plant may stand alone in front of green shrubbery.
HABITAT: Tropical America; in Florida, rather popular in warmest parts.
LIGHT REQUIREMENT: Full sun or high, shifting, pine shade.
SOIL REQUIREMENT: Tolerant of many kinds of soils.
SALT TOLERANCE: Not tolerant.
AVAILABILITY: Retail nurseries in southern Florida offer small plants.
CULTURE: Plant in an enriched site, water a few times, and forget.
PROPAGATION: Cuttage or seedage.
PESTS: Mites and scales.
NOTE: Peregrina (*J. hastata*) is a large, compact shrub with evergreen, fiddle-shaped leaves and conspicuous red flowers. All jatrophas are tender to frost, and are very toxic to human beings.

231
Snow-Bush

Breynia (BRAY-knee-a): for J. Breyn, German botanist of the seventeenth century.
nivosa (nye-VOE-sa): snowy.

FAMILY: Euphorbiaceae.   RELATIVES: Poinsettia and slipper-flower.
TYPE OF PLANT: Shrub.   HEIGHT: 10'. ZONE: C,S
HOW TO IDENTIFY: Dark red, zigzag branches; alternate leaves that are variously mottled with red, pink, and white.
HABIT OF GROWTH: Loose habit unless pruned frequently for compactness.
FOLIAGE: Evergreen, medium-fine in texture, brightly variegated in several colors.
FLOWERS: Inconspicuous, greenish, carried on long pedicels.
FRUITS: Berries that are ½" or less in diameter.
SEASON OF MAXIMUM COLOR: The year around.
LANDSCAPE USES: Snow-bush is very popular for hedges because of its bright, multicolored leaves. Plants may be set 2' apart.

Because of the bright colors and somewhat loose, ungainly habit snow-bush is probably not best to use in foundation planting arrangements. As warm color accents, groups of 3 of a variety together may highlight a bay in neutral green shrubbery. Plant 3' o.c. in this use.

There are many leaf-color arrangements. All breynias are tender to cold.
HABITAT: South Sea islands; in Florida, popular for hedges in warm locations.
LIGHT REQUIREMENT: Full sun for compact habit of growth.
SOIL REQUIREMENT: Light, sandy soils are adequate.
SALT TOLERANCE: Not tolerant.
AVAILABILITY: Most nurseries in central and southern Florida have plants for sale.
CULTURE: After planting in moderately fertile sites, no attention other than pruning for compactness, the usual watering, and fertilization is needed.
PROPAGATION: Cuttage.
PESTS: Mites and caterpillars.

232
Toog

Bischofia (bis-CHOF-ee-a): for G. Bischoff, German botanist.
javanica (ja-VAN-i-ca): Javanese.

FAMILY: Euphorbiaceae.　　　RELATIVES: Croton and crown-of-thorns.
TYPE OF PLANT: Tree.　　　　　　　　　HEIGHT: 40′. ZONE: C,S

HOW TO IDENTIFY: A fast-growing tree with milky sap; shiny, bronze-toned, trifoliate leaves. The bright, shining new growth is particularly striking.

HABIT OF GROWTH: Symmetrical, dense, round head from a huge trunk.

FOLIAGE: Evergreen, compound, of coarse texture and dark green color when mature.

FLOWERS: Inconspicuous.

FRUITS: Black, fleshy, ¼″ in diameter.

SEASON OF MAXIMUM COLOR: Warm weather when bronze new growth appears.

LANDSCAPE USES: In southern Florida where quick, dense shade is needed, toog may serve. The tree grows very rapidly to large size, the dense crown discourages lawn grasses, and the brittle wood is very likely to break in high winds.

HABITAT: Old World tropics; in Florida, sandy soils in most nearly frostless sections.

LIGHT REQUIREMENT: Full sun.

SOIL REQUIREMENT: Widely varying soils are tolerated, acidic or basic.

SALT TOLERANCE: Not tolerant of dune conditions.

AVAILABILITY: Toog is sometimes sold in retail nurseries.

CULTURE: Like most members of its family, toog grows with the greatest of ease in Florida.

PROPAGATION: Cuttage.

PESTS: None of major consequence.

233
Japanese Boxwood

Buxus (BUCKS-us): ancient Latin name.
microphylla (my-crow-PHIL-a): small-leaved.

FAMILY: Buxaceae.　　　　RELATIVES: The genus stands alone.
TYPE OF PLANT: Dwarf shrub.　　　HEIGHT: 5′. ZONE: N,C
HOW TO IDENTIFY: Green, quadrangular, conspicuously winged branchlets bear little evergreen leaves in opposite arrangement.
HABIT OF GROWTH: Very compact.
FOLIAGE: Evergreen, opposite, very fine in texture, medium green in color.
FLOWERS: Inconspicuous.
FRUITS: Usually none are produced in Florida.
SEASON OF MAXIMUM COLOR: Winter, when leaves turn red-bronze.
LANDSCAPE USES: From Tampa northward, Japanese boxwood is one of Florida's very best all-green, dwarf shrubs. For shady, nematode-free soils, it is without superior. For foundation plantings, especially on north walls, set about 2′ apart. For edging walks, plant in double, staggered rows at 1′ intervals. In planters, with English ivy, use the same distance.
HABITAT: China and Japan; in Florida, upper central and northern areas.
LIGHT REQUIREMENT: Shade tolerant; north-side location is ideal.
SOIL REQUIREMENT: Fertile, acid soil free of nematodes is recommended.
SALT TOLERANCE: Not tolerant.
AVAILABILITY: Nurseries in upper Florida sell boxwood in containers of various sizes.
CULTURE: On the peninsula, plant on a north-side location in fertile soil that has been made free of nematodes. On superior soils of the Panhandle, no special precautions are observed.
PROPAGATION: Cuttage.
PESTS: Nematodes, mites, and leaf-miners.
NOTE: Harland boxwood, with narrower, darker foliage, is said to be somewhat resistant to nematodes.

Brazilian Pepper-Tree

Schinus (SKY-nus): Greek for the mastic tree.
terebinthifolius (terry-BIN-the-FOL-ee-us): for the turpentine odor of the foliage.

FAMILY: Anacardiaceae.   RELATIVES: Mango, sumac, and pistachio.
TYPE OF PLANT: Tree or shrub.   HEIGHT: 25′. ZONE: C,S
HOW TO IDENTIFY: Rough, odorous, evergreen, odd-pinnate leaves composed of 7 sessile leaflets complement the bright red fruits that are borne by pistillate individuals during the winter.
HABIT OF GROWTH: Stiffly upright by coarse, thick branches, densely clothed with foliage.
FOLIAGE: Evergreen, aromatic, coarse, dark green above, lighter beneath.
FLOWERS: Inconspicuous, unisexual, in dense, bracteate panicles.
FRUITS: Bright red drupes, 3/16″ in diameter, in heavy clusters, are produced by female plants.
SEASON OF MAXIMUM COLOR: The Christmas season.
LANDSCAPE USES: As a part of a barrier planting for large properties, set Brazilian pepper-trees 5′ o.c., or use a single fruiting specimen as a shade tree for a terrace or patio.
HABITAT: Brazil; in Florida, widely planted in central and southern sections. Thickets of self-sown seedlings are common in some parts.
LIGHT REQUIREMENT: Full sun for best compact habit and full fruiting.
SOIL REQUIREMENT: Grows well in reasonably well-drained, moderately fertile sand.
SALT TOLERANCE: Tolerant of mild salt air back of the front-line dunes.
AVAILABILITY: Select fruiting individuals in containers at your garden center or retail nursery.
CULTURE: After careful planting, no special care is needed as this plant is very well adapted to conditions in central and southern Florida.
PROPAGATION: Seedage; cuttage for superior fruiting individuals.
PESTS: Foliage thrips, mites, scales, and nematodes.
NOTE: California pepper-tree (*Schinus molle*) is not widely planted in Florida.

235
Mango

Mangifera (man-JIFF-er-a): mango-bearing.
indica (IN-dee-ca): Indian.

FAMILY: Anacardiaceae.　RELATIVES: Brazilian pepper-tree and sumac.
TYPE OF PLANT: Tree.　　　　　　　　HEIGHT: 40'. ZONE: S
HOW TO IDENTIFY: Large tree with dense, heavy crown of large, shiny,
　　evergreen leaves that are wine-colored while young. Prominent
　　flower- or fruit-clusters hang well outside the foliage canopy.
HABIT OF GROWTH: Densely compact.
FOLIAGE: Evergreen, coarse, wine-colored while new, dark green when
　　mature.
FLOWERS: Small, ivory or reddish, very numerous, in long, conspicuous
　　sprays.
FRUITS: Large, fleshy drupes that must be classed among the world's
　　most delectable fruits.
SEASON OF MAXIMUM COLOR: Spring, new leaves color; summer, fruits
　　ripen.
LANDSCAPE USES: As freestanding shade trees for southern Florida,
　　mangos are all-time favorites, furnishing relief from the tropical
　　sun, seasonal color interest in the red new growth, and, as special
　　dividends, the fruits that are so highly prized. As avenue trees,
　　seedling mangos can stand 50' o.c.
HABITAT: India-Burma; in Florida, warmest parts of peninsula and the
　　Keys.
LIGHT REQUIREMENT: Full sun for best fruiting.
SOIL REQUIREMENT: Fertile, well-drained soil is best.
SALT TOLERANCE: Not tolerant of dune conditions.
AVAILABILITY: Nurseries in southern Florida sell container-grown,
　　grafted plants in 2 dozen named varieties. Seedlings are not rec-
　　ommended for back-yard planting.
CULTURE: Plant carefully in made-up planting sites; water faithfully;
　　fertilize thrice annually; mulch with leaves; employ a pest control
　　firm to protect mango trees against scales and flower- and fruit-
　　diseases.
PROPAGATION: Graftage.
PESTS: Scales, sooty-mold, anthracnose disease of blossoms and fruits.

American Holly

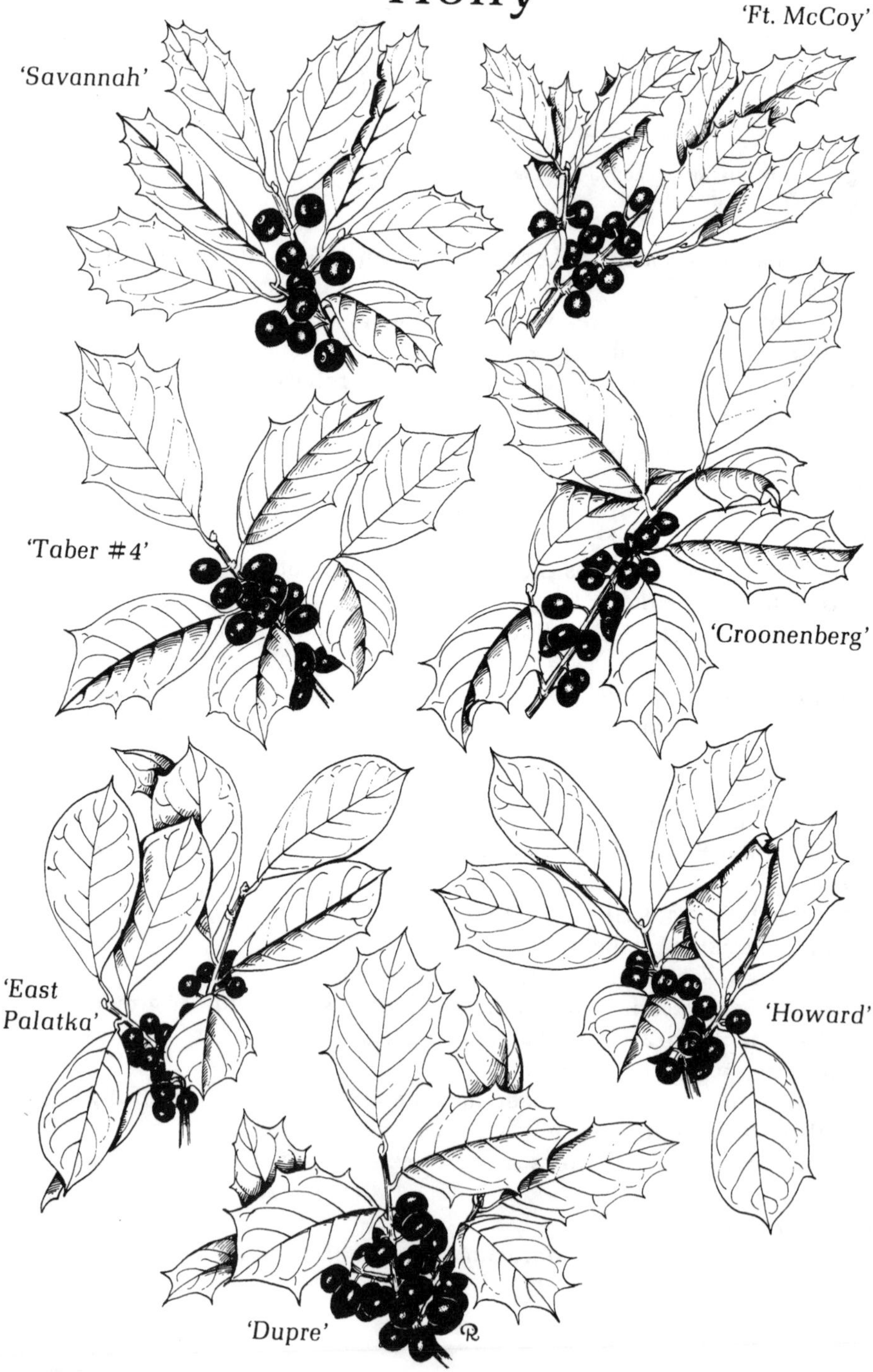

'Savannah'

'Ft. McCoy'

'Taber #4'

'Croonenberg'

'East Palatka'

'Howard'

'Dupre'

American Holly

Ilex (EYE-lecks): ancient Latin name for *Quercus ilex*.
opaca (oh-PAY-ka): shaded.

FAMILY: Aquifoliaceae.

RELATIVES: The hollies.

TYPE OF PLANT: Tree.

HEIGHT: 50'. ZONE: N,C

HOW TO IDENTIFY: Evergreen, alternate leaves, mostly with spines, growing from gray twigs, accompanied by red fruits on female trees during the winter.

HABIT OF GROWTH: Mostly pyramidal-upright with very dense, symmetrical head.

FOLIAGE: Evergreen, alternate, armed, fine to medium in texture, dull green in color.

FLOWERS: Unisexual, inconspicuous, in few-flowered axillary cymes.

FRUITS: Globose, berry-like drupes, usually red, and extremely decorative.

SEASON OF MAXIMUM COLOR: Winter.

LANDSCAPE USES: American holly is one of America's most beloved fruiting trees. Specimens have been used for avenue and yard plantings since the beginning of American history.

There are scores of named clones that exhibit many diverse leaf forms and variation in fruiting habits, fruit color, and other characteristics.

HABITAT: Hammock areas in the upper half of the Florida peninsula and throughout the Panhandle.

LIGHT REQUIREMENT: Broken, shifting shade or full sun.

SOIL REQUIREMENT: Fertile, organic, slightly acid, well-drained soil.

SALT TOLERANCE: Tolerant of salt air back of the dunes.

AVAILABILITY: Nurseries in northern Florida offer holly trees in containers and B & B.

CULTURE: Plant in prepared sites at the same level the trees grew formerly; water faithfully; protect foliage from spittle bugs during hot weather; fertilize twice annually. A mulch over the roots is recommended.

PROPAGATION: Cuttage or graftage.

PESTS: Spittle bugs, scales, and leaf-miners.

Chinese Holly

Ilex (EYE-lecks): ancient Latin name for *Quercus ilex*.
cornuta (cor-NEW-ta): horned, referring to spines on the leaves.

FAMILY: Aquifoliaceae.
RELATIVES: The hollies.
TYPE OF PLANT: Shrub or tree.
HEIGHT: 20′. ZONE: N,C
HOW TO IDENTIFY: Shining, evergreen leaves, often with revolute edges and one or more sharp spines, are closely packed on stout twigs of compact large shrubs or small trees. Fruits are larger than those borne by any holly in Florida.
HABIT OF GROWTH: Shrubby in selected clones, yet seedlings become tree-like with age.
FOLIAGE: Evergreen, shining, armed, of medium texture and dark green color.
FLOWERS: Unisexual, inconspicuous.
FRUITS: Berry-like drupes, scarlet (yellow in one variety), ½″ across.
SEASON OF MAXIMUM COLOR: Fall if fruits mature.
LANDSCAPE USES: Varieties must be listed with the most beautiful evergreen shrubs for upper Florida. In foundation plantings use a 3′ interval between plants; for shrubbery borders, allow 5′. 'Burford', the leading clone, is shrubby, with entire, revolute leaves with single, apical thorns. 'National' is quite similar in appearance. 'Hume' has narrower leaves, and 'Jungle Garden' has yellow fruits. On the Florida peninsula, Chinese holly may not fruit as heavily as it does farther to the north and west.
HABITAT: Eastern Asia; in Florida, gardens of central and northern counties.
LIGHT REQUIREMENT: Full sun or partial shade.
SOIL REQUIREMENT: Superior, well-drained soil that is slightly acid in reaction.
SALT TOLERANCE: Not tolerant.
AVAILABILITY: Container-grown plants of 'Burford' are commonly stocked by retail sales lots; other clones are not widely offered.
CULTURE: On superior soils of northern counties, plant carefully at former depth; water periodically; fertilize twice each growing season; and combat scales and spittle bugs.
PROPAGATION: Cuttage with the aid of root-inducing chemicals.
PESTS: Scales and spittle bugs.

239
Dahoon

Ilex (EYE-lecks): ancient Latin name for *Quercus ilex*.
cassine (cass-SEEN-ee): American Indian name.

FAMILY: Aquifoliaceae.

RELATIVES: The hollies.

TYPE OF PLANT: Tree.

HEIGHT: 40'. ZONE: N,C,S

HOW TO IDENTIFY: A small tree growing in a wet location with conspicuous red fruits in winter. The evergreen leaves are alternate, about 4" long, shining above, pubescent beneath, with a few small teeth near the apex.

HABIT OF GROWTH: Small tree with a narrow, close head of upward-pointing branches.

FOLIAGE: Evergreen or partly deciduous of medium texture and medium green color.

FLOWERS: Inconspicuous, unisexual, clustered on a common stalk.

FRUITS: Globose, berry-like drupes, usually red, occasionally yellow.

SEASON OF MAXIMUM COLOR: The Christmas season.

LANDSCAPE USES: For bright wintertime color in woodland plantings, an occasional pistillate tree of dahoon is very desirable. Home-owners near the peninsula's tip can have true hollies in this species.

Myrtle dahoon is held by some botanists to be a variety of this.

HABITAT: Swamps and lake margins as far south as Biscayne Bay.

LIGHT REQUIREMENT: Reduced light of swamplands.

SOIL REQUIREMENT: Wet, boggy soil of swamps is dahoon's native environment.

SALT TOLERANCE: Tolerant of salt air back of the dunes.

AVAILABILITY: Dahoons are seldom offered for sale in nurseries.

CULTURE: Dig plants from land of a friend; plant in a moist location; after establishment, no further attention is needed.

PROPAGATION: Cuttage or graftage.

PESTS: Spittle bugs and scales.

240
Gallberry

Ilex (EYE-lecks): ancient Latin name for *Quercus ilex*.
glabra (GLAY-bra): not hairy.

FAMILY: Aquifoliaceae.
RELATIVES: The hollies.
TYPE OF PLANT: Clump-forming shrub.
HEIGHT: 10'. ZONE: N,C,S
HOW TO IDENTIFY: Stoloniferous shrub, with evergreen, alternate leaves that are entire or with a few teeth near their apexes. Female plants bear black fruits.
HABIT OF GROWTH: Clump-forming to make huge cultures in the flatwoods.
FOLIAGE: Evergreen, or nearly so, of fine texture and varying tones of green.
FLOWERS: Inconspicuous, unisexual, on current growth; most desirable for honey.
FRUITS: Berry-like, black drupes, ¼" across, produced by pistillate individuals.
SEASON OF MAXIMUM COLOR: Winter, when fruits are colored.
LANDSCAPE USES: For barrier plantings in naturalistic arrangements, gallberry can be used to advantage on certain soils. Set wild clumps 3'–5' o.c. For semiformal, round-topped hedges, set wild clumps 18" o.c. and use the same interval if gallberry bushes are to be planted around the foundations of vacation cottages.

There is a white-fruited gallberry, one with red fruits was once reported, and dwarf clones have been named from time to time.
HABITAT: Flatwoods over much of the state of Florida.
LIGHT REQUIREMENT: Full sun or shade of flatwoods.
SOIL REQUIREMENT: Acid, poorly drained, hardpan soils.
SALT TOLERANCE: Tolerant of light salt drift, well back from the dunes.
AVAILABILITY: Gallberries are not items of commerce.
CULTURE: Cut back stems; set clumps in acid soil; water periodically until well established.
PROPAGATION: Collect wild clumps; selected clones are increased by cuttage.
PESTS: Scales and spittle bugs.
NOTE: Large gallberry (*Ilex coriacea*) grows to a height of 12', but is quite similar to the well-known type.

241
Japanese Holly

Ilex (EYE-lecks): ancient Latin name for *Quercus ilex*.
crenata (cree-NAY-ta): crenate, referring to the leaf margins.

FAMILY: Aquifoliaceae.   RELATIVES: The hollies.

TYPE OF PLANT: Dwarf shrub.   HEIGHT: 5'. ZONE: N

HOW TO IDENTIFY: Alternate, evergreen, scalloped leaves, 1½" or less in length, dull or shiny above, wedge-shaped at the bases. Black fruits are produced by pistillate individuals.

HABIT OF GROWTH: Compact, shrubby, leaves crowded on many small twigs.

FOLIAGE: Evergreen, fine in texture, medium green in color.

FLOWERS: Inconspicuous, unisexual.

FRUITS: Shining black globes, ¼" across, decorative if present in quantity.

SEASON OF MAXIMUM COLOR: Perhaps when fruits mature.

LANDSCAPE USES: For foundation plantings, north or east side, for the smallest structures, this Oriental shrub serves well. Use 2' planting intervals. It is recommended as well for planter bins in constant shade.

Japanese holly is subject to pests (see below) and it is not always entirely satisfactory on landscape jobs, particularly when planted in poor soil in full sun.

There are a number of named clones that display differing leaf forms and growth habits.

HABITAT: Japan; in Florida, shady locations on superior soil.

LIGHT REQUIREMENT: Shade is essential, except on rich soils of the Panhandle.

SOIL REQUIREMENT: Superior soils for best performance.

SALT TOLERANCE: Not tolerant.

AVAILABILITY: Widely available under varietal name, in northern Florida.

CULTURE: Set carefully in fertile sites on the north or east sides, or under trees; water faithfully; mulch the roots, protect the foliage against pests.

PROPAGATION: Cuttage, with root-inducing chemicals.

PESTS: Nematodes, spittle bugs, mites, and scales.

242
Round
Holly

Ilex (EYE-lecks): ancient Latin name for *Quercus ilex*.
rotunda (row-TUN-da): round, referring to the symmetrical head of the tree.

FAMILY: Aquifoliaceae. RELATIVES: The hollies.
TYPE OF PLANT: Tree. HEIGHT: 25′. ZONE: N,C,S

HOW TO IDENTIFY: Attractive, small tree that often has gracefully drooping branches that bear alternate, evergreen, entire, shining green
leaves; pistillate individuals produce heavy clusters of bright, shining red fruits from autumn until late spring.

HABIT OF GROWTH: Compact, central leader, and gracefully drooping
branches.

FOLIAGE: Alternate, evergreen, unarmed, of medium texture and dark
green color.

FLOWERS: Unisexual, inconspicuous, in heavy axillary cymes.

FRUITS: Small, berry-like drupes of glistening red that are highly decorative.

SEASON OF MAXIMUM COLOR: October–April, when fruits are mature.

LANDSCAPE USES: Freestanding specimen for horticultural interest because this beautiful, heavy-fruiting, evergreen holly is one of the
best fruiting trees from abroad. As a framing tree for small houses,
and as a part of a shrubbery border, for skyline interest, *Ilex rotunda* is very good, too.

   Horticultural variety 'Lord', named for a former professor of horticulture at the University of Florida, has been selected, increased
by graftage, and distributed in limited quantity by a nursery in
northern Florida.

HABITAT: Japan; in Florida gardens in northern and central parts.

LIGHT REQUIREMENT: High, shifting, broken shade, or full sun.

SOIL REQUIREMENT: Fertile, organic, well-drained soil, with mulch.

SALT TOLERANCE: Not tolerant.

AVAILABILITY: *Ilex rotunda* is rarely seen in nurseries, unfortunately.

CULTURE: Given reasonable fertility, good drainage, and moderate
water supply, this beautiful holly needs no particular attention
after it becomes established.

PROPAGATION: Cuttage in May, treated with root-inducing chemicals,
or graftage during late winter.

PESTS: Scales and possibly nematodes.

243
Yaupon

Ilex (EYE-lecks): ancient Latin name for *Quercus ilex*.
vomitoria (vom-i-TORE-ee-a): emetic, for the tea made from plant parts.

FAMILY: Aquifoliaceae.

RELATIVES: The hollies.

TYPE OF PLANT: Large shrub.

HEIGHT: 25'. ZONE: N,C

HOW TO IDENTIFY: A shrub with gray-green twigs that bears small, unarmed, scalloped, alternate, evergreen leaves and bright, little red fruits in clusters.

HABIT OF GROWTH: Dense, compact, spreading by stolons to form large cultures.

FOLIAGE: Evergreen, alternate, scalloped, unarmed, very fine in texture.

FLOWERS: Inconspicuous, unisexual, held in axillary cymes.

FRUITS: Glistening red, berry-like drupes, ¼" across, in axillary clusters.

SEASON OF MAXIMUM COLOR: Winter, when fruits assume full color.

LANDSCAPE USES: As a clipped hedge, yaupon cannot be excelled. Plant 18" apart. As a part of an enclosing barrier, this shrub is fine when set 5' o.c. Infusion made from young leaves and twig tips has served as a beverage since the beginning of history. Wild yaupons are protected by Florida statute.

Selection of types of dwarf habit, very fine texture, or special fruiting characteristics will lead to even greater landscape usefulness of this sterling native plant.

HABITAT: Hammocks and stream banks in central and northern Florida.

LIGHT REQUIREMENT: Tolerant of shade.

SOIL REQUIREMENT: Tolerant of widely varying soils.

SALT TOLERANCE: Tolerant of salt, grows on the banks of tidal streams.

AVAILABILITY: Nurseries carry yaupons in containers or B & B. Selected forms are usually sold in pots.

CULTURE: Well-drained soil is essential; transplanting is extremely difficult; spittle bugs must be controlled during warm months.

PROPAGATION: Cuttage, with root-inducing chemicals.

PESTS: Scales and spittle bugs.

Red Maple

Acer (AY-sir): classical Latin name.
rubrum (RUBE-rum): red.

FAMILY: Aceraceae.

RELATIVES: The maple trees.

TYPE OF PLANT: Tree.

HEIGHT: 75'. ZONE: N,C

HOW TO IDENTIFY: Deciduous, opposite, 3-lobed leaves that have V-shaped, shallow sinuses, regular teeth, and red petioles. Conspicuous red fruits are produced in January.

HABIT OF GROWTH: Narrow, upright.

FOLIAGE: Deciduous, 3-lobed, held by red petioles. The texture is medium fine; the color is medium green; the fall color is often a bright red.

FLOWERS: Red in December–January.

FRUITS: Bright red keys in January are highly decorative.

SEASON OF MAXIMUM COLOR: January, keys mature; November, leaves turn red.

LANDSCAPE USES: For seasonal color in naturalistic plantings, set red maple trees 25'–35' apart. As a parking-lot tree in northern areas, set about 35' o.c. This excellent native tree is not widely used because of its short life in civilization; however, with good care, it makes an outstanding specimen.

HABITAT: Swamplands and bayheads.

LIGHT REQUIREMENT: Sun or broken shade of swamplands.

SOIL REQUIREMENT: Low, boggy soil, or rich, upland earth that is kept wet.

SALT TOLERANCE: Not tolerant.

AVAILABILITY: Red maple is seldom offered for sale in nurseries in Florida.

CULTURE: Plant in rich soil; wrap the trunks as protection against borers; keep well watered at all times; fertilize once in late winter.

PROPAGATION: Seedage; clonal selections must be increased vegetatively.

PESTS: Borers and mites.

245
Goldenrain-Tree

Koelreuteria (coal-roy-TEER-ee-a): for J. Koelreuter, a German professor.
formosana (for-mo-SAY-na): of Formosa.

FAMILY: Sapindaceae.　　　RELATIVES: Lychee, soapberry, and akee.

TYPE OF PLANT: Tree.　　　HEIGHT: 30'. ZONE: N,C

HOW TO IDENTIFY: Deciduous leaves, 14" long, composed of 7–15 lobed leaflets; yellow blossoms in autumn, followed one month later by showy, pinkish fruits.

HABIT OF GROWTH: Irregular from a bent, single trunk.

FOLIAGE: Deciduous, much-divided to give a lacy effect. The color is medium green.

FLOWERS: Bright yellow, in 18" panicles in the autumn.

FRUITS: 2" capsules with pinkish, papery walls, which gradually narrow to pointed apexes. These very decorative fruits mature one month after the yellow blossoms fade.

SEASON OF MAXIMUM COLOR: October–November.

LANDSCAPE USES: As a freestanding specimen or as a part of a shrubbery border, goldenrain-tree is rightly popular for its beautiful autumnal display.

　　Because it is so well adapted to northern and central Florida, goldenrain-tree is highly commended to casual, part-time gardeners. As indicated below, seedlings usually are to be found under fruiting trees.

HABITAT: Eastern Asia; in Florida, widely planted in the upper parts.

LIGHT REQUIREMENT: Full sun for best flowering and fruiting.

SOIL REQUIREMENT: Tolerant of many soil types.

SALT TOLERANCE: Not tolerant.

AVAILABILITY: Easily found in nurseries in northern Florida.

CULTURE: Within its climatic range, goldenrain-tree requires little care.

PROPAGATION: Seedage; volunteer seedlings usually grow under old trees.

PESTS: Scales and mushroom root-rot.

246
Lychee

Litchi (LYE-chee): a Chinese name.
chinensis (chi-NEN-sis): Chinese.

FAMILY: Sapindaceae.   RELATIVES: Goldenrain-tree and akee.

TYPE OF PLANT: Tree.   HEIGHT: 40'. ZONE: C,S

HOW TO IDENTIFY: Glossy, evergreen leaves with 2–4 pairs of pinnae; bright red, rough fruits, in hanging clusters that are deliciously edible.

HABIT OF GROWTH: Compact, round-headed tree of attractive appearance.

FOLIAGE: Evergreen, 2–4 pairs of leaflets, each of which is 3"–6" long.

FLOWERS: Small, greenish-white in foot-long, drooping panicles.

FRUITS: Drupes, bright red in color, covered with angular, prominent tubercles, delicious to eat out of hand, highly decorative on the tree.

SEASON OF MAXIMUM COLOR: Late summer, when the fruits turn red.

LANDSCAPE USES: Freestanding specimens in home-ground arrangements, framing trees for small residences, shade tree for the back yard. Lychee is extremely popular, and rightly so, within its climatic zones, because its pleasing habit and beautiful, delicious fruits add interest to back-yard landscape arrangements. Most outdoor living areas would have space for only one lychee tree, considering all the other woody trees and palms that might be wanted.

HABITAT: China; in Florida, warm locations on the peninsula.

LIGHT REQUIREMENT: Full sun for best habit, flowering, and fruiting.

SOIL REQUIREMENT: Sandy soil that has been improved with organic matter.

SALT TOLERANCE: Not tolerant.

AVAILABILITY: Nurseries offer small trees, from air layers, in cans.

CULTURE: With careful planting, in fertile, well-drained soil, regular watering, fertilizing, and spraying, lychee trees are not difficult to grow.

PROPAGATION: Marcottage.

PESTS: Scales.

247
Grape-Ivy

Cissus (SIS-us): Greek for ivy.
SPP.: numerous kinds grow in Florida.

FAMILY: Vitaceae.

RELATIVES: Grape and wood-bine.

TYPE OF PLANT: Vine.

HEIGHT: Variable. ZONE: S

HOW TO IDENTIFY: Tendril-climbing, herbaceous vines, with pubescent new growth and decorative, waxy foliage, often compound.

HABIT OF GROWTH: Vining, to cover shady ground or trellis.

FOLIAGE: Evergreen, waxy, compound or simple, serrate or entire.

FLOWERS: Inconspicuous, of no decorative value.

FRUITS: Small, inedible berries, if present.

SEASON OF MAXIMUM COLOR: Little seasonal change.

LANDSCAPE USES: As a ground cover in densely shaded spots where frost does not occur; as hanging-basket or planter subjects, cissus vines are popular.

HABITAT: Warm parts of the globe.

LIGHT REQUIREMENT: Quite tolerant of reduced light, intolerant of direct sun.

SOIL REQUIREMENT: Tolerant of many soil conditions.

SALT TOLERANCE: Not tolerant.

AVAILABILITY: Most nurseries sell grape-ivies in containers.

CULTURE: Plant stem pieces; water with moderation; fertilize once each summer month.

PROPAGATION: Cuttage and simple layerage.

PESTS: Aphids, mites, and nematodes.

NOTE: Species may number a half dozen, perhaps, but nomenclature may be confused, as additional study in this group is badly needed.

Hibiscus
Hybrids

249
Hibiscus

Hibiscus (hy-BIS-cus): ancient Greek and Latin name.
rosa-sinensis (RO-sa sin-EN-sis): Chinese rose.

FAMILY: Malvaceae.   RELATIVES: Mallow, cotton, and okra.
TYPE OF PLANT: Shrub.   HEIGHT: 15'. ZONE: C,S
HOW TO IDENTIFY: Many-stemmed, robust shrubs hold large, variable, alternate, evergreen leaves and showy flowers almost all the year around.
HABIT OF GROWTH: Shrubby, often upright, often robust, usually many-stemmed.
FOLIAGE: Evergreen, alternate, assuming many forms, mostly dark green in color.
FLOWERS: Bisexual, 5-merous, highly variable, bell-shaped or flaring, very decorative.
FRUITS: Ovoid, beaked capsules, which split at maturity to release seeds.
SEASON OF MAXIMUM COLOR: Much of the year as new growth is made.
LANDSCAPE USES: Hibiscus, queen of shrubs, is used in every conceivable way; as screens, as informal shrubbery borders, as freestanding specimens, as foundation plantings for large buildings. A 5'-planting interval is usually satisfactory. Literally hundreds of named varieties, which bear beautiful blossoms in endless array, are grown by Florida homeowners. Here is, indeed, one of Florida's very best landscape plants.
HABITAT: Asia; in Florida, ubiquitous in gardens on the peninsula.
LIGHT REQUIREMENT: Full sun or broken, high shade for best flowering.
SOIL REQUIREMENT: Moderate moisture and fertility, and a slightly acid reaction make for satisfactory growth.
SALT TOLERANCE: Not tolerant of dune conditions.
AVAILABILITY: Nurseries on the peninsula offer hibiscus plants in containers.
CULTURE: Plant with reasonable care in well-drained, fairly rich earth; fertilize 2 or 3 times during the warm season; water during periods of drought. Some choice clones are not robust and need special care.
PROPAGATION: Cuttage for robust varieties, graftage for poor growers.
PESTS: Aphids, scales, nematodes, mites, and thrips.

250
Fringed
Hibiscus

Hibiscus (hy-BIS-cus): ancient Greek and Latin name.
schizopetalus (skiz-oh-PET-al-us): with cut petals.

FAMILY: Malvaceae.   RELATIVES: Hibiscus, mallow, and Turks-cap.
TYPE OF PLANT: Shrub.   HEIGHT: 12'. ZONE: C,S
HOW TO IDENTIFY: Slim, drooping branches, slender, evergreen leaves, small, fringed red flowers that hang down from long stems.

HABIT OF GROWTH: Scraggly, loose assemblage of many slender, drooping branches.

FOLIAGE: Evergreen, slender, serrate, of medium texture and medium green color.

FLOWERS: Attractive, much-cut red flowers with recurved petals, hanging from long, string-like peduncles.

FRUITS: Long, pointed capsules hanging on long strings.

SEASON OF MAXIMUM COLOR: Much of the warm season.

LANDSCAPE USES: As a point of interest in front of evergreen shrubs, use a clump of three fringed hibiscus, allowing about 3' between plants. This species is too open for foundation plantings.

Fringed hibiscus has been much used in hybridization with the Chinese hibiscus, and its characteristics can be seen in many named hybrids.

HABITAT: Eastern tropical Africa; in Florida, planted where winters are not severe.

LIGHT REQUIREMENT: Full sun or shifting shade from high pines or palms.

SOIL REQUIREMENT: Tolerant of varying types, but moderate fertility is desirable.

SALT TOLERANCE: Not tolerant.

AVAILABILITY: Most nurseries on the peninsula sell plants of fringed hibiscus in containers.

CULTURE: Plant in fertile, slightly acid soil; use care in watering until the plant becomes well established; fertilize three times each year; protect the leaves and branches from scale insects by regular spraying.

PROPAGATION: Cuttage.

PESTS: Scales, nematodes, and deficiencies of minor elements upon occasion.

Rose-of-Sharon

Hibiscus (hy-BIS-cus): ancient Greek and Latin name.
syriacus (see-RYE-a-cus): Syrian.

FAMILY: Malvaceae.   RELATIVES: Mallow, cotton, and okra.

TYPE OF PLANT: Shrub.   HEIGHT: 20'. ZONE: N

HOW TO IDENTIFY: Deciduous, alternate leaves, with palmate veining, that are usually lobed and toothed; usually ascending growth; beautiful mallow-like flowers in summertime.

HABIT OF GROWTH: Shrubby, usually ascending, but habit varies with the clone.

FOLIAGE: Deciduous, alternate, medium-coarse in texture, medium green in color.

FLOWERS: White to bluish, 3" in diameter, flaring, single or double in form.

FRUITS: Capsules 1" long, abruptly short-beaked, split open lengthwise.

SEASON OF MAXIMUM COLOR: Summer.

LANDSCAPE USES: As a part of a shrubbery border, include a clump of rose-of-Sharon, planted 5' o.c. In foundation arrangements for large buildings, use as north-side accents.

Scores of clones that bear beautiful blossoms in different forms and colors are available from nurseries north of Florida.

HABITAT: Eastern Asia; in Florida, gardens in the northern part.

LIGHT REQUIREMENT: High pine shade is beneficial.

SOIL REQUIREMENT: Fertile, heavy, well-drained soils of northern counties.

SALT TOLERANCE: Not tolerant.

AVAILABILITY: Rose-of-Sharon is not important in Florida's nursery industry.

CULTURE: In northernmost areas, rose-of-Sharon grows with a minimum of attention.

PROPAGATION: Cuttage.

PESTS: Nematodes, mites, and scales.

Sea Hibiscus

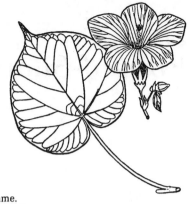

Hibiscus (hy-BIS-cus): ancient Greek and Latin name.
tileaceus (tilly-ACE-ee-us): tilia-like, referring to the foliage.

FAMILY: Malvaceae.　　　　RELATIVES: Mallow, okra, and Turks-cap.

TYPE OF PLANT: Tree.　　　　　　　　　HEIGHT: 35′. ZONE: C,S

HOW TO IDENTIFY: Drooping branches, which may take root where they touch the earth, bear smooth-edged, evergreen leaves about 6″ broad, and flowers which open yellow, turn maroon the same evening. Velvety fruits with persistent calyces follow.

HABIT OF GROWTH: Very dense, close head, with branching to the ground.

FOLIAGE: Evergreen, heart-shaped, very coarse in texture, dark green.

FLOWERS: Mallow-like, yellow with maroon eye in morning, dark red by evening.

FRUITS: Pointed, ovoid, tomentose capsules, ¾″ long, with persistent calyces.

SEASON OF MAXIMUM COLOR: Warm months when blossoms are out.

LANDSCAPE USES: For quick, dense shade, sea hibiscus can be selected, but its very rapid growth and dense head make it unpopular with many homeowners who have acquired it with new homes.

　　Except for seaside locations where it is needed to help build land, this tree is not recommended.

HABITAT: Tropical shores of both hemispheres; in Florida, widely used.

LIGHT REQUIREMENT: Full sun.

SOIL REQUIREMENT: Tolerant of light seaside sand conditions.

SALT TOLERANCE: Tolerant of dune-front locations.

AVAILABILITY: Ease of propagation makes sea hibiscus a popular container item.

CULTURE: After the tree becomes established, frequent heroic pruning is needed to keep it in bounds.

PROPAGATION: Cuttage by huge truncheons.

PESTS: Scales; strap-leaf resulting from deficiency of molybdenum.

Portia-Tree

Thespesia (thes-PEA-sea-a): Greek for divine.
populnea (poe-PUL-nee-a): poplar-like.

FAMILY: Malvaceae.   RELATIVES: Mallow, hibiscus, cotton, and okra.
TYPE OF PLANT: Tree.   HEIGHT: 35′. ZONE: S
HOW TO IDENTIFY: Poplar-like, sharp-pointed, evergreen leaves that are
    1½ times longer than broad; rough trunk bark; faded flowers that
    cling to twigs; leathery, flattened capsules. The leaves are the small-
    est in the tree-hibiscus group.
HABIT OF GROWTH: Very close-growing to form dense thickets by low
    branches.
FOLIAGE: Evergreen, sharp-pointed, medium-coarse in texture, medium
    green in color.
FLOWERS: Hibiscus-like, 3″ across, light yellow with purple-red center
    in the morning, turning to dark red in the afternoon. Old flowers
    hang on the tree for several days.
FRUITS: Flattened, leathery capsules, 1½″ across, with 1 flat and 2
    rounded sides, and persistent calyces.
SEASON OF MAXIMUM COLOR: Warm months.
LANDSCAPE USES: For seaside locations where rapid growth and land-
    holding ability are needed, portia-tree will serve. It is highly recom-
    mended for dune locations, yet it is not well thought of for inland
    homesites because of its very rapid growth and dense head that pre-
    vents the growth of lawn grasses beneath.
    Portia-tree has escaped from cultivation on the Florida Keys.
HABITAT: Old World tropics; in Florida, rather widely planted near
    the sea.
LIGHT REQUIREMENT: Full sun of tropical strands.
SOIL REQUIREMENT: Seaside sands, marl from bay-bottoms and rocks
    of the Keys.
SALT TOLERANCE: Very tolerant of salt; highly recommended for dune
    planting.
AVAILABILITY: Nurseries will have small trees, but there may be con-
    fusion in naming.
CULTURE: No special care is needed for portia-tree.
PROPAGATION: Cuttage or layerage.
PESTS: None of major concern.

Turks-Cap

Malvaviscus (mal-va-VIS-cus): sticky mallow, referring to the fruits.
arboreus (ar-BORE-ee-us): tree-like.

FAMILY: Malvaceae.　　　　RELATIVES: Hibiscus and rose-of-Sharon.

TYPE OF PLANT: Shrub.　　　　HEIGHT: 10′. ZONE: N,C,S

HOW TO IDENTIFY: Robust, branching shrub with green twigs, soft, hairy, evergreen leaves and nodding, closed, hibiscus-like flowers borne during much of the year.

HABIT OF GROWTH: Densely sprawling, but may assume vine form if given support.

FOLIAGE: Alternate, evergreen, soft, long-heart-shaped, light green in color.

FLOWERS: Nodding, petals not flaring, produced in the axils of leaves during much of the year. The usual color is a bright red, but a variety with pink flowers, and one with white blossoms are often seen.

FRUITS: Fleshy, berry-like bodies; these may not form in Florida.

SEASON OF MAXIMUM COLOR: Much of the year, when blossoms are out.

LANDSCAPE USES: Much overused as a clipped hedge and as a foundation plant because of its ease of propagation and culture, Turks-cap is seen in almost every community in central and southern Florida. The myriad blossoms give the plant a bright and cheerful aspect. Plants may stand 2′–5′ apart, depending upon the need. Will freeze back in North Florida.

HABITAT: Tropical America; in Florida, ubiquitous in warmer sections.

LIGHT REQUIREMENT: Full sun for compact habit and full-flowering.

SOIL REQUIREMENT: Any soil is acceptable.

SALT TOLERANCE: Not tolerant.

AVAILABILITY: Retail sales yards on the peninsula offer Turks-cap.

CULTURE: No exotic shrub is of easier culture.

PROPAGATION: Cuttage, employing wood of any size.

PESTS: Caterpillars may chew holes in the leaves.

Bombax

Bombax (BOM-backs): from Greek for silk, for contents of seed pods.
malabaricum (mal-a-BAR-ee-cum): from a district in India.

FAMILY: Bombacaceae.   RELATIVES: Ceiba and shaving-brush-trees.
TYPE OF PLANT: Tree.   HEIGHT: 75'. ZONE: S
HOW TO IDENTIFY: Flaming red or orange blossoms in midwinter; buttressed prickly trunk; compound, deciduous leaves with 5 leaflets.
HABIT OF GROWTH: Stout, buttressed trunk, horizontal branching.
FOLIAGE: Deciduous, compound, of coarse texture and medium green color.
FLOWERS: Very conspicuous flaming red to medium orange; tulip-form.
FRUITS: Capsules, 6" long, woolly within and with woolly seeds.
SEASON OF MAXIMUM COLOR: Winter, when the spectacular blossoms mature.
LANDSCAPE USES: Freestanding specimen for the brave show of the wintertime blossoms.

The bombax family contains numerous species that are characterized by spectacular flowers, heavy buttressed trunks, and prickly bark. These striking trees are great favorites with tourists, yet these are tropical species, rare in cultivation, that probably will never be very widely used in home landscapes. The tulip-like flowers are crowd-stoppers when they appear in wintertime.

HABITAT: Tropics of the Eastern Hemisphere; in Florida, warmest locations.
LIGHT REQUIREMENT: Full sun for best flowering.
SOIL REQUIREMENT: Tolerant of varying soils.
SALT TOLERANCE: Tolerant of light salt drift well back from the strand.
AVAILABILITY: Nurseries stock small trees in cans; there might be confusion in naming.
CULTURE: Plant in well-prepared site in nearly frostless location; water faithfully; fertilize once or twice annually.
PROPAGATION: Seedage.
PESTS: None of major importance.

256
Ceiba

Ceiba (SAY-ba): an aboriginal name.
pentandra (pen-TAN-dra): with five stamens.

FAMILY: Bombacaceae.   RELATIVES: Shaving-brush-trees.
TYPE OF PLANT: Tree.   HEIGHT: 60'. ZONE: S

HOW TO IDENTIFY: Huge, buttressed trunks; branches with spines; deciduous, digitately compound leaves; flowers white or pinkish.

HABIT OF GROWTH: Majestic tree with conspicuously buttressed trunk.

FOLIAGE: Deciduous, digitately compound, 5–6 lobes, the central one the largest.

FLOWERS: Remotely mallow-like, white or pinkish, while the tree is leafless.

FRUITS: Woody, 6" capsules filled with brown seeds and cotton-like fluff which is the kapok of commerce.

SEASON OF MAXIMUM COLOR: Early spring when the blossoms appear.

LANDSCAPE USES: Ceiba is recommended as a freestanding specimen for large public areas where there is plenty of room for full development. One of the tropic's most spectacular trees, this buttressed monarch is a standout in hot countries. In Florida, ceibas should be planted only in most nearly frostless locations, as these trees are easily damaged by cold.

HABITAT: Tropics of both hemispheres; in Florida, nearly frost-free sections.

LIGHT REQUIREMENT: Full sun or broken shade.

SOIL REQUIREMENT: Fertility above the usual Florida grade is required.

SALT TOLERANCE: Ceiba will grow several hundred yards back of the dunes.

AVAILABILITY: Some nurseries in extreme southern Florida stock ceiba trees.

CULTURE: Given reasonably good soil, moderate moisture, and freedom from frost, ceibas grow rapidly.

PROPAGATION: Seedage.

PESTS: None of major importance.

257
Floss-Silk Tree

Chorisia (ko-RIZ-ee-a): Greek for separate or distinct.
speciosa (spee-see-OH-sa): handsome, showy.

FAMILY: Bombacaceae.   RELATIVES: Ceiba and shaving-brush tree.
TYPE OF PLANT: Medium tree.   HEIGHT: 50′. ZONE: S
HOW TO IDENTIFY: Trunk often stout at base; branches green when
   young and covered with spines, often becoming grey and some-
   times losing prickles. The palmately compound leaves have 5–7 leaf-
   lets, which are elliptical with pointed apexes. Flowers are borne in
   small clusters up to 3″ in diameter.
HABIT OF GROWTH: Often as wide as high, but may be conical-shaped.
FOLIAGE: Medium to dark green and coarse-textured. Leaves fall in
   autumn.
FLOWERS: The large, showy flowers are basically pink.
FRUITS: A large capsule; seeds covered with floss. Fruit seldom seen
   in Florida.
SEASON OF MAXIMUM COLOR: October–November.
LANDSCAPE USES: An excellent freestanding specimen tree for small
   properties, mainly for the outstanding show of color in the fall.
HABITAT: Brazil and Argentina.
LIGHT REQUIREMENT: Best show of color is obtained when trees are
   grown in full sun.
SOIL REQUIREMENT: Grows well in most soils of southern Florida.
SALT TOLERANCE: Not for front dunes; will grow inside tidal lagoons.
AVAILABILITY: Occasionally found in containers in some nurseries in
   southern Florida.
CULTURE: Tolerant of adverse conditions when well established.
PROPAGATION: Seedage or cuttage.
PESTS: None serious.
NOTE: Floss from the seeds is used for stuffing pillows. Thin strips of
   bark have been used to make rope.

Shaving-
Brush-Trees

Pachira (pack-EYE-ra): native name in South America.
SPP.: several species are seen in Florida.

FAMILY: Bombacaceae.   RELATIVES: Ceiba and bombax.
TYPE OF PLANT: Tree.   HEIGHT: 30'. ZONE: S

HOW TO IDENTIFY: Coarse trees bear deciduous, digitately compound leaves, with about 7 leaflets on branches that are not prickly. The striking shaving-brush-like flowers have purplish or reddish strap-shaped petals and many conspicuous reddish stamens forming the brushes. These appear in late winter.

HABIT OF GROWTH: Asymmetrical, spreading, from a stout trunk.

FOLIAGE: Deciduous, very coarse in texture, light green in color.

FLOWERS: Linear, purplish petals curl back to reveal many red stamens to make the shaving brush.

FRUITS: Large, woody capsules which contain edible seeds.

SEASON OF MAXIMUM COLOR: Late winter, when blossoms come out.

LANDSCAPE USES: For the curiosity of the shaving-brush blossoms, an occasional freestanding specimen might be wanted, but, like most members of the family, pachiras are tropical trees that should be planted only in protected sites. These rare plants probably will never be widely used in Florida landscapes, but there is no gain-saying that the blossoms are attention-getters.

HABITAT: Tropical America; in Florida, very rare.

LIGHT REQUIREMENT: Full sun or broken shade.

SOIL REQUIREMENT: Fertile, moisture-retentive soils.

SALT TOLERANCE: Not tolerant of front-line dune locations.

AVAILABILITY: Small trees in gallon cans might be found in specialty nurseries.

CULTURE: Plant in prepared sites in frostless locations with care; water periodically; keep lawn grasses back from the roots; fertilize in late winter, perhaps again in summer while the trees are young.

PROPAGATION: Seedage.

PESTS: Scales and mites.

259
Pink-Ball

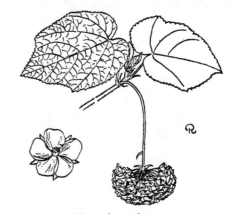

Dombeya (DOM-bay-a): for J. Dombey, French botanist of the eighteenth century.
wallichii (WALL-ick-ee-eye): for N. Wallich, a Danish botanist.

FAMILY: Sterculiaceae.　　　　RELATIVES: Cocoa, cola, and bottle-tree.
TYPE OF PLANT: Tree, usually seen as a shrub in Florida.

HEIGHT: 30'. ZONE: C,S

HOW TO IDENTIFY: Scraggly, upright growth from unbranched canes; huge, heart-shaped leaves that are densely tomentose beneath; bright, pink flowers on long, pendulous peduncles in winter.

HABIT OF GROWTH: Strongly upright, by vigorous unbranched canes.

FOLIAGE: Evergreen, very coarse in texture, medium green in color.

FLOWERS: Dense heads of little pink flowers hang from foot-long stems in winter.

FRUITS: Capsules which split into 5 parts at maturity.

SEASON OF MAXIMUM COLOR: Winter.

LANDSCAPE USES: As a freestanding specimen before hardy, evergreen shrubs, for the curiosity of the wintertime, corsage-like blossoms, pink-ball might be indicated. It is very tender to cold, grows to huge size, and has such very coarse foliage that its use in little back yards should be carefully considered. Nonetheless, people admire the wintertime pink balls and it is much planted despite these qualities.

HABITAT: Madagascar; in Florida, rather widely cultured as a garden shrub.

LIGHT REQUIREMENT: Full sun or high, shifting shade.

SOIL REQUIREMENT: Tolerant of widely varying soils; sands are acceptable.

SALT TOLERANCE: Not tolerant.

AVAILABILITY: Pink-ball is occasionally found in nurseries in southern Florida.

CULTURE: Plant with reasonable care in frostless location; water until well established, and forget.

PROPAGATION: Cuttage.

PESTS: Aphids, soft scales, sooty-mold, and nematodes.

NOTE: A number of new hybrids have been developed by the USDA for South Florida.

'Amabilis'

'Lady Clare'

'Betsy Baker'

Camellia
Hybrids

'C. M. Wilson'

'Pagoda'

'Sarah Frost'

Camellia

Camellia (kam-ELL-ee-a): for G. Kamel, a Jesuit of the seventeenth century.
japonica (jap-ON-i-ca): Japanese.

FAMILY: Theaceae.   RELATIVES: Tea, gordonia, eurya, and cleyera.
TYPE OF PLANT: Shrub.   HEIGHT: 40′. ZONE: N,C
HOW TO IDENTIFY: Alternate, shiny, bluntly serrate, evergreen leaves
    are held by green petioles from brown twigs; handsome flowers on
    current growth in midwinter.
HABIT OF GROWTH: Upright, dense, and compact.
FOLIAGE: Evergreen, alternate, of medium texture and dark green
    color.
FLOWERS: Handsome, variable, red, white, streaked, and blotched;
    appear during wintertime.
FRUITS: Globose capsules about 1″ in diameter with 1–3 seeds within.
SEASON OF MAXIMUM COLOR: Midwinter.
LANDSCAPE USES: Camellia is the aristocrat of southern shrubs, and
    has been in favor for yard planting since antebellum days. As a
    freestanding specimen, as an accent in foundation plantings, as an
    informal hedge (plant 5′ o.c.), camellia is very popular. Specimens
    for exhibition should stand 10′ from other plants.
    Many volumes have been written about camellias, of which there
    are literally thousands of varieties.
HABITAT: Eastern Asia; in Florida, gardens of upper peninsula and
    Panhandle.
LIGHT REQUIREMENT: Full sun in western Florida, broken shade on the
    upper peninsula.
SOIL REQUIREMENT: Superior, well-drained soils that are slightly acid
    in reaction.
SALT TOLERANCE: Not tolerant.
AVAILABILITY: All nurseries within the plant's range market camellias.
CULTURE: Plant carefully at exactly the same level that the plant grew
    formerly in sites made up with rich, acid compost; water faithfully;
    protect the foliage against insects and mites. A mulch is recom-
    mended.
PROPAGATION: Cuttage and graftage.
PESTS: Scales of many species, aphids, beetles, and camellia die-back
    diseases.

262
Sasanqua

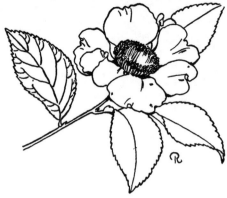

Camellia (kam-ELL-ee-a): for G. Kamel, a Jesuit of the seventeenth century.
sasanqua (sass-ANN-kwa): Japanese vernacular name.

FAMILY: Theaceae. RELATIVES: Tea, gordonia, eurya, and cleyera.

TYPE OF PLANT: Shrub. HEIGHT: 20′. ZONE: N,C

HOW TO IDENTIFY: An evergreen shrub that has downy branchlets that hold alternate leaves, 1″–3″ long, which are bluntly pointed, and hairy on the midrib above. Attractive blossoms appear in early autumn.

HABIT OF GROWTH: Variable with the clone, usually ascending.

FOLIAGE: Evergreen, fine in texture, dark green in color.

FLOWERS: Scented, white, pink, or rose, 2″ in diameter, with 5 or more petals.

FRUITS: Globose capsules, ½″–¾″ in diameter, with 1–3 seeds within.

SEASON OF MAXIMUM COLOR: October–November.

LANDSCAPE USES: For screens, set plants 3′ apart; as an accent in foundation plantings. Gardeners in northern Florida admire this good, hardy shrub, and sasanquas are widely grown in gardens of the upper counties.

HABITAT: China, Japan; in Florida, well distributed in gardens of the upper counties.

LIGHT REQUIREMENT: Full sun on good soils in western Florida, broken shade elsewhere.

SOIL REQUIREMENT: Sasanquas thrive on superior soils, but as a class, they endure less good drainage than do other camellias.

SALT TOLERANCE: Not tolerant.

AVAILABILITY: Sasanquas in cans are widely available.

CULTURE: Plant carefully in holes made up with rich, acid compost; water faithfully; protect the foliage against scales and mites.

PROPAGATION: Cuttage.

PESTS: Scales, mites, aphids, beetles, and camellia die-back disease.

263
Cleyera

Cleyera (CLAY-er-a): for A. Cleyer, a Dutch botanist.
japonica (jap-ON-i-ca): Japanese.

FAMILY: Theaceae.   RELATIVES: Tea, camellia, eurya, and gordonia.

TYPE OF PLANT: Shrub.   HEIGHT: 25′. ZONE: N,C,S

HOW TO IDENTIFY: Upright habit; glossy, alternate, entire leaves sometimes with reddish midribs. Foliage often is clustered toward the
  ends of branches, leaving the plant somewhat open beneath.

HABIT OF GROWTH: Narrow, upright, many branches nearly erect in
  some specimens.

FOLIAGE: Evergreen, alternate, medium-fine in texture, very deep green
  in color.

FLOWERS: White, fragrant, ½″ across, clustered in axils.

FRUITS: Red, roundish berries, not of great decorative value.

SEASON OF MAXIMUM COLOR: When red fruits color.

LANDSCAPE USES: Cleyera can be used as a corner plant in foundation
  groupings, if there are no corner windows. In shrubbery borders,
  it may serve, too, when planted in groups with 3′ between plants.
    Cleyera is hardy to cold and it is worthy of wider usage in north-
  ern areas of our state.

HABITAT: Asia; in Florida, on better soils, particularly, in the northern
  part.

LIGHT REQUIREMENT: Tolerant of shade; can endure north-side locations.

SOIL REQUIREMENT: Thrives on better soils of the upper peninsula and
  the Panhandle.

SALT TOLERANCE: Not tolerant.

AVAILABILITY: Cleyera is generally on lists of nurseries in upper counties.

CULTURE: Plant in enriched, acid sites; water carefully; protect foliage
  from scale insects.

PROPAGATION: Seedage or cuttage.

PESTS: Scales.

264
Eurya

Eurya (YOU-ree-a): of uncertain derivation.
japonica (jap-ON-i-ca): Japanese.

FAMILY: Theaceae.   RELATIVES: Tea, camellia, cleyera, and gordonia.

TYPE OF PLANT: Dwarf shrub.   HEIGHT: 25'. ZONE: N,C

HOW TO IDENTIFY: Evergreen, serrate, short-petioled, alternate leaves, about 1½" long; unisexual flowers, ¼" across; upward-pointing branches.

HABIT OF GROWTH: Compact, with upward-pointing branches.

FOLIAGE: Evergreen, fine in texture, dark green in color.

FLOWERS: White, ¼" in diameter, unisexual, in small clusters.

FRUITS: Globose, black pods, 1/5" across, seldom seen in Florida landscapes.

SEASON OF MAXIMUM COLOR: Little seasonal variation.

LANDSCAPE USES: Eurya is a useful shrub because of its small size, fine scale, and slow growth. In foundation arrangements, use a 3' interval. This is a good north-side plant, as it endures shade well and flowers and fruits are of no importance.

HABITAT: Coastal Asia; in Florida, superior soils of central and northern sections.

LIGHT REQUIREMENT: Broken shade of pine trees or full shade of north-side locations.

SOIL REQUIREMENT: Fertile soils free from nematodes, if possible.

SALT TOLERANCE: Not tolerant.

AVAILABILITY: Euryas in cans in nurseries are rather rare.

CULTURE: Excellent soil, partial or full shade, freedom from nematodes, and protection from scale insects are needed for success. Water and fertilizer must be applied regularly.

PROPAGATION: Cuttage.

PESTS: Many types of scale insects and nematodes.

Loblolly Bay

Gordonia (gore-DOAN-ee-a): for J. Gordon, early English nurseryman.
lasianthus (lay-zee-AN-thus): old generic name.

FAMILY: Theaceae.   RELATIVES: Tea, camellia, cleyera, and eurya.
TYPE OF PLANT: Tree.   HEIGHT: 70'. ZONE: N,C,S
HOW TO IDENTIFY: An upright-growing tree bears evergreen leaves that are shining green on both sides and have shallow teeth along their edges; the twigs are dark brown with a few scattered lenticels. Charming, 5-parted, white flowers on long stalks appear in spring or summer.
HABIT OF GROWTH: Upright tree with cylindrical head and shallow root system.
FOLIAGE: Evergreen, coarse in texture; both surfaces are smooth and shining.
FLOWERS: Showy, white, fragrant, 3″ across on long, axillary pedicels in spring.
FRUITS: Woody capsules, about ¾″ long, which split into 5s.
SEASON OF MAXIMUM COLOR: Spring when flowers open; fall when leaves turn red.
LANDSCAPE USES: In woodland plantings on low ground, loblolly bay is useful for its beautiful white blossoms and red leaves that mature in autumn. This native tree is not widely planted in home landscapes.
HABITAT: Swamps and bayheads as far south as Lake Okeechobee.
LIGHT REQUIREMENT: Diffused light of hammocks.
SOIL REQUIREMENT: Heavy, fertile, moist soils support the shallow root systems.
SALT TOLERANCE: Not tolerant.
AVAILABILITY: Not a nursery item; get a small seedling from a friend.
CULTURE: Select a moist, rich location; plant at the same level as the tree formerly grew; water well until established, thereafter during dry times.
PROPAGATION: Seedage.
PESTS: Borers after periods of drought, sooty-mold after aphids.
NOTE: Famed Franklin tree (*Franklinia altamaha*) is a near relative. This species was discovered by John Bartram in Georgia in 1790 and transported to his garden in Philadelphia.

Tea

Thea (THE-ah): Latinized Chinese name for the tea plant.
sinensis (sin-EN-sis): Chinese.

FAMILY: Theaceae.　　　　RELATIVES: Camellia, eurya, and gordonia.

TYPE OF PLANT: Shrub.　　　　　　HEIGHT: 20′. ZONE: N,C

HOW TO IDENTIFY: Evergreen, alternate, serrate, short-petioled leaves, 2″–5″ long, acute or obtuse; white, nodding, fragrant flowers, 1½″ in diameter, followed by woody capsules.

HABIT OF GROWTH: Compact, dense shrub in Florida.

FOLIAGE: Evergreen, of medium texture and dark green color.

FLOWERS: White, fragrant, nodding, 1½″ across, showing numerous stamens.

FRUITS: Woody capsules rather freely formed.

SEASON OF MAXIMUM COLOR: Wintertime.

LANDSCAPE USES: Tea may be planted as a horticultural curiosity in an informal shrubbery group; allow 5′ of space for each plant.

　　Tea has many of the good qualities of camellia as a garden shrub, yet the latter is rightly preferred because of its gorgeous blossoms. Floridians are not likely to try to grow their own tea in their small back yards, but they may gain satisfaction from telling guests about their tea plants and demonstrating the kinds of leaves that are used in our table beverage.

HABITAT: China; in Florida, sparingly grown as a curiosity in northern and central counties.

LIGHT REQUIREMENT: Tolerant of shifting shade.

SOIL REQUIREMENT: Any reasonably fertile, well-drained soil is adequate.

SALT TOLERANCE: Not tolerant.

AVAILABILITY: Tea is occasionally sold in nurseries.

CULTURE: If given camellia culture, tea should thrive.

PROPAGATION: Seedage in Florida.

PESTS: Scales, twig die-back disease, and mushroom root-rot.

267
Pitch-Apple

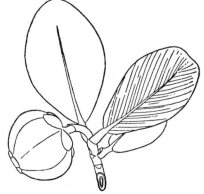

Clusia (CLEW-see-a): from an association of plants growing in flooded places.
rosea (ROSE-ee-a): rosy.

FAMILY: Guttiferae.   RELATIVES: Mangosteen and mamey.
TYPE OF PLANT: Tree, used as a shrub in landscaping.   HEIGHT: 30'.
ZONE: S

HOW TO IDENTIFY: Huge, evergreen leaves, 8″ long x 4½″ wide, leathery, and stiff. Attractive pink or white flowers 3″ across are followed by prominent round fruits, 3″ in diameter, with large, pinkish calyces at their stem ends.

HABIT OF GROWTH: Widespreading, horizontal, irregular branching.

FOLIAGE: Evergreen, 8″ × 4½″, bold in aspect, light green in color.

FLOWERS: Showy, pink or white, in terminal positions.

FRUITS: Prominent, fleshy fruits, 3″ across, which split at maturity to display seeds surrounded by black, resinous material.

SEASON OF MAXIMUM COLOR: Warm months when blossoms are out.

LANDSCAPE USES: To gain a tropical effect, pitch-apple is used as a shrub in informal borders and screens. It is really too large and too coarse to plant in bins, but it is used this way, nonetheless. The clone with the marbled leaves (*C. rosea* 'Variegata') is much in demand because of its unusual and very striking variegated foliage.

HABITAT: West Indian islands; in Florida, possibly the Keys. In gardens, frost-free locations only.

LIGHT REQUIREMENT: Full sun or broken shade from tall palms.

SOIL REQUIREMENT: Tolerant of light, open sands.

SALT TOLERANCE: Very resistant to salt air and salt spray.

AVAILABILITY: Small plants in containers may be found in some nurseries in southern Florida.

CULTURE: Set in holes with fertile compost; water until well established; thereafter, keep lawn grasses back from the root zone.

PROPAGATION: Seedage or cuttage.

PESTS: Scales.

'President Carnot'

'Dew Drop'

'Baby Rainbow'

Rex Begonia

'His Majesty'

Seedling

'Her Majesty'

Seedling

Unidentified

269
Rex Begonia

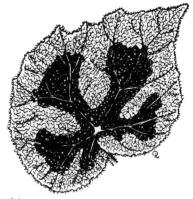

Begonia (be-GO-nee-a): for M. Begon, French botanist.
SPP.: probably several species are represented in Rex begonias.

FAMILY: Begoniaceae.   RELATIVES: The wonderful world of begonias.
TYPE OF PLANT: Herbaceous perennial.   HEIGHT: Variable. ZONE: S
HOW TO IDENTIFY: The fantastic leaves, in their multitudinous forms
   and colors, are the reasons why Rex begonias are among the
   world's most beloved houseplants.
HABIT OF GROWTH: Compact, heavily foliated.
FOLIAGE: Universally appealing in its many forms.
FLOWERS: Attractive, yet incidental in this group of begonias.
FRUITS: Angled pods, often green with red markings.
SEASON OF MAXIMUM COLOR: Warm months when blossoms appear.
LANDSCAPE USES: Since the white man came to Florida, Rex begonias
   have figured prominently in porch and indoor decoration. In late
   years these beautiful plants have come into their own as urn sub-
   jects for Florida rooms and patios.
HABITAT: Warm parts of the world around.
LIGHT REQUIREMENT: Partial shade is best. Protection from wind is es-
   sential.
SOIL REQUIREMENT: Fibrous, organic, slightly acid soil, of moderately
   high fertility is recommended. Begonia soils must drain quickly.
SALT TOLERANCE: Not tolerant.
AVAILABILITY: Nurseries, chain stores, and garden centers sell Rex be-
   gonias in pots.
CULTURE: Water and feed as you do your other house plants; shift to
   larger containers when old plants become crowded.
PROPAGATION: Cuttage, using terminal shoots or whole leaves.
PESTS: Mealy-bugs, mites, and nematodes.
NOTE: On the facing page are diagrams of some Florida favorites;
   above is ever popular 'Iron Cross'.

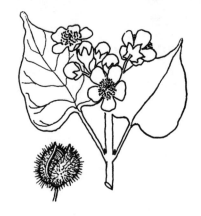

270
Annatto

Bixa (BICK-sa): aboriginal name.
orellana (or-rel-AY-na): ancient name.

FAMILY: Bixaceae.   RELATIVES: This plant stands alone in its family.
TYPE OF PLANT: Tree or large shrub.   HEIGHT: 20′. ZONE: C,S
HOW TO IDENTIFY: Ovate, evergreen leaves, palmately veined, about 7″
   long; attractive pink flowers (sometimes white) in clusters, followed
   by spiny, brown fruits.
HABIT OF GROWTH: Usually a many-stemmed, bushy, small tree.
FOLIAGE: Evergreen, coarse in texture, and light green in color.
FLOWERS: Pink (sometimes white), 2″ across, in large clusters.
FRUITS: Conspicuous, spiny, brown capsules split open in winter to
   display many small seeds that are covered with a pulp that is used
   as a source of yellow dye.
SEASON OF MAXIMUM COLOR: Summer, when flowers open; winter, when
   pods split.
LANDSCAPE USES: For beautiful pink blossoms and unusual spiny fruits,
   annatto can be featured as a freestanding specimen. Advanced
   horticulturists might take pride in explaining to guests that the pulp
   has long been used as a natural dye for foodstuffs and as a body
   paint by aborigines. This tropical plant is injured by cold.
HABITAT: American tropics; in Florida, landscape plantings in warm
   locations.
LIGHT REQUIREMENT: Full sun for best flowering.
SOIL REQUIREMENT: Tolerant of many kinds of soil, from clay to sand.
SALT TOLERANCE: Endures salt air back of the first dunes.
AVAILABILITY: Small trees are in nurseries in southern Florida.
CULTURE: No special problems are encountered where frost is not a
   hazard.
PROPAGATION: Seedage.
PESTS: None of great importance.

271
Buttercup-Tree

Cochlospermum (coch-lo-SPERM-um): snail seed.
vitifolium (vit-i-FOL-ee-um): grape-like leaves.

FAMILY: Cochlospermaceae.

RELATIVES: None in cultivation.

TYPE OF PLANT: Tree.

HEIGHT: 40'. ZONE: S

HOW TO IDENTIFY: Deciduous tree with alternate, palmately lobed leaves which are usually 5-lobed and up to 1' across; lobes toothed. Flowers are borne in terminal clusters before the leaves in late spring.

HABIT OF GROWTH: Open-branched tree.

FOLIAGE: Dull, medium green, medium texture.

FLOWERS: Large, yellow, to 4" across, numerous stamens.

FRUITS: Capsules to 3" long with fine pubescence.

SEASON OF MAXIMUM COLOR: Spring in southern Florida; after the dry period in the tropics.

LANDSCAPE USES: Suitable as a street tree, framing tree, or specimen tree for small properties.

HABITAT: American tropics.

LIGHT REQUIREMENT: Full sun.

SOIL REQUIREMENT: Most well-drained soils.

SALT TOLERANCE: Avoid front-line locations.

AVAILABILITY: Available in some southern Florida nurseries.

CULTURE: Easy to establish and maintain without special attention.

PROPAGATION: Seedage or cuttage.

PESTS: None serious.

NOTE: Double-flowered forms are available.

272
Crab Cactus

Schlumbergera (schlum-ber-GER-a): for F. Schlumberger, European horticulturist (left-hand sketch), and
Zygocactus (zy-go-CACK-tus): cactus with irregular flowers (right-hand drawing).
SPP.: several species in these two genera and their hybrids grow in Florida.

FAMILY: Cactaceae.   RELATIVES: Orchid cactus and prickly-pear.
TYPE OF PLANT: Epiphytic perennials.   HEIGHT: Variable. ZONE: S
HOW TO IDENTIFY: Flat, jointed, leafless stems resemble crabs' legs, and appear to have been clipped at the ends where blossoms appear.
HABIT OF GROWTH: Declinate, segmented stems fall over edges of their containers.
FOLIAGE: Absent.
STEMS: Flat, jointed, unarmed, in various tones of green, with ends that seem to have been sheared. *Schlumbergera* (left) has slight indentations along stem margins. *Zygocactus* (right) has stem joints about 2½″ long by 1″ broad, and the margins are furnished with 2–3 incurved horns. Bigeneric hybrids might be different.
FLOWERS: Borne horizontally at stem ends, irregular, very beautiful, usually in tones of red or orange.
FRUITS: Red berries, if present.
SEASON OF MAXIMUM COLOR: Whenever blossoms mature.
LANDSCAPE USES: For generations, crab cacti have been front-porch favorites. Now they adorn Florida rooms and patios, yet still more use could be made of these epiphytes on lawn trees.
HABITAT: Tropical America.
LIGHT REQUIREMENT: Partial shade in midsummer, but full sunlight is needed in late summer and autumn for flower-bud development.
SOIL REQUIREMENT: Although these are epiphytes, crab cacti are usually grown in fibrous compost by Floridians.
SALT TOLERANCE: Not tolerant.
AVAILABILITY: Nurseries and chain stores stock crab cacti in small pots.
CULTURE: Plant pieces of stems in small pots or baskets; water moderately during midsummer; and fertilize lightly each month. In late summer allow the substratum to be dry as you expose crab cacti to full sunlight to encourage flowering in season.
PROPAGATION: Cuttage or graftage.
PESTS: Mealy-bugs.

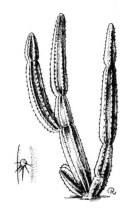

273
Hedge
Cactus

Cereus (SEA-ree-us): a Latin word of uncertain application here.
peruvianus (per-oo-vee-ANE-us): Peruvian.

FAMILY: Cactaceae.   RELATIVES: The true cacti.
TYPE OF PLANT: Succulent shrub in landscape use.   HEIGHT: 25'.
                                             ZONE: N,C,S
HOW TO IDENTIFY: This is a hardy, upright-growing cactus, with ribbed
  stems about 8" in diameter.
HABIT OF GROWTH: Columnar growth with upright, leafless, flanged
  branches.
FOLIAGE: None.
FLOWERS: Spectacular, night-blooming, white, fragrant, almost a foot
  in diameter.
FRUITS: Red, oval, 3" or so in length. Often fruits do not mature on
  this species in Florida.
SEASON OF MAXIMUM COLOR: Summer nights, when blossoms unfurl.
LANDSCAPE USES: As a freestanding specimen to gain a tropical effect
  and as a part of the foundation planting of contemporary houses,
  hedge cactus is very popular. The type with the flanges in spiral
  arrangement is well liked.
     When blossom buds appear in May–June, specimen plants may
  be floodlighted after dark on nights when flowers open. Dramatic,
  nighttime garden displays are possible when lighting is properly
  arranged.
HABITAT: South America; in Florida, widely used in landscape plantings.
LIGHT REQUIREMENT: Full sun or partial shade.
SOIL REQUIREMENT: Tolerant of widely varying soils.
SALT TOLERANCE: Tolerant of moderate salt drift.
AVAILABILITY: Nurseries frequently stock hedge cactus in gallon cans.
CULTURE: Plant in a well-drained site; fertilize at the beginning of
  the rainy season; protect from frost during the first winter or so
  until a heavy root system becomes established.
PROPAGATION: Simply cut a piece of stem and plant where a cactus is
  wanted.
PESTS: None of major consequence.

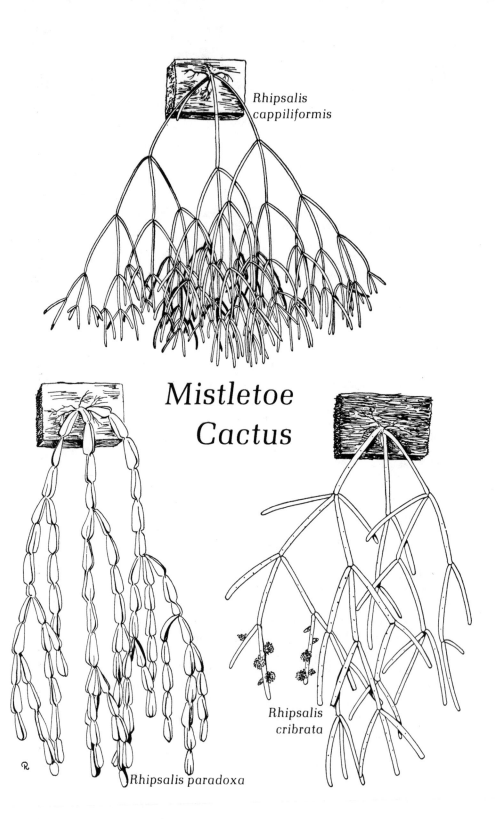

Rhipsalis
cappiliformis

Mistletoe
Cactus

Rhipsalis
cribrata

Rhipsalis paradoxa

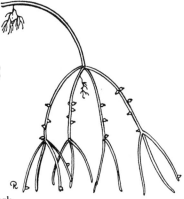

275
Mistletoe Cactus

Rhipsalis (RIP-sal-is): from the Greek for wickerwork.
SPP.: a dozen species and their hybrids grow in our state.

FAMILY: Cactaceae.   RELATIVES: Hedge cactus and organ cactus.
TYPE OF PLANT: Epiphytic perennial.   HEIGHT: Variable. ZONE: S
HOW TO IDENTIFY: Spineless cacti hang from trees like Spanish-moss.
   Quite or nearly leafless plants divide into 3 general classes: round-
   branched, those which hang like rawhide thongs; angle-branched,
   those which have hanging, rooting, angled branches; and flat-
   branched, those with broad stems like orchid cacti.
HABIT OF GROWTH: Branching, leafless, green stems hang downward
   from the substratum.
FOLIAGE: Absent.
STEMS: Evergreen, functioning photosynthetically, rooting as they
   hang. Three arbitrary classes are noted above.
FLOWERS: Small, white, pink, red, or 2-toned.
FRUITS: Small, naked berries, some red, some white, others greenish.
SEASON OF MAXIMUM COLOR: Fall if fruits mature.
LANDSCAPE USES: To help cast the spell of the tropics, mistletoe cacti
   can be hung from trees, rafters, lanai or chickee posts, or other
   stable wooden objects in frostless locations. Very often these curi-
   ous tropical exotics are kept in baskets and pots on porches. Many
   named mistletoe cacti, some of which are delineated across, are
   seen in the Sunshine State. The most widely grown, *Rhipsalis cas-
   sutha*, is illustrated above.
HABITAT: Tropical America.
LIGHT REQUIREMENT: Broken, high shade.
SOIL REQUIREMENT: Osmundine, driftwood, trees, palms, and tree fern
   planks serve as substrata for mistletoe cacti.
SALT TOLERANCE: Tolerant to salt drift well back of the front-line dunes.
AVAILABILITY: A few specialty nurseries offer different kinds of mistle-
   toe cactus in pots.
CULTURE: Hang or tie with a bit of osmundine or tree fern plank where
   wanted; syringe frequently; enjoy. Mistletoe cacti are among the
   least demanding of all tropical exotics.
PROPAGATION: Cuttage.
PESTS: Grasshoppers and roaches eat the succulent stems.

Night-Blooming Cereus

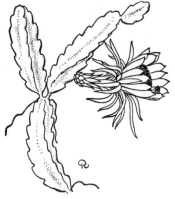

Hylocereus (hi-lo-SEAR-ee-us): Greek for wood and cereus.
undatus (un-DAY-tus): waved.

FAMILY: Cactaceae. RELATIVES: The true cacti.

TYPE OF PLANT: Vine. HEIGHT: 20′. ZONE: S

HOW TO IDENTIFY: Strong, climbing vine that clings to its support by many, twine-like, aerial roots, and produces, during summer nights, spectacular foot-broad, white blossoms.

HABIT OF GROWTH: Vine-like, clinging by many strong roots.

FOLIAGE: Absent. The triangular stems, dark green in color, form interesting patterns.

FLOWERS: Noteworthy, foot-broad, white, funnel-form blossoms at night.

FRUITS: Red berries, 4½″ long, that are highly decorative and edible as well.

SEASON OF MAXIMUM COLOR: Summer nights when blossoms unfurl; fall, when fruits mature.

LANDSCAPE USES: For the tropical effect of the climbing stems and the much-talked-about nighttime blossoms, night-blooming cereus is widely cultured in warm countries. The cactus is planted by palms, walls, and masonry houses, where the tracery effect of its snake-like, clinging stems is much admired by tourists. Here is another tropical plant, very well adapted to our state, that helps to enhance the feeling of the tropics in our southernmost counties.

HABITAT: Tropical America; in Florida, escaped from cultivation in the southern part.

LIGHT REQUIREMENT: Sun or shade.

SOIL REQUIREMENT: Any soil is suitable.

SALT TOLERANCE: Very tolerant of salt.

AVAILABILITY: From a friend, one may obtain a section of stem for planting.

CULTURE: Where frosts seldom occur, culture of night-blooming cereus is simplicity itself. Plant a section of stem and forget it.

PROPAGATION: Cuttage by pieces of mature stems.

PESTS: Scales.

Orchid Cactus

Epiphyllum (ep-i-FILL-um): Greek for on a leaf, alluding to position of flowers.
SPP.: two species and many hybrids bloom in Florida.

FAMILY: Cactaceae. RELATIVES: Crab cactus and night-blooming cereus.

TYPE OF PLANT: Epiphytic perennial.   HEIGHT: Variable. ZONE: S

HOW TO IDENTIFY: Yard-long, flat, leafless stems have crenatures in their margins, some of which produce the huge, glistening, orchid-like blossoms, held by some gardeners to be the most spectacular in the plant kingdom.

HABIT OF GROWTH: Declinate, flat stems hang downward.

FOLIAGE: Absent.

FLOWERS: Foot-broad, day- or night-blooming, white, red, pink, orange, or yellow, emerging from notches along leaf margins.

FRUITS: Red, bracted berries, if present.

SEASON OF MAXIMUM COLOR: Warm months when blossoms appear.

LANDSCAPE USES: Collectors' items, flowers of fanciers, these tropical, rain-forest cacti are cultured as pot specimens, or they may be set on branches of rough-barked trees.

HABITAT: Tropical America.

LIGHT REQUIREMENT: Partial shade, with more light in wintertime.

SOIL REQUIREMENT: Open, fibrous, leafy compost of slight acid reaction.

SALT TOLERANCE: Not tolerant.

AVAILABILITY: Plants of many varieties are found in containers at Florida nurseries.

CULTURE: Plant stem pieces in pots of compost; water always with moderation; apply liquid fertilizer during warm months. When days become shorter, apply less water, but do not allow stems to shrivel.

PROPAGATION: Cuttage.

PESTS: Mealy-bugs; rot diseases if grown too wet.

Prickly-Pear

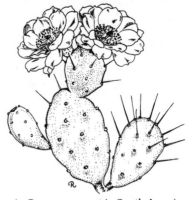

Opuntia (o-PUNT-ee-a): probably from Opus, a town in Greece or a port in South America. SPP.: several species grow in Florida.

FAMILY: Cactaceae.   RELATIVES: Christmas cactus and cereus.

TYPE OF PLANT: Herbaceous perennial.   HEIGHT: 9'–12'. ZONE: N,C,S

HOW TO IDENTIFY: Over 250 species of coarse and awkward plants. The joints usually form flat pads, up to 12" long and 6"–8" wide; most species carry spines and fine bristles, others are naturally spineless. Flowers are borne on the upper margins of the pads.

HABIT OF GROWTH: Low and spreading to irregular upright.

FOLIAGE: Small, cylindrical leaves fall very early, and are rarely seen.

FLOWERS: Large and showy, red, yellow, purple, or white.

FRUITS: Dry or juicy edible berries.

SEASON OF MAXIMUM COLOR: Spring and summer.

LANDSCAPE USES: Excellent for rock gardens, exposed and rocky banks, sandy, waste areas, and seaside locations.

HABITAT: Canada south to Straits of Magellan.

LIGHT REQUIREMENT: Full sun to partial shade.

SOIL REQUIREMENT: Well-drained, sandy soils.

SALT TOLERANCE: Some species thrive on sand dunes near ocean or gulf.

AVAILABILITY: Available in many nurseries in cans.

CULTURE: Require little or no care once plants are established.

PROPAGATION: Joints root readily.

PESTS: None serious.

NOTE: *O. ficus-indica* is grown in the tropics for its edible fruits. Spineless varieties of prickly-pear have been used for cattle feed.

Lingaro

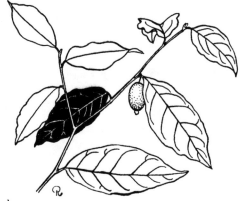

Elaeagnus (ell-ee-AG-nus): ancient Greek name.
philippensis (fill-ip-EN-sis): Philippine.

FAMILY: Elaeagnaceae.   RELATIVES: Silverthorn and oleaster.

TYPE OF PLANT: Shrub or vine.   HEIGHT: 20'. ZONE: C,S

HOW TO IDENTIFY: Long, arching canes with alternate, silvery-scurfy, evergreen leaves.

HABIT OF GROWTH: Sprawling, weeping, can be kept compact by shearing.

FOLIAGE: Medium-fine texture.

FLOWERS: Tiny, scurfy, brown, nodding, fragrant, clustered in leaf axils.

FRUITS: Little pinkish, drupe-like, acid fruits that are edible.

SEASON OF MAXIMUM COLOR: No variation in color.

LANDSCAPE USES: In a foundation planting, set 3' o.c.; as a part of a large, enclosing shrubbery border, lingaro plants can stand 5' o.c. This is a useful shrub for nearly frostless sections of the lower peninsula, because of its weeping habit, medium-fine texture, silvery foliage, and fragrant little blossoms. There are annual crops of the little acid fruits, as extra dividends. For these, this plant was originally introduced.

HABITAT: South Sea islands; in Florida, warmest locations.

LIGHT REQUIREMENT: Full sun for best color, habit, and fruiting.

SOIL REQUIREMENT: Adapted to various soils, except alkaline ones.

SALT TOLERANCE: Tolerant of salt drift.

AVAILABILITY: A few specialty nurseries offer this good shrub.

CULTURE: After careful planting in improved, slightly acid soil, pruning, fertilization, and protection against mites and scales are needed as with most other shrubs.

PROPAGATION: Seedage, cuttage, or marcottage.

PESTS: Mites, scales, and cane die-back disease.

280
Silverthorn

Elaeagnus (ell-ee-AG-nus): ancient Greek name.
pungens (PUN-genz): sharp-pointed.

FAMILY: Elaeagnaceae.   RELATIVES: Lingaro and oleaster.
TYPE OF PLANT: Shrub or vine.   HEIGHT: 20'. ZONE: N,C
HOW TO IDENTIFY: Long, reaching, thorny canes with scurfy bark, often with sharp thorns; alternate, scurfy leaves, silvery beneath, with many brown dots; scurfy, little, brown flowers in winter, followed by scurfy, brown fruits that are edible.
HABIT OF GROWTH: Sprawling, weeping, very amenable to shearing.
FOLIAGE: Evergreen, alternate, silvery beneath, with many brown dots. The texture is medium, the color variable with the clone. Many have leaves variously marbled with white or yellow.
FLOWERS: Tiny, brown, scurfy, fragrant in winter, clustered in leaf axils.
FRUITS: Little, pinkish-brown, scurfy, drupe-like, acid fruits that are edible.
SEASON OF MAXIMUM COLOR: No seasonal changes.
LANDSCAPE USES: In foundation plantings, set 3' o.c.; for a hedge that is to be clipped, have the plants 18" apart; as a part of a large, enclosing shrubbery border, silverthorn plants can stand 5' o.c.
   This is one of Florida's very best broad-leaved evergreen shrubs because it grows well and survives all of Florida's minimum temperatures, yet it may develop deficiencies of minor elements on calcareous soils.
HABITAT: Eastern Asia; in Florida, ubiquitous as a garden shrub.
LIGHT REQUIREMENT: Full sun or light, shifting pine shade.
SOIL REQUIREMENT: Tolerant of varying soils.
SALT TOLERANCE: Very tolerant of salt.
AVAILABILITY: Retail nurseries stock silverthorn plants canned and B & B.
CULTURE: After careful planting and faithful watering for establishment, fertilize once a year; head in long canes by deep pruning; control mites during dry periods.
PROPAGATION: Cuttage. The small plants grow slowly at first.
PESTS: Mites, scales, and cane die-back disease.

Crape-Myrtle

Lagerstroemia (lah-ger-STREAM-ee-a): for M. von Lagerstroem, Swedish botanist.
indica (IN-dee-ca): of the Indies, eastern tropics of Linnaeus' time.

FAMILY: Lythraceae.　　　　　　　　　　　RELATIVE: Cuphea.

TYPE OF PLANT: Tree or shrub.　　　　　HEIGHT: 20′. ZONE: N,C,S

HOW TO IDENTIFY: Deciduous, alternate, glabrous leaves with very short petioles; very smooth, brown bark that sloughs off in large patches; showy spikes of beautiful blossoms in summertime.

HABIT OF GROWTH: Upright, suckering freely at the ground line.

FOLIAGE: Deciduous, alternate, smooth, medium-fine in texture, light green in color. The fall color is yellow and red.

FLOWERS: Showy terminal or axillary panicles of white, pink, red, or purple flowers in summertime. These fringed and clawed blossoms are borne on current wood.

FRUITS: Brown, woody capsules that split from the top.

SEASON OF MAXIMUM COLOR: May, June, and July, when the blossoms are at their best.

LANDSCAPE USES: Crape-myrtle is an old garden favorite that has been a part of Florida home-ground plantings for many generations. It may serve as a freestanding tree, a framing tree, or as a shrub to become a color highlight in a shrubbery border. As a roadside plant, crape-myrtle also excels.

HABITAT: Asia; naturalized in Florida.

LIGHT REQUIREMENT: Full sun for best flowering and habit.

SOIL REQUIREMENT: Tolerant of many different kinds of soils.

SALT TOLERANCE: Not tolerant.

AVAILABILITY: Canned crape-myrtles in full bloom are frequently seen in nurseries.

CULTURE: No special culture is needed for success with crape-myrtle.

PROPAGATION: Cuttage, by long, leafless, hardwood cuttings in early winter.

PESTS: Powdery mildew, mushroom root-rot, and aphids followed by sooty-mold.

282
Queen
Crape-Myrtle

Lagerstroemia (lah-ger-STREAM-ee-a): for M. von Lagerstroem, Swedish botanist.
speciosa (spee-see-OH-sa): showy.

FAMILY: Lythraceae.   RELATIVES: Cuphea and common crape-myrtle.

TYPE OF PLANT: Tree.   HEIGHT: 30′. ZONE: S

HOW TO IDENTIFY: Medium-sized tree with huge, simple, deciduous leaves that resemble those of guava; very spectacular blossoms in summertime.

HABIT OF GROWTH: Dense, bushy, rank-growing.

FOLIAGE: Deciduous, coarse in texture, dark green when fertilized. Fall color, red.

FLOWERS: 3″ across, in large, terminal panicles, pink or mauve, produced in such numbers as to cause the stalks to bend.

FRUITS: Capsules 1″ in diameter, sitting within the withered calyx.

SEASON OF MAXIMUM COLOR: July.

LANDSCAPE USES: As an avenue tree in warmest locations, or as a free-standing specimen in a garden development, queen crape-myrtle is one of the tropics' most spectacular summer bloomers. Additional species are offered by specialists in tropical trees.

HABITAT: Old World tropics; in Florida, yard tree in warmest locations.

LIGHT REQUIREMENT: Full sun or broken, shifting, high shade.

SOIL REQUIREMENT: Tolerant of varying soils.

SALT TOLERANCE: Not tolerant.

AVAILABILITY: Queen crape-myrtle is for sale in cans in many nurseries.

CULTURE: Plant with reasonable care in fertile, acid soil; water faithfully; fertilize twice annually; keep lawn grasses back from root zone. Protection during cold nights is necessary.

PROPAGATION: Cuttage under mist or by sprouts from cut roots.

PESTS: Scales.

283
Cuphea

Cuphea (COO-fee-a): Greek for curved, for beak at base of the calyx tube.
hyssopifolia (hiss-op-ee-FOL-ee-a): with leaves like hyssop.

FAMILY: Lythraceae.   RELATIVES: Crape-myrtle, loosestrife, and henna.
TYPE OF PLANT: Dwarf shrub.   HEIGHT: 1'–2'. ZONE: C,S
HOW TO IDENTIFY: A tiny shrub with close, dense branching; leaves of
    finest scale; attractive little blossoms, colored or white, during
    much of the year.
HABIT OF GROWTH: Very close, tight, and compact; spreading branches.
FOLIAGE: Evergreen, opposite, of finest texture and medium green color.
FLOWERS: Tiny (¼"–½"), axillary, profuse much of the year.
FRUITS: Tiny, oblong capsules enclosed by calyces.
SEASON OF MAXIMUM COLOR: Much of the year.
LANDSCAPE USES: For edgings (1' apart) cuphea is unexcelled in frost-
    free sections; for sunny planters (1' apart) it is favored, and as a
    foundation plant for the smallest buildings, cuphea is approved
    when set at 1½' intervals. The cheerful aspect produced by the
    many diminutive blossoms among the tiny leaves on the wiry stems
    is much appreciated. The various clones exhibit slightly differing
    growth habits, and bear flowers of white or shades of lilac or red.
HABITAT: Highlands of Central America; in Florida, cold-protected
    areas.
LIGHT REQUIREMENT: Full sun or broken, shifting shade from high pines.
SOIL REQUIREMENT: Grows best in soils above average in fertility.
SALT TOLERANCE: Not tolerant.
AVAILABILITY: Cuphea is widely available in containers.
CULTURE: Nematode-free soil is recommended; an organic mulch is
    desirable; abundant watering during dry times and frequent, light
    fertilization are indicated.
PROPAGATION: Cuttage; the tips root readily almost any time of the
    year.
PESTS: Nematodes; occasional attacks by caterpillars.

284
Pomegranate

Punica (PEW-nick-a): from *Malum punicum*, early name for pomegranate.
granatum (gran-AY-tum): old name.

FAMILY: Punicaceae. RELATIVES: Stands alone in its own family.

TYPE OF PLANT: Tree. HEIGHT: 20′. ZONE: N,C,S

HOW TO IDENTIFY: Spiny bush or small tree with square new growth; deciduous, simple leaves that are red at first; bright red blossoms and hard brown fruits about the size of oranges.

HABIT OF GROWTH: Scraggly, much-branched shrub or small tree.

FOLIAGE: Deciduous, opposite, simple, of fine texture; red color at first.

FLOWERS: Showy, orange-red or variegated with white, at tips of axillary shoots.

FRUITS: Berries with thick skin enclosing many seeds surrounded by juicy pulp; sepals persist on the blossom end.

SEASON OF MAXIMUM COLOR: Spring; new growth is red, blossoms are out.

LANDSCAPE USES: For the curiosity of the fruits, which have been so important in history and mythology, and for the cheerful red blossoms, some gardeners like to have a pomegranate tree as a free-standing specimen in the out-of-door living area.

Through the ages the pomegranate has been prominent in art. The plant grows well here, but it does not flower and fruit here as freely as in drier, colder climates.

Several clones have been selected for various characters, increased vegetatively, and sold under name.

HABITAT: Southern Asia; in Florida, widely planted as a yard tree.

LIGHT REQUIREMENT: Full sun for best flowering.

SOIL REQUIREMENT: Tolerant of many different soil types.

SALT TOLERANCE: Not tolerant.

AVAILABILITY: Some nurseries in northern Florida propagate pomegranates.

CULTURE: Plant in reasonably fertile soil; water until well established, thereafter during dry spells; fertilize during late winter; keep mulch over the root area.

PROPAGATION: Cuttage by hardwood, leafless shoots in wintertime.

PESTS: Scales and a leaf-spotting disease.

285
Black-Olive

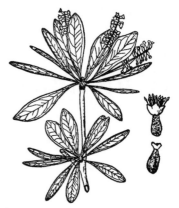

Bucida (bew-SIDE-a): crooked horn, alluding to the fruits.
buceras (bew-SER-as): ox-horned.

FAMILY: Combretaceae. RELATIVES: Combretum and Rangoon-creeper.

TYPE OF PLANT: Tree.   HEIGHT: 40′. ZONE: S

HOW TO IDENTIFY: Evergreen, entire, leathery leaves clustered with thorns, at the ends of twigs; small, black drupes clustered on long spikes.

HABIT OF GROWTH: Dense, round head, very thick foliage, very slow growth.

FOLIAGE: Evergreen, of fine texture and medium green color.

FLOWERS: Inconspicuous, greenish-yellow, on long spikes.

FRUITS: Black drupes, ⅓″ long, clustered on long spikes.

SEASON OF MAXIMUM COLOR: Fruit color is about the only seasonal change.

LANDSCAPE USES: As a street tree, bucida is very fine because of its resistance to salt and wind, and because of its beautiful crown. Plant 25′–35′ apart. As a shade tree for back yards there is nothing superior for the extreme southern part of the state. As a windbreak, when planted 10′ o.c. in double staggered rows, it excels.

HABITAT: Extreme southern Florida.

LIGHT REQUIREMENT: Full sun or broken, high shade.

SOIL REQUIREMENT: Native on calcareous soils of the Florida Keys.

SALT TOLERANCE: Very resistant to salt and to wind.

AVAILABILITY: Some nurseries will have little black-olive trees in cans.

CULTURE: Plant in well-prepared sites; water faithfully; keep grasses back from the roots; fertilize twice each year.

PROPAGATION: Seedage and marcottage.

PESTS: None of major concern.

Combretum

Combretum (com-BREET-um): old Latin name.
grandiflorum (gran-dee-FLOR-um): large-flowered.

FAMILY: Combretaceae.   RELATIVES: Rangoon-creeper and black-olive.
TYPE OF PLANT: Vine.   HEIGHT: Variable. ZONE: S
HOW TO IDENTIFY: Vine with slender, twining branches; slender leaves
    6″ long; showy, red, tubular flowers in one-sided clusters that re-
    semble giant toothbrushes.
HABIT OF GROWTH: Rampant, twining vine.
FOLIAGE: Evergreen, alternate, rough, of medium texture and medium
    green color.
FLOWERS: Red, tubular, in large, one-sided clusters produced in sum-
    mertime.
FRUITS: Papery, winged fruits in clusters.
SEASON OF MAXIMUM COLOR: Summer.
LANDSCAPE USES: To cover a fence, arbor, pergola, or small building,
    combretum is most desirable for southern Florida. It is a great at-
    tention-getter when the blossoms are out. Cut stems with either
    flowers or fruits are very much in favor for arrangements.
HABITAT: West Africa; in Florida, warm sections.
LIGHT REQUIREMENT: Full sun for dense habit and best flowering.
SOIL REQUIREMENT: Tolerant of many different soil types.
SALT TOLERANCE: Not tolerant.
AVAILABILITY: Combretum vines are in retail nurseries in southern
    Florida.
CULTURE: Plant in carefully prepared sites; water faithfully; keep lawn
    grasses back; fertilize twice each year.
PROPAGATION: Seedage and layerage.
PESTS: Scales and mites.
NOTE: There are several other species in this genus, some of which
    are native in our hemisphere.

Rangoon-Creeper

Quisqualis (kwiss-KWALE-is): Latin for who, what sort?
indica (IN-dee-ca): Indian.

FAMILY: Combretaceae. RELATIVES: Combretum and tropical-almond.
TYPE OF PLANT: Vine. HEIGHT: 30'. ZONE: S
HOW TO IDENTIFY: Opposite, deciduous leaves to 6" long; brown fuzz on new growth; terminal clusters of tubular blossoms that turn from white to red, or from pinkish to deep red. New leaves have a brownish cast.
HABIT OF GROWTH: Sprawling vine.
FOLIAGE: Deciduous, opposite, rough, coarse in texture, green in tone.
FLOWERS: Showy, tubular, 1" across, in loose, terminal clusters, white turning to pink, or pinkish turning to deep red.
FRUITS: Leathery pods, conspicuously 5-angled.
SEASON OF MAXIMUM COLOR: Warm months.
LANDSCAPE USES: For the beautiful blossoms that change color, Rangoon-creeper is planted to sprawl over fences, pergolas, or small buildings.

Perhaps one vine of quisqualis would be sufficient in the out-of-door living area of a small home in southern Florida. In large public areas where tropical vines can be displayed adequately, Rangoon-creeper can be used in profusion to give a bright tropical effect, as its blossoms continually change color.
HABITAT: Old World tropics; in Florida, warm locations.
LIGHT REQUIREMENT: Full sun or partial shade.
SOIL REQUIREMENT: Tolerant of varying soils.
SALT TOLERANCE: Not tolerant.
AVAILABILITY: Nurseries in southern part display small vines in containers.
CULTURE: In nearly frostless locations, set vines in fertile soil near strong supports; water until well established; fertilize twice each year; prune after flowering to keep within bounds.
PROPAGATION: Seedage or marcottage.
PESTS: Scales and caterpillars.

288
Silver
Button-Bush

Conocarpus (con-o-car-pus): an aggregate fruit.
erectus (ee-wreck-tus): upright.

FAMILY: Combretaceae. RELATIVES: Combretum and Rangoon-creeper.

TYPE OF PLANT: Tree; frequently shrub. HEIGHT: 60′. ZONE: S

HOW TO IDENTIFY: Silver leaves (made thus by silky down) that are persistent, alternate, and about 4″ long; red-brown, globular button-like fruit, in terminal position; habitat, brackish water or sandy shores.

HABIT OF GROWTH: Shrub-like, somewhat asymmetrical, becoming a tree with age.

FOLIAGE: Evergreen, alternate, medium in texture, silver, in the wanted form.

FLOWERS: Inconspicuous, greenish little flowers in dense heads on terminal panicles.

FRUITS: Reddish-brown, cone-like structures, ½″ in diameter.

SEASON OF MAXIMUM COLOR: No seasonal variation.

LANDSCAPE USES: For ocean-front landscaping in southern Florida and the offshore islands, nothing surpasses silver button-bush. For screens, set wild plants about 5′ apart.

Not all plants of *Conocarpus erectus* have the bright silver foliage; normally one would seek those which do.

All are very tolerant of lime soils.

HABITAT: Shores of tidal watercourses in southern Florida and off-shore islands.

LIGHT REQUIREMENT: Full sun of beaches or broken shade of hammocks.

SOIL REQUIREMENT: Grows in brackish water and on sandy or rocky shores as well.

SALT TOLERANCE: Very tolerant of salt and highly recommended for seaside plantings.

AVAILABILITY: Silver button-bush may not be found in nurseries, but possibly one can obtain wild silver-leaved plants from a friend who has waterfront property. Nurseries should grow bright specimens from cuttings.

CULTURE: Plant; water faithfully; fertilize once or twice a year.

PROPAGATION: Cuttage or marcottage.

PESTS: Sooty-mold.

289
Tropical-Almond

Terminalia (ter-min-ALE-ee-a): from the Latin terminus.
catappa (cah-TAP-a): East Indian name.

FAMILY: Combretaceae.   RELATIVES: Combretum and Rangoon-creeper.
TYPE OF PLANT: Tree.   HEIGHT: 30′. ZONE: S
HOW TO IDENTIFY: A large, symmetrical tree whose branches grow out
   horizontally in tiers from an erect central leader and bear foot-
   long, deciduous leaves at their very tips. The leaves, which turn
   red before falling, give seasonal color to the tree. There are green
   fruits, about 2½″ in length.
HABIT OF GROWTH: Striking, symmetrical, pagoda-like structure.
FOLIAGE: Huge, deciduous leaves, coarse in texture, medium green.
FLOWERS: Rat-tail spikes of tiny, greenish-white flowers in springtime.
FRUITS: Drupes 2½″ long, with 2 angles that are winged.
SEASON OF MAXIMUM COLOR: Autumn, when leaves turn red.
LANDSCAPE USES: As an avenue tree (planting distance 25′) tropical-
   almond is without superior where wind resistance and tolerance
   of salt are considerations. The tiered, pagoda-like effect is much
   to be desired.
      Terminalia trees are very tender to frost. Wild cultures have be-
   come established on Big Pine Key.
HABITAT: East Indian islands; in Florida, planted near salt water in
   frost-free sections.
LIGHT REQUIREMENT: Full sun of tropical beaches.
SOIL REQUIREMENT: Tolerant of sandy soil of acid or alkaline reaction.
SALT TOLERANCE: Very tolerant of the seaside, highly recommended.
AVAILABILITY: Nurseries in southern Florida offer almond trees.
CULTURE: Plant in holes that have been improved by the addition of
   organic matter; water until well established; place mulch over the
   root area; fertilize thrice annually while young, then once a year.
PROPAGATION: Seedage.
PESTS: None of major concern.
NOTE: *Terminalia arjuna* has smaller leaves (2″ × 8″) with 2 round
   glands at the base of the blade and 1″ fruits with 5 vertical wings.
      Terminalia muelleri has 4″ leaves, twigs growing out from the
   upper surfaces of the horizontal branches, and ovoid, dark blue
   fruits.

290
Bottle-Brush

Callistemon (cal-is-STEAM-on): Greek for beautiful stamen.
rigidus (RIDGE-id-us): rigid, possibly referring to the stiff foliage.

FAMILY: Myrtaceae.   RELATIVES: Cajeput-tree, guava, and feijoa.

TYPE OF PLANT: Large shrub.   HEIGHT: 15'. ZONE: N,C,S

HOW TO IDENTIFY: Aromatic, alternate, linear leaves with prominent lateral midveins. Hard capsules surround old stems at intervals following attractive, springtime, red bottle-brushes.

HABIT OF GROWTH: Stiffly upright.

FOLIAGE: Evergreen, aromatic, of fine texture and dark green color.

FLOWERS: Spectacular spikes resembling red bottle-brushes.

FRUITS: Capsules that surround old stems contain many dust-like seeds.

SEASON OF MAXIMUM COLOR: Late spring when flowers open.

LANDSCAPE USES: As a freestanding specimen for horticultural interest, or for a color note in an informal shrubbery border, this hardy, free-flowering plant is recommended.

HABITAT: Australia; in Florida, widely grown in gardens on light, sandy soils.

LIGHT REQUIREMENT: Full sun for best development.

SOIL REQUIREMENT: Tolerant of many well-drained soil types.

SALT TOLERANCE: Tolerant of moderate salt drift.

AVAILABILITY: Small seedlings are sometimes found in cans in retail nurseries.

CULTURE: Small plants from containers only are recommended, as bottle-brushes are notably intolerant of transplanting in larger sizes.

PROPAGATION: Seedage.

PESTS: Mites.

NOTE: Botanical status of bottle-brushes is unclear and confusion in naming is the rule in Florida.

291
Citrus-Leaved Bottle-Brush

Callistemon (cal-is-STEAM-on): Greek for beautiful stamen.
citrinus (sit-RYE-nus): citrus-leaved.

FAMILY: Myrtaceae.   RELATIVES: Feijoa, downy-myrtle, and guava.
TYPE OF PLANT: Small tree.   HEIGHT: 20′. ZONE: C,S
HOW TO IDENTIFY: A tree bottle-brush with evergreen, pubescent leaves that have the odor of citrus when crushed. The bright red, 4″ flower spikes are not very dense; the many little seed capsules that surround the older stems are ovoid, contracted at their summits.
HABIT OF GROWTH: Tree-like, dense, compact, or rangy and weeping.
FOLIAGE: Evergreen, pubescent, of fine texture and medium green color.
FLOWERS: Bright red spikes, about 4″ long, in springtime.
FRUITS: Ovoid capsules, contracted at summits, surround twigs in 4″ clusters.
SEASON OF MAXIMUM COLOR: Spring, when blossoms emerge on new growth.
LANDSCAPE USES: As a freestanding specimen, or as a bright accent in front of all-green shrubbery, bottle-brush is highly regarded. Unfortunately, there is confusion in naming, and the situation is complicated by the fact that many are hybrids.
HABITAT: Australia; in Florida, warmer parts of the peninsula.
LIGHT REQUIREMENT: Full sun for best flowering.
SOIL REQUIREMENT: Thrives in many different soils.
SALT TOLERANCE: Tolerant of mild salt drift, but not recommended for dune planting.
AVAILABILITY: Nurseries offer little bottle-brushes in containers.
CULTURE: Transplant only little trees from containers; plant very carefully; water faithfully until well established; keep back the grass; fertilize twice or thrice annually.
PROPAGATION: Seedage and marcottage.
PESTS: Mites and scales.
NOTE: Weeping bottle-brush, with willowy, pendulous branches and bright red brushes, *Callistemon viminalis*, is popular in South Florida.

292
Cajeput-Tree

Melaleuca (mel-a-LOO-ka): Greek for black and white.
leucadendra (loo-ka-DEN-dra): white tree.

FAMILY: Myrtaceae.   RELATIVES: Bottle-brush, jaboticaba, and myrtle.
TYPE OF PLANT: Tree.   HEIGHT: 50'. ZONE: C,S
HOW TO IDENTIFY: Paper bark tree is a popular name for this plant and
   it is very descriptive of the whitish, soft, many-layered bark that
   is positive identification. There are groups of hard, round seed cap-
   sules at intervals around stems and creamy-white flowers in bottle-
   brush-like clusters.
HABIT OF GROWTH: Ascending, narrow.
FOLIAGE: Evergreen, aromatic, fine in texture, light green in color.
FLOWERS: Showy, creamy-white, in close, terminal clusters.
FRUITS: Capsules ⅛" across surround stems where blossoms have been.
SEASON OF MAXIMUM COLOR: Springtime, when flowers are out.
LANDSCAPE USES: Its small size, tolerance of adverse growing conditions, and resistance to pests make this one of Florida's very best
   landscape trees. As a framing tree, cajeput is highly favored in
   warm parts of the state; as a hedge, it is popular there, too (plant
   3' o.c.). As a street tree, set individuals 25'–35' o.c.
      For a striking effect, plant an allamanda vine by a paper bark
   tree so that the golden trumpets show in upper branches.
HABITAT: Australia; in Florida, very much grown as a yard tree in
   warm locations. Naturalized in southwestern counties.
LIGHT REQUIREMENT: Full sun for compact growth and best flowering.
SOIL REQUIREMENT: Tolerant of differing soils, enduring inundation
   and salinity.
SALT TOLERANCE: Very tolerant of salt wind.
AVAILABILITY: Nurseries stock container-grown and B & B trees in all
   sizes.
CULTURE: This excellent tree is of easiest culture. Plant in prepared
   sites; water moderately during dry periods; keep lawn grasses back
   from the root zone. Freezing temperatures are injurious.
PROPAGATION: Sow seeds on sterilized soil topped with sphagnum moss.
PESTS: None of major concern.
NOTE: Honey made from cajeput blossoms has an unpleasant flavor.
   This tree has escaped and become naturalized in South Florida.

293
Australian Brush-Cherry

Eugenia (you-JEAN-ee-a): for Prince Eugene of Savoy, patron of botany.
paniculata (pan-ick-you-LAY-ta): with flowers in elongate spikes.

FAMILY: Myrtaceae.   RELATIVES: Surinam-cherry, myrtle, and guava.
TYPE OF PLANT: Shrub or tree, depending upon training.

HEIGHT: 25′. ZONE: S

HOW TO IDENTIFY: Slim, narrow, evergreen leaves to 3″ long, that are pinkish while young; compact, yet ascending habit; often seen in sheared forms.

HABIT OF GROWTH: Upright, with ascending branches, and closely packed foliage.

FOLIAGE: Evergreen, of medium texture and dark green color. New growth is pinkish.

FLOWERS: White, about 1″ across, with the many prominent stamens of the myrtle family.

FRUITS: Ovoid berries ¾″ in diameter, rose-purple, excellent in jellies.

SEASON OF MAXIMUM COLOR: Warm months, when flowers and fruits are present.

LANDSCAPE USES: As a sheared specimen for extreme southern Florida, brush-cherry is a favorite plant. As a clipped hedge, it is excellent when planted 18″ apart. As a part of an informal enclosure, brush-cherry is good when set 3′–5′ o.c.

HABITAT: Australia; in Florida, gardens in warmest parts of the peninsula.

LIGHT REQUIREMENT: Full sun for best form, flowering, and fruiting.

SOIL REQUIREMENT: Tolerant of varying soils, but grows best in good soil.

SALT TOLERANCE: Not tolerant.

AVAILABILITY: Brush-cherry is offered in nurseries in warmer parts.

CULTURE: Plant carefully in well-made sites; water moderately; clip frequently; cover the root zone with an organic mulch; apply fertilizer three times a year.

PROPAGATION: Seedage.

PESTS: Scales and mites.

294
Surinam-Cherry

Eugenia (you-JEAN-ee-a): for Prince Eugene of Savoy, patron of botany.
uniflora (you-nee-FLOR-a): single-flowered.

FAMILY: Myrtaceae. RELATIVES: Brush-cherry, myrtle, and guava.
TYPE OF PLANT: Shrub. HEIGHT: 25′. ZONE: C,S
HOW TO IDENTIFY: Evergreen, sessile, shining leaves that are wine-colored while young; solitary, white flowers that are followed by ribbed, red or black fruits during much of the year.
HABIT OF GROWTH: Shrubby, very compact, with closely packed leaves.
FOLIAGE: Evergreen, of medium-fine texture and a dark green color at maturity. New growth is wine-colored.
FLOWERS: Solitary, fragrant, with the many prominent stamens of the myrtle family.
FRUITS: Fluted or ribbed red or black berries crowned by calyx lobes, about 1″ in diameter. Many persons like the fresh fruits for their sprightly, acid flavor. Surinam-cherry preserves are delicious.
SEASON OF MAXIMUM COLOR: Much of the year, when blossoms and/or fruits are out; when reddish new growth appears.
LANDSCAPE USES: For clipped hedges, Surinam-cherry is one of the very best materials within its climatic range. Set the plants 18″ apart. As a part of an informal enclosing border, the plants can stand about 3′–5′ o.c.
HABITAT: Brazil; in Florida, widely distributed where citrus is grown commercially.
LIGHT REQUIREMENT: Full sun for best habit, full bloom, and good fruiting.
SOIL REQUIREMENT: Tolerant of widely varying soils.
SALT TOLERANCE: Not tolerant.
AVAILABILITY: Most nurseries in central and southern Florida offer small seedlings.
CULTURE: Plant carefully in well-made sites; water moderately; clip frequently; cover the root zone with an organic mulch; apply fertilizer three times each year.
PROPAGATION: Seedage.
PESTS: Caterpillars and scales.

Downy-Myrtle

Rhodomyrtus (roe-doe-MUR-tus): Greek for rose and myrtle.
tomentosa (toe-men-TOE-sa): Greek for densely woolly.

FAMILY: Myrtaceae. RELATIVES: Feijoa, callistemon, and guava.
TYPE OF PLANT: Shrub. HEIGHT: 10'. ZONE: S
HOW TO IDENTIFY: All parts of the plant are downy. The attractive pink blossoms, with the many prominent stamens of the myrtle family, are followed by downy, purple berries.
HABIT OF GROWTH: Bush-like, maintained in compact form by heading in terminals.
FOLIAGE: Evergreen, opposite, woolly, of medium-fine texture and gray-green color.
FLOWERS: Showy, rose-pink, ¾" across, with many prominent stamens.
FRUITS: Downy, purple berries, ½" across, esteemed in jellies and pies.
SEASON OF MAXIMUM COLOR: Warm months, when flowers or fruits mature.
LANDSCAPE USES: As a foundation plant for large buildings in southern Florida, downy-myrtle is highly acceptable. Set plants 5' o.c. As a part of an enclosing shrubbery border, use the same planting interval.

   Downy-myrtle attracts a great deal of attention because of its woolly foliage, beautiful pink flowers, and delectable fruits. It is one of the best shrubs for nearly frostless sites.
HABITAT: Eastern Asia; in Florida, warmest locations.
LIGHT REQUIREMENT: Full sun or partial shade.
SOIL REQUIREMENT: Tolerant of many soil types, but moderate fertility makes for best growth, flowering, and fruiting.
SALT TOLERANCE: Tolerant of salt air well back from the surf.
AVAILABILITY: Specialty nurseries in southern Florida will have downy-myrtle plants.
CULTURE: Plant in carefully prepared sites; water faithfully; keep lawn grasses back from the root zone; apply a mulch; fertilize twice each year.
PROPAGATION: Seedage and cuttage under mist.
PESTS: Scales, mites, and mushroom root-rot.

296
Feijoa

Feijoa (fay-JOE-ah): for J. Feijo, a Spanish naturalist.
sellowiana (sell-OH-ee-AY-na): for F. Sello, a German traveler in South America.

FAMILY: Myrtaceae.   RELATIVES: Guava, cajeput-tree, and myrtle.
TYPE OF PLANT: Shrub.   HEIGHT: 18′. ZONE: N,C,S
HOW TO IDENTIFY: Shrub that shows a white tomentum on new twigs and new leaves; bears in April attractive blossoms with many conspicuous red stamens.
HABIT OF GROWTH: Compact, shrubby, with many upward-pointing branches.
FOLIAGE: Evergreen, opposite, entire, of medium texture and of gray-green color.
FLOWERS: Solitary, axillary, with 4 fleshy white petals and many glistening red stamens.
FRUITS: Green berries, the size and shape of bantam eggs. The sweet jelly surrounding the seeds is enjoyed by youngsters and some adults.
SEASON OF MAXIMUM COLOR: April, when blossoms are out.
LANDSCAPE USES: As a dependable, hardy, broad-leaved, evergreen shrub, feijoa has proved its worth for Florida gardens. For informal barriers, use at remote boundary to help gain the illusion of distance brought about by the gray-green color of the foliage. Plant 5′ apart in this use. For foundation planting groups allow 3′ between plants.
HABITAT: Brazil; in Florida, ubiquitous as a garden shrub.
LIGHT REQUIREMENT: Tolerant of partial shade.
SOIL REQUIREMENT: Tolerant of varying soils.
SALT TOLERANCE: Tolerant of light salt drift back of front-line dunes.
AVAILABILITY: Feijoas in containers are to be found in many retail nurseries.
CULTURE: Resistance to pests and complete adaptability to Florida's soils and climate make feijoa one of the best exotic shrubs for landscape use. No special care is needed.
PROPAGATION: Seedage.
PESTS: Wax scale on occasion.

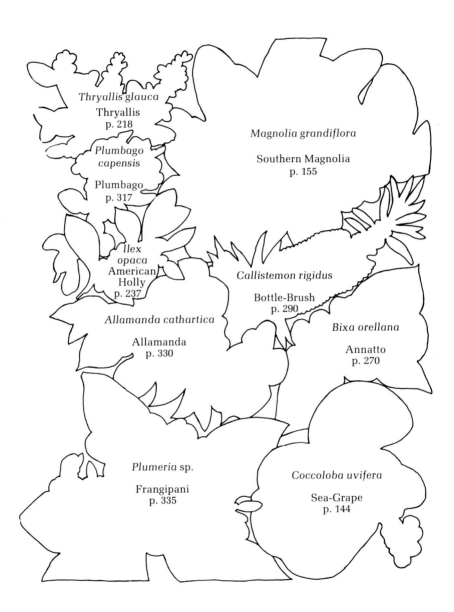

Thryallis glauca
Thryallis
p. 218

*Plumbago
capensis*
Plumbago
p. 317

*Ilex
opaca*
American
Holly
p. 237

Magnolia grandiflora

Southern Magnolia
p. 155

Callistemon rigidus

Bottle-Brush
p. 290

Allamanda cathartica

Allamanda
p. 330

Bixa orellana

Annatto
p. 270

Plumeria sp.

Frangipani
p. 335

Coccoloba uvifera

Sea-Grape
p. 144

Guava

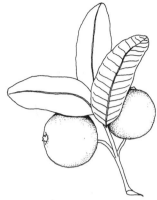

Psidium (SID-ee-um): from *psidion*, Greek name for the pomegranate.
guajava (gwuy-YOB-a): the Spanish name for the fruit in tropical America.

FAMILY: Myrtaceae.   RELATIVES: Feijoa, myrtle, and jaboticaba.

TYPE OF PLANT: Shrub or small tree.   HEIGHT: 30'. ZONE: C,S

HOW TO IDENTIFY: Usually bush-like, with huge (6"), rough, evergreen leaves, light bark that flakes off in large sheets, and conspicuous yellowish fruits, highly odorous, that are present during much of the year.

HABIT OF GROWTH: Usually bush-form; may become tree.

FOLIAGE: Evergreen (cold causes leaves to shed), rough, very coarse in texture.

FLOWERS: White, 1" in diameter, with many conspicuous stamens.

FRUITS: Yellow berries, highly odorous, about 4" long, variable in form.

SEASON OF MAXIMUM COLOR: Warm months when the many fruits are ripening.

LANDSCAPE USES: As a source of tropical preserve fruits in the out-of-door living area, guava, in one of the improved forms, is widely grown in southern Florida. To form a part of an enclosing shrubbery barrier, guava bushes may stand 5' o.c.

Named clones increased by marcottage are 'Ruby' and 'Supreme', large jelly types that mature in summer. 'Redland', an older variety, ripens in wintertime.

HABITAT: Tropical America; escaped from cultivation in southern Florida.

LIGHT REQUIREMENT: Full sun or partial shade of hammocks.

SOIL REQUIREMENT: Tolerant of many soil types.

SALT TOLERANCE: Not tolerant.

AVAILABILITY: Nurseries in southern Florida have guava bushes in cans.

CULTURE: Plant in enriched sites; water faithfully until established, thereafter during periods of drought; mulch heavily; fertilize three times a year.

PROPAGATION: Seedage; marcottage for selected clones.

PESTS: Scales, mites, caterpillars, nematodes, and white-flies, followed by sooty-mold.

298
Cattley
Guava

Psidium (SID-ee-um): Greek name for the pomegranate.
cattleianum (cat-lee-AY-num): for W. Cattley, English horticulturist.

FAMILY: Myrtaceae.　　　　RELATIVES: Feijoa, myrtle, and cajeput-tree.
TYPE OF PLANT: Shrub or small tree.　　　　HEIGHT: 25′. ZONE: C,S
HOW TO IDENTIFY: A much-branched shrub that bears evergreen, opposite leaves that are thick and leathery, about 4″ in length; smooth, brown bark that sloughs off in thin sheets; white flowers with many prominent stamens, followed by showy, red fruits.
HABIT OF GROWTH: Compact, much-branched shrub with closely packed leaves.
FOLIAGE: Evergreen, opposite, medium in texture, very dark green in color.
FLOWERS: White, axillary, 1″ in diameter, with many prominent stamens.
FRUITS: Round berries of bright red color, 1½″ long, delicious to eat.
SEASON OF MAXIMUM COLOR: April, white flowers; midsummer, red fruits.
LANDSCAPE USES: As a part of an enclosing barrier, set at intervals of 5′. In foundation plantings for large buildings, use a 3′ planting distance.
HABITAT: Brazil; in Florida, much planted in warm areas.
LIGHT REQUIREMENT: Full sun for best flowering and fruiting.
SOIL REQUIREMENT: Sandy soils are suitable, but fertility is reflected in good appearance, heavy flowering, and fruiting.
SALT TOLERANCE: Not tolerant.
AVAILABILITY: Nurseries in warmer parts offer small plants in containers.
CULTURE: Plant in enriched sites; water until well established; mulch the root zone; fertilize three times each year. Prune after fruiting, when necessary.
PROPAGATION: Seedage or marcottage.
PESTS: None of major consequence.
NOTE: Yellow Cattley guava, *P. cattleianum* 'Lucidum', has large yellow fruits of delightful, spicy flavor.

299
Jaboticaba

Myrciaria (mer-see-AIR-ee-a): *Myrica*-like.
cauliflora (call-ee-FLOW-ra): stem-flowering.

FAMILY: Myrtaceae.   RELATIVES: Feijoa, guava, and true myrtle.
TYPE OF PLANT: Shrub, becoming tree-like with age.   HEIGHT: 25′.
                                                            ZONE: S

HOW TO IDENTIFY: Very smooth, light brown bark that flakes off in patches; closely packed, lanceolate leaves; flowers and fruits produced on the trunk and main branches during much of the warm season.

HABIT OF GROWTH: Upward-branching, with close, compact head.

FOLIAGE: Evergreen, of very fine texture, and dark green color.

FLOWERS: White, with many prominent stamens borne on trunk and major branches during warm months.

FRUITS: Globular, purple berries, ¾″–1½″ in diameter, produced right on the trunk and large branches. Delightful to eat out of hand or in preserves.

SEASON OF MAXIMUM COLOR: Warm months, at maturity of fruits.

LANDSCAPE USES: As a freestanding specimen for its neat appearance and the curiosity of its delectable, trunk-borne fruits, jaboticaba is commended to advanced gardeners in most nearly frostless sections.

Seedling variation in habit, fruit size, and flavor is notable in Florida.

HABITAT: Southern Brazil; in Florida, sparingly cultured in gardens of advanced horticulturists in southern counties.

LIGHT REQUIREMENT: Partial shade is acceptable.

SOIL REQUIREMENT: Fertile, well-drained, but moisture-retentive soils are needed.

SALT TOLERANCE: Not recommended for planting near the sea.

AVAILABILITY: Specialty nurseries will have jaboticaba trees.

CULTURE: Plant with care at former level in prepared site; water faithfully; keep leaf mulch over the roots; hoe back grass; fertilize thrice annually; control scale insects.

PROPAGATION: Seedage and marcottage.

PESTS: Scales, nematodes, and mushroom root-rot.

300
Myrtle

Myrtus (MUR-tus): ancient Greek name.
communis (com-YOU-nis): growing in a community.

FAMILY: Myrtaceae.   RELATIVES: Bottle-brush, cajeput-tree, and guava.
TYPE OF PLANT: Shrub.   HEIGHT: 10′. ZONE: N,C
HOW TO IDENTIFY: Somewhat open shrub bearing simple, opposite, evergreen, 2″ leaves closely packed near the branch-tips; white flowers in axillary cymes with many prominent stamens, followed by black berries.
HABIT OF GROWTH: Somewhat open below; on superior soils, growth may be compact.
FOLIAGE: Evergreen, simple, fine in texture, dark green in color.
FLOWERS: White, with 4–5 petals and the many prominent stamens of the myrtle family.
FRUITS: Bluish-black berries, sometimes borne in quantity on superior soil.
SEASON OF MAXIMUM COLOR: Springtime, when the blossoms unfurl.
LANDSCAPE USES: For foundation plantings, set plants 3′ o.c.; as a facer shrub in front of larger, leggy plants, space 3′–5′ apart. Profuse flowering may be the rule for well-grown individuals.
  The clone 'Microphylla' has little, closely packed, upward-pointing leaves, while 'Variegata' has mottled foliage. There are other selected clones, too.
HABITAT: Western Asia; in Florida, infrequently planted on better soils.
LIGHT REQUIREMENT: High, shifting pine shade is excellent.
SOIL REQUIREMENT: Superior soils of the upper counties.
SALT TOLERANCE: Not tolerant.
AVAILABILITY: Infrequently offered in retail sales yards.
CULTURE: On the Panhandle, true myrtle grows with little care; on the peninsula, plant in well-made sites, water faithfully, and fertilize thrice annually.
PROPAGATION: Cuttage.
PESTS: Mites, scales, and mushroom root-rot.

301
Princess-Flower

Tibouchina (tib-oo-KINE-a): a native name in Guiana.
semidecandra (sem-ee-da-CAN-dra): with five stamens.

FAMILY: Melastomaceae.　　　　RELATIVES: The melastomes.
TYPE OF PLANT: Large shrub.　　　HEIGHT: 15′. ZONE: C,S
HOW TO IDENTIFY: A rampant, sprawling shrub that has pubescent twigs that bear large, downy, evergreen leaves with 3–7 prominent nerves. The large, flaring, purple flowers are very showy during warm months.
HABIT OF GROWTH: Sprawling, ungainly, almost vine-like, needing support.
FOLIAGE: Evergreen, notably pubescent, coarse in texture, dark green above, lighter beneath.
FLOWERS: Purple, very showy, 5″ across, near branch-ends, subtended by 2 circular bracts.
FRUITS: 5-valved capsules enclosed by persistent calyx-tubes.
SEASON OF MAXIMUM COLOR: Warm months, when flowers mature.
LANDSCAPE USES: For the glory of the purple blossoms to highlight the green of an enclosing shrubbery border, princess-flower is much liked. Plants may be set in clumps of three with 5′ between the individuals. When in full bloom, a clump of princess-flowers is a sight long to be remembered. This is one of the most popular semitropical flowering shrubs at Florida's famous admission gardens.
HABITAT: Brazil; in Florida, popular as a yard shrub in warm areas.
LIGHT REQUIREMENT: Full sun for best flowering.
SOIL REQUIREMENT: Any well-drained soil appears to be suitable if slightly acid in reaction.
SALT TOLERANCE: Not tolerant.
AVAILABILITY: Plants in containers are in most nurseries in central and southern Florida.
CULTURE: Freedom from nematodes is desirable, but princess-flower will grow in almost any soil if it is well watered and fertilized.
PROPAGATION: Cuttage.
PESTS: Nematodes and mushroom root-rot.

302
Aralia

Polyscias (pol-ISS-ee-us): Greek for many and shade, for the abundant foliage.
balfouriana (bal-four-ee-AY-na): for J. Balfour, English botanist.

FAMILY: Araliaceae.   RELATIVES: Ivy, rice-paper plant and false aralia.
TYPE OF PLANT: Shrub.   HEIGHT: 25′. ZONE: S
HOW TO IDENTIFY: Shrub with stiffly upright stems that show many prom-
   inent lenticels and large, circular leaf-scars; compound, evergreen
   leaves, with rounded leaflets about 4″ wide that are splotched with
   white.
HABIT OF GROWTH: Stiffly upright to make one of our narrowest shrubs.
FOLIAGE: Evergreen, coarse in texture, light green with white variega-
   tion.
FLOWERS: Inconspicuous, held on axillary sprays by older plants.
FRUITS: Smooth, round, drupe-like pods when present.
SEASON OF MAXIMUM COLOR: No variation.
LANDSCAPE USES: For a tall, narrow hedge for extreme southern Flor-
   ida nothing surpasses aralia. Stick cuttings about 1′ apart where
   the hedge is wanted. As an urn subject for terrace, patio, or Flor-
   ida room, this upright shrub is also very popular. Aralias run into
   many forms, and botanical status is unclear.
HABITAT: Landscape plantings in the tropics around the globe.
LIGHT REQUIREMENT: Tolerant of shade; grows well in the sun, too.
SOIL REQUIREMENT: Tolerant of many soils, including thin sands.
SALT TOLERANCE: Aralias grow well some distance back from the shore
   line.
AVAILABILITY: Nurseries in southern Florida display aralias in endless
   array.
CULTURE: No particular requirements are noted except to protect the
   foliage against mites and frost.
PROPAGATION: Seedage and cuttage, using any type of wood, at any
   season of the year.
PESTS: Mites, scales, and nematodes.

303
False
Aralia

Dizygotheca (dizzy-go-THEE-ka): double receptable, for the 4-celled anthers.
kerchoveana (ker-chove-ee-AY-na): for O. de Kerchove, a Belgian horticulturist.

FAMILY: Araliaceae.   RELATIVES: True aralia, rice-paper plant, and ivy.

TYPE OF PLANT: Shrub.   HEIGHT: 15'. ZONE: S

HOW TO IDENTIFY: Finely cut, brownish leaves made up of 7–11 leaflets, about ½" broad. The stems have prominent lenticels like true aralia.

HABIT OF GROWTH: Narrowly upright like aralia.

FOLIAGE: Evergreen, digitate, coarse in texture, of mottled brown tones.

FLOWERS: Inconspicuous when present.

FRUITS: Usually not formed.

SEASON OF MAXIMUM COLOR: No variation.

LANDSCAPE USES: For its tropical effect, false aralia may be used as a freestanding specimen or as an urn subject for patio, terrace, or Florida room. False aralia is usually labeled "Aralia elegantissima."

Interesting to most gardeners is the fact that large, mature plants of false aralia will develop two kinds of leaves: the finely cut juvenile type characteristic of young plants, and heavier, broad-bladed, adult foliage that is quite different from the juvenile.

HABITAT: Tropics; in Florida, warmest locations only.

LIGHT REQUIREMENT: Tolerant of shade.

SOIL REQUIREMENT: Very tolerant of varying soils.

SALT TOLERANCE: Not tolerant.

AVAILABILITY: Nurseries in southern Florida and many chain stores offer false aralia in containers.

CULTURE: Partial shade, fertile, well-drained soil, moderate moisture, and freedom from frost are requirements for success.

PROPAGATION: Cuttage, marcottage, graftage, or seedage.

PESTS: Scales and nematodes.

'Green Spear'

'Pedata Variegata'

'Pittsburgh'

'My Heart'

Ivy

'Fringette'

'Green Ripples'

'Gold Dust'

'Marginata'

'Digitata'

305
Ivies

Hedera (HED-er-a): classical name for ivy.
SPP.: more than one species is grown in Florida.

FAMILY: Araliaceae.   RELATIVES: Aralia, rice-paper plant, and fatsia.
TYPE OF PLANT: Vine.   HEIGHT: 40'. ZONE: N,C,S
HOW TO IDENTIFY: Clinging vine with many aerial roots, and leaves of
    varying sizes and patterns held alternately on smooth stems.
HABIT OF GROWTH: Clinging vine.
FOLIAGE: Evergreen, highly variable, usually medium or coarse in tex-
    ture, usually dark green or variegated with white or cream.
FLOWERS: Inconspicuous in terminal umbels.
FRUITS: Black berries, ¼" across, when present.
SEASON OF MAXIMUM COLOR: No seasonal variation.
LANDSCAPE USES: As ground cover for shady locations, ivies excel; for
    planters and to soften north walls, they are without superiors.
        English ivy (*Hedera helix*) is known in more than 40 leaf forms.
    Algerian ivy (*Hedera canariensis*) is said to have twigs that are
    burgundy-red and few, remote aerial rootlets, glossy and pale green
    juvenile leaves. Botanical status is unclear, and great confusion in
    naming is the rule.
HABITAT: Southern Europe and northern Africa; in Florida, ubiquitous
    in shady gardens.
LIGHT REQUIREMENT: Tolerant of very deep shade.
SOIL REQUIREMENT: Tolerant of varying soils.
SALT TOLERANCE: Tolerant of light salt drift well back of the dunes.
AVAILABILITY: Canned or potted ivies are found in most garden centers
    and chain stores.
CULTURE: A shaded location that is well drained, protection from scale
    insects, and occasional fertilization are the simple requirements
    of these excellent vines.
PROPAGATION: Cuttage.
PESTS: Both scales and leaf-spots, on some varieties.
NOTE: *Fatshedera* is a foliage plant that resulted from crossing *Fatsia
    japonica* with ivy. For north walls in northern Florida, this is a popu-
    lar plant of tropical aspect. *Fatshedera* ordinarily requires careful
    support as there are no aerial rootlets.

Fatsia

Fatsia (FAT-see-a): from a Japanese name.
japonica (jap-ON-i-ca): Japanese.

FAMILY: Araliaceae. RELATIVES: English ivy and rice-paper plant.
TYPE OF PLANT: Shrub. HEIGHT: 4′. ZONE: N,C,S
HOW TO IDENTIFY: This is a shrub that bears foot-broad leaves, cut
   below the middle into 5–9 deep lobes. The petioles, about a foot
   in length, stand perpendicular to the stem to hold the leaves in at-
   tractive, horizontal array.
HABIT OF GROWTH: Stiffly upright by thick, green stems.
FOLIAGE: Evergreen, bold and handsome, foot-broad, deeply cleft.
FLOWERS: Terminal clusters of whitish little flowers that add nothing
   to the landscape effect.
FRUITS: Little black globes, if present.
SEASON OF MAXIMUM COLOR: No seasonal changes.
LANDSCAPE USES: As a Florida room urn subject or as a north-side wall
   shrub, both fatsia and fatshedera are in high favor. For Oriental
   effects in gardens or Florida rooms, these shrubs are useful.
HABITAT: Japan.
LIGHT REQUIREMENT: Reduced light of north-side or indoor locations;
   bright sunlight is unsuitable.
SOIL REQUIREMENT: Moderately fertile, slightly acid compost is best.
SALT TOLERANCE: Tolerant of moderate salt drift.
AVAILABILITY: Fatsia is found in cans in retail nurseries.
CULTURE: Plant in an urn or by a shaded patio wall; water with moderation, but do not allow the soil to become dry; fertilize once each
   month during warm weather. As stems elongate, support is needed.
PROPAGATION: Cuttage.
PESTS: Mealy-bugs, scales, sooty-mold, and thrips.
NOTE: In addition to the type, there is a clone with white blotches
   near leaf-tips ('Variegata') and one of French origin of compact
   growth and broader, richer leaves known as 'Moseri'. Most popular
   of all, though, is the intergeneric hybrid *Fatshedera* which was
   man-made by crossing fatsia with ivy. This hybrid has smaller
   (6″) lobed, fatsia-like leaves held by ivy-like stems. These branches,
   however, do not have aerial holdfasts, so they need to be tied to a
   support.

307
Rice-Paper Plant

Tetrapanax (tet-tra-PAN-ax): Greek for four and panax, all healing.
papyriferus (pap-er-IFF-er-us): paper-bearing.

FAMILY: Araliaceae.　　　　　RELATIVES: Aralia, false aralia, and ivy.
TYPE OF PLANT: Shrub, sometimes becoming tree-like.　　HEIGHT: 10′.
　　　　　　　　　　　　　　　　　　　　　　　　ZONE: N,C,S
HOW TO IDENTIFY: Great, lobed leaves, a foot or more across, felty beneath, felty new growth; large, woolly panicles may appear in warm months.
HABIT OF GROWTH: Tall bush or small tree with huge, felty leaves, and the tendency to send out suckers at great distances.
FOLIAGE: Evergreen, very bold in aspect, gray-green in color.
FLOWERS: Yellow-white in many globular umbels on large, woolly panicles.
FRUITS: Small and globular.
SEASON OF MAXIMUM COLOR: Warm months, when felty inflorescences appear.
LANDSCAPE USES: Rice-paper plant is useful in helping to create a tropical atmosphere, but it has a tendency to produce large numbers of suckers at great distances from the plant. These can become a real nuisance, and so many gardeners prefer not to grow this handsome tropical subject. These persons might consider having tetrapanax in decorative containers on the terrace.
　　Plants are killed to ground level by temperatures below freezing.
HABITAT: Orient; in Florida, ubiquitous.
LIGHT REQUIREMENT: Full sun or partial shade.
SOIL REQUIREMENT: Any soil seems to meet the requirements of this plant.
SALT TOLERANCE: Not tolerant.
AVAILABILITY: Suckers which arise from roots are exchanged by neighbors.
CULTURE: No particular attention is needed for success with this frost-tender plant.
PROPAGATION: Transplant suckers.
PESTS: Mealy-bugs.

308
Schefflera

Brassaia (brass-say-ee-a): for W. Brass, English botanist.
actinophylla (ac-tin-oh-fill-a): with leaflets in radial arrangement.

FAMILY: Araliaceae.   RELATIVES: Aralia, ivy, and rice-paper plant.
TYPE OF PLANT: Tree.   HEIGHT: 40′. ZONE: C,S
HOW TO IDENTIFY: Huge, shiny, compound leaves held by 2′ stalks from
   thick, straight trunks with broad leaf-scars. Mature specimens may
   send up showy, red inflorescences.
HABIT OF GROWTH: Upright, usually from a single trunk; leaves held
   gracefully.
FOLIAGE: Evergreen, digitate, of bold pattern, light green in color.
FLOWERS: Spectacular red inflorescences standing above the foliage to
   resemble the arms of an octopus.
FRUITS: Small, round, produced in great numbers by mature trees.
SEASON OF MAXIMUM COLOR: Summer, when in flower.
LANDSCAPE USES: Accent plant; urn subject for terrace, patio, or Florida room. Schefflera is very popular for landscaping in Florida, and
   tens of thousands of seedlings are shipped north each year.
      Schefflera is tender to cold, and use in permanent locations out-
   doors will be restricted, therefore, to warm areas on the peninsula.
   In other places, schefflera specimens can be grown in containers
   and moved in and out with the weather. Public acceptance is ac-
   counted for in part by the appearance of schefflera in so many color
   illustrations of interiors in home and garden magazines.
HABITAT: Australia; in Florida, warmer locations.
LIGHT REQUIREMENT: Tolerates shade, but will not flower well without
   sun.
SOIL REQUIREMENT: Sandy soils are acceptable.
SALT TOLERANCE: At some distance back of the beach, it grows well.
AVAILABILITY: Nurseries, garden centers, and chain stores sell schef-
   flera.
CULTURE: After careful planting in fertile soil, little attention is required
   except for occasional irrigation and fertilization.
PROPAGATION: Seedage, cuttage, and marcottage.
PESTS: Scales followed by sooty-mold.

309
Trevesia

Trevesia (tree-VEE-see-a): for the Treves family, Italian patrons of botany.
palmata (pal-MAY-ta): palmate; lobed in a palm-like fashion.

FAMILY: Araliaceae.

RELATIVES: Aralia and false aralia.

TYPE OF PLANT: Tree.

HEIGHT: 20'. ZONE: S

HOW TO IDENTIFY: This small tree, usually grown as a pot plant in Florida, has handsome, large, deeply cut foliage held by prickly stems.

HABIT OF GROWTH: Compact; prominent central leader with gracefully drooping branches.

FOLIAGE: Evergreen, 2' across, held by 2' petioles. There are 5–9 lobes. Young foliage is tomentose.

FLOWERS: Yellowish, showy flowers, 1" across, are borne in erect clusters.

FRUITS: Large, ovoid berries, if present.

SEASON OF MAXIMUM COLOR: Little seasonal change.

LANDSCAPE USES: This is yet another of the tropical exotics with king-size foliage of bold aspect. As a pot plant, it superficially resembles its more common cousin, rice-paper plant.

HABITAT: Eastern tropics.

LIGHT REQUIREMENT: Reduced light of terrace or patio.

SOIL REQUIREMENT: Moderately fertile, slightly acid compost is suggested.

SALT TOLERANCE: Tolerant of light salt drift back of the front-line dunes.

AVAILABILITY: Trevesias in containers are to be found in some retail nurseries in southern Florida.

CULTURE: After planting in fertile soil, little attention is required except for the usual watering and fertilization of pot plants.

PROPAGATION: Cuttage.

PESTS: Mealy-bugs, scales, and sooty-mold.

NOTE: *Trevesia sundaica* from Java has glossy-green leaves, with lanceolate segments, and smooth, open, rounded sinuses.

310
Aucuba

Aucuba (ow-coo-ba): Latin form of native Japanese name.
japonica (jap-on-ee-ca): Japanese.

FAMILY: Cornaceae.

RELATIVE: Dogwood.

TYPE OF PLANT: Shrub.

HEIGHT: 6'. ZONE: N,C

HOW TO IDENTIFY: Shrub with green stems; large, prominent leaf-scars; opposite, evergreen leaves that resemble those of a serrate-leaved croton. Leaves are crowded at branch-tips, and are green or variegated in various patterns.

HABIT OF GROWTH: Stiffly upright; leaves crowded near terminals.

FOLIAGE: Evergreen, opposite, serrate, pleasing in form, dark green in color.

FLOWERS: Small, purple, in terminal panicles, if present.

FRUITS: Berry-like drupes, if present.

SEASON OF MAXIMUM COLOR: No variation.

LANDSCAPE USES: For use in shaded planters, particularly in outdoor sections of through-the-wall bins, aucuba may serve. Set about 14" o.c. On superior soils in shaded gardens on the Panhandle, aucuba grows satisfactorily as a garden shrub. Full-sun locations are not recommended in Florida. A score of clones exhibit various leaf colors.

HABITAT: Eastern Asia; Florida, shaded sites on superior soils of the Panhandle.

LIGHT REQUIREMENT: Shade, running to low light intensities in Florida.

SOIL REQUIREMENT: Superior, organic soil free from nematodes is recommended.

SALT TOLERANCE: Not tolerant.

AVAILABILITY: Florida nurseries sometimes display aucuba plants.

CULTURE: Aucuba should be indicated with caution, lest it be unsatisfactory for your particular conditions.

PROPAGATION: Cuttage.

PESTS: Scales, nematodes, and soil-borne diseases.

311
Flowering Dogwood

Cornus (CORN-us): Latin for horn, for the toughness of the wood.
florida (FLO-ree-da): flowering.

FAMILY: Cornaceae.   RELATIVES: Other dogwoods and aucuba.
TYPE OF PLANT: Tree.   HEIGHT: 30'. ZONE: N,C

HOW TO IDENTIFY: Deciduous opposite leaves that often turn crimson in parts of Florida; symmetrical, whorled branching; showy, white bracts surrounding flowers in springtime, followed by decorative red fruits in the autumn.

HABIT OF GROWTH: Regular, symmetrical branches in whorls from a central leader.

FOLIAGE: Deciduous, opposite, medium in texture. The color is medium green in spring and summer, red and gold in fall.

FLOWERS: Greenish, inconspicuous, clustered within 4 white bracts.

FRUITS: Scarlet, ½" long, in terminal clusters in fall and winter.

SEASON OF MAXIMUM COLOR: Springtime, flowers; autumn, foliage and fruits.

LANDSCAPE USES: As a freestanding specimen, a background tree, framing tree, or avenue subject, nothing can surpass the dogwood. In northern Florida it is deeply appreciated for its many excellent qualities, and it is widely planted.

HABITAT: Hammocks with rich soil in northern and upper-central Florida.

LIGHT REQUIREMENT: Full sun or high, broken, shifting shade.

SOIL REQUIREMENT: Well-drained, fertile soil high in organic matter.

SALT TOLERANCE: Not tolerant.

AVAILABILITY: Field-grown dogwood trees are offered in retail sales lots during the winter dormant season.

CULTURE: Very careful planting in fertile, well-drained sites with protection of the trunks against borers is essential. Care in watering is needed at all times.

PROPAGATION: Seedage; graftage for superior types.

PESTS: Borers may invade the bark; thrips may destroy the bracts during hot, dry spring days; root-rot disease may cause death on poorly drained soils.

NOTE: Pink dogwoods, so very popular farther north, do not succeed in much of Florida because they do not experience sufficient chilling.

312
Indian Azalea

Rhododendron (roe-doe-DEN-dron): Greek for rose-tree.
simsii (SIMS-ee-eye): for J. Sims, an English botanist.

FAMILY: Ericaceae.   RELATIVES: Mountain-laurel and blueberry.
TYPE OF PLANT: Shrub.   HEIGHT: 10'. ZONE: N,C
HOW TO IDENTIFY: A shrub of robust growth that bears evergreen, alternate, elliptic-lanceolate, hairy, 2" leaves on hairy twigs. The blossoms that appear in late winter are justly famous.
HABIT OF GROWTH: Generally compact, well foliated to the ground.
FOLIAGE: Evergreen, alternate, of medium texture and dark green color.
FLOWERS: Very showy in 2- to 6-flowered clusters in early spring, in all shades of red, orange, pink. There are white varieties, too.
FRUITS: Capsules which split downward from the top.
SEASON OF MAXIMUM COLOR: Late winter or early spring.
LANDSCAPE USES: For enclosing devices, plant 5' apart; for foundation plantings for large public buildings, set at the same interval.
   There are many sterling varieties of Indian azaleas for gardeners in the upper part of Florida, where they appear in many garden arrangements. As a class, Indian azaleas are probably more tolerant of adverse growing conditions than any other group for Florida. Azaleas are most successful when set in large drifts of single colors separated by foils of white. These latter may be azaleas or other shrubs that flower coincidentally.
HABITAT: China; in Florida, much planted as a garden shrub.
LIGHT REQUIREMENT: Full sun in western Florida; shade on the peninsula.
SOIL REQUIREMENT: Fertile, acid, porous, organic soils are requisite.
SALT TOLERANCE: Not tolerant.
AVAILABILITY: Most nurseries in upper Florida offer Indian azaleas.
CULTURE: Set plants in carefully prepared sites; mulch the root area; keep lawn grasses back; water during periods of drought and syringe the foliage when watering to reduce infestation by insects and mites.
PROPAGATION: Cuttage.
PESTS: Thrips, mites, azalea defoliator, azalea flower-spot, and mineral deficiencies.

313
Kurume Azalea

Rhododendron (roe-doe-DEN-dron): Greek for rose-tree.
obtusum (ob-TOO-sum): obtuse, referring to the blunt ends of the leaves.

FAMILY: Ericaceae.   RELATIVES: Mountain-laurel and rose-bay.
TYPE OF PLANT: Dwarf shrub.   HEIGHT: 3'. ZONE: N
HOW TO IDENTIFY: A dwarf shrub bearing 1" leaves that are hairy, closely packed on thin, wire-like twigs that are usually upward-pointing. The bright blossoms are borne in such profusion that foliage is hidden.
HABIT OF GROWTH: Much branched, closely foliated, yet leggy on light soils.
FOLIAGE: Evergreen, alternate, of fine texture and dark green color.
FLOWERS: Very showy, extremely variable blossoms in spring. The petals may be white or in any shade of red. Some clones bear double flowers.
FRUITS: Little capsules which split downward from the top.
SEASON OF MAXIMUM COLOR: Late winter or very early spring.
LANDSCAPE USES: Foundation plantings, allow 2' between plants. To edge walks, plant about 18" apart. In front of green shrubbery, for color interest, Kurume azaleas may be planted 2' o.c. Varieties with colored flowers may be most effective when they are separated by generous drifts of white.

There are many kinds of Kurume azaleas available to gardeners in northern Florida. There are, also, many hybrid azaleas that belong to other horticultural classes.
HABITAT: Kurume, Japan; in Florida, gardens in northern counties.
LIGHT REQUIREMENT: On the Panhandle, full sun; elsewhere, plant in partial shade.
SOIL REQUIREMENT: Fertile, acid, porous, organic soils are requisite.
SALT TOLERANCE: Not tolerant.
AVAILABILITY: Most nurseries in northern Florida offer Kurume azaleas.
CULTURE: Set plants in carefully prepared sites; mulch the root area; keep lawn grasses back; water during periods of drought and syringe the foliage to reduce infestation by insects and mites.
PROPAGATION: Cuttage.
PESTS: Thrips, mites, azalea defoliator, azalea flower-spot, and mineral deficiencies.

314
Native Azaleas

Rhododendron (roe-doe-DEN-dron): Greek for rose-tree.
SPP.: several species are native in Florida.

FAMILY: Ericaceae.　　　　RELATIVES: Mountain-laurel and blueberry.
TYPE OF PLANT: Shrubs.　　　　　　HEIGHT: 15′. ZONE: N,C
HOW TO IDENTIFY: Deciduous shrubs with alternate, pubescent leaves
　　and beautiful, fragrant blossoms in early spring.
HABIT OF GROWTH: Upright, vase-shaped.
FOLIAGE: Deciduous, alternate, of medium texture, medium green.
FLOWERS: Showy, fragrant, of funnel form, 1½″ long with conspicuous
　　stamens.
FRUITS: Little capsules that split from the top.
SEASON OF MAXIMUM COLOR: Early springtime.
LANDSCAPE USES: For massing in informal shrubbery borders, Florida's
　　native azaleas are superb. Set native clumps about 5′ apart. In
　　woodland developments, these plants are almost indispensable.
　　　Rhododendron canescens, wild honeysuckle, is the best known.
　　It occurs in moist areas on acid soil in northern and central Flor-
　　ida. The pink or white flowers come in clusters of 6–15 before the
　　leaves in March.
　　　Rhododendron austrinum, Florida azalea, produces great masses
　　of yellow to orange flowers, in groups of 19–21 before the leaves.
　　This one grows in a restricted area in northwestern Florida.
　　　Rhododendron calendulaceum, flame azalea, though not native
　　in Florida, grows in superior soils of the Panhandle.
HABITAT: Moist areas with acid soil.
LIGHT REQUIREMENT: Broken shade of hammocks.
SOIL REQUIREMENT: Acid, fertile, well-drained, well-aerated soils.
SALT TOLERANCE: Not tolerant.
AVAILABILITY: Native deciduous azaleas are not usually sold by Florida
　　nurseries.
CULTURE: Azaleas are very demanding in the matter of growing me-
　　dium. It must be acid in reaction, well drained, open, porous, yet
　　able to retain water well. Water faithfully; fertilize once in late
　　winter; prune in May to keep plants compact and well shaped.
PROPAGATION: Cuttage in May–June.
PESTS: Mushroom root-rot.

315
Coral
Ardisia

Ardisia (ar-DIS-ee-a): Greek for point, referring to the corolla-lobes.
crenata (cree-NAY-ta): crenate, referring to the edges of the leaves.

FAMILY: Myrsinaceae.   RELATIVES: Myrsine and marlberry.
TYPE OF PLANT: Dwarf shrub.   HEIGHT: 6'. ZONE: N,C
HOW TO IDENTIFY: Straight, leggy stems hold evergreen leaves with
    crisped-undulate, glandular margins; coral-red fruits in decorative,
    hanging clusters in the cool months.
HABIT OF GROWTH: Stiffly upright, from unbranching stems bare near
    the earth.
FOLIAGE: Evergreen, coarse in texture, very dark green in color.
FLOWERS: White or pink, ¼" across, on special lateral branches.
FRUITS: Coral-red (sometimes white), 1-seeded drupes, in decorative
    clusters.
SEASON OF MAXIMUM COLOR: Cool months when fruits color.
LANDSCAPE USES: On the north sides of oak or pine trunks, ardisias
    are very handsome. They serve well, also, in planters that are
    shaded, and in north-side foundation arrangements. This is one of
    several fruiting shrubs called "Christmas-berry" in Florida.
        An occasional plant of the white-fruited form planted in with the
    reds is good for contrast.
HABITAT: Japan and southeastern Asia; in Florida, deep shade of trees.
LIGHT REQUIREMENT: Full shade, north-side locations are recommended.
SOIL REQUIREMENT: Fertile, acid soil relatively free of nematodes is
    best.
SALT TOLERANCE: Not tolerant.
AVAILABILITY: Nurseries stock ardisias in containers.
CULTURE: Even though coral ardisia is very subject to attack by nema-
    todes, it survives to form large cultures near the trunks of oaks and
    pines in wooded areas.
PROPAGATION: Seedage; volunteers abound under old plants in good
    locations.
PESTS: Nematodes, mites, and scales.

316
Marlberry

Ardisia (ar-DIS-ee-a): Greek for point, referring to the corolla-lobes.
paniculata (pan-ick-you-LATE-a): with flowers in pyramid-like clusters.

FAMILY: Myrsinaceae.

RELATIVE: Coral ardisia.

TYPE OF PLANT: Shrub or small tree.

HEIGHT: 20'. ZONE: S

HOW TO IDENTIFY: Shrub or small tree with evergreen, alternate, simple leaves that are held by branches that bend down under the weight of the showy, striped blossoms and shining, black fruits.

HABIT OF GROWTH: A slender crown is supported by slender, branched stems.

FOLIAGE: Evergreen, alternate, simple; of coarse texture and dark green color.

FLOWERS: White with purple lines, ¼″ in diameter, produced much of the year.

FRUITS: Smooth, shining, black drupes ¼″ in diameter are much in evidence.

SEASON OF MAXIMUM COLOR: Springtime, flowers; summer, fruits.

LANDSCAPE USES: This native relative of popular coral ardisia has real merit for informal massing on seaside locations, in which use the plants may stand 5′ o.c. Its complete adaptability to salt, marl, and shell should be carefully considered when beach dwellers are selecting their landscape plants.

HABITAT: Coastal hammocks of southern Florida.

LIGHT REQUIREMENT: Broken shade of hammocks or bright light of dunes.

SOIL REQUIREMENT: Marl, sand, or limestone soils are acceptable.

SALT TOLERANCE: Very tolerant of salt.

AVAILABILITY: Nurseries in southern counties can furnish marlberry plants.

CULTURE: After planting at its former level, water during periods of drought and fertilize annually.

PROPAGATION: Seedage, or collect from the wild, with permission of the owner.

PESTS: None of major consequence.

317
Plumbago

Plumbago (plum-BAY-go): Latin for lead, of doubtful application here.
capensis (cay-PEN-sis): of the Cape of Good Hope.

FAMILY: Plumbaginaceae.   RELATIVES: Statice and thrift.
TYPE OF PLANT: Shrub or vine.   HEIGHT: Variable. ZONE: C,S
HOW TO IDENTIFY: Clustered, evergreen, wavy, spiny-tipped leaves; long-tubed, bright blue, clustered flowers, produced much of the year around.
HABIT OF GROWTH: Sprawling, compact, much-branched; may be trained as a vine.
FOLIAGE: Evergreen, fine in texture, light, yellow-green in color.
FLOWERS: Azure-blue, tubular, clustered, profuse during much of the year.
FRUITS: Elongate, bur-like capsules that cling by many curved spines.
SEASON OF MAXIMUM COLOR: Much of the year.
LANDSCAPE USES: As a foundation plant (2′ o.c.); as a transition plant, and as a hedge, plumbago is central Florida's most popular dwarf flowering shrub. It serves well, also, as a light vine when planted by a metal support. For white flowers, choose variety 'Alba'. Plumbago is killed to the earth most winters in northern Florida.
HABITAT: South Africa; in Florida, ubiquitous in gardens on the peninsula.
LIGHT REQUIREMENT: Full sun for best growth and flowering.
SOIL REQUIREMENT: Adapted to widely varying soils, but may show mineral deficiency in presence of lime.
SALT TOLERANCE: Tolerant of light salt drift well back of the dunes.
AVAILABILITY: Both blue and white forms are offered by nurserymen.
CULTURE: Plant with reasonable care in enriched site; water periodically until well established; fertilize twice each year; prune heavily in late winter for fresh new growth.
PROPAGATION: Seedage and cuttage.
PESTS: Cottony cushion scale, mites, and mineral deficiency on calcareous earth.
NOTE: Red plumbago (*P. indica*) is also excellent for mass plantings. The red flowers are borne in terminal spikes; otherwise the two species are very similar.

318
Egg-Fruit

Pouteria (pooh-TEAR-ee-a): native name.
campechiana (cam-PAY-chee-ANE-a): of Campeche, a province in southern Mexico.

FAMILY: Sapotaceae.   RELATIVES: Sapodilla, sapote, and satin-leaf.
TYPE OF PLANT: Tree.   HEIGHT: 25'. ZONE: S
HOW TO IDENTIFY: Evergreen leaves that are bright, shining green, ovate, about 8" in length; bright yellow fruits, about 4" long, somewhat egg-shaped. The fruit has a distinctive flavor, as described below.
HABIT OF GROWTH: Small, neat tree that grows from a single trunk.
FOLIAGE: Evergreen, 8" long, alternate, coarse in texture, dark green.
FLOWERS: Inconspicuous, greenish-white.
FRUITS: Shaped like large hens' eggs, yellow in color, flavored like hard-boiled egg yolk that has been sweetened, or like a very dry sweet potato with syrup. Seedlings vary in flavor.
SEASON OF MAXIMUM COLOR: Summertime, when the fruits are colored.
LANDSCAPE USES: For the unusual egg-yolk fruits, *Pouteria* could be planted as a freestanding specimen in the grounds of advanced horticulturists who live in nearly frostless locations.

Lucuma nervosa is a name, now held to be an invalid synonym, for the egg-fruit. Nurseries may have their plants labeled thus. There is considerable variation in size, shape, and flavor of egg-fruits, but this is usually unimportant to home gardeners in southern Florida who are mainly interested in them as horticultural curiosities.

HABITAT: Tropical America; naturalized in extreme southern Florida.
LIGHT REQUIREMENT: Full sun or partial shade from tall palms.
SOIL REQUIREMENT: Tolerant of limestone.
SALT TOLERANCE: Tolerant of salt.
AVAILABILITY: Trees in containers may be bought in southern counties.
CULTURE: Plant in enriched soil; water periodically; mulch with leaves; fertilize twice or thrice annually for good fruit production.
PROPAGATION: Seedage.
PESTS: Mites and scales.

319
Sapodilla

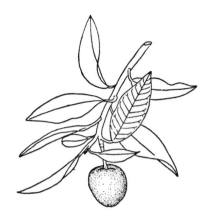

Achras (AK-ras): Greek for pear tree.
zapota (sap-OH-ta): aboriginal name.

FAMILY: Sapotaceae. RELATIVES: Egg-fruit, satin-leaf, and gutta-percha.
TYPE OF PLANT: Tree.   HEIGHT: 35′. ZONE: S
HOW TO IDENTIFY: A symmetrical tree which holds its branches in even
    whorls, with entire, emarginate, evergreen leaves crowded near
    their tips, and rusty, brown, scurfy fruits.
HABIT OF GROWTH: Handsome form by a strong central leader and
    whorled branches.
FOLIAGE: Evergreen, coarse in texture, lustrous green in tone.
FLOWERS: White, ½″ across, not showy.
FRUITS: Rusty, brown, globose berries, 2″–5″ in diameter, pleasant
    tasting to most.
SEASON OF MAXIMUM COLOR: Summer and fall, when rusty fruits ma-
    ture.
LANDSCAPE USES: Storm-fast, salt-resistant sapodilla is most highly
    recommended for nearly frost-free sections of the state. This is a
    beautiful, useful tree that is fully appreciated for its many good
    points. For avenue planting, for shade, for framing, and for back-
    ground it can be planted with confidence.
    This tree is the source of chicle, from which chewing gum is
    made.
    There are several named varieties which bear fruits of superior
    quality. These are increased by graftage.
HABITAT: Central American rain forests; in Florida, landscape plantings
    in warm areas.
LIGHT REQUIREMENT: Full sun for best form.
SOIL REQUIREMENT: Tolerant of many soils, including those of alkaline
    reaction.
SALT TOLERANCE: Very tolerant of salt.
AVAILABILITY: Seedlings and grafted trees under name are offered in
    cans by nurseries in southern Florida.
CULTURE: Once established in frostless locations, sapodilla trees re-
    quire little attention.
PROPAGATION: Seedage; superior forms by graftage.
PESTS: Scales.

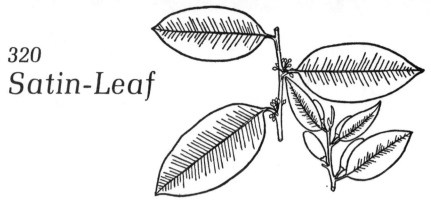

320
Satin-Leaf

Chrysophyllum (cry-so-FILL-um): Greek for golden leaf.
oliviforme ((ol-iv-ee-FORM-ee): olive-shaped.

FAMILY: Sapotaceae.   RELATIVES: Sapodilla, egg-fruit, and star-apple.
TYPE OF PLANT: Tree.   HEIGHT: 30'. ZONE: S
HOW TO IDENTIFY: Large, evergreen leaves that look as though the undersides are of burnished copper.
HABIT OF GROWTH: Somewhat irregular, open-topped, small tree.
FOLIAGE: Evergreen, of coarse texture. The upper surfaces are green; the lower surfaces are of a glowing, bright copper color.
FLOWERS: White, inconspicuous, on fuzzy, brown stalks in leaf axils.
FRUITS: Fleshy berries, green to dark purple, ¾" long, ovate or nearly globose.
SEASON OF MAXIMUM COLOR: No variation.
LANDSCAPE USES: For a freestanding lawn specimen or in shrub borders in frost-free sections, satin-leaf is desirable on account of the beauty of the lower leaf surfaces, which turn up attractively when the wind moves the foliage. This is truly a worthwhile native plant that warrants wider landscape use.
HABITAT: Coastal hammocks of extreme southern Florida, especially on Cape Sable.
LIGHT REQUIREMENT: Broken shade of hammocks.
SOIL REQUIREMENT: Tolerant of varying soils, but fertile soil is best.
SALT TOLERANCE: Not tolerant of dune conditions.
AVAILABILITY: Nurseries in extreme southern Florida sell satin-leaf trees in containers.
CULTURE: Plant in fertile, slightly acid soil; water faithfully; mulch with leaves 6" deep; do not allow grass to grow over the root zone.
PROPAGATION: Seedage.
PESTS: Caterpillars chew the leaves.
NOTE: Star-apple (*C. cainito*), closely related, bears leaves of similar decorative quality and edible fruits that are sometimes as much as 4" long.

321
Fringe-Tree

Chionanthus (kye-oh-NAN-thus): Greek for snowflower.
virginica (vir-GIN-ee-ca): Virginian.

FAMILY: Oleaceae.   RELATIVES: Privet, jasmine, and osmanthus.

TYPE OF PLANT: Shrub-like tree.   HEIGHT: 30′. ZONE: N,C

HOW TO IDENTIFY: Deciduous, entire, opposite leaves narrowing to both ends; brown twigs covered with scattered lenticels; showy clusters of white, narrow-petaled flowers before, or with, the first leaves.

HABIT OF GROWTH: Variable, round-topped or somewhat open and narrow.

FOLIAGE: Deciduous, opposite, coarse in texture, dark green above, paler beneath.

FLOWERS: White, in loose clusters, with four narrow, ribbon-like petals.

FRUITS: Black or dark blue 1-seeded drupes, ¾″ long, in summertime.

SEASON OF MAXIMUM COLOR: Late spring.

LANDSCAPE USES: As a freestanding specimen for late spring blooms and for the curiosity of the black fruits, this little native tree is recommended. Long popular as a front-lawn specimen, fringe-tree is appreciated for its beauty and adaptability.

HABITAT: Moist soils of northern and central Florida.

LIGHT REQUIREMENT: Broken shade of forests or full sun of gardens.

SOIL REQUIREMENT: Fertile moist earth or improved sand.

SALT TOLERANCE: Not tolerant.

AVAILABILITY: Small nurseries in northern Florida may have fringe-trees.

CULTURE: Plant in a moist, fertile spot; water faithfully until well established; thereafter, keep lawn grasses back; fertilize in late winter.

PROPAGATION: Seedage or cuttage.

PESTS: Scales and mites.

322
Downy
Jasmine

Jasminum (JAZZ-min-um): ancient name of Arabic origin.
multiflorum (mul-tee-FLOR-um): many-flowered.

FAMILY: Oleaceae. RELATIVES: Privet, olive, osmanthus, and fringe-tree.
TYPE OF PLANT: Vine, often trained as a shrub.

HEIGHT: Variable. ZONE: C,S

HOW TO IDENTIFY: Densely pubescent, evergreen climber, that has opposite leaves about 2" long that give a slightly gray-green effect; white flowers are very abundant in little axillary clusters. The blossoms are *not* strongly scented. The calyx teeth are densely covered with spreading yellow hairs.

HABIT OF GROWTH: Strong-growing; sprawling or clambering vine if supported.

FOLIAGE: Evergreen, opposite, downy, of medium-fine texture and gray-green color.

FLOWERS: White, axillary, star-like, 1" in diameter, with fuzzy calyx teeth.

FRUITS: Inconspicuous little capsules held within the calyx teeth.

SEASON OF MAXIMUM COLOR: Warm months.

LANDSCAPE USES: In central Florida, where it is known as star jasmine, this plant is very popular as a landscape shrub. For foundation plantings and as a part of shrubbery borders, plant 3' apart.

HABITAT: India; in Florida, much grown in the central section.

LIGHT REQUIREMENT: Full sun for best habit and profuse flowering.

SOIL REQUIREMENT: Sandy soil is adequate.

SALT TOLERANCE: Not tolerant.

AVAILABILITY: In retail nurseries in central and southern Florida.

CULTURE: Set plants in prepared sites; water periodically until well established, thereafter during dry spells; fertilize twice annually; prune as needed to keep within bounds.

PROPAGATION: Cuttage.

PESTS: Scales.

NOTE: *Jasminum gracillimum*, easily confused, has more dense hanging flower clusters; calyx teeth covered sparsely, with close, not spreading, pubescence. Arabian jasmine (*Jasminum sambac*) has 2", very fragrant, usually double flowers and very glossy, broad, prominently veined, dark green leaves.

323
Primrose
Jasmine

Jasminum (JAZZ-min-um): ancient name of Arabic origin.
mesnyi (MESS-nee-eye): for W. Mesny, its collector.

FAMILY: Oleaceae. RELATIVES: Privet, osmanthus, olive, and fringe-tree.
TYPE OF PLANT: Shrub or vine depending upon culture.

HEIGHT: 10'. ZONE: N,C

HOW TO IDENTIFY: A sprawling shrub that has smooth, 4-angled, green branchlets with opposite trifoliolate leaves and yellow flowers in late winter.

HABIT OF GROWTH: Strong vine or declinate shrub that can be clipped to bush form.

FOLIAGE: Evergreen, opposite, trifoliolate, of fine texture and light green color.

FLOWERS: Bright yellow, 2" in diameter, solitary, subtended by leaf-like bracts.

FRUITS: Usually not produced in Florida.

SEASON OF MAXIMUM COLOR: Late winter; best show following considerable cold.

LANDSCAPE USES: One of Florida's most overused shrubs, this very common, yellow-flowered jasmine is seen everywhere over the upper part of the state. In foundation plantings, set 2' o.c.; as a hardy vine on a strong metal trellis plant at the same interval. Primrose jasmine can be planted to help prevent erosion on slopes and banks.

HABITAT: Western China; in Florida, ubiquitous in the upper part.

LIGHT REQUIREMENT: Full sun for compact growth.

SOIL REQUIREMENT: Completely tolerant of all soils.

SALT TOLERANCE: Not tolerant.

AVAILABILITY: This is usually not an item of commerce as there seems always to be an ample supply of planting stock for free acquisition.

CULTURE: Simply plant, water, and forget. Flowering is best after cold winters.

PROPAGATION: Branches root where they touch the earth.

PESTS: Scales and mushroom root-rot.

324
Shining Jasmine

Jasminum (JAZZ-min-um): ancient name of Arabic origin.
nitidum (NIT-i-dum): shining.

FAMILY: Oleaceae.
RELATIVES: Privet and fringe-tree.
TYPE OF PLANT: Vine or shrub.
HEIGHT: Variable. ZONE: C,S
HOW TO IDENTIFY: A strong-growing vine with attractive, evergreen, opposite, glossy, 4″ leaves; flower buds tinted pink; red calyx teeth very prominent, standing perpendicular to the corolla tube at anthesis. Blossoms are fragrant.
HABIT OF GROWTH: Strong, sprawling, twining vine, usually maintained as a shrub by careful, periodic pruning.
FOLIAGE: Evergreen, alternate, very waxy, medium-coarse in texture.
FLOWERS: White, fragrant, 1½″ in diameter, buds tinted pink outside; calyx and calyx teeth are red in cool weather.
FRUITS: 2-lobed berries, if present; frequently lacking in Florida.
SEASON OF MAXIMUM COLOR: Warm months.
LANDSCAPE USES: This, perhaps Florida's most popular landscape jasmine, is much planted in foundation groups, planters, and shrubbery borders in the most nearly frost-free sections. Planting intervals may be 3′ o.c. This sterling landscape jasmine has been known as "Jasminum ilicifolium" and "Jasminum amplexicaule."
HABITAT: Islands of the southern Pacific Ocean; in Florida, much planted in central and southern parts.
LIGHT REQUIREMENT: Full sun or broken shade; on north sides, plants will not bloom.
SOIL REQUIREMENT: Sandy soils, when reasonably well fertilized, are satisfactory.
SALT TOLERANCE: Not tolerant of dune conditions.
AVAILABILITY: This jasmine is widely offered for sale in central and southern Florida.
CULTURE: Set in well-prepared sites; water faithfully during all periods of drought; fertilize thrice annually; mulch and keep out grass.
PROPAGATION: Cuttage.
PESTS: Scales and mushroom root-rot.
NOTE: River jasmine (*Jasminum fluminense*) has trifoliate leaves, the center leaflet being the largest and held on a longer leaf stalk. This species fruits abundantly and volunteer seedlings are numerous.

325
Osmanthus

Osmanthus (oz-MAN-thus): Greek for fragrant flower.
fragrans (FRAY-grans): fragrant.

FAMILY: Oleaceae. RELATIVES: Olive and native devilwood.
TYPE OF PLANT: Large shrub. HEIGHT: 20'. ZONE: N
HOW TO IDENTIFY: Opposite, evergreen leaves, 2½"–4" in length, finely and sharply toothed or entire on the same plant; very fragrant, inconspicuous, white blossoms in winter.
HABIT OF GROWTH: Open, bare stems below; foliage restricted to branch-tips.
FOLIAGE: Evergreen, opposite, medium in texture, dark green in color.
FLOWERS: Small, deliciously fragrant, white flowers in winter.
FRUITS: Bluish, ovoid drupes, ½" in diameter.
SEASON OF MAXIMUM COLOR: No seasonal variation; fragrance is the thing.
LANDSCAPE USES: For generations, osmanthus has been a favorite as a freestanding specimen for the delight of its wintertime blossoms. Plant a group of three (5' o.c.) in a shrubbery bay.
HABITAT: Eastern Asia; in Florida, superior soils of northern counties.
LIGHT REQUIREMENT: Full sun or broken, shifting shade from high pines.
SOIL REQUIREMENT: Superior soils of northern counties.
SALT TOLERANCE: Not tolerant.
AVAILABILITY: Nurseries in northern and western Florida sell canned plants.
CULTURE: On reasonably good soil, osmanthus is usually long lived, in spite of neglect.
PROPAGATION: Cuttage.
PESTS: Scales, mushroom root-rot, and nematodes.
NOTE: Holly osmanthus (*O. ilicifolius*) has opposite, 2½" leaves, with 1–4 pairs of marginal spines and sweet flowers to distinguish it from true hollies. One clone has variegated foliage.

A hybrid (*O. fragrans* × *O. ilicifolius*) is Fortune's osmanthus with 4" leaves that contain 8–10 teeth on each side.

326
Glossy Privet

Ligustrum (li-GUS-trum): ancient Latin name.
lucidum (LOU-sid-um): bright.

FAMILY: Oleaceae.   RELATIVES: Osmanthus, fringe-tree, and olive.
TYPE OF PLANT: Tree.   HEIGHT: 40'. ZONE: N,C,S
HOW TO IDENTIFY: Fast-growing tree with huge, opposite, pear-like, evergreen leaves that have 6–8 pairs of veins. Usually many of the drupe-like black fruits persist over much of the year.
HABIT OF GROWTH: Tree-like, with dense, compact head of bending branches.
FOLIAGE: Evergreen, opposite, pear-like, very coarse in texture, dark green.
FLOWERS: Little, white, odorous flowers in springtime, held up by terminal panicles.
FRUITS: Drupe-like berries, blue-black in color, with bloom, persist much of the year.
SEASON OF MAXIMUM COLOR: Fall, when blue-black fruits mature.
LANDSCAPE USES: Street tree at 40' intervals; as a very large shrub on very poor sandy soil, plant at 5' intervals, and attend to pruning frequently.
    There are numerous named varieties of glossy privet.
HABITAT: Eastern Asia; in Florida, ubiquitous, in landscape plantings.
LIGHT REQUIREMENT: Full sun or partial shade is suitable.
SOIL REQUIREMENT: Tolerant of widely varying soil types.
SALT TOLERANCE: Not tolerant.
AVAILABILITY: Usually sold as a shrub B & B or in containers by most nurseries.
CULTURE: If white-flies are controlled, and the plant is pruned regularly, no additional attention is required.
PROPAGATION: Graftage on *L. quihoui*, as glossy privet is resistant to propagation by cuttage. Seedlings abound under old trees, and these may be used as they are or as grafting stocks.
PESTS: Scales, white-flies, and sooty-mold.

327
Japanese Privet

Ligustrum (li-GUS-trum): ancient Latin name.
japonicum (jap-ON-i-cum): Japanese.

FAMILY: Oleaceae.   RELATIVES: Osmanthus, jasmine, and fringe-tree.
TYPE OF PLANT: Shrub.   HEIGHT: 15'. ZONE: N,C,S
HOW TO IDENTIFY: A shrub with evergreen, opposite, entire leaves that are broad-ovate, nearly flat, with 4–5 pairs of veins and springtime panicles of small, white, odorous flowers.
HABIT OF GROWTH: Upright-spreading, strict, or low-spreading.
FOLIAGE: Evergreen, opposite, medium-coarse in texture in most forms, yet some have fine texture and others coarse. The color is dark green in most all-green varieties, yet there are those that have leaves marbled with yellow.
FLOWERS: White, small, odorous, in terminal panicles in springtime.
FRUITS: Drupe-like berries that are blue-black and few on a panicle.
SEASON OF MAXIMUM COLOR: Early spring, when the blossoms are out.
LANDSCAPE USES: Florida's most overused shrub is seen almost everywhere. As a foundation plant for large buildings, set plant 3' apart; for informal enclosure, allow 5' between plants; for sheared hedges, set the plants 2' o.c.
HABITAT: Japan; Florida's most widely planted broad-leaved, evergreen shrub.
LIGHT REQUIREMENT: Full sun or partial shade is suitable.
SOIL REQUIREMENT: Tolerant of widely varying soils.
SALT TOLERANCE: Not tolerant.
AVAILABILITY: All nurseries market Japanese privet, canned or B & B. There are a dozen or more named varieties from which to choose. Grafted plants are always to be preferred when available.
CULTURE: Grafted plants need little attention save for fertilization twice a year and irrigation during serious droughts.
PROPAGATION: Cuttage or by graftage on *L. quihoui* for protection against harmful nematodes.
PESTS: Nematodes, mushroom root-rot, scales, and white-flies followed by sooty-mold.

328
Butterfly-Bush

Buddleja (bud-LEE-a): for A. Buddle, an English botanist.
officinalis (of-fis-in-ALE-is): medicinal.

FAMILY: Loganiaceae. RELATIVE: Carolina yellow-jasmine.
TYPE OF PLANT: Shrub, sometimes becoming tree-like. HEIGHT: 20′.
ZONE: C,S

HOW TO IDENTIFY: All leaves, twigs, and flowers are densely pubescent; lilac flowers in midwinter are very fragrant.

HABIT OF GROWTH: Large, sprawling, almost tree-like if not frosted.

FOLIAGE: Evergreen, alternate, coarse in texture, light green above, white beneath.

FLOWERS: Tiny, but very fragrant, of lilac color, in panicles 6″ long in midwinter.

FRUITS: Inconspicuous capsules.

SEASON OF MAXIMUM COLOR: Midwinter.

LANDSCAPE USES: As a part of a tall shrubbery border to yield delicious fragrance in midwinter, butterfly-bush will serve. As the plant is frequently frosted to earth, it should stand near hardy evergreen shrubs that can maintain the form of the garden during the winter.

HABITAT: Asia; in Florida, warmer sections.

LIGHT REQUIREMENT: Full sun for compact habit and full flowering.

SOIL REQUIREMENT: Tolerant of light sandy soils, but susceptible to nematode attack.

SALT TOLERANCE: Tolerates salt drift, but not front-line dunes.

AVAILABILITY: Small plants in containers are frequently found in nurseries.

CULTURE: Butterfly-bush grows rapidly, usually recovers after each freezing.

PROPAGATION: Cuttage or marcottage.

PESTS: Nematodes, mites, and caterpillars.

NOTE: Several other buddlejas are sometimes seen in Florida. *B. madagascariensis*, with sprawling habit, white-tomentose branches, and yellow flowers grows in southern counties. *B. davidii*, the most famed of the genus, will grow fairly well in extreme western Florida. *B. asiatica*, of upright habit, and with white, fragrant flowers, grows fairly well in central Florida if protected against nematodes.

329
Carolina Yellow-Jasmine

Gelsemium (gel-SEM-ee-um): Italian *gelsomino* for true jasmine.
sempervirens (sem-per-VYE-rens): evergreen.

FAMILY: Loganiaceae.

TYPE OF PLANT: Vine.

RELATIVES: Butterfly-bush.

HEIGHT: Variable. ZONE: N,C

HOW TO IDENTIFY: Reddish stems which climb by twisting about supports; partially evergreen foliage; showy yellow blossoms in springtime.

HABIT OF GROWTH: Climbing vine by means of twisting stems.

FOLIAGE: Semi-evergreen, opposite, fine in texture, medium green in color, turning rusty during cold months.

FLOWERS: Funnel-form, five-lobed, bright yellow, fragrant; outstanding highlights in Florida hammocks during their season.

FRUITS: Ovoid capsules, ½" long, split at maturity to release seeds.

SEASON OF MAXIMUM COLOR: January–February.

LANDSCAPE USES: For the beauty of the springtime gold, Carolina yellow-jasmine may be planted by trees, fences, or pergolas. This fine-scale native vine seldom gets out of hand to become a nuisance.

HABITAT: Hammocks of central and northern Florida.

LIGHT REQUIREMENT: Reduced light or full sun.

SOIL REQUIREMENT: Hammock soils support best growth and flowering.

SALT TOLERANCE: Not tolerant.

AVAILABILITY: Some nurseries might offer vines in containers; however, rooted layers are usually obtained from friends.

CULTURE: Plant near a support in moderately fertile earth; water periodically; place a mulch over the roots; fertilize once each winter.

PROPAGATION: Layerage, where branches touch the earth.

PESTS: Usually none of great importance.

330
Allamanda

Allamanda (al-a-MAN-da): for F. Allamand, a Dutch professor.
cathartica (cath-AR-tee-ca): cathartic.

FAMILY: Apocynaceae.   RELATIVES: Oleander and lucky nut.
TYPE OF PLANT: Shrub or vine depending upon training.
                            HEIGHT: Variable. ZONE: C,S
HOW TO IDENTIFY: Vining growth; milky sap; evergreen leaves in
  whorls; bright yellow, flaring trumpets during much of the year.
HABIT OF GROWTH: A vigorous vine that may be maintained as a shrub
  by pruning.
FOLIAGE: Evergreen, whorled, coarse in texture, light green in color.
FLOWERS: Handsome, large, golden trumpets produced much of the
  year.
FRUITS: Prickly capsules, splitting to release winged seeds.
SEASON OF MAXIMUM COLOR: Much of the year, when flowers are pro-
  duced.
LANDSCAPE USES: As a vine, as a hedge (set 18″ o.c.), as a freestand-
  ing, clipped specimen, allamanda is an all-time favorite. Planted by
  a cajeput tree to grow as a vine and to flower in the upper branches,
  allamanda is most effective. The brown-bud variety is very popu-
  lar with homeowners and nurserymen.
  All allamandas are VERY POISONOUS; all are tender to cold.
HABITAT: Tropical parts of Brazil; in Florida, warm parts of the penin-
  sula.
LIGHT REQUIREMENT: Full sun for best flowering.
SOIL REQUIREMENT: Tolerant of many soil types.
SALT TOLERANCE: Not tolerant.
AVAILABILITY: Allamandas are offered in most nurseries on the penin-
  sula.
CULTURE: Except for their tenderness to frost, allamandas grow with-
  out major impediment.
PROPAGATION: Cuttage.
PESTS: Caterpillars and mites.

331
Purple Allamanda

Allamanda (al-a-MAN-da): for F. Allamand, a Dutch professor.
violacea (vye-oh-LAY-see-a): violet.

FAMILY: Apocynaceae.   RELATIVES: Confederate-jasmine and oleander.
TYPE OF PLANT: Vine or shrub depending upon training.
                                   HEIGHT: Variable. ZONE: C,S
HOW TO IDENTIFY: Sprawling, declinate stems with milky sap; pubescent leaves in whorls; trumpet-shaped flowers of dull magenta.
HABIT OF GROWTH: Vining; maintained as a shrub by pruning.
FOLIAGE: Evergreen, pubescent, coarse in texture, light green in color.
FLOWERS: Flaring trumpets of magenta-violet that fades to give a two-toned effect.
FRUITS: Prickly capsules that split to release winged seeds.
SEASON OF MAXIMUM COLOR: Warm months.
LANDSCAPE USES: Purple allamanda is sometimes planted as a vine for the curiosity of its violet-magenta flowers. It is not to be confused with *Cryptostegia*.

   Like all allamandas, this species is tender to cold and plants will be killed back to the earth by frosts. Normally roots may survive many winters to produce new tops after the advent of warm weather. All allamandas are POISONOUS.
HABITAT: Warm section of Brazil; in Florida, most nearly frostless regions.
LIGHT REQUIREMENT: Full sun for best flowering.
SOIL REQUIREMENT: Tolerant of widely varying soils.
SALT TOLERANCE: Not tolerant.
AVAILABILITY: Specialty nurseries may have purple allamandas.
CULTURE: Soil of reasonable fertility that is free of nematodes is best. Water faithfully until well established; prune to keep within bounds; offer protection on cold nights.
PROPAGATION: Cuttage.
PESTS: Mites and scales.

332
Pink-Allamanda

Mandevilla (man-de-vill-a): for H. J. Mandeville, English minister at Buenos Aires. *splendens* (splen-dens): from Latin to shine.

FAMILY: Apocynaceae.

RELATIVES: Allamanda and plumeria.

TYPE OF PLANT: Evergreen vine.

HEIGHT: Variable. ZONE: C,S

HOW TO IDENTIFY: A fast-growing vine with opposite, oblong leaves up to 8″ long; climbs by entwining. The large funnel- or trumpet-shaped flowers are borne in small axillary clusters on new growth.

HABIT OF GROWTH: A dense vine.

FOLIAGE: The soft, leathery, evergreen leaves, with entire margins, are medium to dark green.

FLOWERS: Pinkish-lavender, to 5″ long.

FRUITS: Follicles to 8″ long, often in pairs.

SEASON OF MAXIMUM COLOR: Summer, but flowers all year.

LANDSCAPE USES: Excellent screening vine.

HABITAT: Brazil.

LIGHT REQUIREMENT: Full sun for best flowering.

SOIL REQUIREMENT: Thrives on most well-drained soils.

SALT TOLERANCE: Endures salt drift just behind front-line dunes.

AVAILABILITY: Readily available in cans in most nurseries within its climatic range.

CULTURE: Same as for yellow allamanda.

PROPAGATION: Seedage or cuttage.

PESTS: None serious at present.

NOTE: The most common variety in the trade today is Mrs. Alice Dupont. A smaller-flowered vine, *Dipladenia splendens*, is often sold erroneously as *Mandevilla*.

333
Confederate-Jasmine

Trachelospermum (track-ell-oh-SPERM-um): Greek for neck and seed.
jasminoides (jazz-min-OY-dez): jasmine-like.

FAMILY: Apocynaceae.   RELATIVES: Natal-plum and heralds-trumpet.
TYPE OF PLANT: Vine.   HEIGHT: Variable. ZONE: N,C,S
HOW TO IDENTIFY: A twining vine that has milky sap, opposite, thick,
    evergreen leaves and white, fragrant flowers with petals in pin-
    wheel arrangement in springtime.
HABIT OF GROWTH: Twining vine.
FOLIAGE: Opposite, evergreen, medium in texture, dark green in color.
FLOWERS: White, fragrant, 1″ in diameter, in axillary cymes that ex-
    tend well beyond the leaves.
FRUITS: Two long, slender pods, if present.
SEASON OF MAXIMUM COLOR: April–May, when flowers mature.
LANDSCAPE USES: As a vine to train beside and across the top of a
    doorway, this hardy plant cannot be excelled. To cover pergolas,
    fences, and trellises and to add seasonal interest to pine trunks,
    Confederate-jasmine is much planted.
    The little-leaf variety 'Microphylla' is useful as a ground cover
    and for north-side planters.
    There is at least one variety that produces leaves that are mottled.
HABITAT: China; in Florida, this cherished vine is in every community.
LIGHT REQUIREMENT: Sun or shade.
SOIL REQUIREMENT: Tolerant of many soils.
SALT TOLERANCE: Not tolerant.
AVAILABILITY: Widely available in gallon cans.
CULTURE: No special culture is required after well-planted vines be-
    come established.
PROPAGATION: Marcottage or cuttage with root-inducing powders under
    mist.
PESTS: Scales, followed by sooty-mold.

334
Crape-Jasmine

Ervatamia (er-va-TAME-ee-a): from a vernacular name.
coronaria (core-oh-NARE-ee-a): used for garlands.

FAMILY: Apocynaceae.
RELATIVES: Natal-plum and oleander.
TYPE OF PLANT: Shrub.
HEIGHT: 10′. ZONE: C,S
HOW TO IDENTIFY: Green twigs with milky sap bear huge, shining, opposite, evergreen leaves; small, white, ruffled, fragrant flowers, 1½″–2″ across.
HABIT OF GROWTH: Symmetrical, spreading shrub of pleasing form.
FOLIAGE: Evergreen, opposite, of large size and shining dark green color.
FLOWERS: Waxy, white, fragrant, with wavy petals, often much doubled.
FRUITS: Orange-red pods, about 2″ long, with recurved beaks.
SEASON OF MAXIMUM COLOR: Warm months, when in full bloom.
LANDSCAPE USES: As a part of an enclosing shrubbery border, plant 5′ o.c. Thus the shining foliage and the fragrant flowers can be featured.

Crape-jasmine is less hardy than gardenia; therefore, it is less permanent in garden arrangements in cold locations. In northern Florida, *Ervatamia* seldom escapes cold damage.
HABITAT: India; in Florida, ubiquitous in gardens.
LIGHT REQUIREMENT: Tolerant of partial shade.
SOIL REQUIREMENT: Tolerant of many different kinds of soil.
SALT TOLERANCE: Not tolerant.
AVAILABILITY: Small plants in containers are offered in most nurseries.
CULTURE: After establishment, crape-jasmine grows with little attention. One or two applications of fertilizer each year and the maintenance of a mulch over the root zone should keep plants healthy. Plants in exposed locations must be protected on cold nights.
PROPAGATION: Cuttage.
PESTS: Scales, sooty-mold, mites, and nematodes.

Frangipani

Plumeria (plume-ERE-ee-a): for C. Plumier, French botanist.
SPP.: several species are grown in Florida.

FAMILY: Apocynaceae. RELATIVES: Heralds-trumpet and oleander.
TYPE OF PLANT: Tree. HEIGHT: 15'. ZONE: S
HOW TO IDENTIFY: Branches sausage-like, blunt, rough with crowded leaf-scars, and with deciduous leaves crowded at their tips. The blossoms are beautiful, waxy, and very fragrant.
HABIT OF GROWTH: Awkward composition of sausage-like branches.
FOLIAGE: Deciduous, very large, very coarse in texture, of medium-green color.
FLOWERS: Tubular, 2" across, waxy, fragrant, variable in color.
FRUITS: Foot-long twin pods that are brown and leathery.
SEASON OF MAXIMUM COLOR: Summertime.
LANDSCAPE USES: For the fragrance of the beautiful blossoms, frangipanis are among the most popular trees for hot countries. Plant as a freestanding specimen, as a patio tree, or as a part of a shrubbery border.
HABITAT: Tropical America; in Florida, warmest locations.
LIGHT REQUIREMENT: Full sun or high, shifting shade.
SOIL REQUIREMENT: Tolerant of many different soils.
SALT TOLERANCE: Will grow fairly close to salt water.
AVAILABILITY: Many kinds can be found in nurseries in southern Florida.
CULTURE: Set in soil that has been enriched. Water until well rooted in the earth.
PROPAGATION: Cuttage at any time, using any kind of wood.
PESTS: Scales, frangipani caterpillar, and nematodes.
NOTE: *P. rubra* produces flowers in tones of red, and has the largest leaves in the genus (18" long), with conspicuous marginal veins.
    P. alba has white flowers, narrow, lance-shaped leaves with revolute edges.
    P. obtusa has spatula-like leaves with distinctly rounded apexes and white blooms centered in yellow. This one is variable in form and color, to confuse the issue.

Heralds-Trumpet

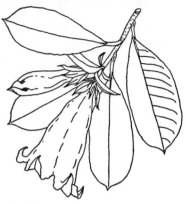

Beaumontia (bo-MONT-ee-a): for Lady Beaumont of England.
grandiflora (gran-dee-FLOR-a): large-flowered.

FAMILY: Apocynaceae.   RELATIVES: Frangipani, Confederate-jasmine.
TYPE OF PLANT: Vine.   HEIGHT: Variable. ZONE: C,S
HOW TO IDENTIFY: Huge, white, Easter-lily-like blossoms; opposite,
   evergreen leaves, 8″ long; milky sap.
HABIT OF GROWTH: Rampant vine that develops very heavy cover.
FOLIAGE: Evergreen, opposite, 8″ long, of very coarse texture and me-
   dium green color.
FLOWERS: Huge trumpets, 8″ long, white, tipped with pink, veined
   with green, without scales at the throat. These trumpets, borne in
   warm weather, are very fragrant.
FRUITS: Long, woody pods which split lengthwise into two parts.
SEASON OF MAXIMUM COLOR: During the hot months.
LANDSCAPE USES: Heralds-trumpet is a breath-taking sight when it is
   in bloom, and the individual trumpets are good for indoor decora-
   tion, too. The vine will cover a pergola or old building, usually to
   exclude the supporting object from view. The growth is so heavy
   that strong supports are needed.
HABITAT: Himalayan region; in Florida, frost-protected areas.
LIGHT REQUIREMENT: Full sun or broken, high shade.
SOIL REQUIREMENT: Moderately fertile, well-drained soil is adequate.
SALT TOLERANCE: Not tolerant.
AVAILABILITY: Specialty nurseries will have vines.
CULTURE: Furnish a very strong support; plant in moderately fertile
   soil; water until well established; fertilize annually. Frost kills the
   vine to the ground, but recovery is the general rule.
PROPAGATION: Marcottage.
PESTS: Mites and scales.

337
Lucky Nut

Thevetia (the-VEE-she-a): for A. Thevet, a French monk who traveled in Brazil.
peruviana (per-oo-vee-AY-na): Peruvian.

FAMILY: Apocynaceae.　　　　　　RELATIVES: Allamanda and frangipani.
TYPE OF PLANT: Shrub or tree.　　　　　　　　HEIGHT: 20′. ZONE: C,S
HOW TO IDENTIFY: Milky sap, evergreen, alternate, linear leaves, to 6″
　　long; bell-like, yellow flowers followed by angled fruits.
HABIT OF GROWTH: Dense, with upright branching.
FOLIAGE: Evergreen, medium-fine in texture, dark, shining green in tone.
FLOWERS: Bell-like, 2″–3″ long, yellow or peach-colored, attractive.
FRUITS: Drupes, about 1″ through, prominently angled, VERY POISONOUS.
SEASON OF MAXIMUM COLOR: Warm months, as flowers unfurl.
LANDSCAPE USES: As a freestanding shrub for its attractive peach-
　　colored flowers and curious angled fruits, lucky nut is rather widely
　　planted. However, all parts of the plant are highly toxic.
　　　　Frost will kill the plants back to the earth, so garden use is re-
　　stricted to warm sections if a permanent effect is desired. Roots
　　tolerate cool soil fairly well and lucky nut plants frequently rally
　　to develop new tops in springtime following cold injury.
HABITAT: Tropical America; in Florida, rather widely planted in all
　　areas.
LIGHT REQUIREMENT: Full sun for best habit and flowering.
SOIL REQUIREMENT: Any soil appears to be suitable for growth.
SALT TOLERANCE: Not especially salt-tolerant.
AVAILABILITY: Frequently found in nurseries on the peninsula.
CULTURE: No special culture is called for, but every precaution must
　　be observed so that children do not put parts of the plant in their
　　mouths.
PROPAGATION: Seedage.
PESTS: Mushroom root-rot.

338
Oleander

Nerium (NEE-ree-um): Greek name for oleander.
oleander (oh-lee-ANN-der): with leaves like olive.

FAMILY: Apocynaceae.   RELATIVES: Allamanda and frangipani.
TYPE OF PLANT: Shrub.   HEIGHT: 20′. ZONE: N,C,S
HOW TO IDENTIFY: Scraggly shrub of many stems bearing long, ever-
    green leaves, mostly in whorls of 3 on heavy, green twigs; an
    abundance of cheerful flowers in spring and summer in red, pink,
    white, or cream.
HABIT OF GROWTH: Stiffly upright by many ascending stems that are bare
    below.
FOLIAGE: Evergreen, lance-shaped, usually in whorls of 3.
FLOWERS: Showy, terminal, branching cymes during much of the warm
    season. The colors may be red, pink, cream, or white.
FRUITS: Hanging brown pods, 7″ long, formed of 2 follicles together.
SEASON OF MAXIMUM COLOR: Warm months.
LANDSCAPE USES: As a heavy, informal screen at the rear of large
    properties, plant oleanders 5′ apart. For waterfront plantings, olean-
    der excels. It is too large and coarse for foundation plantings. All
    parts of the plant are VERY TOXIC.
    There are varieties that have different growth habits and flowers
    of different sizes and colors. At least one clone is grown that has
    variegated foliage.
HABITAT: Mediterranean region; in Florida, ubiquitous.
LIGHT REQUIREMENT: Full sun for compact habit and free flowering.
SOIL REQUIREMENT: Any soil seems to be suitable.
SALT TOLERANCE: Very tolerant of salt; excellent seaside shrub.
AVAILABILITY: Almost all nurseries grow oleanders in cans.
CULTURE: Of easiest culture, oleander nonetheless requires periodic
    pruning and protection against caterpillars.
PROPAGATION: Cuttage, at any season, using any kind of wood.
PESTS: Oleander caterpillar defoliates the plants upon occasion; scales,
    witches' broom, and mushroom root-rot.

339
Natal-Plum

Carissa (car-ɪss-a): African aboriginal name.
grandiflora(gran-di-ғʟoʀ-a): large-flowered.

FAMILY: Apocynaceae.   RELATIVES: Crape-jasmine and ochrosia.
TYPE OF PLANT: Shrub.   HEIGHT: 10′. ZONE: C,S
HOW TO IDENTIFY: Milky sap; stout, bifurcate thorns to 1½″ long, at opposite, evergreen leaves; beautiful, white, fragrant flowers followed by plum-like fruits.
HABIT OF GROWTH: Dense and compact because of much-branched, downward-growing limbs.
FOLIAGE: Evergreen, of medium texture and dark green color.
FLOWERS: White, fragrant, 2″ in diameter, petals overlapping to the left.
FRUITS: Globose or elliptical berry, 2″ long, scarlet; very decorative. The reddish pulp is excellent in jellies. Fruits mature year around.
SEASON OF MAXIMUM COLOR: Much of the year as fruits mature.
LANDSCAPE USES: For ocean-front barriers, plant 5′ o.c.; for foundation plantings for large buildings, plant 4′ apart.

Carissa is one of Florida's very best ocean-front plants. Ordinarily seedlings are used for these plantings. Outstanding dwarf clones 'Boxwood Beauty', 'Linki', and 'Dainty Princess' are available under name for special needs.
HABITAT: South Africa; in Florida, widely planted on sandy soils in warm locations.
LIGHT REQUIREMENT: Full sun for best fruiting.
SOIL REQUIREMENT: Tolerant of sandy soils, even those which contain calcium in excessive amounts.
SALT TOLERANCE: Very tolerant of salt; one of Florida's best seaside plants.
AVAILABILITY: Stocked by most nurseries in southern Florida.
CULTURE: Plant in enriched sites; water moderately; mulch with leaves; keep lawn grasses back. Fertilize 2 or 3 times a year.
PROPAGATION: Seedage for the type, cuttage for named varieties.
PESTS: Scales.
NOTE: Karanda (*C. carandas*), from India, is smaller in all respects, but serves in ocean-front landscaping in extreme southern Florida. The spines are unbranched; the fruits, 1″ long, turn purple-black at maturity. Many nurseries will have seedlings in containers.

340
Ochrosia

Ochrosia (oak-ROSE-ee-a): from ochre, from the yellow color of the flowers.
elliptica (ee-LIP-tee-ca): of oval form, referring to the shape of the fruits.

FAMILY: Apocynaceae.   RELATIVES: Allamanda and Natal-plum.
TYPE OF PLANT: Tree, used as a shrub in landscaping.   HEIGHT: 20'.
                                                              ZONE: S
HOW TO IDENTIFY: Large, leathery, evergreen leaves, opposite or whorled,
    with many transverse veins; scarlet fruits, 2" long, have violet odor
    when crushed.
HABIT OF GROWTH: Shrubby, becoming tree-like with age.
FOLIAGE: Evergreen, of striking pattern in medium-green color.
FLOWERS: Fragrant, yellowish-white, in flat clusters.
FRUITS: Two scarlet drupes, borne end-to-end, each about 2" long.
    These are POISONOUS.
SEASON OF MAXIMUM COLOR: Late summer, when fruits color.
LANDSCAPE USES: For seaside hedges ochrosia can be set 18" o.c. For
    planters, urn subjects, or as freestanding specimen trees for beach
    cottages, this plant may also serve.
        Erroneously known as "Kopsia arborea" in the Miami area, this
    salt-tolerant tree is in wide use. The fruits are POISONOUS.
HABITAT: Tropical islands of the Old World; in Florida, landscape
    plantings of the southern part.
LIGHT REQUIREMENT: Full sun of beaches or broken shade of palm trees.
SOIL REQUIREMENT: Tolerant of many kinds of soils.
SALT TOLERANCE: Very tolerant of salt; recommended for ocean-front
    plantings.
AVAILABILITY: Nurseries stock canned plants regularly.
CULTURE: Make sites with fertile, acid, organic mixture; plant at former
    level; water carefully; fertilize two or three times each year.
PROPAGATION: Seedage.
PESTS: Mites and scales.

341
Giant Milkweed

Calotropis (cal-o-TRO-pis): Greek for beautiful ship's keel.
gigantea (gi-GAN-tee-a): of large size.

FAMILY: Asclepiadaceae.

RELATIVES: Hoya and stapelia.

TYPE OF PLANT: Shrub.

HEIGHT: 15'. ZONE: S

HOW TO IDENTIFY: Erect shrub with opposite leaves; new growth and leaves downy; flowers in small clusters arising from upper leaf axils.

HABIT OF GROWTH: Dense to partially open shrub.

FOLIAGE: The thick, almost stemless leaves are grey-green, up to 10" long, and indented at the base.

FLOWERS: The purple or white flowers resemble small crowns.

FRUITS: Large pods containing silken fibers.

SEASON OF MAXIMUM COLOR: Much of the year round.

LANDSCAPE USES: Accent plant in foundation plantings for large buildings; good for creating a tropical effect. Giant milkweed is used as a freestanding specimen upon occasion.

HABITAT: India.

LIGHT REQUIREMENT: Full sun.

SOIL REQUIREMENT: Tolerates a wide variety of soil types.

SALT TOLERANCE: Tolerates some salt drift back of dunes.

AVAILABILITY: Occasionally found in nurseries and deserves wider use.

CULTURE: Once established, plants require only minimal care.

PROPAGATION: Seedage or cuttage.

PESTS: Favorite plant of monarch butterflies in all stages of development.

NOTE: Flowers are sacred in India so plants play a role in the lives of the gods Siva and Kama. Plants have some medicinal use and the silken floss in the seed pods is used to stuff pillows.

342
Palay
Rubber-Vine

Cryptostegia (crip-to-STEEG-ee-a): Greek for conceal and cover.
grandiflora (grand-ee-FLOR-a): large-flowered.

FAMILY: Asclepiadaceae.   RELATIVES: Milkweed and stephanotis.
TYPE OF PLANT: Vine.   HEIGHT: Variable. ZONE: S
HOW TO IDENTIFY: Milky-sap, evergreen leaves, 4″ long, opposite, gla-
    brous, and shining; lilac-purple flowers, 2″ across; long, pointed
    pods borne in pairs, splitting to discharge "milkweed" parachutes.
HABIT OF GROWTH: Vining.
FOLIAGE: Evergreen, opposite, coarse in texture, dark green in color.
FLOWERS: Very showy, lilac-purple, bell-shaped, 2″ in diameter, calyx
    leafy.
FRUITS: Pods 4″ long, sharply angled, produced in pairs.
SEASON OF MAXIMUM COLOR: Warm months, when flowers are out.
LANDSCAPE USES: As a cover for a fence or small building in southern
    Florida, this tropical vine may serve; as a freestanding, flowering
    shrub maintained by pruning, it is frequently seen, too.
HABITAT: Africa; in Florida, most nearly frost-free locations.
LIGHT REQUIREMENT: Full sun for dense habit and profuse flowering.
SOIL REQUIREMENT: Sandy, well-drained soils are adequate.
SALT TOLERANCE: Reasonably resistant to salt.
AVAILABILITY: Rubber-vines, sometimes erroneously called purple al-
    lamandas, are rather frequently seen in nurseries.
CULTURE: In nearly frostless locations, plant the vines in well-prepared
    sites, water, and by occasional pruning keep within bounds.
PROPAGATION: Seedage, cuttage, and layerage.
PESTS: Scales and mites.
NOTE: Naming is in confusion: *Cryptostegia madagascariensis* has
    reddish-purple flowers with smaller calyx, about ¼″ long, and the
    scales of the crown are not divided.

343
Wax-Plant

Hoya (HOY-a): for T. Hoy, English gardener.
carnosa (car-NO-sa): fleshy.

FAMILY: Asclepiadaceae.   RELATIVES: Carrion-flower and milkweed.
TYPE OF PLANT: Woody vine.   HEIGHT: Variable. ZONE: S
HOW TO IDENTIFY: This slow-growing vine with milky sap bears oppo-
    site, fleshy, 4″ leaves. The profusion of tiny hairs makes these soft
    to the touch. Large, showy clusters of white and pink flowers, ½″
    across, appear in spring and summer.
HABIT OF GROWTH: Sprawling little vine.
FOLIAGE: Evergreen, opposite, thick and fleshy, from short, thick peti-
    oles. Clones with marbled foliage are very attractive.
FLOWERS: Beautiful, waxy, long-lasting, star-shaped, pink-and-white.
    Blossoms come from old flower spurs, which must never be cut off.
FRUITS: Little pods, if present.
SEASON OF MAXIMUM COLOR: Spring and summer when new growth
    matures.
LANDSCAPE USES: Long a hanging-basket favorite, wax-plant can be
    grown to adorn a patio wall, if freedom from nematodes in the
    growing medium is assured.
HABITAT: Eastern tropics.
LIGHT REQUIREMENT: High, broken shade.
SOIL REQUIREMENT: Wax-plants will grow in fibrous compost that has
    been made free of nematodes, or peat or sphagnum moss.
SALT TOLERANCE: Tolerant of salt drift.
AVAILABILITY: Many nurseries offer small assorted wax-plants.
CULTURE: Water with moderation until after flowering, then during the
    cool months allow wax-plants to become dormant by reducing the
    amount of water. As days lengthen after winter, increase water
    and light; fertilize once each month. Since flowers come from old
    spurs, do not cut these structures if blossoms are gathered for ar-
    rangements.
PROPAGATION: Cuttage, layerage, and marcottage.
PESTS: Nematodes and mealy-bugs.
NOTE: Clones with foliage marbled with white are more popular than
    the all-green species. Named hoyas have fantastically beautiful
    leaves that display shades of pink or red.

344
Christmas-Vine

Porana (poe-RAIN-a): native name.
paniculata (pan-ick-you-LATE-a): with stalked flowers in clusters.

FAMILY: Convolvulaceae.   RELATIVES: Cypress-vine and morning-glory.
TYPE OF PLANT: Vine.   HEIGHT: Variable. ZONE: S
HOW TO IDENTIFY: Evergreen, heart-shaped, entire, alternate leaves about 6″ long; showers of wintertime, fragrant, white blossoms in profuse axillary panicles.
HABIT OF GROWTH: Sprawling vine that may veil its support quickly.
FOLIAGE: Evergreen, heart-shaped, of coarse texture and gray-green color.
FLOWERS: Showy, axillary panicles of white flowers, ⅓″ across, in winter.
FRUITS: Hairy capsules about 1/5″ across.
SEASON OF MAXIMUM COLOR: The Christmas season.
LANDSCAPE USES: To cover fences, tree trunks, small buildings, or pergolas, Christmas-vine is popular in warm sections of the lower peninsula.

    The slender stems may reach a length of as much as 30′ and so pruning of vines growing under favorable conditions is needed to keep them within bounds. This cutting back should come just after flowering during the holiday season. During that time masses of blossoms might be cut for Christmas decorations.
HABITAT: India; in Florida, warmest locations.
LIGHT REQUIREMENT: Partial shade is acceptable.
SOIL REQUIREMENT: Tolerant of varying soils.
SALT TOLERANCE: Not tolerant.
AVAILABILITY: Some retail nurseries will have small vines in containers.
CULTURE: Plant in reasonably fertile soil; furnish a strong support; water until well established; fertilize once or twice each year.
PROPAGATION: Seedage or simple layerage.
PESTS: Mites and thrips.

345
Wood-Rose

Ipomea (i-po-MEE-a): like bindweed.
tuberosa (tu-ber-o-sa): having a tuber.

FAMILY: Convolvulaceae.   RELATIVES: Morning-glory and sweet-potato.
TYPE OF PLANT: Rapidly growing, perennial vine.   HEIGHT: Variable.
                                                                            ZONE: S
HOW TO IDENTIFY: Twining, evergreen vine with large, digitately divided
   leaves, usually in 5–7 segments. Flowers borne in axils of leaves,
   funnel form, to 2″ long.
HABIT OF GROWTH: Fast-growing vines completely encompass a tree if
   left alone.
FOLIAGE: Leaves palmately divided into 5–7 narrow segments with en-
   tire, lobed margins; dark green and medium-textured. Leaf petioles
   and new stem growth often reddish-brown.
FLOWERS: Morning-glory-like, yellow, 2″ in diameter.
FRUITS: Woody, rose-like, excellent for dried arrangements.
SEASON OF MAXIMUM COLOR: Flowers when plants are in active growth
   during warm months.
LANDSCAPE USES: Fast-growing screening plant, usually grown for its
   fruits, the wood-roses.
HABITAT: Widespread in the tropics.
LIGHT REQUIREMENT: Full sun.
SOIL REQUIREMENT: Performs best in soils containing some organic
   matter.
SALT TOLERANCE: Ordinarily not planted near ocean or gulf.
AVAILABILITY: Seed is available in many garden centers.
CULTURE: Once established, wood-rose will need little care except
   pruning to keep it within bounds.
PROPAGATION: Can be raised easily from seeds or by cuttage.
PESTS: None serious.
NOTE: The flowers of the miniature wood rose, *Argyreia speciosa*, with
   clusters of smaller wood-roses, are also much sought after for dried
   arrangements.

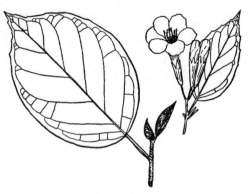

346
Geiger-Tree

Cordia (CORE-dee-a): for V. Cordus, a sixteenth-century German botanist.
sebestena (seb-es-TANE-a): an Arabic name.

FAMILY: Boraginaceae.   RELATIVES: Forget-me-not and heliotrope.
TYPE OF PLANT: Tree.   HEIGHT: 30'. ZONE: S
HOW TO IDENTIFY: Showy, orange-red flowers that resemble geraniums
    at a distance; 8", ovate, evergreen leaves with short-pointed tips,
    roughly downy on the upper surfaces.
HABIT OF GROWTH: Dense, round heads atop crooked trunks about 6"
    in diameter.
FOLIAGE: Evergreen, heart-shaped, fuzzy, of coarse texture and dark
    green color.
FLOWERS: Showy, orange-red or scarlet, 1"–2" long, in open clusters
    like geraniums.
FRUITS: White drupes, ¾" long, enclosed in persistent calyces.
SEASON OF MAXIMUM COLOR: Summer, when blossoms appear.
LANDSCAPE USES: As a freestanding specimen or as a framing tree for
    a home in a tropical setting, this diminutive native is in high favor.
    Occasionally it is seen as an avenue tree standing at intervals of
    about 25'–35'. Geiger-tree is recommended for seaside use, but it
    will not endure frost.
    The common name, according to legend, was bestowed by Au-
    dubon in commemoration of John Geiger, a pilot and Key West
    wrecker of the last century. Geiger-tree is quite universally used
    as the common name for this excellent native tree.
HABITAT: Florida Keys and West Indian islands; on the mainland,
    warmest locations.
LIGHT REQUIREMENT: Full sun or partial shade.
SOIL REQUIREMENT: Tolerant of light, sandy, alkaline soils, rock, or
    marl.
SALT TOLERANCE: Tolerant of salt; recommended for seaside plantings.
AVAILABILITY: Found in nurseries in southern counties.
CULTURE: Plant with reasonable care; water with reasonable regularity;
    fertilize once or twice a year.
PROPAGATION: Seedage and marcottage.
PESTS: Mites, scales, and caterpillars.

347
Beauty-Berry

Callicarpa (cally-CAR-pa): Greek for beauty and fruit.
americana (a-mer-ee-CANE-a): American.

FAMILY: Verbenaceae.   RELATIVES: Verbena and chaste-tree.
TYPE OF PLANT: Shrub.   HEIGHT: 8'. ZONE: N,C
HOW TO IDENTIFY: A shrub with deciduous, opposite foliage, held by fuzzy petioles. Unfurling buds and branchlets are quite tomentose. Lilac blossoms clustered around the stems in springtime are followed by magenta fruits in autumn.
HABIT OF GROWTH: Compact, with outward-pointing branches.
FOLIAGE: Deciduous, opposite, coarse in texture, light green in color.
FLOWERS: Lilac, 1/6" long, in dense cymes around stems in springtime.
FRUITS: Subglobose, berry-like drupes in autumn, usually magenta, rarely white.
SEASON OF MAXIMUM COLOR: Autumn, when the fruits color at maturity.
LANDSCAPE USES: For massing in woodland plantings, this native shrub is excellent, and should be more widely used.

Birds are very fond of the ripe fruits, so beauty-berry will help attract and keep birds where it grows. As with coral ardisia, white-fruited individuals can be planted among the normal type as interesting contrast. Perhaps other colors will appear over the years.
HABITAT: Hammocks and rich woodlands in central and northern Florida.
LIGHT REQUIREMENT: The broken shade of hammocks is optimum.
SOIL REQUIREMENT: Fertile soil of hammocks is best, but beauty-berry tolerates lighter sands.
SALT TOLERANCE: Not tolerant.
AVAILABILITY: This is not a nursery item, but plants might be obtained from friends who have woodlots.
CULTURE: Cut back heavily after fruiting; move in from woodland; water carefully; after the root system has become established, no further attention is necessary.
PROPAGATION: Seedage.
PESTS: Caterpillars may chew leaves.

Bleeding-Heart
Glory-Bower

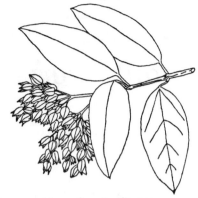

Clerodendrum (cler-oh-DEN-drum): Greek for chance and tree, of no significance.
thomsoniae (TOM-son-ee-ee): for Mrs. W. Thomson, wife of a missionary.

FAMILY: Verbenaceae. RELATIVES: Beauty-berry and lantana.
TYPE OF PLANT: Vine. HEIGHT: Variable. ZONE: N,C,S
HOW TO IDENTIFY: Vine-like growth; evergreen leaves, to 6″ long, that are opposite and prominently veined; flowers in showy racemes, calyces white, bag-like, with bright red corollas extending beyond their tips, stamens and styles extending well beyond both.
HABIT OF GROWTH: Vine-like, stems twining about supports.
FOLIAGE: Evergreen, of coarse texture and dark green color.
FLOWERS: Calyx white, bag-like, enclosing bright red corolla which extends beyond the bag, stamens and styles extending beyond both.
FRUITS: Drupes.
SEASON OF MAXIMUM COLOR: Summer, when blossoms are out.
LANDSCAPE USES: As a temporary, warm-weather vine for the curiosity of the flowers that remind northerners of *Dicentra*, this plant is popular. In warm locations, the vine persists all year around.
HABITAT: West Africa; in Florida, widely planted in all sections.
LIGHT REQUIREMENT: Partial shade seems to be satisfactory.
SOIL REQUIREMENT: Well-drained fertile soil is best and freedom from nematodes is most desirable.
SALT TOLERANCE: Not tolerant.
AVAILABILITY: Many retail sales lots offer small plants.
CULTURE: Set in a rich site that has been made free of nematodes by fumigation or drenching.
PROPAGATION: Cuttage, marcottage, or seedage.
PESTS: Nematodes, mites, and thrips.
NOTE: Turks-turban (*Clerodendrum indicum*) is a huge, upright-growing, tender shrub that is well known for the showy black fruits with their bright red calyces. This one escapes from cultivation to become a real nuisance.

349
Chaste-Tree

Vitex (vye-tex): ancient Latin name.
agnus-castus (ag-nus-cast-us): ancient classical name.

FAMILY: Verbenaceae.   RELATIVES: Verbena and golden-dewdrop.
TYPE OF PLANT: Tree.   HEIGHT: 20′. ZONE: N,C,S
HOW TO IDENTIFY: This little tree bears deciduous, opposite, digitate, pungent leaves, and summertime lilac flowers in terminal spikes.
HABIT OF GROWTH: Ungainly, open, small crown develops a picturesque form.
FOLIAGE: Deciduous, digitate, fine in texture, medium-gray-green in color.
FLOWERS: Terminal spikes, 5″–7″ long, produce lavender or white little fragrant flowers in summertime.
FRUITS: Little drupes with 4 stones enclosing pepper-like seeds.
SEASON OF MAXIMUM COLOR: Midsummer.
LANDSCAPE USES: As a summer-flowering tree for fragrance near a terrace, patio, or porch, chaste-tree is highly desirable. As a part of a shrubbery border, plant 5′ apart in groups and prune to shrub habit.

Chaste-tree has long been a garden favorite because of its delightfully fragrant, lilac-like blossoms in summertime. There is a clone 'Alba' that bears white blossoms, another has variegated foliage, and 'Latifolia' has broad leaflets.

Seeds can be used for seasoning foods.
HABITAT: Southern Europe; in Florida, sparingly planted as a yard tree.
LIGHT REQUIREMENT: Sun or shade.
SOIL REQUIREMENT: Tolerant of various soils.
SALT TOLERANCE: Tolerant of salt drift back from the front dunes.
AVAILABILITY: Small chaste-trees are occasionally found in nurseries.
CULTURE: After establishment, this tree grows without attention except for the usual fertilization. Mulching is always helpful, and watering during dry spells is expected.
PROPAGATION: Cuttage.
PESTS: Scales, mushroom root-rot, and nematodes.

350
Vitex

Vitex (VYE-tex): ancient Latin name.
trifolia (try-FOL-ee-a): with three leaf(lets).
'Variegata' (vare-eye-ee-GAY-ta): variegated.

FAMILY: Verbenaceae.   RELATIVES: Verbena and golden-dewdrop.
TYPE OF PLANT: Shrub.   HEIGHT: 12'. ZONE: C,S
HOW TO IDENTIFY: A vigorous shrub that has gayly variegated, trifolio-
  late leaves and little panicles of blue flowers in summertime.
HABIT OF GROWTH: Very dense and shrubby, but vigorous to become
  tree-like with neglect in warm locations.
FOLIAGE: Evergreen, fine in texture, gray-green to give a hazy tone.
FLOWERS: Tiny blue or lavender flowers with white spots in summer-
  time.
FRUITS: Drupes with 4 stones.
SEASON OF MAXIMUM COLOR: Summer.
LANDSCAPE USES: In warm locations vitex hedge is extremely popular.
  Set plants 1½' o.c. In foundation plantings allow 3' between plants,
  but for informal enclosure set the plants 5' apart. Variegated plants
  are prone to revert to the all-green type, and these vigorous shoots
  must be pruned out lest the plant become all green. Variegated vitex
  will be killed to the ground by frost.
HABITAT: Old World tropics; in Florida, much used as a hedge in warm
  locations.
LIGHT REQUIREMENT: Full sun for very compact hedge.
SOIL REQUIREMENT: Very tolerant of sandy soils.
SALT TOLERANCE: Tolerant of salt air at some distance back from the
  strand.
AVAILABILITY: Nurseries in southern Florida display small plants.
CULTURE: Plant in fairly fertile soil; water faithfully until well estab-
  lished. If the plants are in hedge arrangement, clip frequently for
  compact shape; if they are in foundation plantings, head in vigorous
  shoots to keep the plants in scale with the house.
PROPAGATION: Cuttage.
PESTS: Scales and mushroom root-rot.

351
Chinese-Hat-Plant

Holmskioldia (holm-skee-OLD-ee-a): for T. Holmskiold, Danish scientist.
sanguinea (san-GWIN-ee-a): blood-red.

FAMILY: Verbenaceae.   RELATIVES: Lantana, chaste-tree, and verbena.
TYPE OF PLANT: Sprawling shrub.   HEIGHT: Variable. ZONE: C,S
HOW TO IDENTIFY: Sprawling habit; evergreen, opposite leaves; the outstanding feature of the plant is the showy, orange-red, circular calyx subtending every flower.
HABIT OF GROWTH: Sprawling, becoming a vine with support.
FOLIAGE: Evergreen, opposite, of coarse texture and, often, yellow-green color.
FLOWERS: Small, dark red corollas, subtended by circular, orange-red calyces.
FRUITS: Ovoid, 4-lobed drupes about ⅛″ long.
SEASON OF MAXIMUM COLOR: Springtime, when calyces color up.
LANDSCAPE USES: To sprawl over a white masonry wall (plant 10′ o.c.) is the most effective use of Chinese-hat-plant. Thus, it resembles an orange bougainvillea. As a huge unkempt mound or trained beside and over doorways are other landscape uses. Chinese-hat-plant is very popular with Florida homeowners.
HABITAT: Himalayan region; in Florida, widely planted in protected gardens.
LIGHT REQUIREMENT: Full sun or light shade from tall trees.
SOIL REQUIREMENT: Any reasonably fertile soil.
SALT TOLERANCE: Not tolerant.
AVAILABILITY: Nurseries on the peninsula offer plants in containers.
CULTURE: Plant in reasonably fertile soil; water as needed; fertilize twice a year; prune to keep within bounds. If the plant is to be trained as a vine, offer strong support.
PROPAGATION: Cuttage or marcottage.
PESTS: Scales, mites, and nematodes.

Golden-Dewdrop

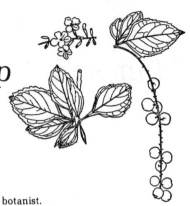

Duranta (dew-ʀᴀɴ-ta): for C. Durantes, an Italian botanist.
repens (ʀᴇᴇ-pens): creeping.

Fᴀᴍɪʟʏ: Verbenaceae.   Rᴇʟᴀᴛɪᴠᴇs: Verbena, lantana, and chaste-tree.
Tʏᴘᴇ ᴏF Pʟᴀɴᴛ: Shrub.   Hᴇɪɢʜᴛ: 18′. Zᴏɴᴇ: C,S
Hᴏᴡ ᴛᴏ IᴅᴇɴᴛɪFʏ: Evergreen, thin, scalloped opposite leaves, each with
   a sharp thorn; blue flowers in hanging clusters followed by bright
   yellow fruits.
Hᴀʙɪᴛ ᴏF Gʀᴏᴡᴛʜ: Informal, ascending mound.
Fᴏʟɪᴀɢᴇ: Evergreen, of medium-fine texture and light green color.
Fʟᴏᴡᴇʀs: Blue flowers hang in loose axillary racemes about 6″ long.
Fʀᴜɪᴛs: Conspicuous, yellow globose, about ½″ in diameter, covered
   by calyx which is closed into a curved beak. The fruits are ᴘᴏɪsᴏɴ-
   ᴏᴜs to humans.
Sᴇᴀsᴏɴ ᴏF Mᴀxɪᴍᴜᴍ Cᴏʟᴏʀ: Warm months, when flowers and/or fruits
   are present.
Lᴀɴᴅsᴄᴀᴘᴇ Usᴇs: For background and screening, set plants 5′ o.c.
   Golden-dewdrop is too large to use as a foundation plant, and in
   much of the state it will be frosted back each winter. Occasionally
   a plant with white flowers is seen. There has been some selection
   for specimens that bear flowers larger than ordinary.
      This beautiful plant is ubiquitous in the tropics where it is dis-
   seminated by birds.
Hᴀʙɪᴛᴀᴛ: Florida Keys, Caribbean islands, Central America.
Lɪɢʜᴛ RᴇQᴜɪʀᴇᴍᴇɴᴛ: Full sun for best flowering; endures partial shade.
Sᴏɪʟ RᴇQᴜɪʀᴇᴍᴇɴᴛ: Tolerant of varying soil types.
Sᴀʟᴛ Tᴏʟᴇʀᴀɴᴄᴇ: Not tolerant.
Aᴠᴀɪʟᴀʙɪʟɪᴛʏ: Golden-dewdrop is available in most nurseries in re-
   ceptacles.
Cᴜʟᴛᴜʀᴇ: After establishment, golden-dewdrop requires no care.
Pʀᴏᴘᴀɢᴀᴛɪᴏɴ: Cuttage or seedage.
Pᴇsᴛs: Scales, caterpillars, and nematodes; birds consume fruits.

353
Lantana

Lantana (lan-TAN-a): old name.
camara (cam-AIR-a): South American name.

FAMILY: Verbenaceae.　　RELATIVES: Verbena and chaste-tree.

TYPE OF PLANT: Shrub.　　HEIGHT: 10'. ZONE: N,C,S

HOW TO IDENTIFY: Square, prickly stems, strongly upward-growing; rough leaves that have an unpleasant odor when crushed; tiny flowers of many colors in terminal, flat, nosegay arrangements, followed by prominent, shiny, blue-black fruits.

HABIT OF GROWTH: Stiffly upright, from many-branched stems.

FOLIAGE: Evergreen, of medium texture and light green color.

FLOWERS: Showy, flat heads of tiny flowers, in tones of red, pink, orange, and yellow.

FRUITS: Fleshy drupes, blue-black in color, ½" across, freely produced, toxic.

SEASON OF MAXIMUM COLOR: Summer months.

LANDSCAPE USES: For gay color in a sunny planter (set 18" o.c.) or against hardy evergreen shrubs, lantana may be used, especially near the ocean. Tender to frost, lantana will die to the ground every year except in warmest locations. Yellow-and-pink-flowered dwarf lantanas are favored by designers.

HABITAT: Tropical and subtropical America, including Florida.

LIGHT REQUIREMENT: Full sun for best habit and free-flowering.

SOIL REQUIREMENT: Any soil appears to be suitable.

SALT TOLERANCE: Quite salt-tolerant; recommended for seashore.

AVAILABILITY: Retail nurseries often sell lantanas in vessels.

CULTURE: Plant in moderately fertile soil; water until established; protect leaves from caterpillars in hot weather; cut back in late winter.

PROPAGATION: Seedage; cuttage for named varieties.

PESTS: Caterpillars chew the leaves; mites make leaves turn brown.

354
Weeping
Lantana

Lantana (lan-TAN-a): old name.
montevidensis (mon-tay-vye-DEN-sis): from Montevideo.

FAMILY: Verbenaceae.   RELATIVES: Verbena and chaste-tree.

TYPE OF PLANT: Dwarf shrub or vine.   HEIGHT: Variable. ZONE: C,S

HOW TO IDENTIFY: Evergreen, opposite, dentate, rugose leaves with pungent odor when crushed; unarmed square twigs; lilac flowers borne through much of the year.

HABIT OF GROWTH: Sprawling over the earth; vine-like if supported.

FOLIAGE: Evergreen, opposite, fine textured, and dark green in color.

FLOWERS: Dense heads at axils on long peduncles, of solid lilac color. There is a white-flowered form.

FRUITS: Usually not formed in Florida.

SEASON OF MAXIMUM COLOR: Much of the year, if there is no frost.

LANDSCAPE USES: Weeping lantana is an excellent ground cover and transition plant when set at 18″ o.c. For sunny planters and to spill over a wall, this little shrub is without peer (plant 18″ o.c.). It is rightfully very popular in sections of Florida where winters are mild. Frost will kill lantana to the earth.

HABITAT: South America; in Florida, ubiquitous in warmer parts.

LIGHT REQUIREMENT: Full sun for compact habit and heavy flowering.

SOIL REQUIREMENT: Tolerant of sandy soils.

SALT TOLERANCE: Not tolerant.

AVAILABILITY: Most retail sales lots display weeping lantanas in vessels.

CULTURE: Within its climatic range, this plant is undemanding in requirements for growth. Fertilize once each spring and water during drought.

PROPAGATION: Cuttage and simple layerage where stems touch the earth.

PESTS: Caterpillars and mites.

355
Queens-Wreath

Petrea (pet-REE-a): for Baron Petre, English patron of botany.
volubilis (vol-OO-bill-is): twining.

FAMILY: Verbenaceae.   RELATIVES: Verbena, lantana, and chaste-tree.
TYPE OF PLANT: Vine.   HEIGHT: Variable. ZONE: S
HOW TO IDENTIFY: Twining vine with evergreen, opposite leaves that
    are so rough to the touch as to feel like sandpaper; conspicuous
    hanging clusters of purple (occasionally white) flowers.
HABIT OF GROWTH: Twining vine.
FOLIAGE: Evergreen, very rough, of coarse texture and gray-green color.
FLOWERS: Purple (sometimes white), 5-petaled, with 5-pointed calyx,
    1½″ wide, in foot-long hanging clusters which resemble wisteria
    when viewed from a distance.
FRUITS: Drupes which include the dried calyces.
SEASON OF MAXIMUM COLOR: Late spring and early summer.
LANDSCAPE USES: To cover an arbor, fence, or small structure, queens-
    wreath is much planted in southern Florida, where it could be con-
    sidered a substitute for wisteria.
HABITAT: Tropical America; in Florida, widely planted in warm areas.
LIGHT REQUIREMENT: Full sun or broken shade.
SOIL REQUIREMENT: Tolerant of soils of open texture and moderate fer-
    tility.
SALT TOLERANCE: Not tolerant.
AVAILABILITY: Nurseries in southern Florida offer queens-wreath in
    containers.
CULTURE: Enrich sandy soil by digging in organic matter; set at its
    former level; water periodically; keep lawn grasses back from the
    root zone. Protect small vines when frost is forecast.
PROPAGATION: Cuttage or marcottage.
PESTS: None of great importance.

356
Woolly
Congea

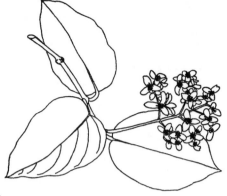

Congea (CON-ghe-a): East Indian vernacular name.
tomentosa (toe-men-TOE-sa): densely woolly.

FAMILY: Verbenaceae.
RELATIVES: Verbena and lantana.
TYPE OF PLANT: Vine.
HEIGHT: Variable. ZONE: S
HOW TO IDENTIFY: Fuzzy twigs hold fuzzy leaves and showy clusters of whitish bracts in winter or spring.
HABIT OF GROWTH: Sprawling, vine-like; may be trained as a vine or as a shrub.
FOLIAGE: Evergreen, opposite, rough, coarse in texture, and light green in color.
FLOWERS: Inconspicuous, in generous clusters, subtended by propeller-like bracts. These white appendages are the showy members as they change to lavender, then to lilac-mauve or dusky-gray over a period of many weeks.
FRUITS: Small drupes.
SEASON OF MAXIMUM COLOR: Late winter or early spring.
LANDSCAPE USES: To clamber over a fence or arbor, to veil a small building, congea is desirable for the wintertime show of the snowy bracts. Cut branches are popular for arrangements indoors, and after maximum flowering has passed, annual heading-in might be needed to keep mature vines from getting too large. As with queens-wreath, extended flowering comes from persistent bracts. These woolly appendages change through tints of pink over several weeks.
HABITAT: Burma; in Florida, warm locations.
LIGHT REQUIREMENT: Full sun for best performance.
SOIL REQUIREMENT: Tolerant of many, varying soil types.
SALT TOLERANCE: Not tolerant of dune conditions.
AVAILABILITY: Some retail sales lots will have small vines in gallon cans.
CULTURE: Plant with reasonable care; attend to watering; supply a strong support; fertilize two times a year; prune after flowering to keep the vine within bounds.
PROPAGATION: Seedage.
PESTS: Mites and scales.

357
Angel's Trumpet

Datura (da-TOUR-a): Indian vernacular name.
arborea (are-BORE-ee-a): tree-like.

FAMILY: Solanaceae.　　　　RELATIVES: Tobacco, potato, and tomato.
TYPE OF PLANT: Succulent shrub.　　　　HEIGHT: 15'. ZONE: C,S
HOW TO IDENTIFY: Pubescent, evergreen leaves in pairs, one of which
　　is a third shorter than the other; nodding, fragrant, 9" white flowers
　　in summer.
HABIT OF GROWTH: Upright, tree-like.
FOLIAGE: Evergreen, soft, tender, of huge size and medium color.
FLOWERS: Spectacular hanging trumpets of white that are very fragrant.
FRUITS: Smooth, broad-ovoid capsules about 2½" long.
SEASON OF MAXIMUM COLOR: Summer and autumn.
LANDSCAPE USES: For the tropical aspect of the plant and the mon-
　　strous, nodding trumpets, datura is planted as a freestanding speci-
　　men.
　　　　ALL DATURAS ARE VERY POISONOUS. Nonetheless, they are widely
　　grown in hot countries for their striking, fragrant blossoms.
HABITAT: Tropical America; in Florida, ubiquitous in all but coldest
　　parts.
LIGHT REQUIREMENT: Full sun or partial shade.
SOIL REQUIREMENT: Tolerant of widely varying soils.
SALT TOLERANCE: Not tolerant.
AVAILABILITY: Small datura plants are sometimes seen in nurseries.
CULTURE: Plant with reasonable care; water until established; and for-
　　get. Protection on cold nights might save datura plants from being
　　killed to the earth.
PROPAGATION: Cuttage and seedage.
PESTS: Nematodes, mites, and thrips.
NOTE: *D. sanguinea* has brilliant orange-red flowers with yellow nerves,
　　without fragrance.
　　　　D. suaveolens may be confused with *D. arborea*. Suaveolens has
　　foot-long, white trumpets on pedicels ¾"–1½" long and calyces
　　that are inflated, angled, obscurely 5-toothed. Suaveolens capsules
　　are unarmed, spindle-shaped, 5" long.

358
Chalice-Vine

Solandra (so-LAN-dra): for D. Solander, Swedish naturalist.
guttata (gut-TAY-ta): spotted.

FAMILY: Solanaceae.   RELATIVES: Tobacco, pepper, and eggplant.

TYPE OF PLANT: Vine.   HEIGHT: Variable. ZONE: C,S

HOW TO IDENTIFY: A rampant tropical vine which produces goblet-shaped flowers about 10″ long which turn to gold.

HABIT OF GROWTH: Vigorous vine that clings by tenacious aerial roots.

FOLIAGE: Evergreen, very bold in aspect, dark green when well fertilized.

FLOWERS: Very spectacular, goblet-formed blossoms that open white and turn golden before they fall. Purple lines decorate the interior; the pistil is prominent. Fragrance of coconut is released at night.

FRUITS: Round berries, 2½″ wide, partially enclosed by the calyces.

SEASON OF MAXIMUM COLOR: Warm months, after good growth.

LANDSCAPE USES: For the tropical aspect of the huge gold cups, this vine is fancied. Strong metal and concrete trellises are needed to support the great weight. Very tender to cold.

HABITAT: Tropical America; in Florida, popular vine in warm areas.

LIGHT REQUIREMENT: Partial shade.

SOIL REQUIREMENT: Moderate fertility is recommended.

SALT TOLERANCE: Not tolerant.

AVAILABILITY: Small vines in cans are in some nurseries on the peninsula.

CULTURE: Once established near a strong steel and masonry trellis, chalice-vine will grow rampantly with little attention.

PROPAGATION: Layerage.

PESTS: Nematodes, mites, and caterpillars.

NOTE: There may be confusion in naming. *Solandra grandiflora* has the slender part of the flower tube not longer than the calyx. Other names are sometimes listed.

359
Night
Cestrum

Cestrum (SES-trum): Greek name for some plant.
nocturnum (nock-TURN-um): night-blooming.

FAMILY: Solanaceae.   RELATIVES: Tobacco, pepper, potato, and tomato.
TYPE OF PLANT: Sprawling shrub.   HEIGHT: 12'. ZONE: C,S
HOW TO IDENTIFY: Half-climbing shrub with green stems that bear
    simple, smooth leaves, 4"–8" long, with broad bases and distinct
    petioles. Greenish-white tubular blossoms with *acute* lobes erect or
    spreading are excessively fragrant at *night*. Fruits are *white*.
HABIT OF GROWTH: Sprawling with declinate stems, to make an untidy
    mound.
FOLIAGE: Evergreen, smooth, of medium texture and yellow-green
    color.
FLOWERS: Greenish-white, with erect or flaring, long-pointed lobes.
FRUITS: Shining white, succulent berries freely produced.
SEASON OF MAXIMUM COLOR: No seasonal change in color.
LANDSCAPE USES: As a part of a shrubbery border in warm locations,
    plant about 5' apart. Nighttime fragrance is overpowering to some
    persons.
HABITAT: Tropical America; in Florida, much planted in warm locations.
LIGHT REQUIREMENT: Full sun for best habit and flowering, but light
    shade is tolerated.
SOIL REQUIREMENT: Tolerates light sandy soil.
SALT TOLERANCE: Not tolerant of dune conditions.
AVAILABILITY: Widely offered in cans at nurseries.
CULTURE: Like other cestrums these grow with but little care.
PROPAGATION: Cuttage and seedage.
PESTS: Mites, scales, and caterpillars.
NOTE: Day cestrum (*C. diurnum*) is somewhat more hardy, with
    thicker leaves, white blossoms with *rounded* lobes, *day* fragrance,
    and *black* berries. These and other cestrums are favorite shrubs
    in dooryards in hot countries the world around.

360
Orange Cestrum

Cestrum (SES-trum): Greek name for some plant.
aurantiacum (are-an-TIE-a-cum): orange-colored.

FAMILY: Solanaceae.   RELATIVES: Tobacco, pepper, potato, and tomato.
TYPE OF PLANT: Sprawling shrub.   HEIGHT: 15'. ZONE: C,S
HOW TO IDENTIFY: Half-climbing shrub with simple, alternate leaves
   and tubular, orange-colored blossoms during warm months.
HABIT OF GROWTH: Sprawling, vine-like, by greenish, succulent stems.
FOLIAGE: Evergreen, of medium texture and medium green color.
FLOWERS: Orange-yellow, tubular, 1" long, with lobes reflexed. The
   terminal panicles usually contain 2–5 blossoms.
FRUITS: Small, succulent berries.
SEASON OF MAXIMUM COLOR: Warm months.
LANDSCAPE USES: As a part of a shrubbery border, in warm locations,
   plant about 5' o.c.
HABITAT: Central America; in Florida, warmest sections.
LIGHT REQUIREMENT: Full sun for best habit and flowering.
SOIL REQUIREMENT: Light sandy soils are acceptable.
SALT TOLERANCE: Not tolerant.
AVAILABILITY: Cestrums are available in nurseries down the peninsula.
CULTURE: All cestrums seem to grow with the least possible care.
PROPAGATION: Cuttage.
PESTS: Mites, scales, and caterpillars.
NOTE: Purple cestrum (*Cestrum purpureum*) is also vine-like, and bears
   nodding clusters of urn-shaped, rose-purple flowers more than 1"
   long.
   Members of this genus, like most members of their family, grow
rapidly to attain maturity rather quickly. All must be pruned after
flowering to keep within bounds. All are tender to cold, but usually
will rally after having been frosted. Cestrums are leading beginners'
plants because they are so easy to increase, so undemanding of the
gardener.

Callicarpa americana

Beauty-Berry
p. 347

Camellia sasanqua

Sasanqua
p. 262

Rhododendron canescens

Native Azalea
p. 314

Fortunella nagami

Nagami Kumquat
p. 209

Tibouchina semidecandra

Princess-Flower
p. 301

Phaius grandifolius

Veiled Nun Orchid
p. 123

Duranta repens
Golden-Dewdrop
p. 352

Bauhinia blakeana

Orchid-Tree
p. 192

Maranta rubranervum

Arrowroot
p. 120

Hibiscus rosa-sinensis

Hibiscus
p. 249

361
Potato
Vines

Solanum (so-LAY-num): Latin, alluding to sedative qualities.
SPP.: several species are grown in Florida.

FAMILY: Solanaceae.   RELATIVES: Potato, tobacco, and tomato.
TYPE OF PLANT: Vine.   HEIGHT: Variable. ZONE: S
HOW TO IDENTIFY: Herbaceous, tropical vines with evergreen, dissected
   leaves, and showy, potato-like flowers.
HABIT OF GROWTH: Vining; requires tying at first.
FOLIAGE: Evergreen, bold in form, dark green when well fertilized.
FLOWERS: Potato-like flowers, usually blue or blue-and-white in showy
   clusters.
FRUITS: Ovoid berries, variable in size and color with species.
SEASON OF MAXIMUM COLOR: Warm months, when flowers expand.
LANDSCAPE USES: For the beauty of the hanging blossoms, solanum
   vines are cultured in hot countries. They may add interest to palm
   trunks, hide fences, or veil small buildings.
      Brazilian nightshade (*S. seaforthianum*) has spineless stems and
   foliage, and blue, star-shaped, 1″ flowers in small clusters.
      Wendland nightshade (*S. wendlandii*) has prickly stems, leaves
   both simple and pinnatifid, lilac-blue flowers 2½″ across in foot-
   wide, forking clusters.
      Solanum jasminoides is spineless and bears attractive little star-
   shaped flowers that are white tinged with blue.
      All solanum vines are very tender to cold.
HABITAT: Tropical America; in Florida, warmest locations.
LIGHT REQUIREMENT: Partial shade.
SOIL REQUIREMENT: Tolerant of many soil types, but subject to attack
   by nematodes.
SALT TOLERANCE: Not tolerant.
AVAILABILITY: Nurseries in southern Florida offer vines in cans of steri-
   lized soil.
CULTURE: Plant carefully in sterilized soil; water until well established;
   offer support and a heavy mulch over the roots; fertilize once in
   late winter.
PROPAGATION: Cuttage or layerage.
PESTS: Nematodes, mites, and scales.

Firecracker-Plant

Russelia (russ-ELL-ee-a): for A. Russell, an English physician.
equisetiformis (eck-we-seat-i-FORM-is): horsetail-like.

FAMILY: Scrophulariaceae. RELATIVES: Angelonia and torenia.

TYPE OF PLANT: Dwarf shrub. HEIGHT: 4'. ZONE: C,S

HOW TO IDENTIFY: This tender shrub is of pendulous habit with rush-like stems that are ridged vertically. The leaves are reduced to bracts, yet the bright red, firecracker-like flowers make up for the paucity of foliage.

HABIT OF GROWTH: Weeping, fountain-like.

FOLIAGE: Usually lacking; branches and bracts are of fine texture and pleasing color.

FLOWERS: Bright red, cylindrical, 2-lipped, 5-cleft, hanging like little firecrackers during much of the year.

FRUITS: Little, hanging capsules.

SEASON OF MAXIMUM COLOR: Summer, when flowers come out.

LANDSCAPE USES: For the cheerful aspect of the bright flowers, and the attractive weeping habit, this plant is much grown. In planters, foundation arrangements, and rock-'n'-sand gardens, it serves well. Use 18" planting intervals.

HABITAT: Tropical America.

LIGHT REQUIREMENT: Full sun or broken, shifting, high shade.

SOIL REQUIREMENT: Tolerant of different soils, but thrives with moderate fertility and regular watering as needed.

SALT TOLERANCE: Not tolerant.

AVAILABILITY: Most nurseries in central and southern Florida offer coral-plants in cans.

CULTURE: When once established, these plants grow with little care. Protection from heavy competition and frost is suggested.

PROPAGATION: Simple layers where stems touch the earth.

PESTS: Chewing insects, nematodes, and mites.

African Tulip-Tree

Spathodea (spath-OH-dee-a): Greek for spathe-like, for the shape of the calyx.
campanulata (cam-pan-you-LATE-a): bell-shaped, referring to the flowers.

FAMILY: Bignoniaceae. RELATIVES: Jacaranda and tabebuia.

TYPE OF PLANT: Large tree. HEIGHT: 50'. ZONE: S

HOW TO IDENTIFY: A tree that bears evergreen, compound leaves made up of 5" leaflets with 2–3 glands at the base; showy, tulip-like, orange-scarlet flowers are held above the foliage in late winter.

HABIT OF GROWTH: Large, ascending, heavy-headed tree.

FOLIAGE: Evergreen, compound, of medium texture and medium green color.

FLOWERS: Orange-scarlet, upward-looking, tulip-like, emerging from 1-sided, recurved calyces.

FRUITS: Flattened capsules about 8" long, when present.

SEASON OF MAXIMUM COLOR: Late winter, when blossoms open.

LANDSCAPE USES: As an avenue tree (25'–35' o.c.) African tulip-tree is admired for the glory of its wintertime blossoms. As a shade tree or as a framing tree it excels in frostless locations, but it is very tender to cold and the brittle wood breaks in strong winds.

HABITAT: Tropical Africa; in Florida, gardens in warm locations.

LIGHT REQUIREMENT: Full sun for good flowering.

SOIL REQUIREMENT: Soil of moderate fertility is recommended.

SALT TOLERANCE: Tolerant of salt air back from the sea.

AVAILABILITY: Rather widely available in nurseries in southern Florida.

CULTURE: Plant in moderately fertile soil in frostless area; water faithfully until well established; thereafter, little attention is needed.

PROPAGATION: Cuttage.

PESTS: None of major concern.

364
Cat-Claw

Doxantha (docks-AN-tha): Greek for glory-flower.
unguis-cati (UN-guis CAT-eye): Latin for cat's claw.

FAMILY: Bignoniaceae. RELATIVES: Trumpet-creeper and flame-vine.
TYPE OF PLANT: Vine. HEIGHT: Variable. ZONE: N,C,S
HOW TO IDENTIFY: Evergreen vine with 3-parted, cat-claw-like tendrils for climbing and yellow trumpets in springtime.
HABIT OF GROWTH: Rampantly clambering by claw-like tendrils.
FOLIAGE: Evergreen, compound, of medium-fine texture and light green color. Three-parted tendrils stand between leaflets.
FLOWERS: Showy, trumpet-shaped, 2″ long, clear, bright yellow with orange lines in throat.
FRUITS: Foot-long, bignonia-type capsules, about ½″ wide.
SEASON OF MAXIMUM COLOR: April.
LANDSCAPE USES: To cover a metal fence or to veil a small building, cat-claw will serve well. Stems root where they touch the earth, thus making the vine a nuisance under some conditions. At best, it is hard to control unless severe freezes cut canes to the earth.
HABITAT: American tropics; in Florida, ubiquitous except in coldest parts.
LIGHT REQUIREMENT: Full sun or broken shade.
SOIL REQUIREMENT: Tolerant of many varying soils.
SALT TOLERANCE: Not tolerant.
AVAILABILITY: This is usually not a nursery item; rather, simple layers are acquired from neighbors.
CULTURE: Of easiest culture, cat-claw grows without attention.
PROPAGATION: Simple layerage where stems touch the earth.
PESTS: Mites and scales.

365
Cape-
Honeysuckle

Tecomaria (teck-o-MARY-a): from Tecoma, an old genus name in the Bignoniaceae.
capensis (cape-EN-sis): of the Cape of Good Hope.

FAMILY: Bignoniaceae.   RELATIVES: Flame-vine and trumpet-creeper.
TYPE OF PLANT: Vine or shrub, depending upon culture.

HEIGHT: Variable. ZONE: C,S

HOW TO IDENTIFY: This is a half-climbing shrub that may be made into a tree or a vine with training. It has flexible, grayish branches, evergreen, compound leaves with 5–9 odd-pinnate, serrate leaflets; dense terminal clusters of orange, trumpet-shaped flowers during much of the year, with heaviest flowering in autumn.

HABIT OF GROWTH: Sprawling shrub, vine, or tree, depending upon training.

FOLIAGE: Evergreen, compound, of fine texture and light green or yellow-green color.

FLOWERS: Orange, bignonia-like, in upright, terminal racemes much of the year. One variety has yellow flowers.

FRUITS: Small bignonia-type capsules, 2″ × ⅓″, rather freely produced.

SEASON OF MAXIMUM COLOR: Warm months, particularly autumn.

LANDSCAPE USES: As a hedge, plant 3′ apart; as an informal shrubbery border, set 5′ o.c.; as a vine or as a tree, Cape-honeysuckle is very popular in warm sections of the state because of its attractive foliage and very showy orange blossoms.

There is a clone with variegated foliage, one with yellow blossoms.

HABITAT: South Africa; in Florida, widely grown where citrus thrives.

LIGHT REQUIREMENT: Full sun for best habit and flowering.

SOIL REQUIREMENT: Tolerant of many soils, including open sands. Good drainage is a requirement for success.

SALT TOLERANCE: Tolerant of light salt drift; not recommended for dune planting.

AVAILABILITY: Widely available in gallon cans.

CULTURE: Once established, Cape-honeysuckle grows freely with little attention in areas that are not subject to sharp frosts.

PROPAGATION: Seedage, cuttage, and layerage.

PESTS: Scales, mites, and nematodes.

Flame-Vine

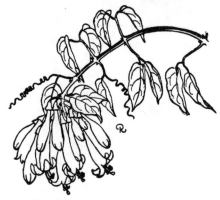

Pyrostegia (pie-roe-STEEG-ee-a): Greek for fire and roof.
ignea (IG-knee-a): fiery.

FAMILY: Bignoniaceae.　　RELATIVES: Cape-honeysuckle and pandorea.

TYPE OF PLANT: Vine.　　　　　HEIGHT: Variable. ZONE: C,S

HOW TO IDENTIFY: Rampant vine, climbing by tendrils; evergreen leaves of 2–3 leaflets; terminal panicles of orange, tubular flowers in wintertime.

HABIT OF GROWTH: Clambering vine that clings tenaciously by tendrils.

FOLIAGE: Evergreen, compound, 2–3 leaflets and 3-parted tendrils, medium in texture, light to medium green in color.

FLOWERS: Conspicuous, bright orange tubular blossoms with 5 points curling back from the mouth. These are borne in panicles during the tourist season. The color does not combine well with red.

FRUITS: Foot-long capsules in Brazil, sometimes not present in Florida.

SEASON OF MAXIMUM COLOR: Late winter and early spring.

LANDSCAPE USES: To cover a fence, pergola, small building, or unwanted tree, flame-vine is central Florida's most popular vine. Landscape use must be indicated with caution, because the vine grows so rampantly that it will soon cover every available support.

HABITAT: Brazil; in Florida, ubiquitous in the central section.

LIGHT REQUIREMENT: Full sun or partial shade.

SOIL REQUIREMENT: Light, sandy soil is quite acceptable.

SALT TOLERANCE: Not tolerant.

AVAILABILITY: Almost all retail nurseries market flame-vines.

CULTURE: Set in reasonably fertile soil; water periodically until established; furnish a strong support; fertilize once each winter; prune immediately after flowering to keep somewhat within bounds.

PROPAGATION: Simple layerage or cuttage.

PESTS: Scales, caterpillars, and mites.

367
Jacaranda

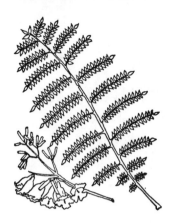

Jacaranda (jack-a-ʀᴀɴ-da): Brazilian name.
acutifolia (a-cute-ee-ғᴏ-lee-a): sharp-leaved.

FAMILY: Bignoniaceae. RELATIVES: Pandorea and flame-vine.
TYPE OF PLANT: Tree. HEIGHT: 50′. ZONE: C,S
HOW TO IDENTIFY: Large, loose-branched, irregular tree with deciduous, 2-pinnate foliage and showy panicles of blue, bignonia-like flowers in late spring.
HABIT OF GROWTH: Awkward, asymmetrical, open head from a bending trunk.
FOLIAGE: Deciduous, very fine in texture, medium green in color.
FLOWERS: Showy, blue trumpets, 1½″ wide, in terminal or axillary panicles.
FRUITS: Capsules, 2″ across, more or less disk-shaped; black at maturity.
SEASON OF MAXIMUM COLOR: April–June.
LANDSCAPE USES: As a tree for summer shade (sun comes through in winter), framing tree, or avenue tree, jacaranda is cherished. It is widely planted in the central section of Florida, but it sometimes gets too large for its position in home landscapes.
HABITAT: Brazil; in Florida, much used in the citrus-producing areas.
LIGHT REQUIREMENT: Full sun for heavy flowering; small trees endure shade.
SOIL REQUIREMENT: Sandy soils of reasonable fertility are acceptable.
SALT TOLERANCE: Not tolerant of salt.
AVAILABILITY: Small jacaranda trees are for sale in most retail nurseries in central and southern Florida.
CULTURE: Plant in reasonably fertile soil of sandy nature; water periodically; keep lawn grasses back from the roots; fertilize along with the citrus trees.
PROPAGATION: Seedage; graftage for named clones.
PESTS: Mushroom root-rot.
NOTE: Superior types have been selected and named. These are increased by graftage. Other species of jacaranda may be seen upon occasion.

368
Pandorea

Podranea (poe-DRAIN-ee-a): anagram of pandorea.
ricasoliana (rick-a-sole-ee-ANE-a): for the Ricasoli gardens in Italy.

FAMILY: Bignoniaceae.   RELATIVES: Sausage-tree and trumpet-creeper.
TYPE OF PLANT: Sprawling vine.   HEIGHT: Variable. ZONE: C,S
HOW TO IDENTIFY: Sprawling vine with pinnate, evergreen foliage and
   attractive pinkish, bell-form blossoms in springtime.
HABIT OF GROWTH: Sprawling vine that needs to be tied until stems
   become established.
FOLIAGE: Evergreen, odd-pinnate, without tendrils, of medium texture
   and medium green color.
FLOWERS: Showy, pinkish, trumpet-like, about 2″ long, lined inside
   with red, borne in hanging, terminal panicles.
FRUITS: Foot-long bignonia capsules which split into two segments.
SEASON OF MAXIMUM COLOR: Springtime.
LANDSCAPE USES: To add color interest to a fence, pergola, small building, or palm trunk, this tropical vine is much planted where winter
   temperatures are mild.
   Of the many vines of the bignonia family, this is held to be the
   most delicately attractive by many experienced gardeners. The
   graceful foliage, delicate coloration of the attractive trumpets, and
   moderate growth rate contribute to its excellence. It is highly commended to those who live within its climatic range.
HABITAT: South Africa; in Florida, in nearly frostless locations.
LIGHT REQUIREMENT: Light shade of high pines or palms is excellent.
SOIL REQUIREMENT: Reasonably fertile soil that is free of nematodes is
   recommended.
SALT TOLERANCE: Not tolerant.
AVAILABILITY: Nurseries in warm areas stock pandoreas in assorted
   vessels.
CULTURE: Nematodes are major parasites, so plant in sterilized, fertile
   soil if possible. Water frequently and train on a support. Frost
   will cut the vine to the ground.
PROPAGATION: Simple layerage where branches touch the earth.
PESTS: Nematodes, mites, scales, and caterpillars.

369
Painted-Trumpet

Clytostoma (cly-toss-to-ma): Greek for splendid mouth.
callistegioides (cal-lis-tee-gee-oy-dez): callistegia-like.

FAMILY: Bignoniaceae.   RELATIVES: Flame-vine and trumpet-creeper.
TYPE OF PLANT: Vine.   HEIGHT: Variable. ZONE: N,C,S
HOW TO IDENTIFY: Evergreen leaves with 2 entire leaflets and a tendril
  that twines around support; showy, lavender, trumpet-like flowers
  in springtime.
HABIT OF GROWTH: Rampant-growing, tendril-clinging vine.
FOLIAGE: Evergreen, of coarse texture and dark green color.
FLOWERS: Trumpets, 3″ long, of attractive lavender color, produced
  during springtime.
FRUITS: Prickly capsules, 3″–5″ long, contain many flat, winged seeds.
SEASON OF MAXIMUM COLOR: Spring, when lavender trumpets open.
LANDSCAPE USES: As a permanent evergreen vine to soften a fence or
  to make shade beneath a pergola, painted-trumpet is very popular.
  This is one of the many bignonia-relatives that grow so well in
  Florida. For persons who live too far north in the state to grow
  pandorea and other tropical bignonia-relatives, painted-trumpet is
  suggested. Many homeowners in upper counties admire it for its
  excellent qualities.
HABITAT: South America; in Florida, ubiquitous as a garden vine.
LIGHT REQUIREMENT: Full sun or broken shade.
SOIL REQUIREMENT: Almost any well-drained soil seems to be adequate.
SALT TOLERANCE: Not tolerant of dune locations.
AVAILABILITY: Retail nurseries stock painted-trumpet vines.
CULTURE: Simply plant in reasonably fertile soil and water periodically
  until well established. This unusually dependable vine requires
  little attention.
PROPAGATION: Simple layerage where branches touch the earth.
PESTS: Scales and mites.

Sausage-Tree

Kigelia (ki-GEE-lee-a): from an African native name.
pinnata (pin-ATE-a): feather-formed, referring to the foliage.

FAMILY: Bignoniaceae.   RELATIVES: Jacaranda and African tulip-tree.
TYPE OF PLANT: Tree.   HEIGHT: 30′. ZONE: S
HOW TO IDENTIFY: A medium-sized tree that bears deciduous, odd-pinnate leaves; claret-colored flowers on long stalks and huge, sausage-like fruits, 2′ long.
HABIT OF GROWTH: Spreading tree of generous size with somewhat open branching.
FOLIAGE: Deciduous, pinnate, of large size and light green color.
FLOWERS: Claret, bignonia-like, 3″ flowers open at night to be pollinated by bats. In Florida, hand pollination by man is practiced to assure fruit setting.
FRUITS: Huge, gourd-like capsules, 2′ long, hanging from long cords. Fruit shape and size varies with the individual tree that bears the fruits and with the pollen source as well.
SEASON OF MAXIMUM COLOR: Blossom-time.
LANDSCAPE USES: As a freestanding specimen in admission gardens, parks, campuses, and arboretums, sausage-tree is popular with all who view it. Moderate size does not preclude its use on large lawns in extreme southern Florida.
HABITAT: Tropical Africa; in Florida, a rarity in show gardens.
LIGHT REQUIREMENT: Full sun for best form, flowering, and fruiting.
SOIL REQUIREMENT: Moderate fertility in soils of many types.
SALT TOLERANCE: Not tolerant.
AVAILABILITY: Small sausage-trees are found in specialty nurseries.
CULTURE: After careful planting in prepared site, water intermittently until well established. Keep mulch over the roots; hoe back grass; and fertilize when other plants are tended.
PROPAGATION: Seedage.
PESTS: Scales, mites, and nematodes.

371
Tabebuias

Tabebuia (tab-bay-BOO-ee-a): a Brazilian name.
SPP.: several species are grown in Florida.

FAMILY: Bignoniaceae. RELATIVES: Jacaranda and flame-vine.
TYPE OF PLANT: Tree. HEIGHT: Variable. ZONE: S
HOW TO IDENTIFY: Showy, flowering trees in the bignonia family, with typical trumpet-flowers, that are widely planted in tropical lands for their bright color.
HABIT OF GROWTH: Mostly awkward, asymmetrical trees or tall shrubs.
FOLIAGE: Mostly deciduous, usually bold in form, usually light green or gray-green in color.
FLOWERS: Usually very colorful and profuse, white, pink or yellow, typically trumpet-shaped, with spreading, irregular, lobed limbs. These may appear over a long period, perhaps more than once each year.
FRUITS: Long capsules of the bignonia family.
SEASON OF MAXIMUM COLOR: Warm months; variable with the species.
LANDSCAPE USES: For the bright clusters of trumpets, tabebuia trees are popular as freestanding specimens and as avenue trees. As a patio tree, *Tabebuia argentea* excels because of its small size, and silvery-gray, contorted branches in picturesque arrangement. Protection overhead will be needed on cold nights. The brittle wood breaks in strong winds.
HABITAT: Tropical America; in Florida, gardens in warmest parts.
LIGHT REQUIREMENT: Full sun or partial shade.
SOIL REQUIREMENT: Tolerant of many soil types and conditions.
SALT TOLERANCE: Some species are quite salt tolerant.
AVAILABILITY: Some specialty nurseries display small tabebuia trees.
CULTURE: Freedom from frost, reasonable fertility, and moderate moisture supply are requirements for success.
PROPAGATION: Seedage, marcottage, and graftage.
PESTS: None of major concern.
NOTE: Of the 100 species of *Tabebuia* known to science, less than half are grown in Florida, these by specialists.

372
Trumpet-Vine

Campsis (CAMP-sis): Greek for curve, referring to curved stamens.
radicans (RAD-ee-cans): rooting, referring to many aerial roots along stems.

FAMILY: Bignoniaceae.   RELATIVES: Painted-trumpet and cat-claw vine.
TYPE OF PLANT: Vine.   HEIGHT: Variable. ZONE: N,C
HOW TO IDENTIFY: Vine clinging tenaciously by root-like hold-fasts; compound deciduous leaves; showy, orange-red, trumpet-like flowers in summertime.
HABIT OF GROWTH: Vining, holding by aerial rootlets.
FOLIAGE: Deciduous, compound of medium texture and medium green color.
FLOWERS: Orange-red trumpets appear in terminal clusters in summertime.
FRUITS: Capsules about 5″ long, keeled and beaked.
SEASON OF MAXIMUM COLOR: Summertime.
LANDSCAPE USES: To cover pine trunks, wooden fences, or small wooden buildings, trumpet-vine has long been popular. Contact with the foliage may cause a skin rash on some persons.
HABITAT: Hammocks in northern and central Florida.
LIGHT REQUIREMENT: Broken shade of hammocks.
SOIL REQUIREMENT: Tolerant of widely varying soils.
SALT TOLERANCE: Not tolerant.
AVAILABILITY: Not many nurseries stock trumpet-vines.
CULTURE: Once established by a pine trunk or wooden fence, the vine needs no attention.
PROPAGATION: Seedage or marcottage; vines root where they touch the ground.
PESTS: None of major importance attack this good native vine.
NOTE: Chinese trumpet-creeper, *C. grandiflora*, grows well in northern Florida, to produce larger, deeper-colored flowers. Hybrids between the two species are known in horticulture.

373
Yellow-Elder

Stenolobium (sten-o-LOB-ee-um): Greek for narrow lobes.
stans (stans): standing upright.

FAMILY: Bignoniaceae.   RELATIVES: Jacaranda and African tulip-tree.

TYPE OF PLANT: Shrub or small tree.   HEIGHT: 15′. ZONE: C,S

HOW TO IDENTIFY: The opposite, compound leaves are borne on green, willowy branches, which turn gray with age. The 2½″ bell-shaped flowers are borne in clusters near branch terminals.

HABIT OF GROWTH: Shrub or small tree.

FOLIAGE: The pinnately divided leaves will have 5–13 leaflets which may be short-stalked or sessile and smooth to almost woolly beneath.

FLOWERS: The yellow, bell-shaped flowers appear on new growth.

FRUITS: Narrow capsules, 8″ long, which split and hang on for months to give an untidy aspect to this tropical shrub.

SEASON OF MAXIMUM COLOR: Flowers on each flush of new growth.

LANDSCAPE USES: May be used as specimen plant or in shrubbery borders.

HABITAT: Native to the American tropics.

LIGHT REQUIREMENT: Best flowering and most compact plants are obtained when grown in full sun.

SOIL REQUIREMENT: Grows on most Florida soils.

SALT TOLERANCE: Tolerant of salt drift back of the strand.

AVAILABILITY: Most nurseries have it in cans.

CULTURE: Requires no special culture; grow as other bignonias.

PROPAGATION: Seedage or cuttage.

PESTS: None serious.

NOTE: It has been reported that Indians used the wood of yellow-elder to make bows.

E. dianthiflora

E. lilacina

E. lilacina 'Viridis'

Episcia

E. cuperata 'Variegata'

E. cuperata 'Silver Sheen'

E. reptans

E. cuperata 'Chocolate Soldier'

E. punctata

375
Episcia

Episcia (ee-PIS-ee-a): Greek for shady, referring to the plant's habitat.
SPP.: more than one species and many cultivars grow in our state.

FAMILY: Gesneriaceae.   RELATIVES: Achimenes and gloxinia.
TYPE OF PLANT: Herbaceous perennial.   HEIGHT: 6″. ZONE: S
HOW TO IDENTIFY: Shade-demanding, hairy-leaved, creeping tropical
   herbs that bear attractive, bright little blossoms are the episcias.
   The copper-toned, quilted leaves are variously marked and lined
   with silver.
HABIT OF GROWTH: Mat-forming by means of rooting stems.
FOLIAGE: Dark, copper shades, usually variegated with silver; also
   green.
FLOWERS: Showy, red, purplish, or whitish, borne during warm months.
FRUITS: Little pods, if present.
SEASON OF MAXIMUM COLOR: Summer, when flowers expand.
LANDSCAPE USES: As hanging basket and pot plants for very shady lo-
   cations, episcias are very popular. They are also used today to
   soften the edges of Florida room planters.
HABITAT: Tropical America.
LIGHT REQUIREMENT: Fairly deep shade is requisite for success. Episcias
   are injured by sunlight, drafts, and low temperatures.
SOIL REQUIREMENT: Fibrous, fast-draining, slightly acid, moderately
   fertile compost that has been sterilized is recommended.
SALT TOLERANCE: Not tolerant.
AVAILABILITY: Episcias in small pots are to be found in some nurseries
   and chain stores.
CULTURE: Plant in containers that can be kept in shady, draft-free,
   warm (above 45°F) locations. Water with moderation and apply
   dilute liquid fertilizer once during each warm month.
PROPAGATION: Cuttage.
PESTS: Nematodes, mealy-bugs, and mites.
NOTE: Pictured above is a popular form of *Episcia cupreata*. On the
   facing page are drawings of other Florida favorites.

Achimenes

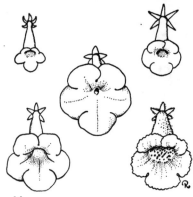

Achimenes (a-KIM-ee-nez): Greek, to suffer from cold.
SPP.: plants seen in collections are of hybrid origin.

FAMILY: Gesneriaceae.　　　　RELATIVES: Cape-primrose and episcia.
TYPE OF PLANT: Rhizomatous perennial.　　　HEIGHT: 2'. ZONE: N,C,S
HOW TO IDENTIFY: Bushy, downy-leaved pot plants grow from little
　　rhizomes during warm months, to produce many attractive, trumpet-
　　shaped flowers in tones of red and violet. Shown above are some
　　of the flower shapes.
HABIT OF GROWTH: Compact, neat, little, leafy mounds.
FOLIAGE: Variable, opposite or whorled, hairy.
FLOWERS: Variable, attractive, trumpet-shaped as depicted above. The
　　colors are in tones of red or violet, seldom white.
FRUITS: Little capsules, if present.
SEASON OF MAXIMUM COLOR: Late summer when blossoms appear.
LANDSCAPE USES: Window box and porch plants par excellence,
　　achimenes have been favorites with homeowners for centuries.
HABITAT: Tropical America.
LIGHT REQUIREMENT: Reduced light of porches or greenhouses. Drafts
　　and cold must be avoided.
SOIL REQUIREMENT: Fibrous, well-drained, moderately fertile, sterilized
　　compost is suggested. Prompt drainage and good aeration must be
　　assured.
SALT TOLERANCE: Not tolerant.
AVAILABILITY: Dormant rhizomes appear in garden centers in season.
CULTURE: Start dormant rhizomes in pots of gritty, fibrous compost;
　　water sparingly until growth is well along; then increase the amount
　　of water daily; do not allow the soil to become dry. Apply liquid
　　fertilizer once during each warm month. Store rhizomes in a dry
　　place when growth matures in the autumn.
PROPAGATION: Division of underground or axillary rhizomes.
PESTS: Nematodes, soil-borne rots, mites, and mealy-bugs.

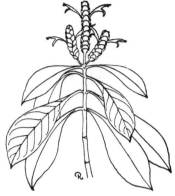

377
Aphelandra
(Zebra-Plant)

Aphelandra (a-fell-AN-dra): Greek for simple anther.
SPP.: numerous kinds grow in Florida.

FAMILY: Acanthaceae.   RELATIVES: Crossandra and sanchezia.
TYPE OF PLANT: Tender bush.   HEIGHT: 5'. ZONE: S
HOW TO IDENTIFY: The strikingly banded foliage is outstanding, yet
    spikes of orange or red flowers are attractive dividends. Easily
    confused with *Sanchezia*, differences in floral characters set the 2
    genera apart.
HABIT OF GROWTH: Stiffly upright by herbaceous stems.
FOLIAGE: Opposite, bold, banded with contrasting colors.
FLOWERS: Showy spikes of bracted flowers, usually in tones of orange
    or red, are warm-weather highlights.
FRUITS: Oblong capsules.
SEASON OF MAXIMUM COLOR: Warm months when new growth pro-
    duces colorful bracted spikes in terminal positions.
LANDSCAPE USES: For the gaiety of the banded or netted foliage, aphel-
    andras may accent groups of all-green tender bushes.
HABITAT: Tropical America.
LIGHT REQUIREMENT: Broken shade is recommended for Florida.
SOIL REQUIREMENT: Sandy soil, of moderate fertility, that drains well
    is usually satisfactory.
SALT TOLERANCE: Not tolerant.
AVAILABILITY: Most nurseries and chain stores display small aphelan-
    dras in pots.
CULTURE: In partially shaded, protected locations, plant with other
    tender exotics. If frosted, cut back to the earth; new shoots will ap-
    pear with the advent of warm weather.
PROPAGATION: Cuttage.
PESTS: Mites and nematodes.

Cardinals Guard

Pachystachys (pack-is-TACK-eez): Greek for thick spike.
coccinea (cock-SIN-ee-a): scarlet.

FAMILY: Acanthaceae.   RELATIVES: Acanthus and crossandra.

TYPE OF PLANT: Herbaceous perennial.   HEIGHT: 7'. ZONE: C,S

HOW TO IDENTIFY: Shade-loving, coarse, spindly perennials bear thick red plumes in terminal positions. These are made up of 2", scarlet, tubular corollas, split nearly to their middles, subtended by conspicuous green bracts.

HABIT OF GROWTH: Upright, many-stemmed.

FOLIAGE: Evergreen, opposite, 8" long, pointed both ends.

FLOWERS: Thick spikes of scarlet; curved, split corollas held within broad, green, entire bracts.

FRUITS: Little pods.

SEASON OF MAXIMUM COLOR: Late summer when flowers mature.

LANDSCAPE USES: For a dash of red in a shaded corner, cardinals guard can stand with other tender tropical exotics.

HABITAT: Caribbean region.

LIGHT REQUIREMENT: Shade is a requirement.

SOIL REQUIREMENT: Moderately fertile, well-drained earth seems to suffice.

SALT TOLERANCE: Not tolerant.

AVAILABILITY: Small plants in cans appear in some nurseries and garden centers.

CULTURE: Plant rooted cuttings in protected, shady spots; water moderately; fertilize lightly thrice annually; cut back hard after blooming.

PROPAGATION: Cuttage.

PESTS: Mites and nematodes.

379
Caricature Plant

Graptophyllum (grap-toe-FILL-um): Greek for write and leaf, for the variegated foliage. *pictum* (PICK-tum): painted.

FAMILY: Acanthaceae.   RELATIVES: Shrimp-plant and strobilanthes.
TYPE OF PLANT: Shrub.   HEIGHT: 8'. ZONE: S
HOW TO IDENTIFY: Glabrous shrub with opposite, shining leaves, 6" long, blotched with cream along the midrib. Purplish-red, tubular flowers appear in compact clusters.
HABIT OF GROWTH: Compact, well-foliated, tender shrub.
FOLIAGE: Evergreen, opposite, blotched with cream around the midrib, of coarse texture and cream-and-green color.
FLOWERS: Purplish-red, tubular, 1½" long, borne in short clusters.
FRUITS: Capsules.
SEASON OF MAXIMUM COLOR: No seasonal variation.
LANDSCAPE USES: As a gay urn subject, caricature plant evokes favorable comment. In frostless gardens it may serve as a warm accent in front of green shrubs. Set in groups 3' o.c.

As a change from croton and gold-dust-tree, both of which it resembles superficially, caricature plant may interest some homeowners in extreme southern Florida. The pattern of variegation about the midribs varies in size and color in several selections. In Latin American gardens this plant is very popular and may be known as *cafe con leche.*
HABITAT: New Guinea; in Florida, warmest locations.
LIGHT REQUIREMENT: Tolerant of reduced light of greenhouses, porches, and patios.
SOIL REQUIREMENT: Fertile, moist, organic soils, free of nematodes.
SALT TOLERANCE: Not tolerant.
AVAILABILITY: Some nurseries in southern Florida will have small plants in receptacles.
CULTURE: Nematode-free, rich, moist soil is suggested for planting; therefore, container- or bin-culture might be best for caricature plant.
PROPAGATION: Cuttage.
PESTS: Mites, nematodes, thrips, and scales.

380
Coromandel

Asystasia (as-is-STAY-see-a): name of doubtful application.
gangetica (gan-JEE-ti-ca): of the Ganges.

FAMILY: Acanthaceae.   RELATIVES: Shrimp-plant and strobilanthes.

TYPE OF PLANT: Herbaceous perennial.   HEIGHT: Variable. ZONE: S

HOW TO IDENTIFY: Trailing, rooting stems bear thin-textured, light green, opposite leaves, and bell-shaped flowers of white, pinkish, or lavender.

HABIT OF GROWTH: Densely sprawling, but may assume vine form if given support.

FOLIAGE: Opposite, 2", light-green leaves are held by long petioles.

FLOWERS: Tubular, white, pinkish or purplish, appearing much of the year.

FRUITS: Little, oblong capsules.

SEASON OF MAXIMUM COLOR: Summer when flowers come out.

LANDSCAPE USES: As a ground cover for partially shaded, narrow, or restricted spaces in frostless sections, this little tropical perennial is fully appreciated. Additional uses can be made of coromandel for planter bins and for covering the bases of tall, leggy, tropical shrubs.

HABITAT: Tropics of the Old World.

LIGHT REQUIREMENT: Partial shade is recommended.

SOIL REQUIREMENT: Moderately fertile, well-drained soil that can be watered as needed is suitable.

SALT TOLERANCE: Not tolerant.

AVAILABILITY: Easily found in nurseries in southern Florida.

CULTURE: Plant rooted cuttings about 1' apart in the partially shaded area to be covered; water periodically; fertilize lightly 3 times during the summer. Heroic pruning will be needed when the mass becomes untidy.

PROPAGATION: Simple layerage, cuttage, and seedage.

PESTS: Nematodes, mites, and leaf-eating insects.

381
Crossandra

Crossandra (cross-AN-dra): Greek for fringed anthers.
infundibuliformis (in-fun-di-bull-i-FORM-is): funnel-form.

FAMILY: Acanthaceae.   RELATIVES: Bears-breech and clock-vine.

TYPE OF PLANT: Herbaceous perennial.   HEIGHT: 4'. ZONE: C,S

HOW TO IDENTIFY: This yard-high perennial may become shrub-like if not frosted to earth. The wavy-margined, smooth leaves are opposite or whorled; above them appear the glowing, soft apricot spikes of bracted flowers during warm months.

HABIT OF GROWTH: Compact, shrub-like, by leafy, green stems.

FOLIAGE: Glossy, opposite, tender, and fragile.

FLOWERS: Showy spikes of bracted, funnel-form flowers of glowing, soft apricot are seen in warm months. No other flower displays this gorgeous tone.

FRUITS: Angled capsules.

SEASON OF MAXIMUM COLOR: Summer, when terminal flower spikes expand.

LANDSCAPE USES: In frostless locations, crossandra is grown with other herbaceous perennials or tender shrubs, usually with some shade here in Florida. As a pot plant, this exotic from India has long been in high favor.

HABITAT: India.

LIGHT REQUIREMENT: Reduced light is recommended in Florida.

SOIL REQUIREMENT: Sandy soil, of moderate fertility, that drains well is usually satisfactory.

SALT TOLERANCE: Not tolerant.

AVAILABILITY: Garden centers frequently offer canned crossandras.

CULTURE: In partially shaded, protected locations, plant with other tender exotics. If frosted, cut back to the earth; new shoots will appear with the advent of warm weather.

PROPAGATION: Cuttage.

PESTS: Mites and nematodes.

Eranthemum (Blue Sage)

Eranthemum (er-ANN-the-mum): Greek for lovely flower.
nervosum (ner-VO-sum): nerved, referring to the puckered leaves.

FAMILY: Acanthaceae.   RELATIVES: Bears-breech and shrimp-plant.
TYPE OF PLANT: Tender shrub.   HEIGHT: 5'. ZONE: C,S
HOW TO IDENTIFY: Axillary *and* terminal spikes of bright blue flowers, ¾″ across, subtended by typical acanthus bracts, strongly nerved, are produced during much of the warm season. The upright-growing shrubs are ungainly and not particularly striking in habit.
HABIT OF GROWTH: Strongly upright, open, and scraggly.
FOLIAGE: Opposite, 4″ long, puckered, usually a deep green on well-grown plants in partially shaded situations.
FLOWERS: Celestial blue, ¾″ across, in axillary *and* terminal spikes, above prominently nerved bracts.
FRUITS: Little capsules.
SEASON OF MAXIMUM COLOR: Winter, when terminal spikes of blue appear.
LANDSCAPE USES: For its flowers of deepest blue, eranthemum has long been prized. This Oriental plant may be massed to provide blue in front of other tropical shrubs in shade.
HABITAT: India.
LIGHT REQUIREMENT: Partial shade is recommended.
SOIL REQUIREMENT: Sandy soil of moderate fertility, that drains readily, is usually satisfactory.
SALT TOLERANCE: Not tolerant of dune conditions.
AVAILABILITY: Nurseries in southern Florida sell container-grown eranthemums.
CULTURE: In partially shaded, protected locations, plant with other tender exotics. If frosted, cut back to the earth; new shoots will appear with the advent of warm weather.
PROPAGATION: Cuttage.
PESTS: Mites and nematodes.
NOTE: *Daedalacanthus* is the old generic name, now held to be invalid, and "blue-sage" is the most popular common designation.

383
Firespike

Odontonema (oh-dont-oh-NEE-ma): Greek, referring to toothed filaments.
strictum (STRICT-um): upright.

FAMILY: Acanthaceae.　　　　　　RELATIVES: Barleria and sanchezia.
TYPE OF PLANT: Herbaceous perennial.　　　HEIGHT: 6'. ZONE: N,C,S
HOW TO IDENTIFY: Straight, smooth, green, herbaceous stems bear opposite, shiny, undulate leaves, and, in autumn, spikes of fire-red, tubular flowers for a period of several weeks. These are among Florida's most showy red flowers of the fall season.
HABIT OF GROWTH: Usually a many-stemmed, compact mound of shining green.
FOLIAGE: Evergreen, opposite, smooth and shining, wavy-margined. Nodes somewhat enlarged, and marked by 2 series of whitish dots.
FLOWERS: Tubular blossoms of fire-red are borne in terminal and axillary spikes in the fall. Those in a given spike do not all open at one time, thus to extend anthesis.
FRUITS: Little pods.
SEASON OF MAXIMUM COLOR: Late summer or autumn, when red spikes appear.
LANDSCAPE USES: For notes of bright red in the fall, firespike is very widely grown throughout our state. Very tender to cold, plants die to earth following first frosts; therefore, firespike should be planted near hardy shrubs. Hummingbirds and butterflies frequent *Odontonema* blossoms.
HABITAT: Central America.
LIGHT REQUIREMENT: Full sun for best habit and heavy flowering.
SOIL REQUIREMENT: Moderately fertile, sandy soil is adequate.
SALT TOLERANCE: Not tolerant.
AVAILABILITY: Nurseries occasionally carry firespike plants in cans.
CULTURE: Plant divisions or rooted cuttings in moderately rich earth near woody shrubs; water and forget. After frost blackens stems, cut them back to the ground line.
PROPAGATION: Cuttage and division.
PESTS: None of major consequence.

384
Jacobinia

Jacobinia (jake-oh-BIN-ee-a): probably a personal name.
SPP.: different species and their hybrids grow in Florida.

FAMILY: Acanthaceae.   RELATIVES: Red justicia and shrimp-plant.

TYPE OF PLANT: Herbs or shrubs.   HEIGHT: 7′. ZONE: C,S

HOW TO IDENTIFY: Thick spikes of curved flowers in tones of red, yellow-apricot, rose-purple, or orange are produced in terminal positions by coarse, tender, herbaceous perennials or shrubs with large, opposite, wavy leaves.

HABIT OF GROWTH: Upright, by heavily foliated green stems.

FOLIAGE: Evergreen, large, wavy, opposite, usually light green in color.

FLOWERS: Decorative thick spikes of curving corollas in tones of red, yellow, apricot, rose-purple, or orange are well liked by gardeners.

FRUITS: Little pods.

SEASON OF MAXIMUM COLOR: Late summer when flower spikes expand.

LANDSCAPE USES: For the handsome spikes, these tender, tropical exotics are cultivated in frostless locations.

HABITAT: Tropical America.

LIGHT REQUIREMENT: Shade is a requirement.

SOIL REQUIREMENT: Moderately fertile, well-drained earth seems to suffice.

SALT TOLERANCE: Not tolerant.

AVAILABILITY: Some nurseries carry canned jacobinias.

CULTURE: Plant rooted cuttings in protected, shady locations with other tender tropical exotics; water moderately; fertilize thrice annually; cut back hard after blooming to maintain compact habit.

PROPAGATION: Cuttage.

PESTS: Mites and nematodes.

Pseuderanthemum

Pseuderanthemum (sue-der-ANN-the-mum): false eranthemum.
atropurpureum (at-roe-purr-PURE-ee-um): dark purple.

FAMILY: Acanthaceae.   RELATIVES: Eranthemum and mackaya.
TYPE OF PLANT: Shrub.   HEIGHT: 4'. ZONE: C,S
HOW TO IDENTIFY: This glabrous shrub has herbaceous, purple twigs
  that hold opposite, shining leaves, 6″ long. These leaves are glow-
  ing wine-purple with shaded blotches of lighter tones that may
  run out to the margins. There may be shallow notches near the apical ends.
HABIT OF GROWTH: Upright, many-stemmed, heavily foliated.
FOLIAGE: Evergreen, opposite, wine-purple with irregular blotches of
  different tones.
FLOWERS: Short spikes of white or purple flowers completely dotted
  with darker tones.
FRUITS: Capsules.
SEASON OF MAXIMUM COLOR: Warm months when new leaves come out.
LANDSCAPE USES: As a gay urn subject, pseuderanthemum (we should
  have a valid common name!) is a change from red-leaved crotons
  and acalyphas. In very warm spots that are free from nematodes,
  this acanthus-relative may grow as a shrub.
HABITAT: Polynesia.
LIGHT REQUIREMENT: Tolerant of reduced light of greenhouses, porches,
  and patios.
SOIL REQUIREMENT: Fertile, moist soils, free from nematodes, are sug-
  gested.
SALT TOLERANCE: Endures salt air back of the first dunes.
AVAILABILITY: Small plants are in nurseries in southern Florida.
CULTURE: Growing techniques that are successful for other pot plants
  will be good for this tropical exotic.
PROPAGATION: Cuttage.
PESTS: Nematodes, mites, scales, and thrips.
NOTE: Sister species, *Pseuderanthemum reticulatum*, has light, yellow-
  green foliage strikingly netted with golden veins. Young leaves unfurl orange-yellow; as they mature they shade through chartreuse
  to become a solid green finally. The white flowers of this species
  are dotted with purple.

386
Sanchezia

Sanchezia (san-CHEZ-ee-a): for J. Sanchez, early Spanish botanist.
nobilis (NOB-ill-is): renowned.

FAMILY: Acanthaceae.

RELATIVES: Acanthus and barleria.

TYPE OF PLANT: Shrub.

HEIGHT: 6′. ZONE: C,S

HOW TO IDENTIFY: Robust, upright-growing shrub with glabrous stems, and, in the types seen in Florida, foot-long, opposite leaves strongly marked with white or cream-colored veins. It is difficult for some gardeners to distinguish between *Aphelandra* and *Sanchezia*, differences being found in the flowers.

HABIT OF GROWTH: Shrubby, usually ascending, open, and coarse.

FOLIAGE: Bold and colorful by virtue of the strongly contrasting veins. Opposite leaves are foot-long, smooth, attached by very short petioles to smooth, squarish stems.

FLOWERS: Terminal spikes of yellow, tubular flowers, 2″ long, are highlighted by bright red bracts.

FRUITS: Little pods.

SEASON OF MAXIMUM COLOR: The year around!

LANDSCAPE USES: Like many another acanthus-relative, sanchezia has long been popular as a pot plant. In tropical locations, it serves as an accent in a shaded shrubbery border.

HABITAT: Northwestern South America.

LIGHT REQUIREMENT: Partial shade is recommended; rather deep shade can be tolerated.

SOIL REQUIREMENT: Moderately fertile, well-drained soil is satisfactory.

SALT TOLERANCE: Not tolerant of dune conditions.

AVAILABILITY: Nurseries on the peninsula offer sanchezia plants in containers.

CULTURE: In partially shaded, protected locations, plant with other tender exotics. If frosted, cut back to earth; new shoots will appear with the advent of warm weather.

PROPAGATION: Cuttage.

PESTS: Mites and nematodes.

Shrimp-Plant

Beloperone (bell-oh-PER-oh-nee): Greek for the arrow-shaped anthers.
guttata (goo-TAY-tah): spotted, referring to the spotted throats of the flowers.

FAMILY: Acanthaceae.   RELATIVES: Cardinals guard and coromandel.
TYPE OF PLANT: Herbaceous perennial.   HEIGHT: 8′. ZONE: N,C,S
HOW TO IDENTIFY: Terete stems bear 2½″ fuzzy leaves; blossom spikes
   with showy, brownish bracts resemble shrimps.
HABIT OF GROWTH: Clusters of slender, terete, herbaceous stems.
FOLIAGE: Evergreen, hairy, of medium texture and light green color.
FLOWERS: Spikes some 3½″ long, made showy by the reddish-brown,
   heart-shaped, hairy bracts which surround the true flowers.
FRUITS: Long-stalked capsules.
SEASON OF MAXIMUM COLOR: Springtime and much of the summer.
LANDSCAPE USES: Shrimp-plant is much used for mass plantings in
   front of shrubbery, and around palms and woody trees; planting
   interval, 18″. For planters and urns, shrimp-plant also is popular.
   Here is another herbaceous perennial that is a favorite with be-
   ginning or casual part-time gardeners because it is so easy to prop-
   agate, so undemanding of its owner. Shrimp-plant has many good
   qualities that make it worthy of the esteem with which it is regarded in Florida. Frost cuts the stems back to the earth.
HABITAT: Mexico; in Florida, ubiquitous in gardens all over the state.
LIGHT REQUIREMENT: Full sun or high, broken pine shade.
SOIL REQUIREMENT: Tolerant of widely varying soils.
SALT TOLERANCE: Not tolerant.
AVAILABILITY: Every retail sales yard offers shrimp-plants in assorted
   vessels.
CULTURE: Plant in fairly fertile soil; water until established; furnish a
   mulch; cut back to the ground after the first frost injures the succu-
   lent herbaceous stems.
PROPAGATION: Cuttage or division of old, matted clumps.
PESTS: Caterpillars.
NOTE: A red and a yellow-green form are also available. The latter
   should not be confused with the yellow shrimp-plant (*Pachystachys
   lutea*), which has clean, bright yellow bracts subtending the flowers.

388
Strobilanthes

Strobilanthes (stro-bill-ANN-thez): Greek for cone flower.
dyerianus (die-er-ee-ANE-us): for W. Thiselton-Dyer, English horticulturist.

FAMILY: Acanthaceae.   RELATIVES: Coromandel and crossandra.

TYPE OF PLANT: Herbaceous perennial.   HEIGHT: 4′. ZONE: C,S

HOW TO IDENTIFY: The puckered, 8″ leaves are bright purple beneath and variegated above in iridescent tints of blue and lilac.

HABIT OF GROWTH: Shrubby, upright, ungainly.

FOLIAGE: Opposite, bold in color, purple below, iridescent lilac and blue above, sessile, puckered, minutely toothed.

FLOWERS: Erect spikes of 1½″ lilac, tubular flowers will appear on plants of some size, but small pot specimens may not bloom.

FRUITS: Little oblong capsules.

SEASON OF MAXIMUM COLOR: Very colorful the year around.

LANDSCAPE USES: Long popular as a pot plant for its colorful foliage, strobilanthes may also serve as a tall planter subject or, on occasion, as a tender shrub in protected spots.

HABITAT: Southeastern Asia.

LIGHT REQUIREMENT: Reduced light is recommended.

SOIL REQUIREMENT: Moderately fertile, well-drained soil is acceptable.

SALT TOLERANCE: Not tolerant.

AVAILABILITY: Retail sales yards on the peninsula offer strobilanthes in cans.

CULTURE: Care given to most popular pot plants should make for success with strobilanthes. Water with moderation and fertilize with a balanced mixture so as to maintain rich foliage tints.

PROPAGATION: Cuttage.

PESTS: Nematodes and mites.

389
Clock-Vines

Thunbergia (THUN-ber-gee-a): after Thunberg, botanist.
SPP.: several species are grown in Florida.

FAMILY: Acanthaceae.   RELATIVES: Shrimp-plant and caricature plant.
TYPE OF PLANT: Shrubs and vines.   HEIGHT: Variable. ZONE: C,S
HOW TO IDENTIFY: Plant may be erect or climbing with opposite, ovate
   to triangular-ovate leaves and with axillary, 5-lobed bracts. There
   are three most commonly seen. *T. erecta* is a small shrub with blue-
   purple flowers. Some cultivars bear white blossoms. *T. alata* is a vine
   with yellow flowers with dark brown centers; black-eyed Susan is
   a common name. *T. grandiflora* is a vine with large blue or white
   flowers. Clock-vine is a vernacular name.
HABIT OF GROWTH: Variable, depending on species.
FOLIAGE: Opposite, evergreen, of medium texture.
FLOWERS: Blue, yellow, or white, 1½"–4" across.
FRUITS: Dry capsules.
SEASON OF MAXIMUM COLOR: Summer and autumn.
LANDSCAPE USES: Screening vines for patios, trellises, and fences.
   T. erecta makes a fine tub specimen and is popular as a clipped
   hedge.
HABITAT: Tropical Africa and India.
LIGHT REQUIREMENT: Best flowering is obtained when plants are grown
   in full sun.
SOIL REQUIREMENT: Thrives on well-drained soils.
SALT TOLERANCE: Not tolerant.
AVAILABILITY: Found in cans in many nurseries in southern Florida.
CULTURE: Once established, plants require little care. *T. grandiflora*
   will outgrow its bounds and will require pruning. One or two fer-
   tilizations per year will suffice.
PROPAGATION: Seedage, cuttage, and layering.
PESTS: None of serious nature.

390
Yellow Shrimp-Plant

Pachystachys (pack-is-TACK-eez): Greek for thick spike.
lutea (LOU-tee-a): yellow.

FAMILY: Acanthaceae.   RELATIVES: Firespike and cardinals guard.

TYPE OF PLANT: Herbaceous perennial.   HEIGHT: 4′. ZONE: C,S

HOW TO IDENTIFY: Evergreen, oval, opposite leaves are borne on green, freely branching stems, topped by a dense spike of flowers subtended by colorful bracts.

HABIT OF GROWTH: Upright, many-branched plants.

FOLIAGE: Dark green, oval to ovate leaves, to 6″ long, of medium texture.

FLOWERS: Narrow, tubular, white flowers to 1½″ long, subtended by bright yellow bracts.

FRUITS: Little pods.

SEASON OF MAXIMUM COLOR: Flowers on each new growth.

LANDSCAPE USES: Tub specimen for patios; for a dash of yellow in the border with other tropicals.

HABITAT: Islands of the Caribbean.

LIGHT REQUIREMENT: Full sun for best flowering and most compact plants.

SOIL REQUIREMENT: Most fertile, well-drained soils.

SALT TOLERANCE: Not tolerant.

AVAILABILITY: Widely grown by foliage nurseries as a pot plant.

CULTURE: Plant cuttings or small plants in soil enriched with peat. Do not allow to dry out excessively or plants will defoliate.

PROPAGATION: Easily raised by cuttage.

PESTS: Scales and spider mites can be problems.

391
Coffee

Coffea (cof-FAY-a): Arabic name of the beverage.
arabica (are-AY-bick-a): Arabian.

FAMILY: Rubiaceae.   RELATIVES: Ixora, serissa, pentas, and gardenia.
TYPE OF PLANT: Shrub.   HEIGHT: 15'. ZONE: S
HOW TO IDENTIFY: An attractive shrub bears shining, wavy-edged,
    evergreen leaves that are 2″ × 6″ and bright red fruits about ½″
    across.
HABIT OF GROWTH: Whorled branching and close-packed foliage makes
    dense habit.
FOLIAGE: Evergreen, opposite, coarse in texture, and dark green in
    color.
FLOWERS: White, star-like, fragrant, in axillary clusters.
FRUITS: Crimson, 2-seeded berries, ½″ long. Seeds are coffee of com-
    merce.
SEASON OF MAXIMUM COLOR: Spring, white flowers; summer, red fruits.
LANDSCAPE USES: For its highly decorative quality and the curiosity
    of its fruits, coffee is well worth having in frost-free gardens. It
    may stand as a free specimen, or groups may be incorporated in
    shrubbery borders.
HABITAT: Africa; in Florida, gardens in frost-free locations.
LIGHT REQUIREMENT: Broken, shifting, light shade is desirable in Flor-
    ida.
SOIL REQUIREMENT: Fertile, acid, organic soil is recommended.
SALT TOLERANCE: Not tolerant.
AVAILABILITY: Some specialty nurseries will have small coffee plants
    in cans.
CULTURE: Plant in carefully prepared holes of fertile, acid compost
    in a partially shaded location. Water carefully during dry times and
    protect when frost is forecast.
PROPAGATION: Seedage.
PESTS: Scales, mites, thrips, caterpillars, and mineral deficiencies.
NOTE: There are several species and many varieties of coffee.

Gardenia

Gardenia (gar-DEAN-ee-a): for A. Garden, a physician of Charleston.
jasminoides (jas-min-OI-dez): jasmine-like.

FAMILY: Rubiaceae.

RELATIVES: Coffee and ixora.

TYPE OF PLANT: Shrub.

HEIGHT: 8'. ZONE: N,C,S

HOW TO IDENTIFY: Evergreen, opposite leaves with interpetiolar stipules, and in springtime, the famed, beloved gardenias.

HABIT OF GROWTH: Compact, shrubby by many stems, with closely packed twigs.

FOLIAGE: Evergreen, of medium texture and dark green color when properly fertilized.

FLOWERS: White, fragrant, solitary in axils in springtime.

FRUITS: Fleshy, orange-colored, sessile, ribbed capsules, about 1½" long.

SEASON OF MAXIMUM COLOR: April–May.

LANDSCAPE USES: Gardenias have been favorites as freestanding specimens with generations of southerners. As a part of an informal shrubbery border, set groups of gardenias with about 5' between plants. Sometimes they are used as urn subjects on terraces.

There are many varieties which display slightly varying characters in the flowers. One clone has variegated foliage, but it is not very widely grown.

HABITAT: China; in Florida, ubiquitous in gardens.

LIGHT REQUIREMENT: Light, shifting, high pine shade is excellent.

SOIL REQUIREMENT: Acid, fertile soil that is free from nematodes is wanted.

SALT TOLERANCE: Not tolerant.

AVAILABILITY: Most retail nurseries sell gardenia plants. In northern Florida, they are own root, B & B, or canned; in southern Florida, canned specimens grafted on stocks of *Gardenia thunbergia* are offered.

CULTURE: Plant in rich, acid, nematode-free soil; water faithfully; spray frequently to control a host of pests.

PROPAGATION: Cuttage in northern Florida; graftage on stocks of nematode-resistant *Gardenia thunbergia* in southern Florida.

PESTS: White-flies, sooty-mold, cottony cushion scale, mealy bugs, and nematodes.

393
Ixora

Ixora (icks-OH-ra): a Malabar diety.
coccinea (cox-IN-ee-a): scarlet.

FAMILY: Rubiaceae.   RELATIVES: Gardenia, coffee, and serissa.
TYPE OF PLANT: Shrub.   HEIGHT: 15'. ZONE: C,S

HOW TO IDENTIFY: Opposite, evergreen leaves with cordate, amplexi-caul bases, often showing chlorosis; tubular flowers of red, yellow, or tones of red during much of the year.

HABIT OF GROWTH: Very compact, much-branched, amenable to shearing.

FOLIAGE: Evergreen, opposite, of medium texture and medium green color; frequently chlorotic.

FLOWERS: Showy, red, yellow or orange, 1½" long, in dense axillary corymbs.

FRUITS: Berries.

SEASON OF MAXIMUM COLOR: Much of the warm season.

LANDSCAPE USES: As a hedge for southern Florida, ixora is a great favorite; set plants 18" apart. In foundation arrangements it is used as a sheared accent and as filler material, too. In the garden, as a part of an enclosing shrubbery border, set ixoras 3' o.c. for color.

HABITAT: Southern Asia; in Florida, warmest parts.

LIGHT REQUIREMENT: Full sun for best habit and profuse flowering.

SOIL REQUIREMENT: Slightly acid soil of high fertility and good drainage. Foliage will become chlorotic in alkaline soils.

SALT TOLERANCE: Endures mild salt air, back of the front-line dunes.

AVAILABILITY: Ixoras are widely available in containers of all sizes.

CULTURE: In protected locations, plant in rich, acid soil that is free of nematodes; water faithfully; spray to control insects; fertilize twice or thrice annually.

PROPAGATION: Cuttage.

PESTS: Nematodes, scales, mushroom root-rot, and deficiencies of trace elements.

NOTE: One of southern Florida's leading flowering shrubs is available in many colors and forms now that hybrids have been introduced. Most spectacular is Malay ixora (*Ixora macrothyrsa*), a species which bears flowers in showy clusters 10" across. Ixoras are very sensitive to cold.

394
Pentas

Pentas (PEN-tass): Greek five, referring to the flower parts.
lanceolata (lan-see-oh-LATE-a): lance-shaped.

FAMILY: Rubiaceae.　　　　　　RELATIVES: Coffee and gardenia.
TYPE OF PLANT: Herbaceous perennial.　　HEIGHT: 4'. ZONE: N,C,S
HOW TO IDENTIFY: Here is Florida's most popular herbaceous member
　of the famed madder family, that great group of plants that con-
　tains so many species important in the tropics. Pentas is a tender
　but vigorous perennial with fuzzy, deeply veined, opposite leaves
　and terminal heads of star-like flowers in tones of red, in lilac, or
　in white during much of the warm season.
HABIT OF GROWTH: Sprawling, leafy mounds usually crowned by bright
　blossoms.
FOLIAGE: Opposite, hairy, deeply veined, 6" long.
FLOWERS: Bright, attractive terminal clusters of star-like flowers, in
　many shades, are produced much of the year.
FRUITS: Little capsules bear many small seeds.
SEASON OF MAXIMUM COLOR: Much of the year, when blossoms are
　out.
LANDSCAPE USES: For splashes of bright color in front of green shrubs,
　pentas is unexcelled. Although some gardeners like to mix plants
　of different shades, best usage suggests that pentas be set in drifts
　of separate colors with generous foils of the white-flowered clone
　to divide these groups.
HABITAT: Tropical Africa.
LIGHT REQUIREMENT: Full sun for best habit and full flowering, though
　light shade from high-headed pines or palms is good.
SOIL REQUIREMENT: Moderately fertile, well-drained earth is adequate.
SALT TOLERANCE: Not tolerant.
AVAILABILITY: Most nurseries have plants in cans for sale.
CULTURE: Plant rooted cuttings in generous drifts by separate colors;
　water moderately; fertilize lightly once each summer month; re-
　move seed heads to keep plants in production for long periods.
PROPAGATION: Cuttage or seedage.
PESTS: Mites.

395
Scarlet-Bush

Hamelia (ham-ALE-ee-a): for H. Duhamel, early French botanist.
patens (PAY-tens): spreading.

FAMILY: Rubiaceae.

RELATIVES: Ixora, gardenia, and coffee.

TYPE OF PLANT: Shrub.

HEIGHT: 12'. ZONE: S

HOW TO IDENTIFY: Bush with reddish hairs on all young parts; ever-green leaves to 6" long in whorls of 3; bright red, tubular flowers with red stalks, followed by black berries, ¼" in diameter, which are edible.

HABIT OF GROWTH: Bushy, from several branching stems.

FOLIAGE: Evergreen, whorled, of bold aspect. The young leaves are reddish from tomentum; the old ones are dark green or tinted with red or purple.

FLOWERS: Tubular, red, very showy, in terminal, forking cymes.

FRUITS: Black berries, ¼" in diameter, almost sessile, edible.

SEASON OF MAXIMUM COLOR: Warm months, when blossoms emerge.

LANDSCAPE USES: As a part of an enclosing barrier, in extreme south-ern Florida, set scarlet-bush 5' o.c. Residents of Dade, Monroe, and Lee counties would do well to consider the use of this calcium-tolerant native in enclosing shrubbery borders. True, the large leaves and considerable height rule out scarlet-bush for founda-tion plantings, but in barrier plantings it can serve well.

HABITAT: Tropical America, including southern Florida.

LIGHT REQUIREMENT: Reduced light of hammocks.

SOIL REQUIREMENT: Tolerant of lime-bearing soils of southern Florida.

SALT TOLERANCE: Tolerant of salt drift back from the ocean front.

AVAILABILITY: Some nurseries might have small scarlet-bushes in cans.

CULTURE: In prepared sites, plant carefully; water faithfully; fertilize twice or thrice each year. Do not allow lawn grasses to encroach upon the root zone.

PROPAGATION: Seedage, cuttage, or marcottage.

PESTS: Scales and mites.

Serissa

Serissa (ser-ɪss-a): from the Indian name.
foetida (ғет-id-a): bad-smelling.

FAMILY: Rubiaceae.

RELATIVES: Coffee, ixora, and pentas.

TYPE OF PLANT: Tiny shrub.

HEIGHT: 2′. ZONE: N,C,S

HOW TO IDENTIFY: Tiny shrub with ½″ leaves that have fetid odor when crushed; tiny white flowers in axillary position much of the year.

HABIT OF GROWTH: Dwarf shrub of several stems with upward-pointing branches.

FOLIAGE: Evergreen, fine texture, dark green or margined with yellow in the clone 'Variegata'.

FLOWERS: Tiny, white, single or double flowers. The unexpanded buds are pink.

FRUITS: Tiny, subglobose drupes.

SEASON OF MAXIMUM COLOR: When flowers are out, which is much of the year.

LANDSCAPE USES: As an edging (set 1′ o.c.) serissa is excellent; for planters it is widely accepted, and for foundation plantings, it has come into its own with contemporary architecture. In this latter use set 2′ o.c.

'Variegata' has leaves margined with yellow, and a variety with double flowers has little all-green leaves that are crowded to give a compact appearance to the plants.

HABITAT: Japan; in Florida, rather widely grown as a garden shrub.

LIGHT REQUIREMENT: Partial shade is desirable in much of Florida.

SOIL REQUIREMENT: A fertile, moisture-retentive soil is recommended.

SALT TOLERANCE: Not tolerant.

AVAILABILITY: Nurseries propagate quantities of this diminutive shrub.

CULTURE: Plant in fertile soil that is free of nematodes, if possible. Water faithfully; keep a mulch over the roots; do not allow grasses to encroach; fertilize once late in the winter.

PROPAGATION: Cuttage.

PESTS: Nematodes, mites, and scales.

397
Glossy
Abelia

Abelia (a-BEE-lee-a): for C. Abel, physician and author.
grandiflora (grand-ee-FLOR-a): large-flowered.

FAMILY: Caprifoliaceae. RELATIVES: Honeysuckle, viburnum, and elder.
TYPE OF PLANT: Shrub. HEIGHT: 10′. ZONE: N

HOW TO IDENTIFY: White, tubular blossoms subtended by reddish calyces which persist for much of the year; opposite, shining leaves on reddish twigs; shredding bark on old stems.

HABIT OF GROWTH: Spreading, tending to become leggy and open below.

FOLIAGE: Evergreen, opposite, shining, of deep green color and finest texture.

FLOWERS: White, tubular, subtended by persistent, reddish calyces.

FRUITS: Usually none.

SEASON OF MAXIMUM COLOR: Summer, white blossoms; later, red calyces.

LANDSCAPE USES: Clipped hedge, set 18″ o.c.; informal screen, plant 3′ apart; foundation plant, arrange at 2′ intervals. Abelia is very useful in northern counties because of its fine texture, attractive foliage, and flowers, but it is not recommended for use south of Gainesville. As one proceeds down the peninsula, abelia becomes less good as a garden shrub.

HABITAT: Gardens of warmer United States; in Florida, western part.

LIGHT REQUIREMENT: Full sun or high, light, shifting shade.

SOIL REQUIREMENT: Fertile, moisture-retaining clay-loams.

SALT TOLERANCE: Not tolerant.

AVAILABILITY: Abelia is offered by nurseries in the northern part.

CULTURE: Plant on fertile, clay-loam soil in western Florida; pinch succulent canes as soon as they appear in springtime; fertilize once each winter.

PROPAGATION: Cuttage by long, leafless, hardwood stems in December–January.

PESTS: Usually none of major concern.

Japanese Honeysuckle

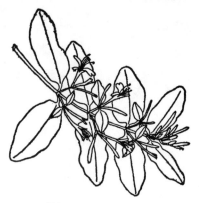

Lonicera (lon-is-er-a): for A. Lonicer, early German naturalist.
japonica (jap-on-i-ca): Japanese.

FAMILY: Caprifoliaceae.

RELATIVES: Viburnum and abelia.

TYPE OF PLANT: Vine.

HEIGHT: Variable. **ZONE:** N,C

HOW TO IDENTIFY: A vigorous, twining, evergreen vine with opposite, simple leaves of dark green color, and fragrant flowers that open white and turn yellow in the clone 'Halliana', which is the one most often seen in Florida.

HABIT OF GROWTH: Vigorously twining.

FOLIAGE: Evergreen, opposite, of medium texture and dark green color.

FLOWERS: Showy, tubular, pubescent, very fragrant, produced in pairs in summer. In 'Halliana', as noted above, the flowers are white at first, aging to yellow.

FRUITS: Showy, black berries are borne in clusters around stems.

SEASON OF MAXIMUM COLOR: Summer, when flowers are out.

LANDSCAPE USES: To veil a fence and add fragrance to the evening air, plant 10' o.c. To prevent erosion on steep slopes, plant 1'–2' o.c. There is always the possibility that Japanese honeysuckle will get out of hand and become a nuisance, especially on rich soil.

HABITAT: Eastern Asia; in Florida, naturalized in some places.

LIGHT REQUIREMENT: Full sun or reduced light of woodlands.

SOIL REQUIREMENT: Tolerant of many soil types, except lightest sands.

SALT TOLERANCE: Not tolerant of conditions near the strand.

AVAILABILITY: This is usually not an item of commerce, but rooted layers may be acquired from friends.

CULTURE: Plant, water, and forget.

PROPAGATION: Simple layerage where stems meet the earth.

PESTS: None of major concern.

NOTE: Trumpet honeysuckle (*Lonicera sempervirens*), with upper leaves joined at their bases and with red trumpets, is native in much of Florida. This one is not as likely to become a nuisance as is the exotic species.

399
Laurestinus

Viburnum (vye-BUR-num): ancient Latin name.
tinus (TYE-nus): ancient name for this plant.

FAMILY: Caprifoliaceae. RELATIVES: Abelia and honeysuckle.
TYPE OF PLANT: Shrub. HEIGHT: 12′. ZONE: N
HOW TO IDENTIFY: Evergreen, opposite, dark green leaves, 3″ long, are entire and have revolute edges; the twigs are somewhat hairy; the growth habit is symmetrical and compact.
HABIT OF GROWTH: Attractive, upright, dense, and compact.
FOLIAGE: Evergreen, opposite, medium in texture, dark green in color.
FLOWERS: White or pinkish flowers are produced in convex cymes in late winter or early spring.
FRUITS: Bright blue drupes in early winter.
SEASON OF MAXIMUM COLOR: Spring, when blossoms are open.
LANDSCAPE USES: Foundation plant for large buildings, set 3′-5′ O.C. Informal enclosure, allow 5′ between plants.

This is the most beautiful evergreen viburnum for Florida, but it is successful only on superior soils of the Panhandle and is not recommended for the peninsula generally.

In states north of the Florida line laurestinus may look even better than it does in our state. Planters in other areas utilize this excellent shrub more fully than do Floridians.

HABITAT: Mediterranean region; in Florida, gardens of the Panhandle.
LIGHT REQUIREMENT: Full sun on superior soils; high shade on sands.
SOIL REQUIREMENT: Fertile soils that are free from nematodes.
SALT TOLERANCE: Not tolerant.
AVAILABILITY: Small canned plants may be in nurseries in northern counties.
CULTURE: In western Florida, no special care is needed after establishment. Mulching is a good practice, of course, and pruning may be needed to keep laurestinus shapely.
PROPAGATION: Cuttage.
PESTS: Aphids, thrips, mites, and nematodes.

400
Sandankwa Viburnum

Viburnum (vye-BUR-num): ancient Latin name.
suspensum (sus-PEN-sum): hung.

FAMILY: Caprifoliaceae.   RELATIVES: Honeysuckle, abelia, and elder.
TYPE OF PLANT: Shrub.   HEIGHT: 12'. ZONE: N,C,S

HOW TO IDENTIFY: Brown twigs that are warty and quite rough to the touch because of prominent lenticels; evergreen, opposite, dark green leaves that have densely crenate-serrate margins.

HABIT OF GROWTH: Shrubby, compact, dense from many stems.

FOLIAGE: Evergreen, opposite, coarse in texture, dark green in color.

FLOWERS: Little white flowers produced in winter and early spring.

FRUITS: Red, subglobose drupes, very sparingly produced in Florida.

SEASON OF MAXIMUM COLOR: Little variation excepting when tiny white blossoms show in January–February.

LANDSCAPE USES: As a part of an enclosing barrier, plant 3' o.c.; as a part of a foundation planting, use the same interval. Sandankwa viburnum is the best of the genus for much of Florida and it is fully appreciated by landscape architects and advanced hobby gardeners here.

HABITAT: Asiatic islands; in Florida, all areas.

LIGHT REQUIREMENT: Tolerant of shade.

SOIL REQUIREMENT: Fertile soil that is free of nematodes is recommended.

SALT TOLERANCE: Not tolerant.

AVAILABILITY: Most retail sales lots offer sandankwa viburnum in cans.

CULTURE: Plant carefully in well-made sites; water diligently; supply with a deep organic mulch. Regular pruning is needed to remove the long, upward-growing shoots.

PROPAGATION: Cuttage.

PESTS: Aphids, white-flies, sooty-mold, thrips, mites, nematodes, and stem canker.

NOTE: There are several native species here that could be used in landscape plantings, notably rusty blackhaw (V. *rufidulum*).

401
Sweet
Viburnum

Viburnum (vye-ʙᴜʀ-num): ancient Latin name.
odoratissimum (o-dor-a-ᴛɪs-a-mum): most fragrant.

FAMILY: Caprifoliaceae.   RELATIVES: Honeysuckle, abelia, and elder.
TYPE OF PLANT: Large shrub.   HEIGHT: 25'. ZONE: N,C,S
HOW TO IDENTIFY: Evergreen, opposite, bright green leaves, 6″ long,
   remotely serrate toward the apex, tufts of brown hairs in axils of
   veins beneath; twigs green and smooth.
HABIT OF GROWTH: Very robust, dense, thick, becoming tree-like with
   age.
FOLIAGE: Evergreen, opposite, coarse in texture, bright green in color.
FLOWERS: Little, white, fragrant flowers in panicles in springtime.
FRUITS: Drupes, changing from red to black at maturity, very sparingly produced in Florida.
SEASON OF MAXIMUM COLOR: None.
LANDSCAPE USES: As an enclosing device, or as a screen, set sweet
   viburnum plants 5' o.c. Use the same interval if this shrub is
   planted by large, multistoried buildings. Very often sweet viburnum
   is allowed to become too big in landscape plantings if regular
   semi-annual pruning is not practiced. Indeed this heading-in twice
   each year can be quite severe. It is always a good plan to prune
   frequently so that comparatively small branches can be cut to
   leave small wounds. When large limbs are removed and big cuts
   are made, disease organisms may enter and cause decline, possibly
   death, of the plant.
HABITAT: Asia; in Florida, every community in the state.
LIGHT REQUIREMENT: Full sun or high, shifting shade from tall trees.
SOIL REQUIREMENT: Tolerant of many, varying soil types.
SALT TOLERANCE: Not tolerant.
AVAILABILITY: Practically every Florida nursery markets sweet vibur-
   num in cans.
CULTURE: No special attention is needed after establishment, except
   for regular pruning to keep the plant within bounds.
PROPAGATION: Cuttage and simple layerage.
PESTS: Aphids, white-flies, sooty-mold, thrips, mites, and stem canker.

402
Mexican Flame-Vine

Senecio (sen-EE-see-o): Latin *senex* for old man.
confusus (con-FUSE-us): uncertain.

FAMILY: Compositae.   RELATIVES: Daisy, calendula, and marigold.

TYPE OF PLANT: Herbaceous vine.   HEIGHT: Variable. ZONE: C,S

HOW TO IDENTIFY: A smooth-stemmed vine that bears alternate, ever-green leaves, 4″ long, with coarse teeth and sharp points. Daisy-like, orange flowers are produced during warm months.

HABIT OF GROWTH: Sprawling vine by herbaceous, green stems.

FOLIAGE: Evergreen, medium in texture, dark green in color.

FLOWERS: Orange daisies about 1″ across with 15-ray flowers that deepen to red with age.

FRUITS: Little, bristled achenes like dandelion fruits.

SEASON OF MAXIMUM COLOR: Warm months, when heavy-flowered.

LANDSCAPE USES: To add interest to palm trunks, to soften fences, or to veil small buildings, Mexican flame-vine is popular in warm sections of the state. This is primarily a home-gardener's vine because of its very easy culture. Variation in flower color may be noted upon occasion, but no named clones have been isolated and increased vegetatively.

HABITAT: Mexico; in Florida, widely grown in warm locations.

LIGHT REQUIREMENT: Full sun or shade from high-headed trees.

SOIL REQUIREMENT: Tolerant of widely varying soils.

SALT TOLERANCE: Not tolerant.

AVAILABILITY: Most nurseries on the peninsula offer Mexican flame-vines.

CULTURE: Of easiest culture, this vine grows without attention. First frosts will usually cut stems to the earth.

PROPAGATION: Seedage, layerage, and cuttage.

PESTS: Nematodes, mites, scales, and caterpillars.

403
Wedelia

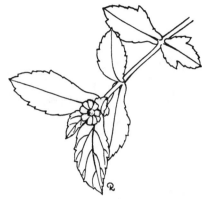

Wedelia (we-DELL-ee-a): for G. Wedel, a German botanist.
trilobata (try-low-BAIT-a): 3-lobed, referring to leaf form.

FAMILY: Compositae.   RELATIVES: Aster, cosmos, and daisy.
TYPE OF PLANT: Creeping herbaceous perennial. HEIGHT: 18″. ZONE: C,S
HOW TO IDENTIFY: Creeping, horizontal stems bear fleshy, toothed or lobed, hairy leaves, and yellow, daisy-like flowers.
HABIT OF GROWTH: Mat-forming by horizontal rooting stems.
FOLIAGE: Fleshy, toothed or lobed, closely packed when plants grow in the sun.
FLOWERS: Yellow, daisy-like, 10–12-rayed, each ray pleated and tipped with 3 lobes. It is hoped that additional colors will appear in the future.
FRUITS: Seed heads typical of the daisy family.
SEASON OF MAXIMUM COLOR: Blossoms open much of the year around.
LANDSCAPE USES: As a ground cover for sunny expanses, even near the sea, wedelia is in high favor in frostless locations. For sunny planters, it excels, as the trailing habit softens the top line and relates the planters and their contents to the earth beneath. Plants may be set 18″ apart.
HABITAT: Tropical America; escaped from cultivation in Florida.
LIGHT REQUIREMENT: Intense light of open, sandy expanses is optimum, yet partial shade from high-headed trees is tolerated.
SOIL REQUIREMENT: Sandy soil of moderate fertility is adequate; yet good soil and plentiful moisture produce beautiful, lush plants of deep-green color.
SALT TOLERANCE: Very tolerant of salt; dune locations are acceptable.
AVAILABILITY: Wedelia is a standard nursery item in central and southern Florida.
CULTURE: After establishment, light fertilization and regular watering will make for good growth. When plantings become thick and heavy, prune drastically with hedge shears or a sharp hoe. Frost kills wedelia to the earth.
PROPAGATION: Simple layerage; stems root where they touch the earth. Unrooted tip cuttings are set where new plants are wanted.
PESTS: Chewing insects and mites.

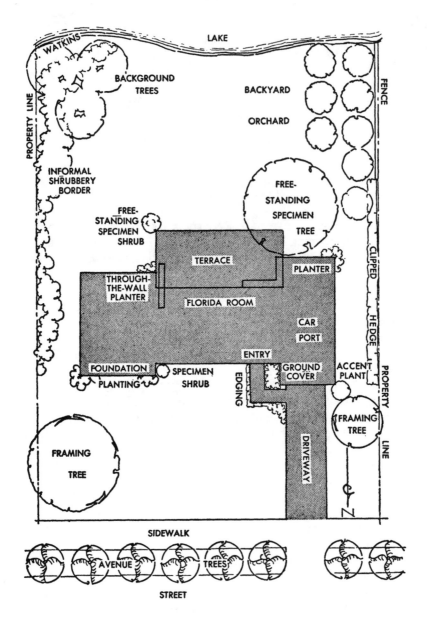

Model plan illustrating uses of landscape plants.

Glossary

ACAULESCENT (aye-call-ES-cent). Stemless, or apparently stemless; sometimes the stem is subterranean or protrudes only slightly.

ACID. Having an excess of free hydrogen ions. Acid solutions taste "sour" and turn litmus red.

ACUMINATE (a-KEW-min-ate). Tapering to a slender point.

ACUTE. Sharp, ending in a point, the sides of the tapered apex essentially straight or slightly convex.

ADNATE (AD-nate). Grown to, organically united with another part; as stamens with the corolla tube or an anther in its whole length with the filament.

ADVENTITIOUS (ad-ven-TISH-us). Arising by chance, or unpredictably, out of the usual place.

AERIAL (AIR-ree-al). In the air; borne above the surface.

AIR-LAYERING. A method of vegetative propagation in which a rooting medium is placed in aerial position. Now commonly done with sphagnum moss and plastic film or aluminum foil.

ALKALINE. Having an excess of free hydroxyl ions, and so a deficiency of free hydrogen ions; basic. Lacking any sour taste, alkaline or basic soils are often called "sweet."

ALTERNATE. Any arrangement of leaves not opposite or whorled; placed singly at different heights on the axis, stem, or rachis.

AMPLEXICAUL (am-PLECKS-e-call). Encircling a stem.

ANTHER (AN-ther). The enlarged tip of the stamen in which pollen is developed.

ANTHESIS (AN-the-sis). Flowering.

APETALOUS (ay-PET-al-us). No petals.

APICAL (A-pick-al). At the apex or tip of a plant organ.

AROID (AIR-oid). A member of the family Araceae.

APPRESSED. Closely and flatly pressed against a surface.

ARMATURE. Any covering or occurrence of spines, barbs, or hooks.

ARIL (A-rill). A special appendage growing from the point of attachment of the seed.

ARMED. Provided with any kind of strong and sharp defense, as of thorns, spines, prickles, or barbs.

ASCENDING. Rising up; produced somewhat obliquely or indirectly upward.

ASEXUAL. Sexless; without sex.

AXIL (ACKS-ill). The angle formed by a petiole with the trunk.

AXIS (ACKS-is). The main or central line of development of any plant or organ; the main stem.

B & B. Balled and burlapped.

BARBED. With bristles that are hooked.

BASAL. At the base of a plant or plant organ.

BASIC. See Alkaline.

BERRY. Pulpy fruit that does not split open.

BIFID (BI-fid). Two-cleft, as in apices of some leaves.

BIFURCATE (BYE-fur-cate). Forked, as some Y-shaped hairs or thorns.

BIGENERIC (bi-gen-ERR-ic). Resulting from crossing two genera of plants.

BLADE. The expanded part of a leaf.

BLOOM. The thin waxy coating, easily rubbed off, on some fruits and on some palm foliage.

BOLE. A strong unbranched stem; the trunk.

BRACT. A modified leaf intermediate between the sepals and vegetative leaves.

CALCAREOUS (cal-CARE-e-us). Having a high content of lime or limestone.

CALYX (KAY-licks). The sepals collectively; the outer of the two series of modified leaves in most flowers.

CAPSULE. Compound pod; a fruit of more than one carpel, usually splitting at maturity along lines.

CATERPILLAR. A worm-like larva of a butterfly or moth that may despoil foliage.

CAUDEX (CAW-decks). Stem.

CAULESCENT (caw-LESS-cent). Having an evident stem above ground.

CHELATE (KEY-late). An organic compound which combines with iron or other heavy metals to release them slowly in the soil for plant use and yet prevents their being tied up in unavailable form by other soil chemicals.

CHLOROSIS (klor-o-sis). Loss of the green color from leaves, leaving them yellowish-green. It may be due to lack of needed nutrient elements, to inability to absorb those elements because of excess water or root disease, or to the direct action of insects or fungi on the leaves.

CILIATE (SILL-ee-ate). Fringed with hairs; bearing hairs on the margin.

CLASPING. Leaf partly or wholly surrounding stem.

CLAY. Mineral matter of exceedingly fine particle size in the soil, colloidal in character and often holding water tenaciously.

CLONE. A group of plants, increased vegetatively, from a single bud; a horticultural variety.

COLLOID (KOLL-oid). Composed of particles too small to be seen with the naked eye, and, by reason of its tremendous surface area, holding water and mineral elements with very great force.

COMA. The leafy crown or head, as of many palm trees.

COMPOST. Partially decomposed plant residues.

CORDATE (CORE-date). Heart-shaped in outline.

COSTAPALMATE (cost-a-PAL-mate). Said of a palmate palm leaf whose petiole continues through the blade as a distinct midrib, as in the cabbage palm.

CROWN. The head of foliage.

CROWNSHAFT. A trunk-like extension of the bole formed by the long, broad, overlapping petiole bases of some palms.

CULTIGEN (CULT-e-jen). Plants known only in cultivation; presumably originating under domestication; contrast with indigen.

CUTICLE (CUTE-e-cal). A waxy coating developed by the epidermis of some plants which reduces somewhat the loss of water through the epidermis. Unlike bloom, it cannot be rubbed off.

CYMBA (SIM-ba). A woody, durable, boat-like spathe that encloses the inflorescence, opens, and persists, as in many palms; see Manubrium.

DECIDUOUS (dee-SID-you-us). Shedding its leaves periodically.

DIOECIOUS (dye-E-shus). Staminate and pistillate flowers on different plants; a term properly applied to plants, not to flowers.

DISTAL (DIS-tal). Farthest from the point of attachment or reference.

DISTICHOUS (DIS-tick-us). Arranged in two vertical rows.

DIVISION. Cutting, tearing, or breaking a plant into two or more independent units.

DRUPE (DROOP). A fleshy, one-seeded fruit.

ELLIPTIC (e-LIP-tick). A flat object that is oval and narrowed to rounded ends and widest near the middle.

EPIDERMIS (ep-e-DER-mis). The skin or outermost layer of cells of a plant.

FIBROUS. Composed of, or resembling, fibers; a root system, as in palms, consisting chiefly of long, slender roots.

FILAMENT. Thread, particularly here, threads on some leaves.

FLATWOODS. Low, level land covered by forest, often under water during some of the rainy season. Flatwoods occupy much of the coastal areas and the north-central part of Florida, and have the saw palmetto and cabbage palm as important species.

FLORIDA ROOM. A room for informal living, usually with glass walls, overlooking the garden.

FOLIAGE. Leaves taken collectively.

FOLLICLE (FALL-ick-al). A dry fruit which splits open only along a single line.

FOUNDATION PLANTING. The shrubs, vines, and trees placed close around a building to soften the abrupt transition from the horizontal ground to the vertical wall.

FREEZE. A condition where plant temperatures below 32°F. result from the inflow of masses of air below this temperature, so that the air is colder than plants or ground.

FROST. A condition where plant temperatures below 32°F. result from radiation of heat from plants and ground, occurring only on still, cloudless nights. The air is coldest next to the ground and may be several degrees above 32° at a few feet above the ground.

FUNGICIDE (FUN-gee-side). A chemical which kills fungi.

FUNGUS. A leafless plant that may parasitize plants. Mildews, rusts, and molds are fungi.

GENUS (JEAN-us). A closely related group of species; the first and always capitalized word in the scientific name of a plant. The plural form is *genera* (JEN-er-a).

GLABROUS (GLAY-brus). Smooth, without hairs or scaly outgrowth.

GLAUCOUS (GLAW-cuss). Covered with a bloom or a whitish substance that rubs off.

GROUND COVER. A plant, other than a grass, used to cover the earth.

HABIT. The general appearance of a plant.

HABITAT (HAB-e-tat). The particular location in which a plant grows, as along stream bank, on the seashore, or in a hammock.

HAMMOCK. A slightly elevated island of hardwoods in a sea of pines or marsh grass.

HERB. A non-woody plant, naturally dying back to the ground on the completion of its (usually) brief season of active growth.

HERMAPHRODITE (her-MAF-roe-dite). A plant which has perfect flowers, each one having stamens and pistils.

HUMIDITY. Water vapor in the air. Of interest is the relative humidity expressed as a percentage of what would saturate the air at a given temperature.

HUMUS (HYU-mus). Decomposed remnants of organic matter in the soil, which undergoes further decomposition only very slowly and so exercises a rather lasting effect on soil properties.

HYBRID. A plant obtained by using pollen of one species on the stigma of another; or, more loosely, the product of crossing any two dissimilar plants.

INDIGENOUS (in-DIDGE-en-us). Native to a given area; not introduced.

INFLORESCENCE (in-flor-ESS-ence). Specialized leafless, flowering shoots.

INSECT. A six-legged organism that may attack and despoil plants.

INSECTICIDE. A chemical which kills insects.

LEAFLET. One part of a compound leaf.

LITTORAL (LIT-o-ral). Growing along the shore of a sea or lake.

LOAM. A very desirable soil for plants, composed of a mixture of clay, silt, sand, and organic matter.

MANUBRIUM (man-oo-bry-um). The long, thin, more or less cylindrical base of certain cymbas or palm spathes.

MARCOTTAGE (mar-cot-TAZH). The same as air-layering.

MARL. A gray soil of claylike particle size, consisting of calcium carbonate plus a little sand and organic matter, which is built of shells and organisms of microscopic size in shallow seas.

MEDIUM. The material in which seeds, cuttings, or plants are placed.

MIDRIB. The main rib of a leaf, a continuation of the petiole.

MINOR ELEMENT. A mineral element needed by plants only in very small amounts, although no less essential than those needed in large amounts. Copper, zinc, iron, manganese, boron, molybdenum, chlorine, and perhaps sodium for some plants, are in this group.

MITE. An eight-legged organism that sucks plant juices from leaves.

MONOECIOUS (mon-EE-shus). Having separate male and female flowers on the same plant.

MULCH. A porous material covering the ground, usually meaning an organic mulch, such as a layer of leaves, straw, pine needles, or sawdust.

NEUTRAL. Of soil or water, being neither acid nor alkaline in reaction.

NODE. The part of a stem from which arises a leaf or branch.

NUTRIENT. A material supplying a chemical element needed by plants.

OBOVATE (OB-o-vate). The reverse of ovate; the terminal half broader than the basal.

o.c. On center.

OOLITE (o-o-lite). A very porous limestone composed of shells of small marine organisms naturally cemented together; found in southern Florida and some adjacent islands.

ORGAN. One of the parts of a plant which has a definite function, as stem, root, or flower.

ORGANIC. As used to describe fertilizers and mulches, this means material derived from the bodies of plants or animals.

OVATE. Egg-shaped in outline; broadened in the basal half.

PALMAN (PAL-man). Undivided part of a palmate leaf between the petiole and segments of the blade.

PALMATE (PAL-mate). With leaf lobes, leaflets, or veins radiating from a common origin.

PANICLE (PAN-i-cal). A branched inflorescence, with flowers being developed toward the tips of the branches as they elongate.

PATIO. A courtyard or outdoor living room with enclosing walls.

PEDICELLATE (ped-DIS-sell-ate). Having a flower stalk or pedicel.

PEDUNCLE (PEA-dunk-cal). Stem of a flower cluster, or of a solitary flower when that flower is the remaining member of an inflorescence.

PEST. An organism which is injurious to plants, including bacteria, insects, mites, fungi, and rodents.

PESTICIDE. A chemical which kills pests.

PETAL. One of the separate parts of the corolla.

PETIOLE (PET-ee-ol). The stalk of a leaf.

pH. A number expressing the degree of acidity or alkalinity of soil or solution. The neutral point is 7.0. Numbers decreasing from 7 indicate acidity; numbers higher than 7 indicate alkalinity.

PITH. The soft, spongy central cylinder of a stem.

PINNA (PIN-a). A primary division or leaflet of a pinnate leaf.

PINNATE. Featherlike; a leaf which has leaflets arranged on both sides of a rachis.

PISTIL. The female organ of the flower, consisting of ovary, style, and stigma.

PISTILLATE. Having a pistil but no stamens; thus a female flower or plant.

PLANTER OR PLANTER-BIN. A masonry box, raised above the grade, used for growing plants.

PLICATE (PLY-cate). Folded, as in a fan, or approaching this condition.

PLUMOSE (PLUME-ose). Plumy; feather-like.

POLLEN. The yellow dust contained in the anthers which must be deposited on stigmas for fertilization to take place. Pollen grains germinate on stigmas, producing tubes which carry male sex cells (sperms) down to unite with egg cells (female) in the ovule.

POLYGAMOUS (poll-IG-a-mus). Bearing unisexual and hermaphrodite flowers on the same plant.

PROXIMAL. Nearest to the point of attachment or reference.

PUBESCENT (pew-BESS-ent). Covered with hairs or fuzz.

RACEME (ray-SEAM). An elongated, indeterminate inflorescence with stalked flowers.

RACHIS (RAY-kiss). The main axis of a palm frond.

RECLINATE (WRECK-lin-ate). Reclining; bent down from the perpendicular.

RECURVED. Bent or curved downward or backward.

RHIZOME (RYE-zome). An underground stem, distinguished from a true root by the presence of nodes, buds, or scale-like leaves.

SALTDRIFT. Air laden with salt water vapor, coming ashore from ocean or gulf.

SCALE. An insect which, in its usual adult form, resembles a tiny bump or excrescence. The insect sucks juice from plant tissues.

SCALECIDE (SCALE-i-side). A chemical which kills scale insects.

SCANDENT (SKAN-dent). Climbing or scrambling without the use of tendrils.

SCAPE. A flower stem, usually leafless, but sometimes furnished with bracts.

SEEDLING. A plant which has been grown from seed.

SEGMENT. One of the parts of a leaf that is divided but not truly compound.

SEPAL (SEE-pal). One of the parts of the calyx.

SERRATE (SER-ate). Saw-toothed; said of leaf margins.

SESSILE (SES-ill). Without a stalk or stem.

SPADIX (SPAY-dicks). A thick flower spike, subtended by a spathe.

SPATHE. A bract subtending a flower cluster.

SPATULATE (SPAT-you-late). Like a spatula blade in outline.

SPECIES. A kind of plant distinct from other kinds and reproducing its characteristics when self-pollinated. The second (usually uncapitalized) word in the scientific name of a plant.

SPHAGNUM (SFAG-num). A type of moss growing in acid bogs and widely used in marcottage and in seed sowing because of its combination of good moisture holding, good aeration, and freedom from disease.

SPICULES (SPIC-yewls). Minute, needle-like crystals.

SPIKE. As used here, a generalized term for an elongated flower cluster.

SPRAY. To apply a pesticide in water under pressure, to emerge as a spray.

STACHYS (STAY-kiss). In Greek compounds, signifying a spike.

STAMEN (STAY-men). The male organ in the flower, consisting of anther (containing pollen) and filament.

STAMINATE (STAM-in-ate). Flowers or plants having stamens but no pistils; male.

STIGMA. The tip of the pistil which receives pollen.

STOLON. A horizontal stem, at or below surface of the ground, that gives rise to a new plant at the tip.

STOMATA (STOH-mat-ta). Openings through the epidermal layer of leaves which allow internal air cavities to communicate with outside air.

STRAND. A shore, especially of the sea.

SUCCULENT (SUCK-you-lent). Juicy; used for plants characterized by the water-conserving and storing capacity of their stems, branches, and leaves.

SYRINGE (SEER-inge). To water plant foliage with a fine, misty spray.

TAXONOMY (tacks-ON-omy). The study of plant classification and relationships.

TERETE (tee-REET). Cylindrical and tapering; round in cross-section.

TERMINAL. At the tip or apex.

TERRACE. A raised platform of earth, preferably paved with masonry.

TERRESTRIAL (ter-ES-tree-al). Earth-dwelling; growing in the ground as opposed to aerial or aquatic.

THRIPS. A tiny insect that may injure plants by sucking juices.

TOMENTOSE (toe-MEN-tose). Densely woolly or pubescent; with matted soft hairs.

TRIGENERIC (tri-gen-ER-ic). A plant resulting from crosses involving three genera.

UBIQUITOUS (you-BICK-wit-us). Found everywhere; growing in a wide variety of habitats.

UNISEXUAL. Of one sex; staminate only or pistillate only.

VARIEGATED. Irregularly colored in patches; blotched.

VARIETY. A plant differing in minor characters from the type species.

VEGETATIVE. The portions of a plant other than the flowers and fruits, i.e., stem, leaves, and roots. Vegetative reproduction must involve plant parts other than seeds.

VIABLE. Alive; said of seeds capable of germinating.

VILLOUS (VIL-us). Provided with long and soft, not matted, hairs; shaggy.

WHORL. The arrangement of three or more leaves, branches, or flowers at one node.

XEROPHYTE (ZARE-o-fite). A plant adapted to living under conditions of very little moisture, as a desert plant.

Index to Plant Families

Index to Common and Scientific Names